JUSTIFYING REVOLUTION

POLITICAL VIOLENCE IN NORTH AMERICA
Gregory D. Miller, *Series Editor*

JUSTIFYING REVOLUTION

Law, Virtue, and Violence in the American War of Independence

Edited by Glenn A. Moots *and* Phillip Hamilton

UNIVERSITY OF OKLAHOMA PRESS : NORMAN

Library of Congress Cataloging-in-Publication Data

Names: Moots, Glenn A., editor. | Hamilton, Phillip, 1961– editor.
Title: Justifying Revolution : Law, Virtue, and Violence in the American War of Independence / edited by Glenn A. Moots and Phillip Hamilton.
Description: Norman : University of Oklahoma Press, 2018. | Series: Political violence in North America ; volume 1 | Includes index.
Identifiers: LCCN 2017052789 | ISBN 978-0-8061-6013-9 (hardback)
Subjects: LCSH: United States—History—Revolution, 1775–1783—Moral and ethical aspects. | Just war doctrine—History—18th century. | War (Philosophy)—History—18th century. | BISAC: HISTORY / United States / Revolutionary Period (1775–1800).
Classification: LCC E209 .J87 2018 | DDC 973.3—dc23
LC record available at https://lccn.loc.gov/2017052789

Justifying Revolution: Law, Virtue, and Violence in the American War of Independence is Volume 1 in the Political Violence in North America series.

The paper in this book meets the guidelines for permanence and durability of the Committee on Production Guidelines for Book Longevity of the Council on Library Resources, Inc. ∞

1 2 3 4 5 6 7 8 9 10

CONTENTS

ACKNOWLEDGMENTS

The idea for this collection began as a panel organized by Mark David Hall (George Fox University) at the American Political Science Association's annual meeting. Henrik Syse (Peace Research Institute Oslo), editor of the *Journal of Military Ethics,* attended the session and, in subsequent conversations with Glenn Moots, concluded that the topic of the American Revolution and just war theory deserved a special issue. Glenn served as guest editor. We thank Mark and Henrik for planting the seed for this volume and for enabling a first run at the subject in the premier academic journal on just war theory.

We then wondered if there was sufficient interest in the topic to merit an entire conference, with different participants. We soon discovered both a strong interest in such a gathering as well as a fine spirit of camaraderie among Revolutionary Era scholars, many of whom are contributors to this volume. Their enthusiastic agreement to participate often came with recommendations of others who should also join us. As a result, our list of participants practically came together on its own. Even those who could not attend endorsed the idea and encouraged us to move forward. As a result, our two-day conference at the Union League of Philadelphia in October 2015 proved to be engaging and rewarding. All of our participants, moreover, immediately endorsed the idea of an edited collection. We deeply thank our contributors and are honored to be included among them. Indeed, all credit for the merits of this volume belongs to them. Its shortcomings, of course, rest with us.

We could not have organized this event without Kelly Hanlon's invaluable assistance. A true professional, Kelly not only saw the value of our conference but also secured support from the Agora Institute at Eastern University and handled the meeting's logistical and financial details. Without her, this conference (and this volume) would not have happened. Alongside Kelly was Leah Sioma, who ably assisted in making the conference a success. We also want to thank Mark Henderson, who served as our member sponsor at the Union League, thus allowing us to discuss and debate the American Revolution in a magnificent venue whose historical origins and artifacts reminded us of the moral significance of warfare.

A number of additional scholars joined us in Philadelphia as discussants or as presenters but could not be part of the edited collection. Benjamin Lyons of Columbia University and Don Johnson of North Dakota State University were presenters. Our discussants, Tim Demy (U.S. Naval War College), Robert Ingram (Ohio University), Jessica Choppin Roney (Temple University), Jim Stoner (Louisiana State University), and James Vaughn (University of Texas at Austin), kept our conversations lively and honest. We are indebted to them for their participation.

Generous funding for the project came from the Agora Institute, the Institute for Humane Studies, and the Charles Koch Foundation. The Agora Institute generously provided the bulk of the funding for the conference. Support from the Institute for Humane Studies enabled students to attend from Penn, Villanova, and the Templeton Honors College at Eastern University. The Charles Koch Foundation graciously provided funding to move the edited collection toward publication. We are grateful for this support.

Our contributors, Mark Edward Lender and James Kirby Martin, recommended the University of Oklahoma Press, for which we are very grateful. We also thank Adam Kane and Steven Baker, both of the University of Oklahoma Press, for their enthusiastic support and for skillfully shepherding this volume toward publication. Our copyeditor, Kevin Brock, received many well-deserved commendations from contributors. We are grateful, furthermore, to our anonymous readers for their many helpful suggestions and endorsements. We are especially pleased to be the first title in this new and valuable series on political violence.

Additionally, Glenn owes continued thanks to his wife, Michelle, and children, Rebekah and Andrew, for their loving support of his endeavors. Whatever one is researching, it is even more interesting when your family supports your engagement and enthusiasm, joins you for the occasional trip or pilgrimage, and reminds you that scholarship is both a means and an end. He is also indebted to Northwood University for travel funds and to Rochelle Zimmerman for the occasional interlibrary-loan errand.

Phillip Hamilton also owes a deep debt of gratitude to his wife, Chris, and children, Tommy and Jake, all of whom continue to generously understand the time that scholarship and the academic life take away from family. They have, moreover, always cheerfully participated in our many family trips to historical sites, museums, and battlefields. Lastly, Phil thanks Nancy Wilson, the administrative assistant for the History Department at Christopher Newport University, for her repeated assistance in solving his computer problems and word-processing issues.

JUSTIFYING REVOLUTION

INTRODUCTION

Glenn A. Moots and Phillip Hamilton

Since 1783, Americans have largely regarded their war for independence more as a political idea or movement than as a real war. The passage of time, the accumulation of legend, and the mythos of the founding of the United States suggest the Revolution's outcome was destined to be. Indeed, the two fundamental ideals associated with the Revolution, liberty and equality, have marched from victory to victory to become the zeitgeist of our age. Numerous best-selling books celebrate the Founders and their achievements. Costumed actors and park rangers entertain audiences with replicas of period muskets and cannons, all safely shorn of deadly bayonets and murderous iron projectiles. Alexander Hamilton has recently inspired a successful hip-hop musical about the nation's founding, though how can any stage production honestly portray the bloody destruction of British and Hessian troops that Hamilton orchestrated with grapeshot and bayonet at Trenton, Princeton, and Yorktown? Does not all of this distract us from the real violence experienced by both soldiers and civilians alike throughout the American Revolution? The United States was not a near mythic invention of great men, nor was it an inevitable social movement whose outcome was preordained. Rather, the nation was enabled in large part by a hard, bloody, and destructive war.

The Revolutionary War lasted eight tumultuous years and raged across many fronts. Its outcome was always uncertain, and victory came only after innumerable trials by fire and steel endured by combatants and noncombatants alike. For soldiers, battlefield horrors were commonplace: wounds were usually fatal, and surgeons lacked anesthesia and even the most basic medicines to prevent shock and ease suffering. Evacuations to safe, clean hospitals were also largely unknown. Those captured by the enemy faced new terrors and deprivations. Beyond the conflict's battlefields, the war unleashed devastating diseases upon soldiers and civilians, while rapine at the hands of enemy forces destroyed many homes and enormous quantities of property. Mob violence, military occupation, and conflicting allegiances forever displaced tens of thousands of people. The war introduced new difficulties for members of particular races, ethnicities, and religious denominations. Swiss jurist and philosopher Emer de Vattel, the most significant just war theorist at the time of the American Revolution, rightly asked regarding such destruction, "What price can be set on all the blood that has been shed, the loss of such a number of citizens, and the ruin of families?"[1] Indeed, how did participants justify not only their enormous sacrifices but also their own violent acts against the enemy? What limits, if any, did soldiers and political leaders attempt to impose upon the war and its destructiveness?

In examining the justice of *any* war, there is no shortage of arguments on which to draw. Moral justifications for warfare exist in both Western and non-Western traditions. In the Western tradition, moral reasoning about both war and rebellion began in the classics that American and British leaders learned as children. John Adams, for example, surely knew one of the earliest examinations of the ethical dilemmas of war, Thucydides's famous "Melian Dialogue."[2] Adams's fondness for Cicero, one of the first Western philosophers to propose seminal legal and moral boundaries for war, is legendary. Both he and Jefferson certainly read Cicero's judgments about war and tyrannicide in *De Officiis,* Jefferson having read it as a young student with the Reverend James Maury. Across the Atlantic, many British officers were also familiar with the great works of classical Greece and Rome. While attending Eton College or Clare College, Cambridge, Charles Cornwallis surely parsed the same Ciceronian passages as Jefferson and Adams. Thomas Gage undoubtedly read Cicero as part of his education in the classics at Westminster School.[3]

Reasoning about the ethics of warfare continued to develop under Christendom, the waning years of which still influenced the Anglo-American eighteenth century. When it came to warfare, Christian theologians found themselves suspended between Augustine's two cities. On the one hand, Christians sought to serve the Prince of Peace.[4] On the other hand, their civic vocations called on them to mimic David's "mighty men" of the Old Testament and fight. Medieval Christendom gave way to early modernity, however, and imperial conflict, global colonization, and internecine wars brought new complications and challenges to the robust debate over war's justifications.

Despite considerable progress by medieval jurists and theologians in defining the moral parameters of war, the merciless brutality dispensed by supposedly Christian nobles and their soldiers demonstrated that additional limits on war's violence were needed. Early modern political and legal theorists such as Francisco de Vitoria and Francisco Suárez carried forward the next phase of moral and legal reasoning about armed conflict. In the seventeenth and eighteenth centuries, jurists and philosophers such as Hugo Grotius and Vattel articulated new and influential approaches to the conduct of warfare as part of a maturing system of international law.[5]

Yet even though this fecund period of legal and philosophical reasoning created a rich intellectual backdrop shaping the statesmen and commanders on both sides of the Revolutionary War, no monograph has yet examined that conflict in the context of just war theory. Such an oversight is not attributable to a lack of interest in either the war itself or in reasoning about just war. During the past several decades, scholars across disciplines have shown deliberate interest in the interrelated issues of war, law, justice, and violence in general. Indeed, more than forty book-length studies of just war theory have been published in the past decade alone, evincing a sustained interest in this topic among both general readers and specialists. Scholars writing on the legal and moral ramifications of war owe much to two classic works, James Turner Johnson's *Just War Tradition and the Restraint of War* and ever-updated editions of Michael Walzer's *Just and Unjust Wars: A Moral Argument with Historical Illustrations*.[6] These foundational studies have provided readers with a basic framework for understanding ethical reflections on warfare; they also offer a well-focused lens through which to view justifications, rationalizations, and standards of behavior for decision makers and combatants. Yet neither work significantly advances our understanding of just war's relationship to the American Revolution.

Historians of eighteenth-century Europe, meanwhile, have produced dedicated studies of the Enlightenment's influence on European warfare. Did this intellectual movement lead to more-restrained or "civilized" conflicts across the continent? Historians' research reveals a complex and oftentimes-contradictory picture: military violence and brutality certainly did not end, and European soldiers committed atrocities throughout the late seventeenth and then eighteenth centuries. At the same time, however, civilian governments and military leaders increasingly recognized the common humanity of soldiers. Articles of war adopted by Europe's nation-states, together with gentlemanly codes of conduct among its officer classes, succeeded in imposing some restraint on combatants as they conducted operations against civilian populations as well.[7]

Though mostly fought by European armies organized according to European patterns of military organization, the American War for Independence has attracted surprisingly little attention in studies of early modern just war theory. There is no lack of interest in the American Revolution, of course. General histories of the war and of its various military campaigns, many of them commercial successes, continue to be published. Unfortunately, the waning interest in military history within academic history departments means that fewer scholarly volumes on the Revolutionary War are published.[8] Few of these academic studies, let alone the ones targeted at general readers, explicitly juxtapose questions of strategy, morality, legality, and justice within the just war tradition. There are only a few significant exceptions, but few of even these devote much attention to the ideas of just war theory itself.[9] While relevant academic social histories of the period are more common and have their virtues, these narratives usually distance themselves from the broader intellectual history. When the justice or legality of the Revolution is considered in light of just war theory, these arguments have been largely confined to journals.[10]

Justifying Revolution is the first study of the American Revolution dedicated to exploring the conflict's relationship to just war theory. Its contributors collectively explore and evaluate how and why American and British leaders purposefully deployed violence to further specific political and military goals. More than a survey of strategy and decision making, however, these essays situate the soldiers and statesmen within the context of just war theory as it existed in the late eighteenth century in legal, philosophical, and religious terms. Chapters are organized into three parts, each exploring a traditional subfield of just war theory: *jus ad bellum* (right or justice in going to war, including the legality of taking up arms), *jus in bello* (right or justice in conducting war, including legal codes governing military conduct), and *jus post bellum* (right or justice in concluding war).[11] Readers can therefore reconsider the Revolution with an eye to the ethics and legality of going to war, the choices made by military officers and soldiers in deploying force throughout the conflict, and finally the attempts to arrive at defensible terms of peace.

Part 1, "*Jus ad Bellum*," examines the precedents of just war theory for the American Revolution, including legal, political, historical, and religious arguments. The first three essays remind us that at the time of the Revolution, just war theory was a combination of legal theory and philosophical and theological reasoning. International legal doctrine, based on the law of nations, or *jus gentium*, was in a period of transition from natural law to positive law. This transition would not be complete until the nineteenth century with the creation of "international humanitarian law."[12] Until then, just war theory was the product of a long and complex intersection of traditions. Medieval jurists and theologians answered the challenge of just war by carrying forward the Roman *jus gentium* and combining it with scriptural and canon law. By the time of the Reformation, the discussion became even more complex. Streams of medieval canon law and natural law were combined to address the rise of multiple sovereign kingdoms, the fragmentation of Christianity, and the rise of secular legal theory. With the emergence of the nation-state, sovereigns essentially became equals whose legal claims, without a common superior to judge among them, resembled those made by competing parties in a duel.

Though without a superior to evaluate their competing claims, nations were nevertheless bound to heed reason and morality. They were also bound to natural law among all nations, just as it determined the merits of competing claims among individuals in the state of nature. Divine law continued to be acknowledged, of course, though rising confidence in human reason (coupled with a growing skepticism about divine revelation) made these two sources of law equally important.[13] The first three chapters of this book, therefore, explore how American revolutionaries deployed the language and reasoning of the late eighteenth century—built upon both secular and sacred authorities—to assert their case for independence and equality before the international community. Such a defense was the fundamental obligation of every sovereign nation under the early modern *jus gentium*.

Andreas Aure's opening chapter casts the legal context for just war theory when the British-American crisis erupted in the 1760s. Exploring international principles regarding declaring and practicing war in the mid-eighteenth century, Aure focuses on the seminal contribution made by the Swiss legal theorist Emer de Vattel in his book *Law of Nations* (1758). Anchoring his ideas upon natural-law principles and building upon the maxims articulated by the seventeenth-century Dutch philosopher Hugo Grotius, Vattel articulated the moral and ethical standards for taking up arms and conducting military operations. At the time of the Revolution, Vattel's ideas and principles were authoritative on both sides of the Atlantic and remain influential today.

Given that religious arguments were also a coin of the intellectual realm for all classes in eighteenth-century America, Valerie Morkevičius and Glenn Moots survey the Protestant justifications for war, particularly rebellion and civil war. In chapter 2, they examine arguments by Reformation theologians such as Martin Luther, John Calvin, and John Knox as well as those made by Protestant legal theorists Samuel Pufendorf, Grotius, and Vattel. They also consider the arguments of social-contract theorist John Locke, long considered a significant influence on Patriot thinking. They then demonstrate the significance of these assertions for Patriot clergy who deployed them in sermons, the most prolific type of political pamphlet. By recovering how Protestantism integrated both religious and legal reasoning, Morkevičius and Moots enable the reader to place Patriot arguments in the context of two centuries of Protestant legal and theological tradition.

Building and expanding upon the previous chapters' conclusions, Theodore

Christov returns to Vattel in chapter 3. He argues that the legal theorist's *Law of Nations* not only deeply influenced the Founders in their efforts to justify armed rebellion and independence but also provided American political leaders with fundamental guidance as they looked ahead to assuming sovereign control after the war. Christov demonstrates how reasoning about *jus ad bellum, jus in bello,* and *jus post bellum* was sometimes delineated only in theory. He also shows how concepts of sovereignty in the maturing doctrines of international law were central to American justifications for the Revolution.

Jack Greene brings part 1 to a close in chapter 4 by turning to the often-heated political debates before and during the conflict. He examines the extraordinary pamphlet literature published on both sides of the Atlantic and how it sought to defend independence or the suppression of rebellion. With a particular focus on the debates within Great Britain, he explains that proponents of force against Americans fervently believed their actions to be just, righteous, and morally correct. At the same time, however, a substantial and vocal portion of the British population decried the drift toward violence and denounced the costs and sacrifices that armed conflict would inflict upon the empire. Greene's examination of these debates through these largely unexamined tracts recovers the breadth and complexity of these important arguments and their significant influence upon the war's course. Exposing the moral ambiguity that exists when sovereign nations claim the principled high ground, Greene concludes, "The justice or injustice of any war lies in the eye of the beholder."

As chapter 4 illustrates, debates concerning the righteousness of a war hardly cease once hostilities commence. After the initiation of combat, leaders and participants had to confront a host of new questions and decisions. How was the war to be organized and conducted? What levels of violence could win independence or suppress the uprising? How did European principles and laws apply to a civil war, especially one partially conducted on the lawless American frontier? How were civilians to be treated in such a conflict? The chapters in part 2, "*Jus in Bello,*" therefore explore how participants in the conflict faced challenging military and political decisions demanding both moral and prudential choices.

John Roche's chapter 5 reveals that, in truth, the British army encountered *jus in bello* questions long before April 1775. Focusing on the Crown's military occupation of Boston, Roche finds that British officers, particularly the two commanding generals during this time, Thomas Gage and William Howe, were well versed in the international laws of war articulated by Grotius and Vattel. They also knew the European martial traditions governing the actions of occupying troops. Although Patriot propagandists excoriated the king's army for establishing a tyrannical military regime in the city (particularly after the Boston Massacre in 1770), Gage and Howe both conscientiously sought to manage civil affairs in a just manner. Indeed, Roche finds that the generals scrupulously protected civilian lives and property and attempted to maintain strict discipline among their soldiers.

In chapter 6, Phillip Hamilton provides a biographical study of Washington's famed artillery commander Henry Knox. The case of Knox demonstrates how influences other than legal theories and philosophies led Americans not only to embrace the Patriot cause but also to attempt to fight the war along civilized lines. A Boston bookseller before the war and a voracious reader, Knox nevertheless seems to have been neither influenced by nor even familiar with the works of Grotius or Vattel. Rather, he concluded that the Revolution was a just cause due to his own experiences in prewar Boston, which included being present at the Boston Massacre. Furthermore, Knox's determination to fight according to just principles stemmed from his deep reading of eighteenth-century military books, including textbooks and manuals. Such works stressed not only the formal rules for war but also the gentlemanly codes of honor that shaped European officers' actions toward one another: how the enemy was to be treated and how unnecessary violence was to be restrained. Hamilton illuminates the various ways in which the Revolution's participants came to see the justice of the war and the just manner in which it was to be fought—even though this view was not explicitly informed by famous just war theorists.

James Kirby Martin and Mark Edward Lender present a revisionist view of the Revolution's violence in chapter 6. Instead of focusing on *jus in bello* in terms of limits and restraints, they argue that many of the Revolution's combatants perceived the war as a conflict for their society's very existence—in other words, they believed themselves locked in an "existential war." In order to preserve the existence of their families, communities, and nation, combatants practiced war with brutality and ferocity and without restriction or restraint. They paid little or no heed to the norms of military conduct. Indeed, in military operations involving American Indians as well as Patriot and Loyalist militia forces, normal distinctions between soldiers and civilians all but disappeared; brutal tactics and inhumanity on the battlefield dramatically escalated. As a result, the Revolutionary War turned into, as one contemporary put it, "a contagion of violence."

Turning to the widespread destruction of homes, property, and occasionally entire communities by the British, Benjamin Carp also emphasizes the Revolution's unchecked violence in chapter 8. Because just war legal theorists always drew a rather blurry line between "military necessity" and inexcusable barbarity, Carp finds that the king's officers and soldiers alike often engaged in widespread destruction that caused considerable upheaval and dislocation. Throughout the war, however, both Britons and Americans publicly claimed that they were the true practitioners of civilized warfare, concealing their own atrocities while exploiting for propaganda the destructive acts perpetrated by the enemy.

William Tatum, on the other hand, argues that British commanders did attempt to follow *jus in bello* principles, particularly regarding the protection of civilians and their property. Looking closely at British courts-martial records in chapter 9, Tatum discovers that such ideals were oftentimes situational. During active military operations, for instance, civilian lives and property posing a threat to soldiers or to the success of a campaign could legitimately be targeted for violence. Yet when armed forces stood down or were not under direct danger, commanders worked hard to avoid excesses, especially with regard to physical assaults against civilians. He concludes, therefore, that British commanders not only understood *jus in bello* ideals to be an important guide to their actions but also realized such principles could not always be practiced amid the painful realities of war.

Concluding part 2, Cole Jones's chapter 10 further explores this divide between principles and practices as they were applied to prisoners of war. Looking at the treatment of British soldiers captured at Yorktown in 1781, he finds that Washington and other officers of the Continental Army sincerely wanted generous treatment for their subjugated foes. The majority of Americans, on the other hand, demanded vengeance. Therefore, Congress consigned the prisoners to an arduous captivity in Virginia, Maryland, and Pennsylvania, where cruel guards, inadequate funding, and chronic food shortages resulted in one third of the men dying of disease or malnutrition. By recovering the details of this neglected story, Jones illuminates how political and military decentralization as well as the ad hoc nature of the American war effort made it difficult to enforce *jus in bello* norms.

The six chapters comprising the section "*Jus in Bello*" both enlighten and complicate our understanding of the Revolutionary War and the role that just war values played in its conduct. As these authors demonstrate, most military commanders recognized that both law and right necessitated the humane treatment of enemy combatants and civilians and often worked to practice war according to such dictates. Paralleling these moral and legal obligations, the eighteenth century's martial code of honor for officers placed additional pressure upon commanders to lead their men with restraint and to limit any unnecessary destruction of lives or property. The American desire to be regarded as a sovereign power within the family of nations made it even more imperative that its officers adhered strictly to *jus in bello* doctrines. Likewise, British commanders hoped to retain the hearts and minds of Loyalists and even win back (if they could not force back) the allegiance of rebels. These imperatives helped sustain the rules of ritualized violence, including limited (though pitched) battle, what James Q. Whitman calls "the verdict of battle."[14]

Such ideals, however, were unavoidably situational and involved judgments of prudence and expedience. Indeed, the Revolutionary War's general officers never believed themselves to be absolutely bound by *jus in bello.* When certain circumstances presented themselves—such as "military necessity" during active campaigns or if locked in an "existential" war against "savage" or "barbarous" foes—these standards could be, and frequently were, discarded. Likewise, those outside of the military codes of law and honor rarely felt constrained by just war ideals. Unshackled from military laws, values, and discipline, civilians and irregular fighters sometimes gave freer vent to their anger and desire for vengeance, particularly as the sacrifices of the Revolution mounted to levels unimagined in 1775.

The final chapters explore *jus post bellum,* and in three very different approaches to this subject, the authors explore how just war principles were applied during the confusing final years of the Revolution and the first years of peace. It is important to note, however, that this third category of just war theory was largely undeveloped at the time of the Revolution. In fact, as a separate branch of modern theory, *jus post bellum* is still quite young, and its exact meaning continues to be debated.[15] *Jus post bellum* was originally *jus victoriae,* or "the right of the victor."[16]

Medieval theorists initially posited that in each conflict there was only one just side endowed with a preexisting right to victory, a right rooted in natural law.[17] When the justified belligerent prevailed militarily, the victor served as both "judge and executioner in his own cause."[18] This meant, as Stephen Neff describes it, a "law of dictates" in which the victor imposed punishments on the loser. It was not, in other words, a "law of treaties," with a negotiated conclusion among legal equals. Of course, even the preexisting moral right of the victor did not grant impunity in the conduct of war nor in the imposition of terms.[19] Indeed, Augustine, Gratian, and Vitoria all demanded Christian mercy, piety, and humility from a just victor pursuing its right to fair compensation and reliable limits on future aggression. Neither did the presumption of moral right allow a belligerent to do whatever it wished. For example, in the 1530s Vitoria argued against Pope Innocent IV and Charles V that Spain's king could not presume to conquer the West Indies in the name of ending cannibalism; he had no civil jurisdiction there. Such legalistic concepts of sovereignty progressed in the more modern philosophy and jurisprudence articulated by Pufendorf, Grotius, and Vattel.

For *jus post bellum,* a gradual transition to positive law also meant that there was no longer a moral superior engaged with an immoral offender. There was instead an international community of equals, all without a common superior. As this "international community" began to germinate in the era of Christian Wolff and Vattel, the law of dictates evolved into a law of treaties. Moreover, the Christian pieties of Augustine, Gratian, and Vitoria gave way to the more general and generous concept of compromise. Vattel echoed this subtle but significant shift when he wrote: "A treaty of peace can be no more than a compromise. Were the rules of strict and rigid justice to be observed in it, so that each party should precisely receive every thing to which he has a just title, it would be impossible ever to make a peace."[20] Just as Plato had long ago counseled the Greeks to fight like those who would one day be reconciled, Vattel knew that the goal of war must ultimately be peace. Like Plato's Greeks, the British and Americans were blood relations who would eventually have to reconcile.

The fluid nature and meaning of *jus post bellum* at the time of the American Revolution is reflected in our concluding essays. *Jus* during the eighteenth century, for example, was not simply interpreted as "law," it was also a concept of justice and morality. Furthermore, the circumstances of the Revolution placed it outside the boundaries of traditional *jus victoriae.* Americans sought not to conquer but to be independent, whereas the British sought to regain what they thought was theirs by right of possession. Both sides had constructed elaborate arguments about their legal rights and presented those claims before (to use Thomas Jefferson's words) "a candid world." As the chapters of the first two parts demonstrate, there was no universally compelling moral claim held by either side in the Revolution. And though one could argue that the "verdict of battle" had been decided at Yorktown, diplomacy and compromise were still necessary to bring the war to a conclusion.

With these facts in mind, Jonathan Den Hartog returns to a biographical approach with his incisive look at Founder John Jay in order to examine the thinking of one of the key U.S. diplomats who negotiated the Treaty of Paris of 1783. Indeed, Jay's life during the revolutionary crisis and war provides an excellent window into the moral reasoning and reflection prompted by the long and acrimonious conflict. As Den Hartog explains in chapter 11, Jay initially favored reconciliation with England; after independence was declared, however, he gradually became a strong advocate for nationhood provided that justice, reason, and Christian principles characterized America's efforts. Jay's work in Paris focused on bringing the war to such a conclusion as well as on having the United States be accepted as an equal nation among the European powers. In other words, influenced by both Grotius and Vattel, he wished to see the new republic as fully operating within *jus gentium*. Jay also reflected the longstanding Christian hope that God would grant victory to the nation that demonstrated its pious virtue. His postwar efforts to establish strong and virtuous governing constitutions further demonstrates his ongoing concerns with justice as the American nation gradually transitioned to peace.

The Revolutionary War's end from the British perspective, of course, looked very different. In chapter 12, William Anthony Hay addresses how principles of *jus ad, jus in,* and *jus post bellum* were related during the Revolution. He explains how British leaders were forced to accept not only American independence but also a fundamental reassessment of Parliament's constitutional sovereignty over the entire empire. Although George III and his ministers fiercely guarded this principle throughout the revolutionary crisis—indeed, it served as the war's crux—Hay skillfully analyzes how winning the Revolutionary War militarily proved more daunting than London officials had expected. By the time of Yorktown, they finally acknowledged that their forces could not achieve victory, at least in North America. Moreover, policymakers conceded the practical wisdom of agreeing to American independence while also recognizing the tangible benefits of accepting the United States into the international community of sovereign nations. Granting the former colonists their freedom would relieve the Crown of the great costs of defending America's vast territories and coastline while retaining the benefit of ongoing commercial ties. In agreeing to end the quarrel, British diplomats granted dominion to the United States and moved their own nation toward a conception of empire aspiring to economic rather than to military or political dominance. Although both sides entered the war with righteous anger, the resulting peace exemplified the principle articulated by Vattel: treaties are usually "no more than a compromise" falling short of strict justice—at least the "strict justice" that combatants surely sought at the beginning of the conflict.

Daniel Brunstetter's final chapter spotlights the crucial subjects of race, American Indians, and *jus post bellum* principles. In 1783, most white Americans congratulated themselves on their triumph over Great Britain. Their former imperial rulers had granted the United States its independence and ceded to it the frontier lands between the Appalachian Mountains and Mississippi River. At the same time, however, leaders and citizens of the United States considered the Indian tribes of North America, most of whom had attempted to remain neutral throughout the conflict, to be outsiders or even "merciless savages." Returning to Vattel's *Law of Nations,* Brunstetter points out that the Swiss theorist had argued that while a just peace could be sought with "civilized" nations, similar agreements could not be concluded with "savages." This was important because racial tensions between whites and Indians had significantly increased throughout the conflict. In fact, many U.S. leaders had perceived the tribes as insincerely neutral or actual impediments to American military progress; even worse, some had actually fought alongside the British. As a result, many Americans concluded that the Indians—as an entire race—deserved to be placed outside the norms of "civilization" and that wars of extermination and removal in the western territories could be lawfully pursued. Thus, heightened racial prejudices, intensified by the Revolutionary War and legitimized through *jus post bellum* ideas, set the stage for bitter frontier wars in the decades ahead, warfare that often made all progress in moral and legal reasoning seem to be of little consequence.

By recalling the role of just war theory in the American Revolution, the authors herein offer something essential for both scholars and general readers—a fresh approach to a popular subject that sometimes feels all too familiar. Most of them specialists in the revolutionary period, they avoid anachronism in the evaluation of their subjects. They do not recycle the era's propaganda, offer any definitive word on the conflict's status as a good or bad war, or append new arguments to political debates long since concluded. Rather, these scholars remind us that wars can be rightly understood only within their own social, rhetorical, and intellectual contexts. These chapters also remind us that moral judgments about the conduct of war mean the difference between life and death.

NOTES

1. Emer de Vattel, *The Law of Nations; Or, Principles of the Law of Nature, Applied to the Conduct and Affairs of Nations and Sovereigns, with Three Early Essays on the Origin and Nature of Natural Law and on Luxury,* edited and with an introduction by Béla Kapossy and Richard Whitmore (Indianapolis: Liberty Fund, 2008), 4.2.18 [book.chapter.section].
2. Adams told Thomas Jefferson in their famous exchange of letters during retirement that he had read Thucydides so many times during his life, "I Seem to be only reading the History of my own Times and my own Life." "John Adams to Thomas Jefferson, 3 February 1812," *Founders Online,* National Archives, last modified July 12, 2016, http://founders.archives.gov/documents/Jefferson/03-04-02-0361 (from *The Papers of Thomas Jefferson,* Retirement Series, vol. 4, *18 June 1811 to 30 April*

1812, ed. J. Jefferson Looney [Princeton, N.J.: Princeton University Press, 2007], 473–76).

3. In 1776 the Royal Military Academy at Woolrich assigned Thucydides in French to new cadets. On the reading habits of British officers in general at the time of the Revolution, including their familiarity with classical works, see Ira D. Gruber, *Books and the British Army in the Age of the American Revolution* (Chapel Hill: University of North Carolina Press, 2010), 3, 17.
4. Christian participation in the Roman army likely increased after the empire became more Christianized, though there is evidence of such enlistments before Constantine. Consider also biblical references to soldiers who sought moral direction from Christ or the apostles in Luke 3:14; Matthew 8:5–13; and Acts 10:1–48.
5. Many of our contributors address these modern classics of just war theory and their influence on commanders and statesmen on both sides of the Revolution. We know, for example, that some British officers on campaign in the eighteenth century brought along copies of Hugo Grotius's *De jure belli ac pacis* or *Laws of War and Peace.* British general William Tryon possessed a 1759 edition of Vattel's *Law of Nations* in his library; his indiscriminate destruction of property in raids in New York and Connecticut invites speculation about his actual reading or interpretation of it, however. See Gruber, *Books and the British Army,* 31, 111–13, 127–28, 135, 227.
6. James Turner Johnson, *Just War Tradition and the Restraint of War* (Princeton, N.J.: Princeton University Press, 1981); Michael Walzer, *Just and Unjust Wars: A Moral Argument with Historical Illustrations* (New York: Basic Books, 1977). Walzer's book is now in its fifth edition.
7. Among the key works on warfare in the age of Enlightenment, see especially Christopher Duffy, *The Military Experience in the Age of Reason, 1715–1789* (New York: Barnes & Noble, 1997); Armstrong Starkey, *War in the Age of the Enlightenment, 1700–1789* (Westport, Conn.: Praeger, 2003); and Patrick Speelman, *Henry Lloyd and the Military Enlightenment of Eighteenth-Century Europe* (Westport, Conn.: Greenwood Press, 2002).
8. On the decline of military history in academic departments, see John A. Lynn, "The Embattled Future of Academic Military History," *Journal of Military History* 61, no. 4 (1997): 777–89; and Robert M. Citino, "Military Histories Old and New: A Reintroduction," *American Historical Review* 112, no. 4 (2007): 1070–90.
9. Wayne E. Lee, *Barbarians and Brothers: Anglo-American Warfare, 1500–1865* (New York: Oxford University Press, 2011); Patrick Griffin, Robert G. Ingram, Peter S. Onuf, and Brian Schoen, eds., *Between Sovereignty and Anarchy: The Politics of Violence in the American Revolutionary Era* (Charlottesville: University of Virginia Press, 2015); John Resch and Walter Sargent, eds., *War & Society in the American Revolution* (DeKalb: Northern Illinois University Press, 2007); Harry M. Ward, *Between the Lines: Banditti of the American Revolution* (Westport, Conn.: Praeger, 2002); and Harry M. Ward, *George Washington's Enforcers: Policing the Continental Army* (Carbondale: Southern Illinois University Press, 2006). Notable for their focus on violence in the Revolution are Holger Hoock, *Scars of Independence: America's Violent Birth* (New York: Crown Publishers, 2017); Maya Jasanoff, *Liberty's Exiles:*

American Loyalists in the Revolutionary World (New York: Alfred A. Knopff, 2011); and Alan Taylor, *American Revolutions: A Continental History 1750–1804* (New York: W. W. Norton, 2016). Though targeted at an evangelical Christian audience and drawing normative conclusions, see also George Marsden, *The American Revolution: Partisanship, "Just Wars," and Crusades in the Wars of America: Christian Views,* ed. Ronald A. Wells (Grand Rapids, Mich.: William B. Eerdmans, 1981); and Mark Noll, *Christians in the American Revolution* (Washington, D.C.: Christian University Press, 1977).

10. See Armstrong Starkey, "Paoli to Stony Point: Military Ethics and Weaponry during the American Revolution," *Journal of Military History* 58 (1994): 7–27; Armstrong Starkey, "War and Culture, a Case Study: The Enlightenment and the Conduct of the British Army in America, 1755–1781," *War and Society* 8 (1990): 1–28; Glenn Moots, ed., "The American Revolution 240 Years Later: Was it a Just War?" special issue, *Journal of Military Ethics* 14, no. 1 (2015); John Keown, "America's War for Independence: Just or Unjust," *Journal of Catholic Social Thought* 6, no. 2 (2009): 277–304; Stephen Conway, "To Subdue America: British Army Officers and the Conduct of the Revolutionary War," *William & Mary Quarterly* 43, no. 3 (1986): 381–407; and Stephen Conway, "'The Great Mischief Complain'd Of': Reflections on the Misconduct of British Soldiers in the Revolutionary War," *William & Mary Quarterly* 47, no. 3 (1990): 370–90.
11. These are the standing contemporary divisions within just war theory, though it is defensible to say that they are longstanding categories in the tradition going back to seminal thinkers such as Augustine, Vitoria, Suárez, and Grotius. See Carsten Stahn, "Just Post Bellum: Mapping the Discipline(s)," in *Jus Post Bellum: Towards a Law of Transition from Conflict to Peace,* ed. Carsten Stahn and Jann Kleffner (Cambridge: Cambridge University Press, 2008), 93–94.
12. International humanitarian laws establishing formal rules for the conduct of war and the treatment of both combatants and noncombatants began to be adopted during the first Geneva convention of 1864. At this meeting more than a dozen nations agreed to adhere to certain standards of behavior in the treatment of wounded combatants and the civilian medical personnel who attended them. This was soon followed by other international conferences and additional multinational agreements.
13. Consider, for example, Grotius's famous statement in his prologue to *De jure belli ac pacis* in which he argues that the principles of natural justice would oblige us, "even if we should concede (*etiamsi daremus*) that which cannot be conceded without the utmost wickedness, that there is no God, or that the affairs of men are of no concern to Him" (sec. 11).
14. Whitman argues that such pitched but relatively limited battles were a more humane means of limiting destruction and determining victory, using the term "*jus victoriae.*" James Q. Whitman, *The Verdict of Battle: The Law of Victory and the Making of Modern War* (Cambridge, Mass.: Harvard University Press, 2012).
15. For instance, Larry May and Andrew T. Forcehimes have recently asserted: "The emerging field of *jus post bellum* scholarship is still in its formative years. Indeed, the very idea of *jus post bellum* is itself contested, in terms of its meaning and its

usefulness." See "Introduction," in *Morality, Jus Post Bellum, and International Law*, ed. Larry May and Andrew Forcehimes (New York: Cambridge University Press, 2012), 1. Modern theorists have prescribed a variety of ambitions for *jus post bellum:* e.g., the punishment of human rights violations or atrocities, the duty to reconstruct or nation build, adjudication by international courts, and installment of liberal political institutions. Such diverse ambitions confirm what Carsten Stahn has said about *jus post bellum,* calling it "unsatisfactorily narrow and overly broad at the same time"—it is more metaphor than moral or legal concept. See Stahn, "The Future of Jus Post Bellum," in Stahn and Kleffner, *Jus Post Bellum,* 231, 233.

16. The term *jus victoriae* is used differently here than Whitman used it as the determination of victory by the trial of a limited but pitched battle. Here it refers to the right possessed by the morally justified combatant in a just war.
17. Though the medieval worldview presumed a greater role for Providence in the outcome of battles and warfare, it did not equate victory with virtue. Might did not make right, and God sometimes gave the victory to an unjust combatant. This medieval perspective on victory was also a departure from the Roman presumption that victory meant divine favor.
18. Stephen Neff, "Conflict Termination and Peacemaking under the Law of Nations: A Historical Perspective," in Stahn and Kleffner, *Jus Post Bellum,* 77–78.
19. Stephen C. Neff, *War and the Law of Nations: A General History* (Cambridge: Cambridge University Press, 2005), 66–68.
20. Vattel, *Law of Nations,* 4.2.18.

PART I
Jus ad Bellum

1 JUST WAR THEORY IN THE IMAGE OF EMER DE VATTEL

Andreas Harald Aure

The Origins of Just War Theory

William Tecumseh Sherman, one of the most controversial generals in American history, called warfare "the last remedy on earth."[1] The pioneering Dutch humanist Hugo Grotius (1583–1645) asserted something quite similar more than two hundred years earlier when he established the basis of early modern just war theory. Grotius asserted that the justice of war rests on its status as a remedy or the right that everyone has to defend one's own (*suum*)—a concept commonly understood as one's natural rights.[2] Of course, those who initiate this remedy of warfare, either offensively or defensively, usually presume to have justice on their side; they believe that their action is justified. The challenge is how to make an objective assessment of the conditions justifying the commencement of such a powerful remedy. What are the legitimate grounds for warfare, and what are its limits? This is the task of just war theory, a *via media* between the theories of realpolitik (for example, the ideas of Niccolo Machiavelli or Thomas Hobbes) and pacifism, and a prevalent alternative to cosmopolitanism (for example, the goals of Immanuel Kant or Karl Marx).

Just war theorists of the early modern period were ethicists. They attempted to apply objective moral principles knowable to reason (traditionally known as "natural law") both to the conditions for war (*jus ad bellum*) and to the conduct of war (*jus in bello*). Their influence upon those who commenced and fought on both sides in the American Revolution was significant. The idea of just war, however, goes back at least to Cicero and the Roman *ius fetiale*. In the fifth century A.D., Augustine of Hippo established the foundations for a Christian theory of just war. Traditional conditions for a just war in the West were famously identified by Thomas Aquinas as right authority (*auctoritas principis*), just cause (*iusta causa*), and right intent (*intentio bellantium recta*). The Ciceronian and medieval traditions of *bellum justum* saw war as an act of dispensing justice between parties of unequal moral status, often legitimized by intrinsic or divine revelation.

During the sixteenth and seventeenth centuries, just war theory began a profound transformation that moved it away from relying on divine revelation and toward a purely philosophical and secular argumentation, which coincided with developing theories of natural rights. The late scholastics, such as Francisco Vitoria, who were developing elementary ideas of natural right, heralded the basic conditions or tenets of modern *bellum justum* in the background of the Spanish wars with the American Indians. In the seventeenth and eighteenth centuries, justice in the context of war became primarily about evaluating the legitimacy of protecting or defending one's rights (*jus*—justice). In this next stage of development, just war also obliged doing that which is right (*rectum*—the honorable) in a more extensive way.[3]

Grotius provided the most important breakthrough for the possibility of a philosophically grounded ethical justification for war and establishment of its moral limits. He insisted in his seminal work *De jure belli ac pacis libri tres* (Three Books on the Law of War and Peace) that the basic principles of natural law would have full validity even if (*etiamsi daremus*) there were no God ruling the universe.[4] Grotius launched a wave of philosophically rigorous arguments about politics and international relations that encouraged future intellectual giants such as Thomas Hobbes, Baruch Spinoza, Samuel Pufendorf, and John Locke. In the generations after his death, Grotius became the leading authority on natural law and just war and eventually was heralded as the father of just war theory as a subsection of international law. Following his lead, philosophers and authors studiously theorized about war and its nature, justification, bounds, and effects.[5]

Yet it took many generations—indeed, 150 years—before Grotius was superseded in the field of just war theory. In 1758 the Swiss diplomat Emer de Vattel published his celebrated *Le droit de gens* (The Law of Nations), and it immediately became the most impressive example of Enlightenment natural law in both form and content.[6] Vattel quickly became the most influential voice concerning just war theory among eighteenth-century leaders at the time of the American Revolution.

The Theoretical Development of Just War

Beginning with Francisco de Vitoria (c. 1483–1546), the late scholastics started to argue that war was not necessarily governed by intrinsic or divine concepts, rather it could be seen as subjectively just by both sides (*bellum iustum ex utraque parte*).[7] Yet the perception of justice corresponded to each side's understanding of justice. Therefore, despite opposing perceptions, a particular war was ontologically or materially just only on one side. But it was hard to decipher which side was truly justified, especially if both parties viewed themselves as working in good faith.

A consequence of this change was a gradual shift away from the idea of war as a form of dispensing justice and toward a new focus on its formalities distinct from such substantive issues as just cause and right intent. Carl Schmitt describes this evolution as *Hegung des Krieges,* meaning a way of limiting war by formal criteria.[8] In other words, the legality of war became a function of fulfilling certain formal criteria defined by certain conditions of competence, especially the legal competence of the political sovereign (*auctoritas principis*). The idea of two belligerents with equal status, both qualifying as *hostes iusti* (just enemies), was introduced. In such a scheme, lawful belligerents are those who hold supreme governing power (*summum imperium* or *summa potestas*), encountering each other legally as equals, just as opponents would do in a duel. By this conception, war is much less about the execution of justice, instead becoming a *bellum publicum solenne*—a formal or solemn public war.

Bellum justum and *bellum solenne* are archetypes. In theory and practice during the seventeenth and eighteenth centuries, they are closely interconnected and exist as two perspectives of one concept of a just war, which should ideally fulfill both substantive and formal criteria.

Generally, one perspective tends to be dominant in comparison to the other, thus shaping historical conceptions of war: *bellum justum* is dominant in medieval Christian thought, whereas *bellum solenne* becomes more dominant in the eighteenth and nineteenth centuries. In the sixteenth and seventeenth centuries, with the continuous development and influence of the states system and concepts of sovereignty, the idea of seeing *bellum solenne* as the legally relevant type of war becomes increasingly appealing in theory and practice. This has especially to do with the rise of the modern state. If certain formal criteria are fulfilled, the legal or external effects of war will increasingly be determined independently of the substantive cause by the fortunes of war. In this sense a conflict would be called just and trigger legal effects regardless of whose side the substantive justification lies or is claimed to lie upon.

The duality between (substantial) just war and solemn war is reflected most intensely, and some would say confusingly, in Grotius's *De jure belli ac pacis.* This dualism expressed a doctrine of just war more in accordance with the practical demands and realities on the ground—or how these realities would be judged in courts of law, such as admiralty courts. At the same time, the ideals of true justice according to natural law were never forgotten and continued to be fundamental to the concept of just war. Actually, it is possible to argue that discourse on substantive justice was strengthened when it became obvious which political actors were carriers of sovereignty (*summum imperium/summa potestas*).[9] But when the substantive conception of just war was in conflict with human necessities, peace, or the interests of all mankind (*societas gentium* or *magna universitas*), the theoretical ideals were relegated to the consciences of the belligerents as a matter to be settled with themselves and with God.

Eighteenth-century just war theorists continued to speak of the tribunal of conscience (*tribunal de la conscience*). Though sovereign nations "acknowledge no superior," as Vattel argued, sovereigns still were expected to obey the dictates of their conscience: what did their duties or moral obligations require of them, and what could they do or could they not do with the protection of the law? The need to defer authority (via the concept of *bellum solenne*) to the tribunal of conscience was necessary in order to avoid an incessant chain of war as well as to discourage others from entering a conflict. Vattel summarized well his approach by his statement that, on the one hand, everybody should themselves observe the precepts of substantive natural law, while on the other hand, everybody should allow others to avail themselves of the precepts (and effects) of formal war.[10]

Emer de Vattel (1714–67) and *Le droit de gens*

The leading theorist of just war at the time of the American Revolution, Vattel was born in 1714 in Neuchâtel, a principality ruled by the king of Prussia. From 1728 to 1730, he was enrolled as a student of the humanities at the University of Basel. In 1733 he went to Geneva to study theology and metaphysics. One of his teachers was the influential legal theorist Jean-Jacques Burlamaqui (1694–1748), under whose tutelage the young man began his study of the principles of natural law and the law of nations.[11]

Vattel's works became immensely influential in the learned discourse of the eighteenth century and served, like Grotius's work, as blueprints for the policies of kings and political leaders of that age and beyond—to this day the U.S. Department of Defense cites Grotius and Vattel multiple times in its *Law of War Manual*.[12] Vattel's *Le droit de gens* soon became, as the editors of its most recent modern edition have asserted, the "most important book on the law of nations in the eighteenth century."[13] On many questions of international relations, simply citing Vattel was enough to establish conclusive authority and force. Indeed, Charles G. Fenwick stated a century ago that the treatise "was the manual of the student, the reference work of the statesman, and the text from which the political philosopher drew inspiration."[14] An English translation in 1760 further advanced Vattel's authority in the British Empire.

Vattel's motivation to write *Le droit de gens* was to improve on Christian Wolff's *Jus Gentium Methodo Scientifica Pertractum* (1749). According to Vattel, Wolff (1679–1754) should be recognized for conceiving a "system of natural law of nations," which he praises in the preface to *Le droit de gens.* He laments, however, that Wolff's theory of the law of nations was so dependent on that author's voluminous works on philosophy and the law of nature, writing, "it is necessary to have previously studied sixteen or seventeen quarto volumes which precede [Wolff's work]. Besides, it is written in the manner and even in the formal method of geometrical works." Such liabilities convinced Vattel to make these ideas more accessible, especially to those whom the knowledge and principles of the law of nations are "most important and desirable."[15] Vattel uniquely possessed both the philosophical knowledge and practical experience to take on this challenge. His intelligence and legal knowledge came through his schooling, and his experience came through his long work as a diplomat.

Law of Nations Defined

Vattel's systematic approach to international law is rather complex and often quite misunderstood.[16] His preliminary definition of the law of nations (*droit des gens*) is "the science which teaches the rights subsisting between nations or states, and the obligations correspondent to those rights." What makes his conceptual framework hard to grasp is the supreme role he gives to free, independent, and equal commonwealths (*Les Etats*). For Vattel, "the law of nations is the law of sovereigns."[17] This means that scholars and philosophers (such as himself) are indeed asked to guide the sovereigns. Ultimately, however, since nations possess equal rights, they are themselves the final arbiters in the administration of their affairs.[18] *Le droit de gens* is a moral code for the just and prudent action of international actors rather than a manual or code of law in the sense of a command given by God.[19]

Just and Necessary Conditions for War (*Jus ad Bellum*)

According to Vattel, a war is "that state in which we prosecute our right by force." As a subject of the law of nations, only an openly declared public war is proper. Vattel writes, "Public war is that which takes place between nations or sovereigns, and which is carried on in the name of the public power, and by its order." Such war, he argues, is either defensive or offensive. Echoing traditional just war theory, Vattel further stipulates that a just war had to satisfy two main criteria: (1) the motivation had to satisfy the proviso of just cause, and (2) the commencement of hostilities had to satisfy the proviso of necessity. In other words, war is morally acceptable *only* as a last resort and when every other option proves ineffectual.[20]

The reasons given by a sovereign to make war, Vattel asserts, are of two classes—justificatory reasons and motives. Justificatory reasons come under the heading of justice. Motives must always be founded on fitness and utility, and they can be proper or vicious. Proper motives are those that advance the good of the state (*bien de l'Etat*) and the safety and common advantage of its citizens. Vicious motives are those that do not have such benefits as their object, but rather ambition or maliciousness: a thirst for riches, territorial conquest, hatred, or revenge. Such viciousness of motives makes the expressed cause no more than a pretext. For Vattel, pretexts are those reasons put forward as justificatory but that are really justifications only in appearance, or worse, totally destitute of moral foundation. Pretexts are also characteristic of reasons that are in themselves true and well-founded but are not of sufficient importance for undertaking a particular conflict. These are then used to mask ambition or other insidious motives. But a belligerent who has just grounds for taking up arms "cannot indeed be charged with injustice" even if the war is actually undertaken merely from advantage.[21]

In general, the right of employing force or making war belongs to nations no further than is necessary for their own defense and for maintaining the rights of the people. The basis or cause of every just war is injury, either already done or threatened to be done. In order to judge whether a war is just, one must consider whether he who undertakes it has *in fact* received an injury, or if he is truly threatened with one. To determine what qualifies as an injury, one must be acquainted with a nation's rights, that is to say, the people's perfect rights. Whatever strikes at these rights is an injury and may serve as a just cause for war.[22]

Only those to whom an injury is done or threatened have a right to make war. This excludes punishment as an independent cause for hostilities. According to Vattel, punishment cannot serve as a *just cause,* but it may be properly inflicted if an actual injury has been suffered.[23] If satisfaction cannot be obtained, a penalty capable of correcting the offender and serving as an example to others is justified *if* this is indeed the only remaining option. Such a right to punish is "evident," Vattel argues, though stressing that a third party has no right of punishing an independent nation for faults that are not its own concern. Nor may a nation set itself up as the defender of the cause of God, its sovereigns taking "upon them[selves the duty] to punish the moral depravity or irreligion of a people not committed to their superintendency."[24]

If a nation succeeds in conquering another, its rights to punishment are likewise limited. The whole right of conquest, Vattel asserts, is derived only from justifiable self-defense and the prosecution of one's rights. Justice allows for indemnification for expenses and damages necessitated by warfare. One's enemy may even be punished to render it incapable "of doing mischief in the future." But harming an adversary is "no farther authorized by the law of nature, than in the precise degree which is necessary for justifiable self-defense, and the reasonable security for the time to come." From the moment the danger is over, the right of conquest ends. At that point everything should be "conformable to the rules of a wise government and the duties of a good prince."[25]

Elucidating on this theme of defense against injury as a motive for just war, Vattel lists the following as permissible objectives: (1) to recover what belongs or is due to a belligerent, (2) to provide for one's future safety by punishing the aggressor or offender, and (3) to defend or protect from injury by repelling unjust violence.[26] The first two are the objects of an offensive war, the third of a defensive war. Offensive war may not be waged unless a nation is thoroughly assured of its right. Examples of evidently just causes for an offensive war are the recovery of property, the assertion of a clear and incontestable right, or the attainment of due satisfaction for a manifest injury. If justice cannot be obtained otherwise than by force of arms, then offensive war becomes lawful. But again, nature allows this measure only as a last resort, when all other means fail.[27]

The outcome of a conflict itself does not decide the substantial justice of that war; victory only compels the vanquished to subscribe to the treaty terminating hostilities. It is therefore an error to suppose that war's purpose is to decide controversies between those who acknowledge no superior judge—as would seem to be the case with sovereign nations. Victory ordinarily is a consequence of strength and prudence rather than of right and justice.[28]

Of War in Due Form

For a remedy as dreadful, destructive, and grievous as war, the law of nature allows its use only in the last extremity. A declaration of war, in which "the reasons which have induced us to take up arms" are announced, is therefore necessary "as a further effort to terminate the difference without the effusion of blood."

Improving on Grotius, Vattel states that there are only two requirements for a legitimate war to acquire due form (*justum bellum*). Legitimate or lawful war is distinguished from an illegitimate one, undertaken without any right or even without an apparent cause.[29] Hostilities ought to be authorized by the sovereign and accompanied by certain formalities, which consist of the demand of just satisfaction and a declaration of war. These conditions are required "in every war which shall, according to the law of nations, be a legitimate one, that is to say such a war as nations have a right to wage." A conflict in due form is also called a regular war (*guerre reglèe,* or in Latin, *bellum solenne*).[30]

Vattel stipulates the following requirements for a *bellum solenne*: (1) a nation have a just cause of complaint, (2) a reasonable satisfaction must have been denied that nation, and (3) the ruler of the nation must gravely consider whether it be for the *advantage* of the state to prosecute this right by force of arms.

Vattel shows that these conditions of regular war have their roots in Roman *fecial law.* The declaration serves as instruction and direction for both the nation it is directed at and for the instigator's own subjects. It also determines the so-called effects of war, such as the status and distribution of property rights *post bellum* or the claims of reparation. Regarding the timing of the declaration, the law of nations does not demand that it be given before entering the enemy's territories, though it must "necessarily precede the commission of any act of hostility." Defensive war, however, requires no declaration.[31]

The Rights of Nations and Persons in War (*Jus in Bello*)

Vattel argues that the right conduct in war (*jus in bello*) is conjoined with the right of making war; it is permissible to use the means necessary to attain just ends. Actions that go beyond those means, however, are faulty and condemnable at the tribunal of conscience (*tribunal de la conscience*).[32] For example, while all the subjects of an opposing nation are public enemies, those who make no resistance should not be maltreated or killed. Therefore, the prudent and humane general should punish the ungovernable soldier who offends by acts that "violate female chastity, [or] massacre women, children, and old men." The same goes for those who make war on "public ministers of religion, men of letters, and other persons whose mode of life is very remote from military affairs."[33]

An enemy who lays down his arms can no longer be killed with moral approbation. Whereas Samuel Pufendorf and John Locke still subscribed to the idea that enslaving prisoners of war was legitimate, Vattel prohibits this with one exception: If prisoners have rendered themselves guilty of some crime deserving the death penalty, it is lawful to enslave them in exchange for their lives.[34]

Vattel condemns treachery in warfare. In particular, he excoriates the use of assassins, arguing that they are both contrary to the necessary law of nations and pernicious to human society. Such killers, moreover, cannot be considered among the reasonable "surprises," which Vattel argues are "very allowable in war."[35] Assassination is different insofar as it is treacherous murder, wherein the perpetrator executes his perfidy by introducing himself "as supplicant, a refuge, a deserter, or, in fine, as a stranger." As a universally detested historical example, Vattel notes the assassination of William, Prince of Orange (1584). Similarly, he condemns the treacherous use of poisons. Regarding the use of poisoned weapons, Vattel concedes that if there is no clandestine machination, this may be excused or defended with a little more plausibility. But he reasons that since the use of poisoned weapons is pointless, it is contrary to the laws of war. Similarly, a general unanimity prevails against the illicit poisoning of waters, wells, and springs.[36] Vattel does argue that reprisals may be necessary in order to oblige one's counterpart or enemy to observe the laws of war. For example, if an enemy general, without any just reason, ordered some prisoners to be hanged, "we hang an equal number of his people."[37] From this example it becomes clear that Vattel does not grant the protection of the laws of war to those who themselves do not adhere to them.

Civil War

The discussion of Vattel's just war theory thus far has presumed a war between sovereign states. The United States did assert its sovereignty with the Declaration of Independence, and the new nation's leaders had Vattelian notions of sovereignty in mind. (For more on this, see chapter 3.) Likewise, George Washington expected his soldiers to be treated in accordance with existing conventions of war that existed among sovereign states and condemned breaches of those codes by the British under the excuse that the Americans were prosecuting a rebellion. Nevertheless, the American Revolution was a revolt against established authority and constituted a civil war. What are a sovereign's or a nation's rights in handling internal disturbances? Moreover to Washington's point, when might rebels obtain the status of waging a just war and claim protection of established international laws?

Vattel defines rebels as subjects who take up arms unjustly against the ruler of a society. Rebellious action can express itself in the form of "popular commotion" (*l'emotion populaire*). An instance of this is rioting against tax collectors. If the rage is leveled particularly at the magistrates, and people proceed to acts of open violence, it is called a sedition. When the violence infects the majority of the inhabitants of a city or province to the extent that even the sovereign is no longer obeyed, such disorder is designated an insurrection (*soulèvement*).

In discouraging such insurrection Vattel urges people "to patiently endure evils which are not insupportable, rather than disturb the public peace." Jefferson seems to echo this when he writes in the Declaration of Independence that "mankind are more disposed to suffer, while evils are sufferable, than to right themselves by abolishing the forms to which they are accustomed." Vattel argues that only harms that have become intolerable, accompanied by "oppression great and manifest," can excuse the use of force by citizens. Likewise, he asserts that "subjects who rise against their prince without cause, deserve severe punishment." That said, clemency may be called for in certain circumstances. For example, a sovereign may extend clemency on account of a great number of delinquents. Even if the insurrection is unjustified, it may be necessary to grant amnesty when the offenders are numerous. A good prince can even commend virtuous patriots who have resisted him, provided that their zeal is tempered with moderation and prudence. Furthermore, Vattel argues that promises to rebels, even to those who have revolted without reason or need, must be kept. This is necessary in order to avoid fostering despair on the part of insurgents or to minimize the risk of even more extreme bloodshed. In most cases, however, the safest and most just method of precluding sedition is to give the people satisfaction.[38]

Vattel is very careful to define the circumstances of justifiable civil war and its conduct. Civil war (*guerre civile*) is defined by the creation of a party formed within the state that no longer obeys the sovereign and are possessed of sufficient strength to oppose him. Likewise, if the nation is divided into two opposite factions and both sides take up arms, this is also called a civil war. Vattel applies the term "rebellion" *only* to such an insurrection against lawful authority if it is void of all appearance of justice.[39] Is the sovereign bound to conform to the established laws of war (*les loix communes de la guerre*) in a civil war? Yes, because the parties must, at least for a time, be considered to constitute two separate bodies and two distinct peoples. As elsewhere, Vattel recognizes the subjective nature of justice in warfare between separate sovereignties when he asks, "Who shall judge them? Who shall pronounce on which side the right or the wrong lies?" After all, "On earth they have no common superior." The resulting consequence of such disagreement between two contending parties is appeal to the sword. Each ought therefore to submit themselves to the same rights and duties as any other belligerents in warfare.[40]

Vattel also speaks to intervention in such cases (obviously relevant regarding the intervention of France in the American Revolution). He argues that foreign nations ought not to interfere in the internal affairs of an independent state.[41] But if they are not bound by any treaty, they are at liberty to judge the merits of a conflict and support either of the contending parties just as they would consider the merits of sovereign states in a conflict. Therefore, a nation has the right to succor a people who implore assistance to resist an unjust and oppressive sovereign. This was the case when the English applied for assistance to the United Provinces, leading to the demise of James II. For Vattel, the Dutch assistance "of brave people who defended their liberty" was clearly an act of justice and generousity.[42] As to the allies of a state distracted by civil war, they would have to look for direction from what he calls their "engagements," likely their treaties and agreements. They would also have to look to relevant existing circumstances.[43]

Conclusion

A substantial amount of philosophical and legal reasoning had been directed at the conduct of warfare by the time of the American Revolution. Vattel's work was the most comprehensive and authoritative, however, fortuitously appearing during the Seven Years' War and just prior to the troubles in North America, beginning with the Stamp Act crisis. Vattel and other just war theorists were read by commanders on both sides. It would be entirely speculative to imagine what precise judgments he might have rendered concerning the moral justice of the American Revolution or to suppose with any certainty how the war's statesmen and military leaders interpreted and applied his principles. As early modern just war theory itself recognizes, moral ambiguity always exists on both sides of a conflict.

That said, one can hear speculative echoes of Vattel in the origins and conduct of the Revolutionary War. With regard to *jus ad bellum,* just war theorists, including Vattel, Grotius, Pufendorf and many Protestant theologians, argued that subjects and citizens are never denied the right of self-defense; nor are they denied the power to hold magistrates accountable to the law. The Americans supplied important statements akin to Vattel's declaration of war and demand of just satisfaction when they wrote and disseminated the Olive Branch Petition, the Declaration of the United Colonies, and the Declaration of Independence. One can see in these documents Vattel's justified use of natural law and the law of nations in defense of a people's rights.

At the same time, however, one may also presume to hear Vattel in the British response. American protests were perceived at first to be little more than an unjust commotion over taxes, a protest that became a sedition directed by malcontents against officials and property and then an insurrection that exploded into a violent and illegal rebellion. Were not the rights of loyal British subjects to be protected from mob violence, civil disorder, and the destruction of property? Though the Americans claimed to be a separate sovereign power authorized by the creation of ersatz authorities such as the Continental Congress, it was not in Great Britain's interest to recognize such claims in their own conduct of the war.

The ambiguous legal status of American soldiers led by contested sovereign authority made the existing challenges of *jus in bello,* already difficult in any war, even more complicated. (Such moral quandaries, relevant for both sides, are addressed in part 2, particularly the treatment of combatants and noncombatants.) Vattel and his predecessors were concerned with these matters as well. And ultimately, Vattel was relevant for the conclusion of the war and the recognition of the new United States of America. Warfare, "the last remedy," was only the means to an end, just war theory a subset of international law. Only by respecting international law before, during, and after the conflict could the United States hope to join a community of sovereign nation-states with equal legal and moral status.

NOTES

1. William T. Sherman to Miss P. A. Fraser, Memphis, Oct. 22, 1862, in *Sherman's Civil War: Selected Correspondence of William T. Sherman, 1860–1865,* ed. Brooks D. Simpson and Jean V. Berlin (Chapel Hill: University of North Carolina Press, 2013), 319.
2. Hugo Grotius, *De jure belli ac pacis libri tres: In quibus ius naturae et gentium item iuris publici praecipua explicantur,* ed. B. J. Kanter-van Hettinga Tromp (1939), reprinted with additional notes by Robert Feenstra et al. (Aalen, Germany: Scientia-Verlag, 1993).
3. Cf. Andreas Harald Aure, "Der säkularisierte und subjektivierte Naturrechtsbegriff bei Hugo Grotius," *Forum Historiae Iuris* (2008), accessed Aug. 2016, http://www.forhistiur.de/fr/2008–02-aure/abstract/?1=en. For both an abridged and extended English version, see Andreas Harald Aure, "Hugo Grotius: Individual Rights as the Core of Natural Law," in *Philosophy of Justice,* ed. Guttorm Fløistad, Contemporary Philosophy: A New Survey (Dordrecht, Netherlands: Springer, 2015).
4. "Prolegomena," in Grotius, *De jure belli ac pacis libri tres,* sec. 11.
5. For a study of this reception, see Andreas Harald Aure, *The Right to Wage War (Jus ad Bellum): The German Reception of Grotius 50 Years after* De jure belli ac pacis (Berlin: Berliner Wissenschaftsverlag, 2015).
6. On Vattel's life, see Béla Kapossy and Richard Whatmore, "Introduction," in Emer de Vattel, *The Law of Nations, Or, Principles of the Law of Nature, Applied to the Conduct and Affairs of Nations and Sovereigns, with Three Early Essays on the Origin and Nature*

of Natural Law and on Luxury (1758), ed. Béla Kapossy and Richard Whatmore (Indianapolis: Liberty Fund, 2008), ix–xxiv, available at Online Library of Liberty, http://oll.libertyfund.org/titles/2246/212414. For a very good English introduction to his ideas on just war and his conceptual framework, with references to important studies of Vattel, see Simone Zurbuchen, "Vattel's *Law of Nations* and Just War Theory," *History of European Ideas* 35 (2009): 408–17. Excellent also is Ernst Reibstein, "Die Dialektik der souveränen Gleichheit bei Vattel," in *Zeitschrift für ausländisches öffentliches Recht und Völkerrecht* 19 (1958): 607–36, available at www.zaoerv.de. For an important essay on Vattel's highly innovative anthropology and foundation for his natural law theory, see Petter Korkman, "The Vital String of Mankind—Sociability and the Foundation of Natural Law and Universal Rights," in *Universalism in International Law and Political Philosophy,* ed. P. Korkman and V. Mäkinen (2008), 5–34, available at HELDA, University of Helsinki, http://hdl.handle.net/10138/25788. See also *Grotiana* 69 (2010), a collection of essays on Vattel.

7. This section relies heavily on the introduction of Aure, *Right to Wage War.*
8. Carl Schmitt, *Der Nomos der Erde im Völkerrecht des Jus Publicum Europaeum,* 4. Aufl. ed. (Berlin, Germany: Duncker and Humblot, 1997), 123.
9. See Pärtel Piirimäe, "The Wesphalian Myth and the Idea of Sovereignty," in *Sovereignty in Fragments: The Past, Present, and Future of a Contested Concept,* ed. Hent Kalmo and Quentin Skinner (Cambridge: Cambridge University Press, 2010), 78–79.
10. Vattel, *Law of Nations,* 3.12.188 [book.chapter.section], 590. Vattel stresses, "If an unjust war cannot, in its effect, confer any right, no certain possession can be obtained of any thing taken in war, until some acknowledged judge (and there is none such between nations) shall have definitively pronounced concerning the justice of the cause."
11. Kapossy and Whatmore, "Introduction," ix–x.
12. Office of General Counsel, Department of Defense, *Department of Defense Law of War Manual,* (Washington, D.C., June 2015), 36, accessed Aug. 2016, https://www.defense.gov/Portals/1/Documents/pubs/Law-of-War-Manual-June-2015.pdf.
13. Kapossy and Whatmore, "Introduction," ix.
14. Charles G. Fenwick, "The Authority of Vattel," *American Political Science Review* 7 (Aug. 1913): 395–410. As Theo Christov demonstrates in chapter 3, Vattel greatly influenced American statesmen before, during, and after the Revolution. Other contributors to this volume note how Vattel's work guided British leaders as well.
15. Vattel, *Law of Nations,* Preface, 12.
16. For an excellent elaboration, see Reibstein, "Die Dialektik der souveränen Gleichheit bei Vattel."
17. Vattel, *Law of Nations,* 1.1.12, 85.
18. Ibid., Preliminaries 21, 75–76.
19. Vattel grounds obligation in self-interest, not in duty. "Our expediency and our well-being . . . is the first principle of all *obligation*" (emphasis original). Vattel, "Essay on the Foundation of Natural Law and on the First Principle of the Obligation Men Find Themselves under to Observe Laws," in Vattel, *The Law of Nations, Or, Principles*

of the Law of Nature, Applied to the Conduct and Affairs of Nations and Sovereigns, with Three Early Essays on the Origin and Nature of Natural Law and on Luxury (1758), ed. Béla Kapossy and Richard "Whatmore (Indianapolis: Liberty Fund, 2008), 747–71, here at 754. Cf. Korkman, "Vital String of Mankind."

20. Vattel, *Law of Nations,* 3.1.1 and 5, 469, 471; ibid., 3.3.37, 488.
21. Ibid., 3.3.24–34, 482–87.
22. Ibid., 3.3.26, 483.
23. A well-crafted article outlining Vattel's approach to punitive war and the question of intervention is Simone Zurbuchen, "Vattel's *Law of Nations* and the Principle of Non-Intervention," *Grotiana* 31 (2010): 69–84.
24. Vattel, *Law of Nations,* 3.3.41, 490.
25. Ibid., 3.12.201, 598–99.
26. Ibid., 3.3.28, 484.
27. Ibid., 3.3.38, 488.
28. Ibid., 489.
29. Ibid., 3.3.68, 508.
30. Ibid., 3.4.66, 507.
31. Ibid., 3.4.51–60, 500–504.
32. Ibid., 3.8.137, 542.
33. Ibid., 3.4.145–46, 549–50.
34. Zurbuchen, "Vattel's *Law of Nations* and Just War Theory," 8; Vattel, *Law of Nations,* 3.4.152, 556.
35. Vattel, *Law of Nations,* 3.4.155, 559.
36. Ibid., 3.4.156, 562–63.
37. Ibid., 3.8.142, 545.
38. Ibid., 3.18.290–91, 642–44.
39. Ibid., 3.18.292, 645.
40. Ibid., 3.18.293–94, 645–47.
41. Ibid., 2.4.54ff.
42. Ibid., 2.4.56, 290. "Quand un peuple prend avec raison les armes contre un oppresseur, il n'y a que justice et génerosité à secourir de braves gens, qui défendent leur liberté."
43. Ibid., 3.18.295–96, 647–49. On the duties of allies, see ibid., 2.12, esp. 2.12.196–97.

2 JUST REVOLUTION

Protestant Precedents for Resistance and Rebellion

Glenn A. Moots and Valerie Ona Morkevičius

Tyranny and the Loss of Sovereign Authority

Just war theory asks three questions *ad bellum* to determine whether a war may be justly initiated: (1) Is the war declared by a legitimate authority? (2) Does the war have a just cause? (3) Is the authority declaring war motivated by the right intent? Intriguingly, authority is *always* the first question in the traditional formulation, as opposed to the more familiar contemporary accounts found in the works of Michael Walzer and his successors.[1] Legitimate authority is generally presumed to reside with the sovereign, and sovereign authority is traditionally fixed in only one office. Thus, a seminal argument in Western political thinking reasons that if the sovereign is no true sovereign but instead a tyrant, then some other actor may legitimately assume the mantle of authority. The justness of the American Revolution hinges on this logic because (1) Patriots asserted that British sovereignty was forfeit and (2) organizing elements of the Revolution (such as the Continental Congress) claimed legitimate authority to lead it.

Given the authority that the Bible and Protestant religious traditions held in America at the time of the Revolution, we survey Protestant approaches to the question of legitimate authority and rebellion. These examinations always deployed secular legal justifications alongside religious ones. Therefore, we also survey arguments on legitimacy and rebellion articulated by prominent legal theorists or philosophers (also in the Protestant tradition, though perhaps nominally) who developed seminal just war theories prior to the American Revolution: Samuel Pufendorf, Hugo Grotius, Emer de Vattel, and John Locke. We conclude with a brief survey of the Protestant character of the Revolution. Our approach exhibits how American revolutionaries followed the Protestant pattern of integrating theological and secular arguments to legitimize rebellion against established authorities deemed tyrannical. While there was a relevant argument for just revolution in the Protestant tradition that American colonists could deploy in defense of their actions, we do not take a position on whether the Revolution was just or not.

Protestant Theological Approaches

Given that many colonists, especially Patriots, traced their particular religious traditions to some variant of Lutheran or Reformed theology, we begin with Martin Luther and John Calvin. While both saw the magistrate's authority as delegated by God, they differed in their understandings of just how far that secular authority reached. These differences led them to divergent views on the permissibility of rebellion. Luther mostly followed the Augustinian tradition, discouraging rebellion, and argued that God empowered temporal leaders with authority only over secular affairs. A broader Lutheran tradition, however, articulated the first Protestant theories of active resistance to civil authority. Reformed theologians, including Calvin, were disparate in their approaches to revolution yet were united in calling for a greater ecclesiastical role for the sovereign than Lutherans had sought. This enlarging of the sovereign's responsibility increased the potential for charging de facto or de jure abdication against a ruler and thereby enlarged the grounds for resistance and rebellion by the people or by other magistrates.

THE SECULAR MAGISTRATE

In his early writings Luther cast earthly government as a limited good necessitated by human sinfulness. True Christians would be guided by love, he argued, and hence would have no need of government.[2] In a fallen world, however, where "there are few who believe, and even fewer who behave like true Christians," government is necessary to prevent men from acting like beasts.[3] Recognizing humanity's moral frailty, God conferred political authority on earthly princes—even heathen ones.[4]

The just magistrate's duty, according to Luther, is to maintain earthly order and leave spiritual matters to the church.[5] Any official who legislates on matters of faith becomes a tyrant, "commanding where [he has] neither right or power."[6] Conversely, he argued that spiritual leaders should refrain from claiming secular authority.[7] This strict division between spiritual and secular has had mixed consequences for resistance theory. On the one hand, it cedes secular authority to the state in ways that limit the possibility of legitimate resistance. On the other hand, it seems to recognize the possibility of a purely *political* tyrant by Luther's assertion that such rulers may "do violence or injustice in making their demands."[8] Luther's primary concern was that rulers "demand nothing contrary to God."[9] This opens the opportunity for spiritually driven resistance because "where secular authority takes it upon itself to legislate for the soul, it trespasses on . . . God's government, and merely seduces and ruins souls."[10]

Luther counseled, however, that the appropriate response to such tyranny is not armed rebellion, but rather some more passive type of resistance. The overriding principle was that no one should act contrary to conscience. Should one decide to resist and suffer civil consequences for their faith, they would be blessed for suffering at the hands of an impious magistrate.[11] Ultimately, Luther elaborated two distinct arguments against *initiating* rebellion. One is prudential. "A wicked tyrant is more tolerable than a bad war," he cautioned readers, and while a mob might change a government, "it is difficult to get one that is better, and the danger is that you will not."[12] This conservatism is not surprising, given the complicated political landscape and Luther's desire to distance himself from those who threatened to overturn traditional government, whether radical reformers (some Anabaptists, for example) or peasants in revolt.

Luther's other argument is normative, rooted in his theory of government. The people lack the authority to discipline their leaders: "The fact that the rulers are wicked and unjust does not excuse disorder and rebellion, for the punishing of wickedness is not the responsibility of everyone, but of the worldly rulers who bear the sword."[13] While this latter point prefigures a common line of resistance theory, Luther warned ambitious nobles as well.[14] The right to punish tyrannical leaders lies ultimately with God, who uses rulers to chastise his people.[15]

Nonetheless, neither prudence nor submission to God prevented Luther, Philip Melanchthon, or other Lutheran theorists from allowing self-defense against unlawful or immoral force. Nor did it preclude princes or nobles from protecting their jurisdictions from imperial overreach in ecclesiastical matters.[16] Justifications for such actions wed selected Bible passages with legal arguments (civil and natural) from both scholasticism and the *Corpus Juris Civilis* to argue that a tyrant's naked use of force both lacked moral authority and undermined his ability to honor good works and be a terror to the bad as defined in Romans 13.[17]

This interpretation of Romans 13:1–7, a key passage also used by *opponents* of resistance and rebellion, was critical to the development of resistance theory. First, it transformed a passage explicitly commanding obedience into one that justified *disobedience* against those who did not exemplify Saint Paul's definition of a magistrate. Second, it empowered other magistrates to lead the people in their resistance, thereby fulfilling their ordained function by punishing wrongdoers—those rulers who did not fulfill their divine charge.

Such argumentation and exegesis became even more robust in the Reformed, or Calvinist, tradition.[18] Reformed Protestants such as Peter Martyr, Theodore Beza (Calvin's successor in Geneva), and John Knox all alluded to the right of self-defense first asserted by Lutheran magistrates against imperial law in the Magdeburg Confession of 1550. Encouraging magistrates to oppose other magistrates also became a significant part of Reformed resistance theory.[19]

THE FAITHFUL MAGISTRATE

While there were Lutherans in America (including Peter Muhlenberg) who were enthusiastic supporters of the Revolution, many of the English, Scots-Irish, French, Germans, and Dutch who came to the New World subscribed to the Reformed Protestant tradition.[20] Sydney Ahlstrom's landmark religious history of North America suggests that by 1776, three quarters of Americans shared a moral and religious background in Reformed Protestantism. This theological movement's theory of resistance and rebellion was even more robust than that of the Lutheran tradition.

The Reformed tradition imagined earthly government in more positive terms than the Lutherans and hence awarded it a broader mandate. In Calvin's view, for example, government lays the seeds for the "heavenly kingdom," creating opportunities for transcending the mortal and reaching toward "immortal and incorruptible blessedness."[21] Put simply, the government's temporal and spiritual responsibilities are interlocked even though the delegated powers of the magistrate and the clergy were distinct. A government cannot establish a stable and secure society without setting about "to foster and maintain the external worship of God, to defend sound doctrine and the condition of the Church, to adapt our conduct to human society, to form our manners to civil justice, to conciliate us to each other, [and] to cherish common peace and tranquility."[22] Calvin's most important colleague in Zurich, Henry Bullinger, likewise sought a close partnership between the magistrate and the church.[23] The Scottish reformer John Knox charged the "godly magistrate" with the obligation to reform the church and to protect it from "tyranny and bondage," thereby ensuring its survival.[24] Likewise, the influential English Puritan William Ames argued that the Lord's business and the Crown's business were not in conflict: "the care and knowledge of the things which are Gods, may well belong to the King."[25] A similarly robust but somewhat nuanced charge to the magistrate is found in chapter 23 of the Westminster Confession of Faith (1647) as well as other Reformed confessions. So, whereas Lutheran theorists recognized the rights of princes or nobles to *defend* piety and doctrine in their territories, Reformed Protestants wanted rulers to *establish* piety and doctrine.[26]

Such a broad charge to the magistrate meant that earthly governments must prevent and punish idolatry, blasphemy, and heresy just as readily as they would punish crimes against lives and property. This was Calvin's position in his *Institutes*.[27] Similarly, Knox argued that a magistrate who fails to suppress heretical clergymen who "murder the souls" is no better than one who tolerates self-serving judges.[28] For Ames, the duty to care for the spiritual health of the community may even outweigh other concerns. In his view, promoting the "true Religion" and repressing impiety should be the "chief care of the Magistrate."[29]

It must be emphasized that Reformed theologians, like the Lutherans and other magisterial reformers, sought to distance themselves from what they perceived as Anabaptist anarchy and Roman Catholic subterfuge. They agreed with Lutherans not only that a tyrant was one who failed to uphold the good and punish the bad but also that people get the government they deserve. While the faithful may be blessed with a good ruler, God also chastises the sinful by imposing tyrants.[30] Calvin insisted, for example, that the people owe "reverence" and obedience to their leaders, "be their characters what they may."[31] Even if "cruelly tormented," "rapaciously pillaged," "neglected," or "persecuted," the people should remain obedient, pleading to God for help rather than taking matters into their own hands.[32] He discouraged rebellion elsewhere in his writings, including his commentaries on Genesis, Psalms, Acts, and Romans.

Although Calvin urged public prudence and restraint, he also famously asserted that God may send "manifest avengers" to rescue the oppressed.[33] These liberators could be foreign princes, who often intervene for their own private purposes, or domestic magistrates, who have a *duty* to "check the undue license of kings."[34] "Magistrates," writes Calvin, "ought to do their utmost to prevent the liberty, of which they have been appointed guardians, from being impaired, far less violated." Those who fail to do so "are perfidious traitors to their office and their country."[35] This famous reference to "the lesser magistrates" and their right of interposition is a precise permission, however. Calvin indicated in his *Institutes* and elsewhere that this was intended only where such constitutionally warranted checks exist (as he explicitly suggested by citing Greek, Roman, and medieval precedents).[36] Bullinger was quicker than Calvin to condemn tyranny, though, insisting that the devil, not God, was the author of oppression.[37] When Knox approached each for approval of armed resistance by Protestant nobles against Catholic rulers, however, the responses of both Bullinger and Calvin were more circumspect and cautious than he had anticipated.[38] Knox, a Scottish clergyman who had found refuge in Geneva during the Marian exile of Protestants, had hoped for their unequivocal support against the Roman Catholic authorities who then ruled England and Scotland.

Even if Knox did not get the approval he wanted from the de facto ecclesiastical leaders of Geneva and Zurich, his arguments have been of enduring interest to scholars and laymen. Knox's *Faithful Admonition* is full of angry, violent language and charges Mary Tudor with idolatry and treason. In Knox's view tyranny stems from two possible causes: rulers failing to perform their duties, or usurping authority from its rightful holder. In the first case Knox declares that wicked kings do not bridle impiety and therefore do not govern at all. This makes them tyrants.[39] In the second, he argues against those who usurp the royal seat through conspiracy (as was alleged against Mary Tudor). Knox further condemns all female leadership, stating that any woman claiming a right to rule is guilty of "treason and conspiracy" against the laws of God and nature because woman "is not born to rule over man."[40]

Angry rhetoric aside, Knox does not advocate outright rebellion by the public.[41] Instead, he believes that the nobility, as civil magistrates, are entitled to exercise such authority.[42] For Knox, the nobles have the "duty . . . to defend innocents" and to "bridle and repress" the rages of a tyrant.[43] Thus, he imagines that the faithful nobility should push for political change, while the common people should practice nonviolent resistance, including tax strikes.[44] Knox even goes so far as to write, in regard to English succession, that nobles have a duty to "without further delay remove from authority all such persons as by usurpation, violence or tyranny" who claim the throne—simply put, to rebel against Mary Tudor.[45]

Other Reformed Protestants like Knox, hard pressed by Roman Catholic monarchs in England and Scotland, articulated diverse and eclectic political theories on questions of sovereignty, authority, resistance, and rebellion. Bishop John Ponet's anonymously published *A Shorte Treatise of Politike Power* (1556), while directed primarily at ecclesiastical authorities rather than civil ones (it never mentions Mary Tudor), provides a justification for tyrannicide, combining biblical passages with arguments derived from classicism, scholasticism, and common law. Ponet locates the locus of political power in the people, condones popular revolution, and advances private property rights against tyrannical appropriation.

Knox's fellow exile in Geneva, Christopher Goodman, likewise wrote a notable treatise on resistance.[46] Published there in 1558, *How Superior Powers Ought to be Obeyed* advocates tyrannicide and popular rebellion from both scripture and law. Goodman aggressively deploys Reformed Protestantism's ecclesiastical charge to the magistrate to argue that those officials who betray their responsibilities forsake legitimacy altogether. Drawing on themes of covenantal judgment, Goodman contrasts human and divine authority, presaging what Thomas Jefferson would include on his personal seal and, together with

Benjamin Franklin, propose as the seal for the United States: "Resistance to Tyrants Is Obedience to God."[47] Ponet, Knox, and Goodman thus transformed Calvin's right of resistance into a duty, if not an outright call for rebellion.[48]

Facing hostile Catholic authorities in France, Reformed Protestant Huguenots similarly developed elaborate theories of resistance, blending scripture and tradition with rich, sometimes inventive, histories; humanist precedents; and legal arguments. The *Vindiciae, Contra Tyrannos* posits the existence of a multipart covenant that, once betrayed by the sovereign, justifies taking up arms. The list of acts defining tyranny include ignoring counsel, abusing taxation to fund extravagance, and the lawless persecution of subjects. The *Vindicae*'s anonymous author (possibly Philippe de Mornay) not only gives permission for resistance but also considers it a duty. The use of Roman and canon law in *Vindiciae, Contra Tyrannos* is so richly integrated with covenant theology that scholars debate whether it is not better classified as a work of late (and largely secular) medieval political thinking.[49]

Francis Hotman's *Francogallia* (1573) and Beza's *Du droit des magistrats* (1574, published anonymously) preceded the more famous *Vindiciae.* Hotman provides an elaborate constitutional and legal argument from French history, whereas Beza discerns an elaborate constitutional and contractual obligation that kept the king faithful to the law by force if necessary. Both find extensive precedent for these obligations in humanist and biblical sources. Most notable for comparison with the American Revolution is the way that Beza justifies magistrates taking the initiative *without* the king—should he not call the estates (a kind of representative authority or constitutional check)—to organize themselves in opposition to him, much as Huguenot aristocrats did in the *assemblées politiques.* This action arguably paralleled the American colonists' appointment of authorities such as the Continental Congresses to mediate and organize opposition to imperial policy.

The common practice in these works of blending secular and sacred sources should not be surprising given the legal and humanistic training of many reformers. Calvin himself had argued that politics, as an earthly pursuit, should be informed by reason and human wisdom.[50] Scottish Covenanter Samuel Rutherford, an opponent of Charles I and defender of the parliamentary cause, was an encyclopedia of political thought, drawing on more than seven hundred authors both sacred and secular without prejudice.[51] Ames also invoked a natural-law conception of government as a sort of social contract. In Ames's view, God had instituted the *general idea* of magistrates, but the specific form a particular government took was "the device of man."[52] Thus, he asserted, officials do not have a right to absolute power—they are always limited by the will of God and the will of man (through the laws).[53] A ruler who transgresses these limits ceases, by definition, to be a sovereign and devolves into a tyrant; his state likewise ceases to "constitute a City of Body Politick" but instead devolves into "monstrous slavery."[54] In a similar vein, Presbyterian George Buchanan's *De jure regni apud Scotos* (1579) declares that kings are accountable to the people. Such arguments demonstrate the influence of republican thought on Reformed Protestantism overall.

International Legal Approaches

Beyond this Protestant theological tradition, British and American thinkers over two centuries had availed themselves of an increasingly influential discussion of international law, or *jus gentium*. This legal tradition also addressed resistance, rebellion, and civil war.[55] As in the cases of English and French Protestants, other dissenting Protestants deployed a host of secular, legal, historical, and philosophical arguments in their baptism of revolution. Many secular theorists of international law likewise invoked scripture or God. Furthermore, the four jurists and philosophers surveyed below (Grotius, Pufendorf, Vattel, and Locke) were all Protestants themselves, and there are certainly echoes of that theology in their works. Though some of their ideas are summarized elsewhere in this volume, we briefly do so here to show how theological and legal arguments can be complementary. Theologians emphasized obligations to God *in addition* to questions of law and political theory, while the legal and political theorists focused *almost exclusively* on questions of law and political theory apart from theology.

Grotius, Pufendorf, Vattel, and Locke all saw governmental authority as rooted in social relations. But differences in the ways they framed these relationships affected their judgments on obedience and rebellion. For Grotius, states are a rational way to protect certain natural rights, namely life, liberty, property, and contract.[56] For the more explicitly contractarian Pufendorf, governments arise from a three-step process in which subjects not only agree to submit to authority for the sake of protection but also establish a particular form of government.[57] And as for Vattel, individuals enter into political associations not just for the creation of social order but also to perfect themselves (and their societies).[58]

Because an "indiscriminate right of resistance" would undermine the rational basis of the state's existence, Grotius was reluctant to permit *active* rebellion.[59] Pufendorf believed that the creation of sovereignty by an irrevocable act of association did not preclude the possibility that a sovereign could later effectively forfeit his authority.[60] Vattel's view, by contrast, considered the social contract as an ongoing plebiscite, reserving for the people the right to change their constitution at will.

Grotius and Pufendorf both understood the origin of the magistrate's authority in political terms. Rather than imagining the magistrate as a divine institution, Grotius claims in *On the Law of War and Peace* that humans accept governance rationally "of their own free Will, out of a Sense of the inability of separate Families to repel Violence."[61] From this perspective, the primary function of the government is to establish a peaceable and orderly society that protects property and lives, guarantees promises, and "[inflicts] just punishment."[62] Pufendorf's view is traditionally Christian in his writings, deeming civil authority to be divinely ordained.[63] But this ordination is not direct; people's God-given reason compels them to establish civil states for the sake of peace and order.[64] Sharing Luther's pessimistic reading of human nature, in *On the Duty of Man and Citizen,* Pufendorf identifies the purpose of the state as protecting citizens "from the losses and injuries which they may, and so often do inflict on each other."[65]

While mindful of civil concerns, the first generation of Protestant theologians emphasized *religious* concerns in their definition of tyranny. Early modern legal scholars like Grotius and Pufendorf emphasized the violation of certain basic rights to life, liberty, property, and contracts as constituting tyranny. In short, the state's civil sovereignty must be limited. Grotius imagines that at inauguration, a ruler can make binding promises to God or his subjects, "even such Things as respect the Government of the State," and hence limit his authority, including by the observation of certain laws.[66] For Pufendorf, sovereignty emerges from the political constitution between the people and their government, which determines the extent of the latter's authority.[67]

While this idea of constitutional constraint echoes Luther's division between secular and religious authority, Grotius and Pufendorf's version is much broader—in principle, a society can choose to limit the scope of its rulers' authority in any way it pleases. This broadens the universe of cases in which rebels could claim legitimacy by arguing that the sovereign had violated the contractual terms.[68] Simply put, any leader who transgresses the established limits acts unjustly.[69]

Despite arguing that sovereign authority can be sharply constrained, however, Grotius and Pufendorf's theories do not lend themselves easily to justifying rebellion. Both emphasize the subjects' duty of obedience. In this one hears echoes of the Protestant theological reminder that the value of order may trump justice. If government is established for the sake of order, it would be irrational to permit an "indiscriminate right of resistance."[70] This even precludes, in contrast to Calvin, a right of resistance for lesser magistrates.[71] Furthermore, subjects ought to forgive the faults committed by the leaders out of "Fear, Anger, or some other Passion," rather than rashly labeling them as tyrants.[72] Pufendorf likewise finds it "morally wrong" for citizens to resist legitimate government commands and urges citizens to be "content" with the status quo rather than contemplate revolution.[73] Like Grotius, he warns that it is "a folly and impudence to oppose a Prince for every fault," encouraging subjects instead to "overlook [his] pardonable failings."[74]

Nonetheless, like Luther and Calvin, Grotius and Pufendorf permit nonviolent resistance to leaders who issue orders against divine or natural law. If a king abuses his power and orders something "manifestly unjust," then the people are not obligated to obey.[75] As Grotius puts it, sovereign political authorities cannot rightfully require anything contrary to the "Law of Nature, or the Commands of God."[76] Pufendorf similarly requires citizens to obey the civil laws "so far as they are not openly repugnant to divine law."[77] If public authorities, however, overstep their bounds, subjects have a duty to disobey.[78] Yet this grants nothing more than a right to resist, not a right to rebel (or in Grotius's words, "to compel the King, or to command him").[79] If the sovereign punishes his people for their resistance, they "ought rather to bear it patiently, than to resist by force."[80]

What of cases where the sovereign goes even further, threatening lives with unjust force? Are subjects obliged to uphold "the Law of Non-resistance," Grotius asks, even if it puts them in "the most extreme and inevitable danger"?[81] Logically, if security is the original purpose for which humans enter civil society, the formation of a state cannot "impose on all Citizens the hard Necessity of dying, rather than to take up Arms in any case, to defend themselves against the higher Powers."[82] Grotius thus opens the possibility of armed self-defense against a tyranny "unless the Resistance would infallibly occasion great Disturbance in the State, or prove the Destruction of many Innocents."[83] In permitting rebellion *so long as the consequences are not worse than the cause,* Grotius is actually echoing the idea of prudential rebellion found not only in Protestant thought but also in medieval precedent, including Thomas Aquinas.[84]

Grotius argues that fighting a tyrant is not by definition rebellion because an oppressor has no legitimate authority.[85] As "an Enemy to the whole Nation," the tyrant relinquishes his right to rule.[86] A sovereign can also cede his authority in other ways, by abdicating, abandoning the government, or handing it over to another power.[87] In all these cases, resistance "is not directed against a sovereign and therefore cannot violate any sovereignty rights."[88] The Protestant theologians we surveyed above had made similar arguments.

Yet Grotius's belief that sovereignty could be constitutionally constrained (a more secular legal iteration of the covenantal restraint in the *Vindiciae*) also generates the possibility of positive law justifying resistance.[89] This includes situations where free peoples retain the right to choose their sovereign at will. It also encompasses cases where the ruler violates an explicit clause of an act conferring sovereignty or deprives the people of "some part of natural liberty" expressly reserved to them.[90] Notably for the American revolutionary context, Grotius specifically mentions cases where sovereign power is divided (as between a king and a parliament), and the ruler invades "that part which is not his own."[91] Unlike Calvin, he does not restrict resistance in such cases to lesser magistrates. Instead, he permits "all private persons, or a small Part of the People" who find themselves "reduced to the last Extremity," a right to defend themselves so long as it is for the "publick Good."[92]

Pufendorf's logic follows Grotius, permitting an individual right to self-defense.[93] If the king directs injustice at particular individuals, threatening "the worst and most cruel injuries," Pufendorf argues that a good response is to flee or hide.[94] Indeed, if legitimate resistance would threaten the health of the commonwealth, individuals "ought rather to be killed than to kill."[95] If, however, the sovereign injures the whole people by failing to defend the state against external enemies or failing to establish domestic order through law, he has "plainly abdicated the government."[96] Revolutionaries in America used this abdication argument, most famously in the Declaration of Independence: "He has abdicated government here, by declaring us out of his protection and waging war against us."

More than a half century after Grotius and Pufendorf, Emer de Vattel shared many of the same underlying beliefs about the origins of political authority as his predecessors, imagining civil society as arising out of a sort of contract. His treatise *The Law of Nations*, first translated anonymously into English in 1760, describes the purpose of civil society as procuring for citizens "the necessities, the conveniences, the accommodations of life, and, in general, whatever constitutes happiness."[97] Happiness for Vattel was not a hedonistic pursuit, but rather a reflection of the duty of individuals—and states—to "perfect" themselves in all regards.[98]

Like Grotius and Pufendorf, Vattel asserts that societies can constitutionally define the nature and reach of the public institutions entrusted with defending and perfecting the state.[99] As his predecessors did, Vattel opens the possibility of at least passive resistance. If a constitutional monarch exceeds "the bounds prescribed him, commands without any right, and even without a just title: the nation is not obliged to obey him, but may resist his unjust attempts."[100] Here he injects more-contractual language: in thus "[attacking] the constitution of the state, he [the monarch] breaks the contract which bound the people to him: the people become free by the act of the sovereign, and can no longer view him but as an usurper who would load them with oppression."[101] Indeed, even if the constitution had created an absolute monarchy, the society cannot be understood as having "irrevocably [surrendered] itself and all its members to the discretion of a cruel tyrant."[102]

Paraphrasing Grotius, Vattel asserts that the nation always holds in "tacit reserve" the condition that the sovereign's authority is to be used "for the safety of the people, and not for their ruin"; if he acts against the people's interest, then he "is no better than a public enemy."[103] Vattel theoretically opens the door to revolution wider by arguing that the nation maintains "an indisputable right to form, maintain, and perfect its constitution,—to regulate at pleasure everything related to the government,—and that no person can have a just right to hinder it" since the "government is established only for the sake of the nation."[104]

Like his predecessors, Vattel permits resistance in cases where the sovereign's demands conflict with the law of nature or with sacred law.[105] If the "injuries are manifest and atrocious,—when a prince, without any apparent reason, attempts to deprive us of life, or of those things, the loss of which would render life irksome," then the citizen has the right and duty to disobey.[106] Such a prince, who would "take away the life of an innocent person," thus "divests himself of his character, and is no longer to be considered in any other light than that of an unjust and outrageous enemy, against whom his people are allowed to defend themselves."[107]

Given the amount of residual authority held by the public, it is not surprising that Vattel permits nonmagistrates to act in self-defense against tyranny. But he injects an explicit note of caution: his use of "the nation" is not intended to "authorize a few malcontents or incendiaries to give disturbance to their governors by exciting murmurs and seditions. None but the body of a nation have the right to check those at the helm when they abuse their power."[108] This precludes what Vattel calls "the monstrous and absurd doctrine, that a private person is permitted to kill a bad prince."[109] Elsewhere he reiterates that "it is of the utmost importance to observe, that this judgment can only be passed by the nation, or by a body which represents it."[110] This move is aimed at ensuring that revolutions will be rare occurrences—responses to cases of grave tyranny, not mere discontent.

Furthermore, as the Protestant theologians did, Vattel argues that prudential reasons rightfully constrain the recourse to rebellion. When resistance is possible in cases of limited sovereignty through the body of a legislature, the bar is relatively low: "when mild and innocent remedies can be applied to the evil, there can be no reason for waiting until it becomes extreme."[111] But resisting an absolute prince, he says, "cannot be done without raising great disturbances in the state" and hence "ought to be attempted only in cases of extremity." Enduring the status quo must be deemed worse than civil war.[112] Likewise, Vattel warns that in "doubtful cases" subjects should not resist, but rather obey; after all, to oppose the prince at every turn is to return to the state of nature.[113] Citizens ought, therefore, "to patiently suffer from the prince, doubtful wrongs, and wrongs that are supportable," sacrificing themselves "to the peace and safety of the state, on account of the great advantages obtained by living in society."[114]

As for Locke, it should first be noted that he agreed with the arguments of Grotius in *On the Law of War and Peace* and Pufendorf in *Of the Law of Nature and Nations.* In *Some Thoughts Concerning Education,* Locke recommends both, together with Pufendorf's *On the Duty of Man and Citizen* (though he gives preference to *Of the Law of Nature and Nations*). Locke prescribes both Grotius and Pufendorf as instruction in the "natural rights of men, and the original and foundations of society."[115] Yet he also articulates his own influential ideas concerning both war and rebellion. We shall focus primarily on his ideas regarding rebellion, not warfare overall.

Locke's argument for resistance and revolution in his *Two Treatises on Government* is well known. There are terms under which the social (political) contract is formed. This contract exists to spare persons from the inconveniences (and bloodshed) of the state of war. If the terms of the contract are breached, the authority of government devolves to the people, the state of war resumes, and the rights of citizens may be asserted against the abuses of their legislature or executive.[116] Locke's argument is essentially that the legitimate use of force relies on the rule of law. He declares, "Whosoever uses force without right, as every one does in society, who does it without law, puts himself in a state of war with those against whom he so uses it; and in that state all former ties are cancelled, all other rights cease, and every one has a right to defend himself, and to resist the aggressor." [117] With the dissolution of the social contract, the parties involved revert to the state of nature that existed prior to the creation of government and civil society. It is particularly interesting how Locke's individuals in the state of nature (whether before the creation of government or after its dissolution) resemble nations as described in the ideas of international law budding in the seventeenth and eighteenth centuries. Both individuals and nations are essentially equals contesting claims of right without a common (earthly) superior to adjudicate them.[118]

Locke gives specific conditions for just resistance against a ruler. People are free to resist a tyrant who abuses prerogative power, denies government by consent, necessitates justified self-defense, or threatens the people's religion.[119] Locke condemns *rebellion* as an offense before God. Echoing not only Pufendorf and Grotius but also arguments extending to antiquity, Locke contends that magistrates become rebels themselves should they betray the good of the people (*salus populi*) for whom they were empowered; this is what he means by "force without right."[120] It should be emphasized that political threats against religion are also a cause for just revolution. Though only mentioned twice in the *Second Treatise,* this is consistent with the emphasis that Locke places upon the immortal soul, eternal happiness, and divine favor as the "highest obligation that lies upon mankind" in his *Letter Concerning Toleration.* If a ruler enforces religious impositions contrary to "the constitution of the government granted him, nor ever was in the power of the people to grant," the people have the right to meet that dictate with force. God alone, Locke declares, is the judge in such disputes. In a passage with clear implications, he admonishes that "the chief care of every one ought to be of his own soul first, and, in the next place, of the public peace." Even if the magistrate will likely prevail in such a clash, the people still possess the right to initiate that conflict forcefully for the sake of their own souls.[121]

Because there is no earthly judge to resolve such contests between rulers and the citizens, God is ultimately the judge in such cases.[122] It is notable for our purposes that Locke defends revolution with both reason and scripture and calls it an "appeal to heaven" in the context of the latter (Judges 11:27).[123] Men must judge whether or not they are in a state of war; but having judged themselves that they are, God is the judge of right in such cases.[124] In short, people must be prepared to answer to God for their decision to resist. Though Locke makes this point about divine judgment soberly, one would infer that those convinced of their rights in such contests could rally (or claim to have rallied) God to their cause. American revolutionaries did as much in deploying the phrase "An Appeal to Heaven" on a flag.[125]

Protestantism in the Revolution

Though historians disagree about the *precise* role of Protestant religion in the Revolution, there is sufficient reason to agree with John Coffey's recent argument that John Pocock's "British Revolutions" (1641, 1688, and 1776) are better labeled "Protestant Revolutions."[126] It is also significant that David Ramsay and Joseph Galloway, two of the earliest historians of the Revolution, identified

Protestantism as an important contributor to Patriot justifications for war.[127] Likewise, Patriot leader John Adams, in his three-volume defense of the U.S. Constitution, cited both Bishop Ponet (republished in England in 1642) and the French *Vindiciae, Contra Tyrannos* (published in England in 1581, 1648, and 1689) as essential influences on Anglo-American ideas of liberty.[128]

CONTINUITY OF PROTESTANT REVOLUTIONS

Protestant ministers certainly looked back to the 1641 and 1688 revolutions as precedent for the American Revolution. Perhaps the most famous political sermon of the eighteenth century is the Reverend Jonathan Mayhew's 1750 discourse against "unlimited submission and nonresistance." Mayhew was celebrating the centennial of Charles I's execution following his usurpation by Reformed Protestants.[129] Mayhew targeted the doctrine of "passive" or "unlimited" obedience and "nonresistance" that many Anglican clergy had advanced.[130] In hindsight many have associated Mayhew's sermon with the American Revolution. John Adams for one connected Mayhew's sermon with American independence, fondly recalling it as a "catechism" of "armed" resistance "read by everybody"; historians have followed Adams's cue.[131]

Patriot ministers also recalled the Glorious Revolution (1688) as justification. In 1774 the Reverend Samuel Sherwood likewise took aim at "nonresistance," arguing that if the American colonists were in the wrong, then the Glorious Revolution was equally wrong; if so, Britain might as well return the monarchy to the Stuarts. "These," Sherwood chided, "are the genuine consequences of the doctrine of *passive obedience and non-resistance.*"[132] Drawing upon a hodgepodge of historical precedent, the minister argued that neither revolution was an unjust revolution so long as they were motivated to protect rights and liberties.[133]

Older Reformed Protestant literature on resistance even reappeared during the American Revolution. Some Americans looked back to Knox, as evidenced by the republishing of his 1558 *First Blast* in Philadelphia in 1766—most likely in reaction to the Stamp Act, the Declaratory Act, or both. In 1783 someone also reintroduced a Scottish Presbyterian sermon, *A Hind Let Loose* (1687), essentially plagiarizing it (a loose concept in the eighteenth century) and publishing it pseudonymously as *Defensive Arms Vindicated.* It is particularly interesting that this Reformed Protestant work cites Grotius's argument for self-defense against a king who attempts the destruction of his people or denies the necessity of their consent to his action.[134]

The precedent of these Protestant Revolutions for the Americans was also testified to by their opponents, who likewise saw parallels with Protestant uprisings in 1641 and 1688. Recalling the role of Presbyterians in the Wars of the Three Kingdoms, the 4th Earl of Orford, Horace Walpole, wrote to a friend, "One has griefs enough of one's own, without fretting because cousin America has eloped with a Presbyterian parson."[135] Peter Oliver noted the role played by clergy when he decried James Otis's appeal to a "black regiment" of rebellious ministers, writing, "Like their Predecessors of 1641 they have been unceasingly sounding the Yell of Rebellion in the Ears of an ignorant & deluded People."[136] Oliver, like other Loyalists, also recalled Samuel Butler's *Hudibras*, a royalist satire of parliamentary forces during the English Civil War. British political cartoons likewise associated the revolt in America with past Protestant revolutions, especially the English Civil War.[137]

THE PRECEDENT OF COLONIAL WAR

Not only did the Protestant Revolutions serve as precedent for *jus ad bellum* arguments during the American Revolution, but the colonial wars did as well, likewise possessing a distinctly Protestant character. American pastors, especially those in the Reformed and Anglican traditions, enthusiastically baptized constitutional liberties and self-defense as justifications for war during the eight decades between the Glorious Revolution and the French and Indian War (1754–63). Such arguments were also combined with sectarian arguments that emphasized Protestant identity. Colonial wars in particular empowered ministers with legal arguments as they advanced the idea of a "Protestant Interest" or "Protestant Cause" against Roman Catholic adversaries France and Spain. In hundreds of sermons preachers presented Anglo-American Protestantism as the last hope of British constitutional rights and liberties against the "tyrannical" and "arbitrary" abuses of "Popery" or "Papism." Clergy told troops departing for brutal frontier warfare that the dual cause of Protestantism and the British Constitution demanded a bloody fight to the death. In 1755, for example, Samuel Davies told a group of soldiers embarking for the frontier, "You are engaged in a cause of the utmost Importance—to protect your Brethren from the most bloody Barbarities—to Defend the Territories of the best of Kings against the Oppression and Tyranny of arbitrary Power, to secure the inestimable Blessings of Liberty, British Liberty . . . to preserve your Estates . . . [and] to guard your Religion, the pure Religion of Jesus."[138]

American ministers, even in the early years of the Revolution, likewise drew these same parallels between "unjust" ecclesiastical and "unjust" civil authorities. It is significant that as late as 1777, most Anglo-American Protestants still considered the difference between Protestantism and Roman Catholicism as the difference between liberty and tyranny. Samuel Sherwood's much-studied 1776 sermon *The Church's Flight into the Wilderness,* for example, argues that civil tyranny is simply another form of popery condemned in Revelation 13. While such associations may seem absurd two centuries later, they were an essential part of the *jus ad bellum* justification of the Revolution for many Americans.[139]

Ministers who defended the British constitution in these colonial wartime sermons became adept at legal and constitutional arguments; it is therefore not surprising to see many sermons and tracts in the 1770s consisting almost entirely of legal arguments echoing colonial defenses of constitutional rights and liberties. Some even compared the constitutional crises to the bloody colonial wars. For example, some ministers asserted that the repeal of the Stamp Act (a far less bloody threat) was a greater deliverance by God than victory over the their "Papist" foes in the French and Indian War just a few years prior.[140] Preaching to a Boston artillery company more than four decades before the Revolution, Nathaniel Appleton argued: "A war is lawful, when it is entered into, not for the gratifying of our own lusts, but for opposing the lusts of others that are injurious to us. A war is lawful when it is for the necessary defense or recovering of our just rights."[141] Using a common sermon theme of "The Curse of Meroz" (that is, inexcusable inactivity or neutrality), Samuel Finley told his congregation in Pennsylvania in 1757, "If it is just, and our Duty, to defend ourselves against domestic Robbers, it cannot be the Contrary, when we have to deal with foreign ones."[142] Two years earlier John Lowell even went so far as to praise preemptive war under certain circumstances, arguing:

> Can it be a serious doubt . . . whether the estates, laws, liberties, lives, and religion of people are to be defended at the utmost hazard, when they are unjustly and violently attempted, when we are sure to have a Right to these great Blessings from God the great Proprietor? . . . Not only is the defense of those great aforementioned articles a sufficient warrant for drawing the sword, and what will make war sometimes just, but an offensive war may be justifiable in case any of our just Rights are invaded, our properties encroached upon, and detained.[143]

Obligatory sermons for days of fasting and prayer during these colonial wars inspired ministers to articulate such arguments. When they made similar arguments during the American Revolution, many also came in sermons prepared for proclaimed days of prayer and fasting.

Colonial wars became recurring occasions for preachers to hone other *jus ad bellum* arguments. In an unpublished sermon, the Reverend Samuel Cooper of the Brattle Street Church in Boston reminded his audience that war must be just. He drew on the traditional argument that combat must be a last resort, telling his listeners in 1756:

> Nothing can be more plain than that war in certain circumstances is just, and that there are some circumstances that not only allow, but oblige, even the disciples of the Prince of Peace to take up arms. . . . We should contend only for that which after deliberate and impartial examination we are persuaded is just; nor should proceed, even in case of injuries, to the last and dreadful remedy of war, but where the necessity called for it, and after other means, for the procuring of justice are insignificant.[144]

In this sermon Cooper argues that judgments about going to war "chiefly belong to princes," thereby echoing the traditional just war argument about proper authority. Given that he preached from this manuscript again *in 1776,* without apparent modification to this section of the sermon, he must have approved of the use of ad hoc colonial authorities to make such determinations for the Americans. The newly created authorities had become the new "princes" to decide the moral rationale for war.

DEPLOYMENT OF *JUS AD BELLUM* ARGUMENTS BY REVOLUTIONARY CLERGY

Ministers were, as Otis celebrated and Oliver lamented, a significant force for articulating justifications for the American Revolution. Sermons composed roughly 80 percent of published political literature. Ministers were the mediators and interpreters of scripture, making the Bible the most cited source in political literature during the 1770s. Donald Lutz has notably asserted that "one cannot but be struck by the extent to which biblical sources used by ministers and traditional Whigs undergirded the justification for the break with Britain, the rationale for continuing the war, and the basic principles of Americans' writing their own constitution."[145] The main instrument of preachers, the Bible, was such a powerful rhetorical tool that Thomas Paine, a religious skeptic, deployed it to blockbuster effect in *Common Sense.* Paine the skeptic arguably "preached" the greatest "sermon" of the Revolution; his arguments resembled those already used by faithful Protestants, though his predecessors had not argued (as Paine did) that monarchy was *prima facie* contrary to scripture.

Taking cues from ideas articulated by Vattel, Pufendorf, Grotius, and Locke, ministers approached government as a contractual and consensual arrangement wherein civil authority was conditional upon fulfilling specific terms. The Reverend Moses Mather provides a prime example of such hybrid reasoning in his combination of self-defense, contract-based constitutionalism, and scripture:

> The king by withdrawing his protection and levying war upon us has discharged us of our allegiance, and of all obligations to obedience. For protection and subjection are mutual, and cannot subsist apart. He having violated the compact on his part, we, of course, are released from ours; and on the same principles, if we owed any obedience to parliament (which we did not) we are wholly discharged of it. We are compelled to provide, not only for our own subsistence, but for defense against a powerful enemy: Our affections are weaned from Great-Britain, by similar means and almost as miraculously as the Israelites were from Egypt.[146]

Many other ministers deployed similar arguments, seamlessly weaving political, legal, and biblical assertions.[147] Some Patriot pastors credited their arguments explicitly to Locke.[148]

The Continental Congress proclaiming a day of fasting and prayer for July 20, 1775, (after Lexington and Concord) spurred ministers such as the Reverend David Jones to draw on arguments from self-defense as a justification for recent hostilities. Jones devotes more than half of his sermon, *Defensive War in a Just Cause Sinless,* to arguments from scripture that defensive war is justified, but he also hinted at an impending transition away from the apocalyptic rhetoric of a Protestant-vs.-Catholic rivalry. Jones argues that every nation, "whether composed of Jews or Gentiles, Barbarians or Christians," has considered defensive war innocent.[149] Like the arguments used by Sherwood and other ministers, justifications now longstanding, Jones goes on to equate spiritual and political tyranny: that is, wars to defend against religious tyranny are not substantially different from a war to defend against political tyranny. Directly citing arguments from Luther and Calvin for rebellion against religious imposition, Jones asserts: "Names change but not the nature of things. If despotism is bad in a Papist, it cannot be good in a Protestant. If it may be resisted in one, it ought to be in the other."[150]

Ecclesiology continued to play an important role prior to the Revolution—even beyond the longstanding Protestant-vs.-Catholic rhetoric. During the Great Awakening (1730–50), the defense of itinerant preaching against civil or ecclesiastical sanctions became another training ground for ministers to make political arguments. Defenders of roaming revivalist preachers advanced arguments for civil and religious rights that would become relevant for the Revolution's defense of liberty and political rights. These arguments reinforced increasingly popular arguments for limits on power and for the protection of individual rights.[151] Likewise, a decades-long controversy over the establishment of an Anglican bishop in the colonies (beginning in 1741) along with an accompanying fear of ecclesiastical courts—especially in the wake of the Stamp Act—advanced conscience-based arguments for resistance and revolution against the British. Perhaps not coincidentally, the Reverend Jonathan Mayhew was one of the fiercest opponents of the appointment of an Anglican bishop in America. The Reverend Charles Chauncy, another vociferous opponent of the Stamp Act, was also an intransigent opponent of the plan for an American bishop.

A "last straw" for some colonists, hearkening back to the old Protestant cause, was the 1774 passage of the Quebec Act (part of the Intolerable Acts), which removed the requirement of Protestant faith from the oath of allegiance in neighboring Quebec and facilitated Catholic tithes together with the practice of Roman Catholicism there. These religious provisions were so startling that the Continental Congress considered it an establishment of the "Roman Catholick Religion." The Quebec Act also reassigned land that Americans had considered theirs since the French and Indian War. This created a perfect storm for reviving *jus ad bellum* arguments hearkening back centuries, combining both threats to Protestantism as well as the "equitable system of English laws."

The question of authority remained, however, as Patriot leaders attempted to create interposing magistrates of their own making, such as the Continental Congress or the Continental Association. This question of popular resistance versus the interposition of lesser magistrates had been debated since the sixteenth century. Who had the right to decide the question that Cooper raised about just war? Mayhew considered the question in 1766, perhaps foreseeing the installation of British troops in Boston. He argued from law, self-defense, and conscience. His placement of just authority, however, is circumspect and evident only between the lines. At one point in his sermon, Mayhew tells his audience: "I will not meddle with the thorny question, whether, or how far, it may be justifiable for private men, at certain extraordinary conjunctures, to take the administration of government in some respects into their own hands. Self-preservation being a great and primary law of nature, and to be considered as antecedent to all civil laws and institutions which are subordinate and subservient to the other, the right of so doing, in some circumstances, cannot well be denied." At another point, however, Mayhew suggests that *individuals* have considered running all risks and tempting all hazards "if things were driven to extremity." He argues that some preferred "death itself to what they esteemed so wretched and inglorious a servitude." This, Mayhew declares with some histrionics, was the result of the mental "perplexity" forced by the "novel taxation" of the Stamp Act.[152]

Seven years after Mayhew's sermon, in 1773, John Allen appears to vest the right of action in the people. Allen deploys a variation on the longstanding argument that illegal use of authority is no authority at all. Therefore, rebellion in the colonies was not ascribed to those fighting against the king; rather, it was what the king had committed in acting against the law. This made George III the true (and unjust) rebel, Allen asserts:

> Has not your Lordship a right to oppose any power that may assault your Lordship's person, right or privilege, without its being deemed rebellion against the king and state? Yes, sure you have! Then surely, my Lord, an American has the same right to oppose every usurping power (let it be from whom it will), that assaults his person, or deprives him of his own law or liberty as an American. . . . Besides my Lord, what is rebellion? If I understand it right, they are persons rising up with an assumed authority and power to act, dictate, and rule in direct violation to the laws of the land.[153]

Combining the prior Protestant arguments about resistance as a duty to God, including its ready use of natural law, Allen draws a firm conclusion: "Shall a man be deem'd a rebel that supports his own rights? It is the first law of nature, and he must be a rebel to God, to the laws of nature, and his own conscience, who will not do it."[154] Whereas a "king is the guardian and trustee of the rights of the people," a tyrant destroys those rights. Allen here comes full circle to the theological and legal arguments used by Protestants in prior centuries.

NOTES

1. James Turner Johnson, *Ideology, Reason, and the Limitation of War: Religious and Secular Concepts, 1200–1740* (Princeton, N.J.: Princeton University Press, 1975), 26.
2. Martin Luther, "On Secular Authority," in *Luther and Calvin on Secular Authority,* ed. Harro Höpfl (Cambridge: Cambridge University Press, 2010), 9.
3. Ibid., 10.
4. Martin Luther, "Dr. Martin Luther's Warning to His Dear German People," in *Luther: Selected Political Writings,* ed. J. M. Porter (Philadelphia: Fortress, 1974), 87. See also Philip Melanchthon, "The Apology of the Augsburg Confession, article XVI(55)," in *Triglot Concordia: The Symbolical Books of the Evangelical Lutheran Church* (St. Louis: Concordia Publishing House, 1921).
5. Luther, "On Secular Authority," 12.

6. Ibid., 29.
7. Ibid., 3.
8. James Turner Johnson, *Sovereignty* (Washington, D.C.: Georgetown University Press, 2014), 61–62.
9. Martin Luther, "Freedom of a Christian," in *Martin Luther: Selections from His Writings,* ed. John Dillenberger (New York: Anchor Books, 1962), 79.
10. Luther, "On Secular Authority," 23.
11. Ibid., 29. Philip Melanchthon similarly argues that love requires people to "bear with" the "tyrannical commands" of government "when nothing can be done about it short of a disturbance or sedition." See Melanchthon, *Commonplaces: Loci Communes 1521,* trans. Christian Preus (St. Louis: Concordia Publishing House, 2014).
12. Martin Luther, "Whether Soldiers, Too, Can Be Saved," in *Luther: Selected Political Writings,* 109.
13. Martin Luther, "Admonition to Peace: A Reply to the Twelve Articles of the Peasants in Swabia," in *Luther: Selected Political Writings,* 72. See also Luther, "Whether Soldiers, Too, Can Be Saved," 110.
14. Luther, "Admonition to Peace," 83–84.
15. Ibid., 78.
16. *Cuius regio, eius religio.* The Peace of Augsburg established the principle of "whose realm, his religion" within the Holy Roman Empire in 1555.
17. See Luther, "Dr. Martin Luther's Warning to His Dear German People," Melanchthon's second edition of his "Prolegomena to Cicero" (1542), or reaction of Lutheran theorists to Charles V's attack on the Schmalkaldic League after 1546. See also Quentin Skinner's critique of Michael Walzer on this point in "The Origins of the Calvinist Theory of Revolution," in *After the Reformation: Essays in Honor of J. H. Hexter,* ed. Barbara C. Malament (Philadelphia: University of Philadelphia Press, 1980).
18. See, for example, Samuel Rutherford, *Lex, Rex; or The Law and the Prince: A Dispute for the Just Prerogative of King and People . . .* (1644; reprint, Harrisonburg, Va.: Sprinkle, 1982), 34, 144.
19. Interposition was also advanced in ecclesiastical disputes within England, as the Admonition to Parliament (1572) demonstrates.
20. Sydney Ahlstrom suggests that this figure could even approach 90 percent, depending on how it is calculated. The figure is not without its problems, however. Ahlstrom uses the category "Puritanism," which would exclude most Anglicans. A more accurate category would be "Reformed Protestantism" insofar as Continental Reformed theology (e.g., Calvin, Bullinger, Martyr, and others) deeply influenced the wider Anglican tradition. The Church of England owed much of its theology to the Continental Reformed tradition even though the association with it, and subsequent understanding of that relationship, was soured by Puritanism's revolt against Anglicanism. In any case, Protestants in America were more closely associated with the Reformed tradition than with any other. Sydney E. Ahlstrom, *A Religious History of the American People* (New Haven, Conn.: Yale University Press, 1972), 124.
21. John Calvin, *Institutes of the Christian Religion,* vol. 2, trans. John Allen (Philadelphia: Philadelphia Presbyterian Board of Publication and Sabbath School Work,

1902), 4.20.2 [book.chapter.section]. Most quotations from the *Institutes* are from this edition.

22. Ibid.
23. A summary of Bullinger's position is in chapter 30 of his Second Helvetic Confession (1566).
24. John Knox, "First Book of Discipline," VII, in *The History of the Reformation of Religion in Scotland, to which Are Appended Several Other Pieces of His Writing,* ed. William McGavin (Glasgow, Scotland: Blackie, Fullarton, 1831), 498. See also Knox, "The Appellation," ibid., 382, 386. Knox's position, as well as that of other Scottish Reformers, is expressed in chapter 24 of the Scots Confession of 1560.
25. William Ames, *Conscience with the Power and Cases Thereof* (Leyden and London: W. Christiaens, E. Griffin, J. Dawson, 1639), 5.25.1.8 [book.chapter.question.section].
26. We have omitted consideration of the more Erastian position of the Church of England that gave even more significant ecclesiastical authority to the magistrate. We have also omitted notable differences between Calvin and Huldrych Zwingli (1484–1531) over Calvin's insistence on independent church discipline—an insistence that made "Papists" and "Puritans" the same as far as many Anglicans were concerned. Finally, we have omitted from this discussion resistance theory in the Church of England, which was complicated not only by a standing distaste for Papists and Puritans but also by the threat of Jacobite rebellions. The variety of Anglican opinions on resistance was reflected in the variety of positions taken by Anglican clergy during the American Revolution.
27. Calvin, *Institutes of the Christian Religion,* 4.20.3.
28. Knox, "Letter to Mary, Regent of Scotland," in *History of the Reformation of Religion in Scotland,* 366–67.
29. Ames, *Conscience with the Power and Cases Thereof,* 5.25.1.8.
30. For example, see Calvin, *Institutes of the Christian Religion,* 4.20.29.
31. Ibid., 4.20.4.
32. Ibid., 4.20.29.
33. Ibid., 4.20.30.
34. Ibid., 4.20.31.
35. Ibid., 4.20.8.
36. Ibid.
37. The contrast between Calvin and Bullinger is further explained in Glenn A. Moots, *Politics Reformed: The Anglo-American Legacy of Covenant Theology* (Columbia: University of Missouri Press, 2010), 57–60.
38. Jane Dawson, *John Knox* (New Haven, Conn.: Yale University Press, 2015), 86. Calvin likewise discouraged acts of rebellion in almost every other case, including some by Huguenots threatened with persecution. His only exception appears to be a rebellion with clear constitutional authority. See Calvin, "Homilies on the First Book of Samuel," in *John Calvin Opera quae supersunt omnia,* ed. Guilielmus Baum, Eduardus Cunitz, and Eduardus Reuss, vol. 29 (Brunsvigae : C. A. Schwetschke, 1863), 552; and "To the Admiral De Coligny," Apr. 16 1561, DLXXXVIII, in *Letters of John Calvin: Compiled from the Original Manuscripts and Edited with Historical Notes,* vol. 4,

ed. Jules Bonnet, trans. Marcus Robert Gilchrist (Philadelphia: Presbyterian Board of Publication, 1858), 175–76.

39. Knox, "Appellation," 388.
40. Knox, "The First Blast of the Trumpet, against the Monstrous Regiment of Women," in *History of the Reformation of Religion in Scotland,* 458–59.
41. Dawson, *John Knox,* 160.
42. Scott Dolff, "The Two John Knoxes and the Justification of Non-Revolution: A Response to Dawson's Argument from Covenant," *Journal of Ecclesiastical History* 1 (Jan. 2004): 65.
43. John Knox, "Letters to the Regent and Nobility," in *Knox: On Rebellion,* Roger A. Mason, ed. (Cambridge: Cambridge University Press, 1994), 153; Knox, "Appellation," 390.
44. Knox, "Letters to the Regent and Nobility," 159. A tax strike meant withholding of tithes from the church.
45. Knox, "First Blast of the Trumpet," 459.
46. Goodman, like Knox, thought that female rule was against nature and scripture. The presence of Goodman and Knox in Geneva ruined Calvin's relationship with Elizabeth I, even though Calvin did not endorse their arguments.
47. Christopher Goodman, *How Superior Powers Ought to be Obeyed* (1558; reprint, Whitefish, Mont.: Kessinger, 2004), 44, 71–72. Goodman did not say it this succinctly, but he essentially argued that Christians in certain circumstances had a duty, rather than a right, to resist—something else presaging Jefferson and the Declaration of Independence.
48. Quentin Skinner characterizes Goodman, Ponet, and Knox as arguing that those who fail to resist tyrants would be damned. Skinner, *The Foundations of Modern Political Thought,* vol. 2, *The Age of Reformation* (Cambridge: Cambridge University Press, 1978), 234–37.
49. Anne McLaren, "Rethinking Republicanism: Vindiciae, Contra Tyrannos in Context," *Historical Journal* 49, no. 1 (2006): 23–52; George Garnett, "Law in the Vindiciae, Contra Tyrannos: A Vindication," *Historical Journal* 49, no. 3 (2006): 877–91.
50. Calvin, *Institutes of the Christian Religion,* 2.2.13.
51. John Coffey, *Politics, Religion, and the British Revolutions: The Mind of Samuel Rutherford* (New York: Cambridge University Press, 1997), 70.
52. Ames, *Conscience with the Power and Cases Thereof,* 5.25.2.4.
53. Ibid., 5.25.3.3.
54. Ibid., 5.25.1.5.
55. As Theo Christov demonstrates in chapter 3, American statesmen frequently cited Vattel. For the influence of Grotius, Pufendorf, and Vattel, see Brian Richardson, "The Use of Vattel in the American Law of Nations," *American Journal of International Law* 106, no. 3 (July 2012): 547–751.
56. Andreas Harald Aure, "Hugo Grotius—Individual Rights as the Core of Natural Law," in *Contemporary Philosophy: A New Survey,* ed. Guttorm Fløistad, vol. 12, *Philosophy of Justice* (Dordrecht, The Netherlands: Springer, 2015), 75, 80.

57. Thomas Behme, "Pufendorf's Doctrine of Sovereignty and its Natural Law Foundations," in *Natural Law and Civil Sovereignty,* ed. Ian Hunter and David Saunders (New York: Palgrave Macmillan, 2002), 48.
58. Emer de Vattel, *The Law of Nations,* ed. Béla Kapossy and Richard Whatmore (Indianapolis: Liberty Fund, 2008), 1.1.1 [book.chapter.section].
59. Frank Grunert, "Sovereignty and Resistance: The Development of the Right of Resistance in German Natural Law," in Hunter and Saunders, *Natural Law and Civil Sovereignty,* 124, 125.
60. Behme, "Pufendorf's Doctrine of Sovereignty," 51.
61. Hugo Grotius, *The Rights of War and Peace,* ed. Richard Tuck (Indianapolis: Liberty Fund, 2005), 1.4.7 [book.chapter.section].
62. Aure, "Hugo Grotius," 83; Grotius, *Rights of War and Peace,* 1.2.3.
63. Behme, "Pufendorf's Doctrine of Sovereignty," 52–53.
64. Samuel Pufendorf, *Of the Law of Nature and Nations* (London, 1729), 7.3.2 [book.chapter.section]. A scan of John Adams's personal copy of *Of the Law of Nature and Nations* is available online at https://archive.org/details/oflawofnaturenat00pufe.
65. Samuel Pufendorf, *On the Duty of Man and Citizen,* ed. James Tully (Cambridge: Cambridge University Press, 1991), 2.2.7.
66. Grotius, *Rights of War and Peace,* 2.3.15.
67. Pufendorf, *On the Duty of Man and Citizen,* 2.2.6.
68. Pufendorf, *Of the Law of Nature and Nations,* 7.2.9.
69. Ibid., 1.3.15.
70. Grotius, *Rights of War and Peace,* 1.4.2.1, cited in Grunert, "Sovereignty and Resistance," 124.
71. Grunert, "Sovereignty and Resistance," 125.
72. Grotius, *Rights of War and Peace,* 1.4.4. Grotius is citing Seneca here.
73. Pufendorf, *On the Duty of Man and Citizen,* 2.18.3. Indeed, it is a "sin to oppose a lawful ruler . . . acting within the limits of his authority." Pufendorf, *Of the Law of Nature and Nations,* 8.8.1.
74. Pufendorf, *Of the Law of Nature and Nations,* 7.8.5.
75. Grotius, *Rights of War and Peace,* 1.1.3.9. See also Grunert, "Sovereignty and Resistance," 125.
76. Grotius, *Rights of War and Peace,* 1.1.4.1. Grotius here may be read to parallel Jefferson's remarks in the Declaration about "the law of nature and nature's God."
77. Pufendorf, *On the Duty of Man and Citizen,* 2.12.8. See also *Of the Law of Nature and Nations,* 4.8.6.
78. Grotius, *Rights of War and Peace,* 1.1.3.8, 1.3.7.4, 1.7.1.7.
79. Ibid., 1.1.3.9.
80. Ibid., 1.1.4.1. See also ibid., 1.1.4.3–4.
81. Ibid., 1.4.7.2.
82. Ibid., 1.1.4.7.
83. Ibid.
84. Ibid. In the *Summa Theologiae,* Thomas Aquinas argues that the "disruption of such a government therefore does not have the character of sedition, unless perhaps the

tyrant's rule is disrupted so inordinately that the community subject to it suffers greater detriment from the ensuing disorder than it did from the tyrannical government itself." See Aquinas, *Summa Theologiae,* IIaIIae42, art. 2, ad. 3, in *Aquinas: Political Writings,* ed. R. W. Dyson (Cambridge: Cambridge University Press, 2000), 250.

85. Grotius, *Rights of War and Peace,* 1.4.4.11; Aquinas, *Summa Theologiae,* IIaIIae42, art. 2, ad. 3. Aquinas asserts that "disruption of such a government . . . does not have the character of sedition."
86. Grotius, *Rights of War and Peace,* 1.4.4.11.
87. Ibid., 1.4.4.9–10. Grotius avows some caution about relinquishing authority to another power.
88. Grunert, "Sovereignty and Resistance," 127. These sorts of complaints are suggested in the Declaration of Independence's articulation of grievances beginning in its fourth paragraph and continuing to the conclusion.
89. Ibid.
90. Grotius, *Rights of War and Peace,* 1.4.4.8, 14.
91. Ibid., 1.4.4.12.
92. Ibid., 1.2.4.7.
93. Pufendorf, *Of the Law of Nature and Nations,* 7.8.5.
94. Ibid.
95. Ibid.
96. Ibid., 7.8.4.
97. Vattel, *Law of Nations,* 1.11.15.
98. Forrest McDonald, *Alexander Hamilton: A Biography* (New York: W. W. Norton, 1982), 56. See also Stéphane Beaulac, "Emer de Vattel and the Externalization of Sovereignty," *Journal of the History of International Law* 5 (2003): 257; and Richardson, "Use of Vattel in the American Law of Nations," 550.
99. Vattel, *Law of Nations,* 1.3.27. See also ibid., 1.3.45.
100. Ibid., 1.4.51.
101. Ibid.
102. Ibid.
103. Ibid.
104. Ibid., 1.3.30–31.
105. Ibid., 1.4.54.
106. Ibid.
107. Ibid.
108. Ibid., 1.3.32.
109. Ibid., 1.4.50.
110. Ibid.
111. Ibid., 1.4.51.
112. Ibid.
113. Ibid., 1.4.51, 54.
114. Ibid., 1.4.54.
115. John Locke, *Some Thoughts Concerning Education,* ed. John Yolton (Oxford: Oxford

University Press, 1989), §186. See also Locke, "Thoughts Concerning Reading," in *Political Essays,* ed. Mark Goldie (Cambridge: Cambridge University Press, 1997), 351; and "Mr. Locke's Extempore Advice &c," in *Some Thoughts Concerning Education,* 322.

116. John Locke, *Second Treatise of Government,* in Locke, *Two Treatises of Government,* ed. Peter Laslett (New York: Cambridge University Press, 1988), §222.

117. Ibid., §202, §232.

118. Ibid., §232.

119. Ibid., §20, §21, §87, §168, §175, §176, §179, §209, §210.

120. Ibid., §196, §227, §232.

121. John Locke, *Letter Concerning Toleration in Two Treatises of Government and A Letter Concerning Toleration,* ed. Ian Shapiro (New Haven, Conn.: Yale University Press. 2003), 241–44.

122. Locke, *Second Treatise,* §241, §242.

123. Ibid., §21.

124. Ibid., §241, §242.

125. This was the so-called "Pine Tree Flag" or "Washington's Cruisers" flag that featured the "Appeal" phrase over the pine tree, a common symbol for New England.

126. John Pocock, *Three British Revolutions: 1641, 1688, 1776* (Princeton, N.J.: Princeton University Press, 1980); John Coffey, *Exodus and Liberation: Deliverance Politics from John Calvin to Martin Luther King Jr.* (Oxford: Oxford University Press, 2014), 19.

127. David Ramsay, *History of the American Revolution* (Philadelphia, 1789), 1, 8–9; Joseph Galloway, *Historical and Political Reflections on the Rise and Progress of the American Rebellion* (London: G. Wilkie, 1780), 54–55. Ramsay served with the South Carolina militia as a field surgeon; Galloway was a loyalist who fled in 1778. Page Smith gave Ramsay credibility due to his proximity to the event. See Smith, "David Ramsay and the Causes of the American Revolution," *William and Mary Quarterly,* 3rd ser., 17 (Jan. 1960): 51–77.

128. John Adams, "A Defense of the Constitutions of Government of the United States of America, Against the Attack of M. Turgot," in "His Letter to Dr. Price, Dated the Twenty-Second Day of March, 1778," in *The Political Writings of John Adams,* ed. George Carey, vol. 3 (Washington, D.C.: Regnery Gateway, 2000), 224–25.

129. Puritans and Scottish Presbyterians were both Reformed Protestants.

130. For the Anglican attempt to retain this doctrine even in the face of the Glorious Revolution, see Gerald M. Straka, *Anglican Reaction to the Revolution of 1688* (Madison: State Historical Society of Wisconsin, 1962). Patriots vilified "nonresistance" so much that the state constitution of New Hampshire explicitly rejected it; those of other states did likewise.

131. Jonathan Mayhew, *Discourse Concerning Unlimited Submission and Non-Resistance to the Higher Powers* (Boston, 1750); John Adams, *The Works of John Adams,* ed. Charles F. Adams, vol. 1 (Boston, Little Brown, 1856), 287–88. Mayhew did not live to see the American Revolution, preaching this sermon twenty-six years before Lexington and Concord. His sermon has been erroneously cast by some as innovative and departing from a Protestant tradition that preached unconditional obedience.

Not only has this chapter demonstrated that Mayhew was not innovative in his interpretation of Romans 13, but Mayhew's criticism of "passive obedience" and "nonresistance" was not even new in America. George Whitefield had mocked these ideas in his celebration of the Louisburg victory in 1746, going so far as to yoke them with "transubstantiation, purgatory, works of supererogation, . . . and all the other abominations of the Whore of Babylon." George Whitefield, *Britain's Mercies, and Britain's Duties* (1746), in *Political Sermons of the American Founding Era: 1730–1805,* ed. Ellis Sandoz, 1st ed. (Indianapolis: Liberty Fund, 1991), 127. For the most recent study of Mayhew's significance for the Revolution, see J. Patrick Mullins, *Father of Liberty: Jonathan Mayhew and the Principles of the American Revolution* (Lawrence: University Press of Kansas, 2017).

132. Samuel Sherwood, *Scriptural Instructions to Civil Rulers* (New Haven, 1774), in Sandoz, *Political Sermons,* 396. I have silently modernized most of the grammar and spelling in the sermons.

133. On this point of "nonresistance" in the Anglican tradition, Anglicans themselves disagreed about this obligation to passive obedience. In 1775 Christ Church rector Jacob Duché defended war in self-defense, preaching one of the most impassioned justifications of taking up arms. Fellow Anglican minister Jonathan Boucher fired back with a sermon on the virtues of "civil liberty, passive obedience, and non-resistance." Duché, *The Duty of Standing Fast in Our Spiritual and Temporal Liberties* (Philadelphia, 1775); Boucher, *On Civil Liberty, Passive Obedience, and Nonresistance,* in *A View of the Causes and Consequences of the American Revolution* (London: G. G. & J. Robinson, 1797). Mayhew credited his aforementioned sermon to Benjamin Hoadly, an Anglican bishop, who had been influenced by Locke.

134. This was Locke's argument as well, of course. The author of *Defensive Arms Vindicated* (plagiarizing *A Hind Let Loose*) writes: "First, Barclay, contra monarchum, is cited by the Apal Relat, and Jus Populi, asserting, 'That if a king will alienate, and subject his kingdom, without his subjects' consent, or be carried with a hostile mind to the destruction of his people, his kingdom is actually lost, and the people may not only lawfully resist, but also depose him.' *Grotius* de jure Belli, lib. 1, cap. 4, asserts the same, and adds, 'If he but attempt to do so, he may be resisted.'" *Defensive Arms Vindicated,* in Sandoz, *Political Sermons,* 731.

135. Peter Cunningham, ed., *The Letters of Horace Walpole,* vol. 6 (London: Bickers and Son, 1880), 234. British elites often cared little for the difference between Congregationalists and Presbyterians, seeing them as similarly "Puritan" denominations.

136. Douglass Adair and John A Schutz, eds., *Peter Oliver's Origin and Progress of the American Rebellion: A Tory View* (Palo Alto, Calif.: Stanford University Press, 1961), 29. Oliver's "black regiment" may or may not have been a reference to the black clerical gown in the style of Geneva.

137. *An Attempt to Land a Bishop in America,* engraving from *(London) Political Register,* Sept. 1769; *The Yankie Doodles Intrenchments near Boston 1776,* etching, copyprint, British Museum, London.

138. Samuel Davies, *Religion and Patriotism the Constituents of a Good Soldier* (Philadelphia, 1756), 13–14.

139. Glenn A. Moots, "Samuel Cooper's Old Sermons and New Enemies: Popery and Protestant Constitutionalism," *American Political Thought* 5, no. 3 (Summer 2016): 391–420.
140. Jonathan Mayhew, *The Snare Broken* (Boston, 1766), in Sandoz, *Political Sermons,* 245–46. In an unpublished sermon of the same year, the Rev. Eli Forbes called victory in 1760 a comparatively "small" deliverance because the Stamp Act would have made Americans "slaves" while possessing "an undoubted right to freedom." Forbes called this a fate "worse than death." Eli Forbes, Sermons 1752–1804, Mss. Boxes F, American Antiquarian Society, Worcester, Mass.
141. Nathaniel Appleton, *The Origin of War Examin'd and Applied* (Boston, 1733), 21.
142. Samuel Finley, *The Curse of Meroz; or, The Danger of Neutrality, in the Cause of God, and Our Cou*ntry (Philadelphia, 1757), 23.
143. John Lowell, *The Advantages of God's Presence with His People in An Expedition against Their Enemies* (Boston, 1755), 10.
144. Samuel Cooper Papers, CO 157, Huntington Library, San Marino, Calif.
145. Donald S. Lutz, *The Origins of American Constitutionalism* (Baton Rouge: Louisiana State University Press, 1988), 140–42. For a detailed treatment of sermons and the use of scripture, see James P. Byrd, *Sacred Scripture, Sacred War: The Bible and the American Revolution* (New York: Oxford University Press, 2013).
146. Moses Mather, *America's Appeal to the Impartial World* (Hartford, 1775), in Sandoz, *Political Sermons,* 489. Another notable example of a dense political argument presented by a minister is the Rev. John Joachim Zubly, *An Humble Enquiry* (1769) in Sandoz, *Political Sermons,* 265–99.
147. Some ministers, such as Duché and John Joachim Zubly (Presbyterian), ardently supported violent defense of American rights but not independence.
148. For a study of how ministers drew from Locke, see Steven M. Dworetz, *The Unvarnished Doctrine: Locke, Liberalism, and the American Revolution* (Durham, N.C.: Duke University Press, 1990).
149. David Jones, *Defensive War in a Just Cause Sinless* (Philadelphia, 1775), 7.
150. Ibid., 16.
151. For example, sermons of Elisha Williams (Congregationalist) and Isaac Backus (Baptist) both advanced an explication of Romans 13 in such a way as to limit civil jurisdiction and authority. Williams does this, for example, in *The Essential Rights and Liberties of Protestants* (1744), in Sandoz, *Political Sermons,* 51–118, esp. 59, 67, 70–72, 79–80, 83–84, 114–17. John Dunn testified to the radical political significance of Williams's ideas. See Dunn, *Political Obligation in Its Historical Context* (Cambridge: Cambridge University Press, 1980), 73.
152. Mayhew, *The Snare Broken,* 248–49, 263.
153. John Allen, *An Oration upon the Beauties of Liberty* (New London, 1773), in Sandoz, *Political Sermons,* 308–9.
154. Ibid., 307–9, 323.

3 EMER DE VATTEL'S *LAW OF NATIONS* IN AMERICA'S INDEPENDENCE

Theodore Christov

It comes as a surprise that a man known for his diligence and integrity failed to return to the library two volumes due on November 2, 1789. Borrowed from the New York Society Library at Wall and Broad Streets, one of only three libraries in what was then the nation's capital, the books were Emer de Vattel's *Law of Nations* and volume twelve of the fourteen-volume collection *Common Debates,* which contained transcripts of debates from the House of Commons, Britain's lower house of Parliament.[1] It was not until 1934, however, that the charge-out ledger, which had the names of all borrowers between July 1789 and April 1792, was discovered in the library's basement; for almost 150 years, no one could have possibly suspected the misdeed.[2] The other borrowers, including Aaron Burr, Alexander Hamilton, and John Jay, all returned their library books. But one conspicuous patron (who was not even a paying member of the library and whose October 5, 1789, entry was written with a quill pen and recorded simply as "President") never returned his two books. These two books must have proved indispensable for a man preoccupied with the business of creating a new nation and learning how to be its first president. Anecdote even has it that he was found consulting Vattel's book by visitors on his first day in office after his inauguration in New York on April 30, 1789. When Philadelphia became the capital city the following year, the president merely took the books with him, never to return them to the library. The Vattel book was eventually found, some 220 years later, and returned to George Washington's Mount Vernon Library in 2010, the overdue fine of $300,000 waived.

So what story, or event, could possibly have prompted the first president of the United States, who had been in office for a mere five months, to send out a messenger from his Cherry Street home down to the New York Society Library in Federal Hall to fetch Vattel's book? The *New York Daily Gazette* of October 5, 1789, which Washington certainly must have read when he requested the volume, reads like a global chronicle of stories covering four continents: it contains a letter on the "Revolutions of Paris" and allusions to "the Russians," the English, the "Turkish armies," the "States of Holland," an "African Prince," a "Jamaican planter," and of course "the General Assembly" in Philadelphia.[3] Published as one of two dailies in the city, the newspaper was anything but local in its coverage, and the inclusion of foreign affairs on its pages merely reflects how America saw its place in the world. As a nascent state, trying to remain neutral during Europe's political turmoil and to emerge as a fully fledged sovereign on the world stage, the United States was inextricably becoming part of a wider community of customs and conventions practiced internationally. Such an outward orientation naturally demanded philosophical support from political treatises. The work of Vattel for decades provided indispensable intellectual ammunition to the defenders of the Republic surrounding the birth and adolescence of the new American nation.

In the hands of the early republicans, the *Law of Nations*—written largely for a European audience—would serve a twofold purpose: to justify war for independence from the British and to weave the unique American political experiment into the larger fabric of the European experience of liberty. Without its author's intention, the book would effectively link both sides of the Atlantic ideologically. Well before the founding, Vattel's argument—through its call for sovereignty, autonomy, and recognition, made, not least, in a lucid language—provided justification for war in order to gain independence. It relied on a comprehensive understanding of the law of nations, extending back to Roman antiquity in the thought of Cicero and linking that history to the present in the customs of nations. Through their acts of oppression, the British had violated the law of nature as applied to nations and, for that reason alone, could rightly be considered, what Vattel generally calls, "infractors of the law of nations." Such an abrogation of the "laws of natural society" endangers "the safety of all states," and in using their "perfect right," they must now ensure their own preservation.[4]

The use of force indeed can be justified on grounds of not observing the general laws of conduct among nations, and Vattel establishes commensurability between such a violation and the level of force necessary to contain it. "All nations have therefore a right to resort to forcible means," he affirms, "for the purpose of repressing any one particular nation who openly violates the laws of the society which nature has established between them, or who directly attacks the welfare and safety of that society." In its attractively simple formula, the generic template of justifiable force to "repress" violators of the law of nations would resonate with the Founders in their quest for resisting the British. In some exceptional cases and "only in extremities," it would even be acceptable and entirely justifiable "for a just and wise nation" to resort to force.[5] A war for independence from foreign rule would be a moral and political requisite and hence consistent with the general welfare of those seeking to overthrow tyranny. In addition to endorsing the use of force for violations of the law of nations, Vattel's writings simultaneously provided the Founders with arguments about the common purpose of a single humanity and the call to uphold justice among nations.

The seemingly insignificant discovery of Washington's failure to return the borrowed book reveals less about the character of the president than a great deal more about the role that European thinkers would come to exercise on the evolution of his thinking as a leading statesman of the newly founded country. Faced with political and religious turmoil that threatened the very fabric of their societies, many political authors over the course of the eighteenth century dismantled older European monarchical arguments and fervently defended new constitutional regime based on the rights of citizens. While their arguments in favor of political models of legitimate sovereignty and statehood emerged from a distinctly intra-European context of civil and religious wars, they still contained a broad appeal to the universality of human experience and rightful demands for political self-governance. That universality proved critical in making arguments not only in defense of political autonomy domestically but also in the promotion of international sovereignty, including formal recognition for the United States by outside actors. Independent states—the hallmark of Vattel's legacy—must be sovereign both in relation to themselves and, crucially, to each other.

Vattel's treatise served as an indispensable guidebook in the hands of the framers, including the first president, who consulted it in situating independence within the larger context of statehood. It also helped address the question of how a declaration of independence from Great Britain served simultaneously as a proclamation of interdependence to the world of states. Scholarship has generally tended to acknowledge Vattel as the most cited author in legal documents and court proceedings in the early American Republic after 1789—especially throughout the nineteenth century—but the story of his influence before and around 1789 has been generally overlooked.[6] His authority as a preeminent political thinker consulted in favor of overthrowing British dependence can be traced as far back as 1762, almost a quarter century before the drafting of the Constitution. When he requested a copy of the *Law of Nations* in 1789, Washington had already been familiar with its arguments for independence and sovereignty for many years. As early as 1773 he seems to have known about (and almost certainly to have read) Vattel's work. In a shipment request dated October 6, 1773, he submitted a list of authors that included Francis Hutcheson, Adam Ferguson, Hugo Grotius, Adam Smith, Montesquieu, John Locke, and of course Vattel.[7] Fluent in French and versed in Latin, many of the Founding Fathers engaged with political writings that derived the rights and duties of states from those of individuals placed in their natural condition of perfect equality. The essential analogy between free persons and sovereign states provided the ideal context for making claims for the independence of the newly founded United States.

I

From Thomas Hobbes to Samuel Pufendorf, through Richard Cumberland, Christian Wolff, Hutcheson, and Jean-Jacques Burlamaqui, European political thinkers preoccupied the minds of many participants in the central debate over revolution and independence; as Bernard Bailyn reminds us, "[c]itations, respectful borrowings from, or at least references to, the eighteenth-century European illuminati are everywhere in the pamphlets of Revolutionary America."[8] Connected by similar experiences of oppression and dependence, Europeans and Americans could not have been brought any closer in their ideological proximity by addressing the fundamental question of how to secure a free and independent state and by laying out the subsequent criteria for the justification for war, or *jus ad bellum,* when basic rights have been infringed upon. The political theory of Locke, whom Thomas Jefferson called one of "the three greatest men that have ever lived, without any exception," and the influence that his *Second Treatise of Government* exercised on the Virginian's own political worldview have been widely noted and still taken for granted by many.[9] The "unalienable rights" of "life, liberty and the pursuit of happiness" enshrined in the Declaration of Independence continually get attributed to Locke's "life, liberty and estate," but few would link Vattel's language of rights, sovereignty, and independence with that of the founding document.[10] Part of the explanation for the conventional acceptance of Locke's influence in America lies in chronology: most scholars and statesmen alike have tended to emphasize the influence of Vattel only after the Revolutionary War—this was particularly true between 1789 and 1820—and some have continued to stress his importance well into the present day. Even the U.S. Supreme Court affirmed, in a 1978 decision, that Vattel was the "international jurist most widely cited in the first fifty years after the Revolution."[11] On the crucial debate of how to relate America's independence to the practice of the law of nations, Vattel casts a longer shadow than that of Locke.

Writing his introduction to Vattel's book in 1916, Albert de Lapradelle concurs that the fathers of independence "were in accord with the ideas of Vattel" and found in his work "all their maxims of political liberty." From the mid-1770s, "the more the United States progressed, the greater became Vattel's influence," so that "in 1780 his *Law of Nations* was a classic, a textbook in the universities," having already been taught at King's College (now Columbia University) as early as 1773.[12] But the history of Vattel's presence in America extends further back by about a decade to the early years of the 1760s. Much less acknowledged has been the contribution of his thought to the intellectual debates over independence of the American Republic in the years leading up to 1776. While scholarship has generally tended to engage with the English translation of the original French edition of the *Law of Nations,* there is no compelling reason for privileging the one over the other, since historical accounts show the extensive use of both editions.

In its first edition, published in two volumes in 1758 in Neuchâtel, the *Law of Nations* appeared in French—one of a few treatises at the time written in the vernacular rather than the widely used Latin. The first English translation was published anonymously in London in 1759, followed by another English edition in 1760. Only two years later, in the autumn of 1762, the French and English editions of Vattel's treatise were imported from London and made available for purchase from Garrat Noel, the first New York bookseller, located on Dock Street in Manhattan. From his shop, Noel also operated a "Circulating Library" of "several thousand volumes of choice books" for "those who delight in reading." Almost certainly the *Law of Nations* would have been among the selections, which would have made it even more widely accessible to readers without the means to own a copy of it themselves.[13]

John Adams, a delegate to the Continental Congress and later the second U.S. president, must have been one of the very first customers to have purchased the *Law of Nations.* In his diary on February 1, 1763—or just two months after the book was made available on this side of the Atlantic—he recorded that after spending the day frivolously, "I employed however, too little of my Time in Reading and in Thinking. I might have spent much more. The idea of M. de Vattel indeed, scowling and frowning, haunted me."[14] While one may only speculate which specific idea of the treatise may have "haunted" Adams, it would be plausible to suggest that he may have sought to appropriate Vattel's arguments within the larger context of the colonial crisis over the future of the British Empire (which had been brewing since at least 1763). In reading Vattel, he must have surely been preoccupied with establishing the proper relationship between Britain's legitimate power in the colonies and the rights of the Americans: can the rights of British subjects in the imperial periphery be reconciled with government at the core? As one of the most learned and widely read among the Founding Fathers, Adams had not only read (and was impressed with) Vattel extensively but also was familiar with the works of those compatriots who had made use of his ideas.[15] One of the—if not *the*—earliest colonial defenders to employ Vattel in political arguments about the power and limits of Parliament in the case of the colonies was the Massachusetts lawyer James Otis, whom the young Adams both knew and admired.

Educated at Harvard College, James Otis "was well versed in Greek and Roman history, philosophy, oratory, poetry, and mythology," as Adams described him, a man whose "classical studies had been unusually ardent, and his acquisitions uncommonly great." He was considered "a great master of the laws of nature and nations . . . [and] had read Pufendorf, Vattel, [and] Heineccius [*sic*; Daniël Heinsius]."[16] Arguing the famous writs of assistance case for five hours at the Old State House in Boston in 1761 and challenging the authority of Parliament on behalf of fifty-three Boston merchants twice that year, Otis made a dramatic speech, holding that ultimately the general writs were contrary to both natural law and English practice. The twenty-six-year-old Adams was present as an eyewitness (and a scribe) during the actual speech and was so impressed with what he heard that he described the event—some fifty-six years later—as "the first scene of the first act of opposition to the arbitrary claims of Great Britain. Then and there the child Independence was born."[17] Vattel soon emerged as a political thinker whose treatise provided grounds for resistance against arbitrary power, and he would subsequently get incorporated into the larger discourse on the origin of government and the rightful forms of rule as founded on reason and the practice of the law of nations.

Otis expanded his argument that "the Colonists are by the law of nature free born, as indeed all men are, white or black," and in *The Rights of the British Colonies Asserted and Proved,* published in July 1764, he extensively cited Vattel in support of his claims that "the authority of the Parliament of *Great Britain* is circumscribed by certain bounds, which if exceeded their acts become those of mere *power* without *right,* and consequently void." Such a "doctrine is agreeable to the law of nature and nations," he declares, quoting Vattel as the authority on the subject. Rights are derived from nature rather than consent, and as Vattel had shown, any violation of the constitution or natural law, which served as its foundation, amounted to a breach of contract. Critics of the very idea of consent, who objected to the voluntary nature of civil government, dismissed such arguments as merely "chimerical and unsupported by reason or experience": already born into the political compact of society, they claimed that citizens may not renounce the very protection that binds them together. In response Otis challenged, "those who want a full answer [to the question why consent is the basis of any political community] . . . may consult Mr. Locke's discourses on government, M. De Vattel's law of nature and nations, and their own consciences."[18]

The reference to Vattel in support of the basic claim that any political government rests on the consent of its citizens, who have the right to resist when that trust is violated, is unequivocally endorsed as the voice of reason and the free exercise of one's conscience. Otis's inclusion of Vattel within the ranks of Locke and other major political thinkers would canonize the Swiss jurist as a principal support for resistance against British rule and in support of waging a just war against it. The reliance on Vattel as an indisputable authority in a major pamphlet of the American Revolution paved the way—as early as 1764—for a long trajectory of his influence on how the revolutionaries framed their arguments for independence, one that resonates among legal scholars today.

Underpinning the debate over the right of the colonists to demand the same rights as the inhabitants of the home islands was the protection of their sacred liberty. "No people have been more wisely jealous of their liberties and privileges than the British nation," Oxenbridge Thacher writes in his pamphlet *The Sentiments of a British American,* published in the same year as Otis's work. "It is observed by *Vattel* that 'their present happy condition hath cost them seas of blood; but they have not purchased it too dear.'"[19] Liberty was made central to good rule and a major ingredient in the exercise of sovereignty. The colonists understood perfectly well that any claim to a right of self-government would also need to appeal to Great Britain's own experience of liberty, and they clearly followed Vattel's favorable view that "the English furnish us an example highly worthy of attention. That illustrious nation distinguishes itself in a glorious manner by its application to every citizen in a situation that enables him to contribute to this great end [of liberty]." Of all modern nations, Britain—with its "admirable constitution"—had come closest to the reputable position as the leading country in Europe, one whose citizens experienced simultaneously the liberty of being citizens of their own country and that of the universal society of mankind.[20] Separated from their motherland, American colonists were denied the liberty of both, and their insistence on using the language of liberty and independence made their invocation of Vattel ever more pressing.

Some of the most widely circulated and cited pamphlets of the American Revolution made use of Vattel's argument for sovereignty in order to advance claims for independence based on the idea of sovereignty. "Every nation that governs itself, under what form soever, without dependence on any foreign power, is a *sovereign state*," Vattel declares. He then defines sovereignty in almost negative terms as the absence of foreign interference: "To give a nation a right to make an immediate figure in this grand society, it is sufficient that it be really sovereign and independent, that is, that it govern itself by its own authority and laws." The call for liberty went hand in hand with the demand for sovereignty, two sides of the same political expression. As "the soul of abilities and industry," liberty could flourish only when individuals could exercise their own autonomy as citizens and where public welfare had been procured for the benefit of all.[21]

Vattel's argument in defense of political liberty and independence was not confined to political pamphleteers in New England nor localized to publishers in Boston; later in the same year it had spread south to North Carolina. The *North-Carolina Gazette,* established by printer James Davis—a Virginia émigré who moved south at the behest of the North Carolina Colonial Assembly—was first published in 1751 and in many ways served as North Carolina's newspaper. Urgently needing a local printer to disseminate revised laws (rather than depending on the *Virginia Gazette* for this as well as news), North Carolina was the last remaining colony to acquire a printing press. As customary with most newspapers at the time, the *Gazette*'s successor, the *North-Carolina Magazine,* was filled with extensive extracts from the works of religious writers and historians as well as essays and texts of important legislative acts. In the July 1764 issue, a long history of the Roman Empire was inaugurated and continued in installments through several succeeding issues, only to be followed in September by a celebration of a "genius" whose "Book is reckoned among the first for Learning, Erudition, and sound Reasoning." It is not entirely coincidental that commentaries on Roman history and Vattel's *Law of Nations* appeared consecutively: both subjects consider liberty and autonomy as foundational to a free society.

The central theme of the review of *Law of Nations,* despite the inclusion of long, various, and carefully selected extracts, is the nature and scope of sovereignty: who possesses political authority in a civil society whose end is public happiness? While "the prince derives his authority from the nation"—in the words of "the learned author"—who "has strictly and simply invested him with sovereignty," his "*regal prerogatives*" are limited to the wellbeing of his subjects and "regulated by the fundamental laws." Roman history shows that when supreme authority, such as that of Nero, is abused and its holder "becomes the scourge of the state" and effectively "a public enemy," then "the nation may and ought to defend itself." If a monarch "attacks the liberties and privileges of his subjects," then he may "be abridged of his power" and the people "may resist him, try him, and withdraw from his obedience." When the contract between the people and their public authority is breached, "a nation" may consequently "curb an insupportable tyrant, call him even to an account, respecting in his person the majesty of his rank, and withdraw itself from his obedience." As soon as a monarch, "on leaving the bounds prescribed him, commands without any right, and even without a just title; the nation then is not obliged to obey him; but may resist his unjust enterprizes." Such a violation of public trust and transgression of popular sovereignty effectively "breaks the contract which bound the people to him; the people become free by the act of the sovereign, and see nothing in him but an usurper who would load them with oppression."[22] Obedience to authority is based on the consent of the governed and established for their common good. Here Vattel is being employed as a political defender of resistance, whose theory is derived from his larger moral theory of personhood.

II

Benjamin Franklin apparently met Charles Guilliam Frederic Dumas, a German-born Swiss who resided in The Hague, during his visit to the Netherlands in 1766, a meeting that led to a correspondence extending from 1768 until Franklin's death in 1790. Acting as a secret agent of the American colonies from 1775 and serving as their de facto chargé d'affaires at The Hague, Dumas devoted his life to the cause of America's independence (although he never crossed the Atlantic) and designed the first diplomatic cipher to mask correspondence between the Continental Congress and its foreign agents in Europe. In the view of John Bassett Moore, the first American judge to serve on the Permanent Court of International Justice, "with the exception of Adams, Franklin, and Jay," Dumas "rendered to the American cause in Europe services more important than did any other man."[23] Versed in the ancient classics and skilled in many modern languages, Dumas edited the original 1758 edition of Vattel's *Law of Nations* (published in Amsterdam in 1775) specifically to aid his American friends and sent Franklin three copies (in French) that same year with instructions to distribute "one for your own library, another for that of Philadelphia, and a third for such other library and colony as you may choose."[24] He reinvigorated Vattel's arguments for independence and brought out the relevance of the idea of external sovereignty in the context of the law of nations: statehood demanded independence and international recognition.

The three copies Dumas sent were considered "a most timely gift which was pounced upon by studious members of Congress, groping their way without the light of precedents [in international law]."[25] Upon their receipt in Philadelphia, Franklin wrote to Dumas on December 9, 1775:

> I am much obliged by the kind present you have made us of your edition of Vattel. It came to us in good season, when the circumstances of a rising state make it necessary frequently to consult the law of nations. Accordingly that copy, which I kept, (after depositing one in our own library here, and sending the other to the College of Massachusetts Bay, as you directed,) has been continually in the hands of the members of our Congress, now sitting, who are much pleased with your notes and preface, and have entertained a high and just esteem for their author. Your manuscript *Idee sur le Gouvernement et la Royaute* is also well relished, and may, in time, have its effect. . . . But we wish to know, whether any one of them [the countries of Europe], from principles of humanity, is disposed magnanimously to step in for the relief of an oppressed people; or whether, if, as it seems likely to happen, we should be obliged to break off all connexion with Britain, and declare ourselves an independent people, there is any state or power in Europe, who would be willing to enter into an alliance with us for the benefit of our commerce.[26]

The fate of the copy that Franklin kept for himself is not known.[27] The Harvard copy of Dumas's edition contains a handwritten commentary, written by Dumas himself, in which he shares his "idea upon government and royalty" and effectively endorses the urgency of Vattel to the American context of independence. "Impracticable, and consequently useless and dangerous to discuss in Europe, I thought that, sowed in America, it [*Law of Nations*] would take root there, germinate and fructify some day." The third copy Franklin presented to the Library Company of Philadelphia. On "Oct. 10, 1775," the minutes of the library's director reads, "Monsieur Dumas having presented the Library with a very late edition of Vattel's *Law of Nature and Nations* (in French), the Board direct the secretary to return that gentleman their thanks."[28] Of all three copies, the third one must—almost certainly—have been the most heavily used.

The study of the law of nations by the delegates to the Continental Congress, whose task was, in Franklin's language, to inquire into "the circumstances of a rising state," reflected the spirit of the Declaration of Independence itself. The document's central assertion, that governments are instituted to fulfill the "inalienable rights" of "life, liberty, and the pursuit of happiness," owed intellectual debt to Vattel's argument on the legitimacy criteria for a people to overthrow a tyrannical sovereign. Governments may not be usurped for transient and trivial causes, but they can be overthrown after a long chain of abuses to citizens' basic political and civil rights and mounting requests for redress of grievances. After repeated appeals to the "British Brethren," who remained "deaf to the voice of justice and consanguinity," the Americans were prepared to declare their independence from the British Crown, with the full rights of a sovereign government "to levy war, conclude peace, contract alliances, establish commerce, and to do all other acts and things which Independent States may of Right do." The *Law of Nations* not only assured legitimacy to the claims for independence but also provided a blueprint for the practice of statehood in a world of sovereigns. The newly founded United States, in a confluence of intended acts and fortunate circumstances, would become the first state to make international independence the hallmark of statehood.

Vattel's work on the sovereignty and independence of states influenced not only the delegates to the Continental Congresses in formulating a singular policy toward the British but also the debates on the framing of the Constitution. In letters dated November 8 and 10, 1777, Elbridge Gerry (who was to become the fifth vice president of the United States) and Daniel Roberdeau (a Pennsylvania delegate to the Continental Congress), respectively and independently of each other, divulged that "Vattell's Law of Nations" is "much wanted by some Gentlemen of Congress" and pleaded with Thomas Wharton (the first president of Pennsylvania) "for the Immediate Loan" of this work and that it "may be sent by express, if a good Opportunity does not very soon offer."[29]

During the following year, the demand for Vattel grew even wider. On January 1, 1778, James Lovell, a Massachusetts delegate to the Continental Congress and a signatory of the Articles of Confederation, wrote to Adams that Vattel's ideas can be used as powerful intellectual ammunition "to support reason & common sense or to destroy both." The power of ideas, he continued, can be as poignant as that of any military greatness to solve the "*just* Grounds" upon which "the weighty matters now in dispute between Great Britain and these States" can be resolved.[30] Vattel's opinions on the law of nations were frequently read and debated, not simply informatively for guidance in matters of public practice (which they accomplished quite well), but also—if not primarily—in order to stimulate action in the recipient's mind. While reading Vattel was certainly considered a leisurely delight (by most accounts it was, given that the reader did not have to struggle with Latin but engaged the accessible French), and it was simultaneously used with the purpose to induce a course of action.

The *Law of Nations* had been so popularized by late 1770s that the title and its author had become recognizable among leading statesmen. The thirst for owning, or at least borrowing, this work can only be compared to arming oneself with proper ammunition against the ignorant opinion of those who defended servitude toward the British.[31] "Will you permit me now to ask a very great favor of Your Lordship, design'd more for the public benefit than for my private convenience or amusement," wrote Henry Laurens, who succeeded John Hancock as president of the Second Continental Congress, to Major General William Alexander in 1788, "that your Lordship will endeavor to procure for me as early as may be, one or two Copies of Vatell's Law of Nations. I would rather have two than one." By word of mouth, statesmen would notify each other whenever they had knowledge about any means to acquire the *Law of Nations.* "Mr. Elliot, of New York . . . says he has met one copy of Vattel's works, which is among some books in cases which are unpacked, but has the promise of it as soon as they can conveniently get at it," wrote Lord Stirling to Laurens in 1778. "I have heard of another copy in this State, but it is in a similar situation, packed up and sent back into the country." The Senate session of March 10, 1794, concluded its meeting with the order that "the Secretary purchase Blackstone's *Commentaries,* and Vattel's *Law of Nature and Nations,* for the use of the Senate." In light of ongoing debates about the nature of sovereignty, which ultimately hinged on the organization of power itself, it should be hardly surprising that these two books were requested at the same time: they prescribed different conceptions of the nature and location of power in the state. By the mid-eighteenth century, the Whig defense of a sovereign Parliament, formulated by William Blackstone, with "a supreme, irresistible, absolute, uncontrolled authority, in which the *jura summi imperii,* or the rights of sovereignty, reside," became the standard claim of the English against the Americans.[32]

Dumas himself directed that one of the three copies be sent to a library in one of the colonies (though he had not specified which one), and a few months later Franklin "put into Mr. Adams's Hands . . . [the delivery of] the new Edition of Vattel [to James Bowdoin]. When you have perus'd it," he instructed the recipient, "please to place it in your [Harvard] College Library."[33] The only plausible reason for Franklin to have chosen Harvard over any other library in the colonies is his high esteem for the college. When Bowdoin, then president of the Massachusetts Provincial Congress's executive council (thus, the de facto governor) and a member of the Massachusetts Convention of 1788, received the book, he reported that when he had "looked over it," he would send "Vattel's *Droit des Gens*" to "the President of Harvard College as a present to the Library" in accordance with Franklin's instructions.[34] "At a meeting of the President & Fellows at the President's House," the college-board records of September 30, 1776, record a vote "[t]hat the Thanks of this Board be given to the Honle. Dr. Franklin for a fresh Instance of his Regard to the College by the Present of Les Droits de Gens par Monsr. De Vattel to our Library."[35] Even though Franklin's name had been entered as the book's donor, it should have more appropriately been that of Dumas himself.

The years of the American Revolution coincided with a smallpox epidemic that spanned North America and claimed more than 130,000 lives in just a few years. While it is impossible to know with certainty whether the British practiced germ warfare against the Americans or not, a series of letters from Washington to Congress, written in December 1775, reveal that the threat of biological warfare was sufficiently real in his mind to merit mention in his official reports. In a diary entry from that month, Richard Smith, a New Jersey delegate to the Continental Congress, noted that "much of the Day was spent upon" responding to Washington's fear that soldiers from the British army may have been deliberately infected with smallpox so that they may pass the disease to the Americans. During their deliberations, the delegates held "learned Debates" and relied on "[a]uthorities from Vattel" for addressing the British threat, agreeing that "such Matters ought to be tried . . . by the Course of the Law of Nations [and] not of the Municipal Law." Rendered a respected and reliable source in the unchartered waters of international law, Vattel quickly emerged as the main authority for how the new nation should conduct itself as an independent state in its relations with foreign powers. He "helped to influence our course in the early years of the Republic under Washington and Jefferson," scholars recognized more than a century later, "and even afterwards, in moulding the expansion of the Law between Nations."[36]

Like all of the other Founding Fathers, who did not demarcate the domestic sphere from that of the foreign, Jefferson "eventually accumulated nearly all of the fundamental treatises on the subject [of natural law]," including Burlamaqui, Grotius, Pufendorf, Wolff, and "two different editions of Emer de Vattel's *Le Droit des Gens*."[37] Into his earlier edition of Vattel, Jefferson even inscribed marginal references to Wolff's *Institutions* and Burlamaqui's *Principes de Droit Natural.* Jefferson's copy of a later edition of *Law of Nations* (which he loaned to Richard Dobbs Spaight, a representative from North Carolina, and to David Howell, a representative from Rhode Island) reveals that he cross-referenced Vattel with the work of the German jurist Georg Friedrich von Martens. In referencing Vattel's work to that of Jean Bodin, Jefferson positioned the theory of domestic sovereignty within the larger context of the relations between independent states and that of the law of nations more generally. Sovereignty as independence—the main justification for waging a war against British oppression—was located in the larger discourse of the relations between states and the applicable laws of nature.

One important reason why the delegates of the First and Second Continental Congress chose to meet in Carpenters Hall (against the objections of Joseph Galloway) was that the building also housed the Library Company of

Philadelphia. Its director, Francis Daymon, reported that Vattel was one of the main sources consulted by the delegates during the First Continental Congress, which met from September 5 to October 26, 1774. "Philadelphia has become another Cairo," William Bradford wrote to James Madison on October 17, "with this difference that the one is a city swarming with Merchants [and] the other with politicians & Statesmen." The representatives debated "like philosophers; for by what I was told, Vattel, Barlemaqui Locke & Montesquie[u] seem to be the standar[d]s to which they refer either when settling the rights of the Colonies or when a dispute arises on the Justice or propriety of a measure." The Library Company already owned a copy of the 1760 English translation of the first French edition of 1758, which may have been received at any time before 1763. The authority of Vattel on questions of the law of nations thus had been well established by the early 1770s. A few months prior to the congressional debates, on December 28, 1773, the Library Company informed Benjamin Franklin that its "books (enclosed within wire lattices) are kept in one large room" and were available for the delegates to consult. By the time Dumas's own copy of Vattel reached Philadelphia in 1775, the earlier English edition had already been in heavy use by American statesmen for years.[38]

III

When writing to the king of Prussia in 1777, Arthur Lee, serving as an envoy to Prussia at the time, made a case in favor of "deciding for the independence of America" as a fact "authorized by the laws of nations." In support of his claim he cited authoritatively a long paragraph from Vattel affirming "the right of the people" to rule themselves and "the independence of nations."

Luther Martin, a Maryland delegate to the Constitutional Convention, lamented the ascension of the powers of the federal government over the states and for that reason even refused to sign the Constitution; in his view it effectively violated states' rights. "Individuals, by natural right, are equal," Martin argued. "This equality is in some degree lost when they become members of a society. . . . Confederation of such States is for the good of the whole, and their individual rights must be safeguarded without consideration of size or importance. Vattel, Locke, and other authorities on public law, agree upon this point."[39] A staunch antifederalist, Martin relied on Vattel's authority to defend the natural equality among states as a fundamental precondition for a strong Union. The role of the federal government was meant merely to preserve state governments rather than to govern individuals, and its powers should be circumscribed to narrow limits that can be expanded only if inconvenience demands it. "States like individuals were in a State of nature equally sovereign and free," Madison observed of Martin's speech at the convention in his diary entry dated June 27, 1787. "In order to prove that individuals in a State of nature are equally free and independent he [Martin] read passages from Locke, Vattel"; to show "that the case is the same with States till they surrender their equal sovereignty, he read other passages in Locke and Vattel."[40]

In his *Opinion on the French Treaties,* submitted in April 1793, Jefferson considers the question, does the newly established United States "have a right to renounce their treaties with France, or hold them suspended till the government of that country shall be established?" Such an inquiry pertains to the domain of the law of nations, and Jefferson follows Vattel's own tripartite division of the law of nations into three branches: "1. The Moral law of our nature. 2. The Usages of nations. 3. Their special Conventions." In considering the laws that govern international conduct, statesmen treat them as the laws of nature as applied to states and intermixed with established practices and conventions that already exist. "Those who write treatises of natural law," Jefferson affirms, "can only declare what their moral sense and reason dictate in the several cases they state. Such of them as happen to have feelings and a reason coincident with those of the wise and honest part of mankind, are respected and quoted as witnesses of what is morally right or wrong in particular cases. Grotius, Puffendorf [*sic*], Wolf[f], and Vattel are of this number."[41]

The authority of Vattel, along with that of his major predecessors, had been well established for at least two decades by 1793. Jefferson's opinion represented precisely the kind of serious political treatise writing that the Founding Fathers not only esteemed for its intellectual rigor but also actively used for its practical application in engaging in foreign affairs. The framers of the early American Republic endorsed Vattel's argument over the rights of governments, the duties of citizens, and their application to external affairs, especially in relation to their former colonial masters. They also sought to appropriate them in the transatlantic context precisely at a time when the emergence of the United States of America provided Vattel's theory with the richest ground for the creation of new states around the globe, free of tyranny and independent of foreign rule.

NOTES

I am grateful to The John W. Kluge Center at the Library of Congress for awarding me a Kluge Fellowship, during which time this chapter was written.

1. The other two libraries were King's College (now Columbia University) and the Union Library.
2. For a brief history of New York Society Library in its first years, see Frank Monaghan and Marvin Lowenthal, *This Was New York: The Nation's Capital in 1789* (Freeport, N.Y.: Books for Libraries, 1943), 135–67.
3. *Eighteenth-Century American Newspapers in the Library of Congress,* vol. 822 (Oct. 1–Dec. 31, 1789).
4. Emer de Vattel, *The Law of Nations, Or, Principles of the Law of Nature, Applied to the Conduct and Affairs of Nations and Sovereigns, with Three Early Essays on the Origin and Nature of Natural Law and on Luxury* (1758), ed. with an introduction by Béla Kapossy and Richard Whitmore (Indianapolis: Liberty Fund, 2008), 76.
5. Ibid., 76–77, 483.
6. On Vattel's influence on the early American Republic, see Thomas Gray, "Origins of the Unwritten Constitution: Fundamental Law in American Revolutionary Thought," *Stanford Law Review* 30, no. 5 (May 1978): 843–93; Daniel Lang, *Foreign Policy in the Early Republic: The Law of Nations and the Balance of Power* (Baton Rouge: Louisiana State University Press, 1985); Michael Morley, "The Law of Nations and the Offenses Clause of the Constitution: A Defense of Federalism," *Yale Law Journal* 112, no. 1 (Oct. 2002): 109–43; and Suzanna Sherry, "The Founders' Unwritten Constitution," *University of Chicago Law Review* 54, no. 4 (Autumn 1987): 1127–77.
7. "To Robert Cary & Company," in *The Papers of George Washington Digital Edition,* ed. Theodore J. Crackel (Charlottesville: University of Virginia Press, 2008), 344. No record has been found of Washington's receiving any shipment from Cary after 1773.
8. Bernard Bailyn, *Pamphlets of the American Revolution, 1750–1776,* vol. 1 (Cambridge, Mass.: Harvard University Press, 1965), 24.
9. "Thomas Jefferson to John Trumbull, February 15, 1789," in *The Portable Thomas Jefferson,* ed. Merrill Peterson (Harmondsworth, U.K.: Penguin, 1975), 434; Carl L. Becker, *The Declaration of Independence: A Study in the History of Political Ideas* (New York: Harcourt, Brace, 1922), 27; Thomas Pangle, *The Spirit of Modern Republicanism* (Chicago: University of Chicago Press, 1988); Michael Zuckert, *The Natural Rights Republic* (Notre Dame, Ind.: University of Notre Dame Press, 1996), 73–85. Francis Bacon and Isaac Newton were the other two of Jefferson's "three greatest men." Others, however, have noted that Jefferson and Locke stand at "two opposite poles" in their political philosophy: Ray Forrest Harvey, *Jean Jacques Burlamaqui: A Liberal Tradition in American Constitutionalism* (Chapel Hill: University of North Carolina Press, 1937), 120.
10. John Locke, *Two Treatises of Government,* ed. Peter Laslett (Cambridge: Cambridge University Press, 1988), 323. One notable exception is David Armitage, *The Declaration of Independence: A Global History* (Cambridge, Mass.: Harvard University Press, 2008).

11. United States Steel Corp. v. Multistate Tax Commission, 434 U.S. 452 (1978), 462n12.
12. Albert de Lapradelle, introduction to *The Law of Nations; or, The Principles of Natural Law* (Washington, D.C.: Carnegie Institution of Washington, 1916), xxx.
13. *New-York Gazette,* Nov. 29, Dec. 6, 1762, Aug. 29, 1763.
14. John Adams, *The Works of John Adams, Second President of the United States: with a Life of the Author, Notes and Illustrations, by his Grandson Charles Francis Adams,* ed. Charles Francis Adams, 10 vols. (Boston: Little, Brown, 1856), 2:73.
15. Zoltan Haraszti, *John Adams and the Prophets of Progress* (Cambridge, Mass.: Harvard University Press, 1952). I owe this reference to Will Slauter.
16. Bailyn, *Pamphlets of the American Revolution,* 410.
17. "John Adams to William Tudor, March 29, 1817," in Adams, *Works,* 10:247–48.
18. James Otis, *Rights of the British Colonies Asserted and Proved* (1764), in *Collected Political Writings of James Otis,* ed. Richard Samuelson (Indianapolis: Liberty Fund, 2015), 140, 121, 175–76.
19. Oxenbridge Thacher, *The Sentiments of a British American* (Boston, 1764). For additional background, see Bailyn, *Pamphlets of the American Revolution,* 490. While Otis referenced an anonymously translated 1759 edition of the *Law of Nations,* it appears that Thacher must have used a different edition (probably the original French). Bailyn, *Pamphlets of the American Revolution,* 124, 724nn45, 47,726n1. Multiple editions of Vattel's work clearly were in circulation in the colonies by the early 1760s, when booksellers advertised copies of *Law of Nations* for sale in the *New-York Gazette* (November 29 and December 6, 1762) and the *Pennsylvania Journal* (October 13, 1763).
20. Vattel, *Law of Nations,* 89.
21. Ibid., 83, 89.
22. *The (New Bern) North-Carolina Magazine; or, Universal Intelligencer,* Sept. 7–14, 14–21, 1764.
23. John Bassett Moore, *American Diplomacy: Its Spirit and Achievements* (New York: Harper and Brothers, 1905), 23.
24. Charles Guilliam Frederic Dumas to Benjamin Franklin, 1775, in *Publications of the Colonial Society of Massachusetts, Volume 20: Transactions 1917–1919* (Boston, 1920), 7n1
25. James Parton, *Life and Times of Benjamin Franklin,* vol. 2 (Boston: Mason and Hamlin, 1867), 111.
26. "Benjamin Franklin to Charles William Frederic Dumas (Philadelphia, 9 December, 1775)," in *Letters of Delegates to Congress, 1774–1789,* ed. Paul H. Smith, 26 vols. (Washington, D.C.: Library of Congress, 1976–2000), 2:465–66.
27. Some have speculated that "Franklin's own Vattel has vanished." See *Publications of the Colonial Society of Massachusetts: Transaction, 1917–1919,* vol. 20 (Boston, 1920), 9.
28. Lapradelle, introduction to *Law of Nations,* xxx.
29. "Elbridge Gerry to Thomas Wharton (York, PA, 8 November 1777)," in *Letters of Delegates to Congress,* 8:242.

30. "James Lovell to John Adams, January 1, 1778," in *Letters of Delegates to Congress,* 2:514.
31. Apparently, delegates to Congress would insert their own correspondence within the circulating copies of *Law of Nations:* in a letter to Joseph Jones, James Madison wrote, "The inclosed [unidentified] letters were found between the pages of Vattel." James Madison to Joseph Jones, Oct. 17, 1780, in *The Papers of James Madison,* vol. 2, ed. William T. Hutchinson and William M. E. Rachal (Chicago: University of Chicago Press, 1962), 139.
32. "Henry Laurens to William Alexander, November 29, 1778," in *Letters of Delegates to Congress,* 11:265; Lord Stirling to Henry Laurens, Dec. 16, 1778, in *Correspondence of Henry Laurens of South Carolina* (1861; reprint, London: Forgotten Books, 2103), 128; *Journal of the Senate, 1789–1873,* 44; William Blackstone, *Commentaries on the Laws of England in Four Books,* vol. 1 (1753; reprint, Philadelphia, 1893), 49.
33. "Benjamin Franklin to James Bowdoin (Philadelphia, 24 March, 1776)," in *Letters of Delegates to Congress,* 2:435.
34. "James Bowdoin to Benjamin Franklin (Boston, 19 August, 1776)," in *Collections of the Massachusetts Historical Society* (Boston, 1897), 400.
35. Denys P. Myers, "A Franco-American Memento," *Harvard Alumni Bulletin* 21 (1918): 106.
36. "Richard Smith's Diary," in *Letters of Delegates to Congress,* 2:486; *Publications of the Colonial Society of Massachusetts,* 9.
37. Kevin J. Hayes, *The Road to Monticello: The Life and Mind of Thomas Jefferson* (Oxford, U.K: Oxford University Press, 2008), 83.
38. *Journals of the Continental Congress, 1774–1789,* ed. Worthington C. Ford et al., vol. 1 (Washington, D.C., 1904–37), 27; Edmund Cody Burnett, *The Continental Congress* (New York: Macmillan, 1941), 33–34; Austin K. Gray, *Benjamin Franklin's Library: A Short Account of the Library Company of Philadelphia, 1731–1931* (New York: Macmillan, 1936), 27–28. The Dumas copy would get so heavily used that it had to be "rebound" with "more modern kind of paper than that upon which the book" was originally printed. *Publications of the Colonial Society of Massachusetts,* 7.
39. Luther Martin, in *American Debate: A History of Political and Economic Controversy in the United States, with Critical Digests of Leading Debates,* ed. Marion Mills Miller, vol. 1 (New York: G. P. Putnam's Sons, 1916), 217.
40. "The Debates in the Several State Conventions on the Adoption of the Federal Constitution," in Jonathan Elliot, *The debates in the several state conventions on the adoption of the federal Constitution, as recommended by the general convention at Philadelphia, in 1787. Together with the Journal of the federal convention, Luther Martin's letter, Yates's minutes, Congressional opinions, Virginia and Kentucky resolutions of '98–'99, and other illustrations of the Constitution . . . 2d ed., with considerable additions. Collected and rev. from contemporary publications,* 5 vols. ("Pub. under the sanction of Congress," 1836), 5:248–49. Rufus King similarly records that "every man out of society is equal, in Freedom, and every other quality of man- Locke, Vattel, and others prove this position." *The Records of the Federal Convention of 1787,* ed. Max Farrand, vol. 1 (New

Haven, Conn.: Yale University Press, 1911), 442. In his notes from the same day, Robert Yates concurs that, according to Martin, "Vattel, Rutherford and Locke, are united in support of this position, that states, as to each other, are in a state of nature." Ibid., 440.

41. Thomas Jefferson to George Washington, "Opinion on the French Treaties, April 28, 1793," in Thomas Jefferson, *The Papers of Thomas Jefferson,* vol. 25, *1 January–10 May 1793,* ed. John Catanzariti (Princeton, N.J.: Princeton University Press, 1993), 613.

4 JUSTIFYING FRATRICIDAL WAR

The American Revolution as a Case Study

Jack P. Greene

So horrendous are the human and material costs of wars that many polities considering a resort to force have felt compelled to explain and defend this action to the individuals and groups called upon to bear those costs, to engage their wills and energies, to justify their sacrifices and deprivations, and ultimately to persuade observers and posterity of the nobility of their cause. In constructing these defenses, advocates of the use of force have drawn upon religion, law, history, and accepted codes of civil behavior and appealed to collective fears and resentments arising out of perceived political slights and supposed violations of customary rights and authority to make the case that the proposed war is both just and unavoidable. In a free society, however, these constructs are open to challenge from those who have and use political voice, and these challenges mount quickly if the war aims prove elusive and the costs reach insupportable levels. The justice or injustice of any war lies in the eye of the beholder—the Revolutionary War is no exception.

In 1763, barely a dozen years before the event that contemporaries in Great Britain knew as the American War and that American historians would subsequently label the War for American Independence broke out on April 19, 1775, at Lexington and Concord, those on both sides of the Atlantic destined to become the belligerent parties would have laughed at any suggestion that the British Empire might at any point in the foreseeable future be riven by civil war. Resounding victories in the Seven Years' War (1756–63) on three continents (Europe, North America, and Asia), in the West Indies, and on the high seas had brought Britain claims to vast new possessions in North America, the West Indies, Bengal, and the west African coast. As enthusiastic celebrants throughout the British Empire proclaimed, these acquisitions rendered it the largest and most successful empire in history. Because so much of the war had been fought in North America and most of the British continental colonies had made substantial contributions of men and money to the war effort, their inhabitants were happier than ever to be British, taking enhanced pride in their heritage and seizing every occasion to express their longstanding affection for the metropolitan state and their connection to it.

To be sure, wartime experiences had served to confirm a preexisting concern among London authorities about their tenuous authority over those distant provinces that had, especially over the previous half century, contributed so substantially to Britain's commercial and internal economic development and defensive capabilities through their consumption of British goods, their heavy demand for African slaves, and their stimulation of the development of Britain's maritime resources. Specifically, widespread colonial evasions of metropolitan trade laws during the war evoked demands for stricter enforcement, while the refusal of provincial legislatures to adhere to any restrictions on their authority over their respective domestic affairs inspired demands for a new model for colonial government. The chicanery of Indian traders and the relentless encroachment of a prolific settler population upon Indian lands also seemed, if peace were to be maintained on North American frontiers, to require metropolitan direction of both Indian affairs and territorial expansion. If a profound appreciation of the commercial utility of the colonies underlay such demands, few if any of the advocates for such measures expected that the colonies had the capacity, the will, the cohesion, or the disaffection to mount any serious resistance, especially not when the metropolis had a sizeable military contingent scattered through many of the colonies and a powerful navy to help enforce its directives.

For scholars of this post–Seven Years' War era, the paramount questions have always been how and why, over the next dozen years, this manifest colonial affection for Britain could break down to the point that those who favored using force to defend the colonies from British measures that they interpreted as denials of their inherited rights could carry the day and rather quickly turn their resistance into a movement for independence. For historians of late eighteenth-century Britain and the British Empire, the central questions have been how and why over the same period the British political nation, notwithstanding its manifest appreciation of the commercial and strategic utility of the colonies to the parent state, persisted in a policy that led to colonial alienation and provoked a bloody civil war in which proponents of force on both sides of the Atlantic fervently believed that justice was on their side.

What historians on both sides have often missed or inadequately taken into account is that a substantial population in Great Britain and a sizeable population in North America opposed the use of force, lamented the degeneration of an imperial family disagreement into a bloody civil war among fellow nationals, and decried the unnatural—the fratricidal—character of such a conflict and the high costs and injustices it produced. The debate leading up to and continuing throughout the war thus involved, not two, but four differing perspectives on the question of whether the war was a just one. Any discussion of the American Revolution as a just war should include a consideration of all four perspectives. Accordingly, this short chapter will examine the intensive debates in Britain over the legitimacy of using force against fellow subjects and, less fully, the debates in the colonies over, on the one hand, the legitimacy of resisting that force and, on the other, the legitimacy of coercing provincial populations into joining or complying with such a resistance. Mainly through an analysis of two sources—the extensive pamphlet literature published on the American question in Britain and the reports of parliamentary debates—it will consider both the issues and considerations that drove those debates and the rationales developed to justify or oppose the drift toward and the continuation of war.[1]

I

In Britain, the American colonies' massive resistance to the Stamp Act and their explicit denial of parliamentary authority to tax and legislate for their internal affairs effectively split the political nation into two general and contending persuasions, one advocating coercion and the other, conciliation. On two essential points they did not disagree: first, that Parliament's authority to legislate for the colonies was full and complete, and second, that the economic and strategic value of the colonies required that they remain within the British Empire. But the two camps disagreed profoundly about the best strategy to secure the colonial connection.[2]

Thoroughly outraged by the extent, vigor, and character of colonial resistance, the "coercionists" opposed any modification of the Stamp Act, were appalled by proposals for its repeal, and demanded a swift and effective exertion of metropolitan authority to enforce it. For them, the solemn petitions and strident resolutions adopted by colonial legislatures denying Parliament's authority over the internal affairs of free British polities in America, the spirited and substantial pamphlet and newspaper literature produced by individual colonial writers exploring in detail the issues raised by those challenges, the systematic intimidation of officials charged with implementing the Stamp Act by informal vigilante groups calling themselves "Sons of Liberty," the wanton destruction of the personal property of some British officials in Boston and Newport by rioting mobs, and the convocation of a general congress by a majority of the continental colonies to formulate their objections and bring economic pressure on the metropolis by endorsing the adoption of a general boycott on British goods all exhibited a flagrant disregard for metropolitan authority and levels of ingratitude, disloyalty, and dissatisfaction with metropolitan constraints that fell but little short of outright rebellion and expressed long-smoldering aspirations for total independence.

As one coercionist explained it, the "*Americans*," having "been increasing in Riches for these Thirty Years . . . and having obtained immense Territory, and a Security from those Enemies, the *French* and *Indians*, who served to keep them in awe," had "become at our Expence, and for which we are now starving, proud, lordly, and ambitious; or rather, from their former Circumstances, and their vain Persuasion that we are in no Condition to dispute their Wills, have suffered these Seeds of Rebellion to break forth, and discover their long smothered Inclinations and Designs of setting up an Empire, independent of *Britain*." To give in to colonial demands, said another analyst, would "make *Americans* our Masters" and, declared another analyst, Great Britain nothing more than "a province to her own colonies."[3] Hence, coercionists called upon the "*British* Senate" not to "suffer *English* Glory to fade, to be blasted by *American* breath; their Trade to be ruined by rebellious Subjects, nor *Englishmen* to become Slaves to *Creoles*."[4]

Nor was the use of force missing from the coercionists' agendas. Many talked boldly about "compelling the Execution" of the Stamp Act "by Force of Arms" and reckoned that a mere "ten thousand of our Regular Troops" could easily "drive all the Colonies before them."[5] "Our news papers and coffee-house politicians," an advocate for a more conciliatory approach complained in early 1766, "have been lately full of invectives against the disposition and conduct of the Americans, and using foul mouthed reproach" accused them of "insolently claiming an independency" and declared them "guilty of treason" and thoroughly deserving "to be treated as rebels." Calling for "the most violent methods," they seemed "to be endeavoring to drive matters to the worst and last extremity, a civil war" that would "be immediately entered into and pursued with rigour and vengeance against" Britain's very own "descendants and subjects."[6] Merely for standing up for their liberty, lamented still other writers opposed to extreme retaliatory measures, the colonists had succeeded only in eliciting charges that they were seeking nothing less than "pure natural liberty, and absolute uncontroulable independence" and in unleashing "BRITTANIA's hate" to such an extent that "a golden fury . . . rages in each breast."[7]

Branding the advocates of coercion as "enemies to the Peace and Prosperity of this Nation," those favoring conciliation argued that "as fellow subjects," colonists ought to be treated "with tenderness and liberality," urging Parliament to approach the "critical situation we are in" with "deliberation" and an "air of

Good-will," "not rashness and violence." Contending that the principal objective in sponsoring colonizing schemes had been "the establishment and extension of the commerce of [all] the British dominions," they queried whether "levying taxes upon them" was not entirely "contrary to sound policy" and called upon Parliament to consider the colonies' prominent role in enriching and strengthening Britain and the loyal "disposition" they had always displayed toward it. So far from deserving metropolitan disrespect "as a set of vagabonds and transports," as so many coercionists had asserted, the colonists, conciliationists argued, had brought their respective provinces into "a respectable importance" and deserved recognition as "an industrious, honest and free people." Declaring that it was "bad policy in free states" to treat their "colonies with severity," exponents of conciliation contended that Britain had established such settlements to create "a dominion founded on freedom," not "an uncontroulable power over slaves." Especially in view of the colonists' "unanimous" expression through "the Remonstrances of their Assemblies" of their settled determination not to submit to the Stamp Act, they cautioned against measures that through "injury or oppression" might produce further "resentments" and advocated modification or repeal of the offending law. "Not abject Submission," but "wise and proper Management" designed to encourage "a liberal obedience" and "filial affection" along with, following the Irish model, "a very cautious . . . exercise" of parliamentary authority were the best means to restore colonial respect for that authority, retain the colonies within the imperial orbit, and promote their "gradual assimilation" to the British state.[8]

For conciliationists, the use of force was completely inappropriate. In early 1766 the anonymous author of a pamphlet entitled *The General Opposition of the Colonies to the Payment of the Stamp Duty* examined at extended length "the Consequence of Enforcing Obedience by Military Measures." He asked his readers to consider "whether the terror of arms ever convinced the judgment, and conciliated the affections, and whether the Americans can, or will, ever be cordially united to you, if moderation, the best means of governing, is called pusillanimity, and looked upon as below the dignity of authority." Although he thought "it probable that Great Britain would at last be triumphant" in any military altercation, he provided a long history of the successful Netherlands revolt against Spain in the late sixteenth and early seventeenth centuries to alert readers to the possibility that Britain's "most vigorous efforts may be baffled; notwithstanding the greatness of her power, and the weakness of America." "Every war is doubtful," he observed, power having "frequently ruined itself by confidence, and weakness grown strong by despair."[9]

Urging "the Advocates for military Measures" seriously to examine "the Obstacles, as well as the Advantages that may occur in the Execution of any violent Measure," another anonymous writer that same year elaborated upon the prudential objections to resorting to force. With up to seventy thousand able-bodied men who were thoroughly familiar with and acclimatized to the country and schooled in "the *Indian* method of Bush-fighting," the colonists, especially if they had been "enthusiastically misled to imagine they fight for liberty," might be troublesome to subdue and able to retard the "Reduction of each Colony," while a force would be required in each of them sufficient "to keep them in proper Obedience after we have conquered them." On the improbable assumptions that no European rivals would intervene on the colonial side and that the extensive use of the Royal Navy could effectively blockade North American ports, he said, ridiculing his opponents' superficial understanding of the problem, it might take no more than "ten or twelve Years at farthest . . . either to conquer their stubborn Spirits, or [to] extirpate them absolutely." Given the magnitude of these obstacles, he concluded, force was not the answer. Now that the colonies had "grown to maturity," he declared, "they should be held by stronger Bands, I mean those of mutual Friendship and reciprocal Advantage, without which no obligation of Gratitude on account of former care and tenderness, no coercive power, however properly employed, can possibly insure more than a temporary Acquiescence. For whenever there is sufficient Power, or opportunity to shake off Dependence," he added, "I fear there is no other hold to be relied on than that of strong interest."[10]

The repeal of the Stamp Act in 1766 during the few months in which, for the whole of the 1760s and 1770s, such moderates were in control of Parliament represented a victory for the forces of conciliation as did, to a lesser extent, the partial repeal of the Townshend duties in 1771. At the same time, however, continuing resistance in the late 1760s and early 1770s only served to deepen the convictions of advocates for repression that the repeal of the Stamp Act had been a huge mistake; that the colonies, especially New England, were dominated by turbulent politicians who were aiming at independence; and that decades of metropolitan neglect had fostered the development of such sentiments as well as of the groundless constitutional arguments the upstart colonials employed to justify their resistance.

II

Resistance to the Tea Act of 1773 powerfully reinforced such sentiments, inaugurated a new phase in the debate over the use of force, and contributed to the demand for strong measures to bring the colonials to obedience. The avowed intention of the metropolitan government in the Coercive Acts of 1774, after the Boston Tea Party, was to make an example of Massachusetts Bay, unilaterally closing the port of Boston and changing the colony's constitution and its system of justice. Through the imposition of a naval blockade of Boston, these measures represented the first instance of government-mandated force against any of the colonies. While the administration stopped short of actually authorizing the use of an extensive military establishment stationed in the city to quell resistance, neither the government nor its supporters exhibited much interest in conciliation. The colonists' widespread and wholesale resistance to the Coercive Acts, in particular their calling of a continental congress that laid out a case for the unconstitutionality of those measures, sanctioned a boycott of British imports, and approved military preparations to combat any metropolitan effort to force compliance, produced a groundswell of opinion in Britain in favor of naval and military coercion.

Denying that taxation was tyranny, refusing to consider any colonial petitions challenging the authority of Parliament to legislate for all British dominions, assigning all responsibility for the controversy to colonial resistance, and "glowing with a spirit of revenge," coercionists justified the resort to force primarily on grounds of necessity and honor.[11] A fictional character in a mock dialogue published a year after hostilities had begun at Lexington and Concord in April 1775, *Aristocratus* put the administration's case for forceful intervention succinctly. Shall Britain give in or shall it "act with a vigour that becomes the dignity of Great Britain, her immense resources, the might of her invincible fleet, the irresistible bravery of her troops, and conduct of her generals and those troops who have traversed the world with victory," he asked, "and shall not that arm which has subdued the power of two of the most formidable monarchies of Europe united against her, chastise the mad insurrection of her infatuated provinces, who owe all their strength to the power they resist, and who must learn that duty by force, which they will not otherwise be taught."[12] "Can it be thought that *Great-Britain,* whose Government has been insulted, whose constitutional Supremacy has been denied, whose Dominions have been invaded," asked another government spokesman, "will crouch to Subjects in Rebellion? Can *Englishmen* wish to see their Country so far degraded as to make ignominious Concessions under such multiplied Instances of Provocation?" Nothing less than Britain's international standing seemed to be at stake, and Britain had to quell the revolt to preserve its stature as the preeminent imperial power and to save face among its Continental rivals. "The Eyes of all *Europe* are upon us," the author noted, concluding that "*France* and *Spain* would no doubt be well pleased" to "behold a rival State disarmed, by the Partizans of a rebellious Congress."[13] The "sword alone," declared still another writer, "must decide . . .

whether Great Britain shall hereafter in fact give laws to her transmarine provinces, or perhaps even retain her own proper empire in Europe."[14]

Considerations of expediency—striking while the colonies were still too weak and divided to resist British military and naval forces—and of utility—maintaining Britain's ability to continue to subordinate colonial economies to the commercial interests of the metropolis—also informed the decision to employ force; overt considerations of justice, however, were marginal to the government case. Even Alexander Carlyle's 1777 pamphlet, *The Justice and Necessity of the War with our American Colonies Examined,* the only such missive to foreground the word *justice* in its title, was principally concerned with arguing for the *necessity* of war.[15] This observation is not to suggest that proponents of force doubted the justice of their advocacy, only that the point seemed too obvious to be made. No full supporter of the North American war in any way questioned its justice.

III

Such was not the case among the large conciliationist minority, who, opening themselves to recurrent charges that they were encouraging and enabling rebellion in America, mounted a substantial and extended critique of the resort to force both in and out of Parliament, one they kept up from 1774 until 1782, when the loss of an army at Yorktown and the heavy fiscal costs of the conflict drove the North administration out of power. Pointing out in detail the uncertainties of the outcome of any war and the difficulties of controlling a conquered territory of such a huge extent as the North American colonies, these conciliationists insisted that the "very idea" of subduing the colonists "by naval or military force," as an anonymous writer declared in early 1774, was "absurd," nothing more than "a palliative, shuffling, temporary expedient, which may for some time controul, but never can strike at the root of the disease." He continued, "a dominion founded on *Fear,* and maintained through *Compulsion*" could "last no longer than 'till the controuling power is distressed by a general war." "Not force," he insisted, but only "the gentle cords of Humanity and Love" could draw the colonies into a permanent attachment to Britain.[16]

Conciliationists blamed successive administrations for the provocations that had led to the controversy. They denied that problems arising out of the Seven Years' War and its outcome required parliamentary taxation and other interventions or repressive changes in colonial management. Ignoring both the commercial and libertarian principles upon which the empire had been constructed, they charged, one ministry after another had undertaken "new plans for our old Colonies" that revealed a total "unacquaintance" with "the true spirit of commerce" and could only "be seen" by the colonists "in the invidious light of innovations" that would deprive them of the traditional liberties they all had long enjoyed.[17] Before "the aera of the fatal stamp-act," said Henry Cruger in Parliament in restating a line of argument to which the conciliationists had long adhered, "no country" had "been more happy in its colonies than Great Britain." Thus "connected by mutual interests," the empire had "flourished in an intercourse of amity, protection, and obedience" and had exhibited "no instances of disobedience to your laws, no denial of the jurisdiction of Parliament, no marks of jealousy and discontent."[18] But the principal precondition for colonial obedience, advocates of conciliation insisted, was the enjoyment of a considerable measure of British liberty in managing colonial domestic affairs. "So accustomed" were "the people of each government to have its interior oeconomy settled, and its taxes laid on by its own representatives, to look upon its own assembly as its own legislature in either, and even to regard its sister colony as a separate state," declared one pamphleteer in May 1776, "that to turn any of those matters into another channel" invariably, in colonial eyes, appeared to be "bringing about a revolution, a thing seldom attempted where the people are not better disposed to it than [were] the Americans."[19] Indeed, declared Manassah Dawes the following January, from this point of view, it was "our *Administration that is in rebellion,* not the Americans," who had "broke[n] no law, whereto they were parties," while the administration, by breaking "thro' their charters" and committing "violence to our own constitution, by stirring up a war so destructive to common humanity, so offensive to christianity," had assumed the character of "rebels," and "the poor Americans" had become "the oppressed people, against whom their rebellion is made."[20]

Moreover, as many adherents of this position observed, the war proponents severely underestimated the breadth, depth, and character of American resistance. After the colonists had continued their protests for a dozen years and were now so obviously "unanimous in their opposition to government," declared a writer using the pseudonym Janus, only the most "strangely infatuated" people in Britain could persist in believing "that such a universal dissatisfaction could prevail in the colonies" unless the colonists "sensibly felt some real cause; unless they labored under some grievances unredressed."[21] "Is it reasonable or just to conceive," asked another writer, "that a body of people, of at least three millions, many of them of distinguished and acknowledged abilities and genius, whose commerce was in the most thriving situation, whose internal resources were great and valuable, whose families enjoyed peace and plenty, affluence and ease, should, deliberately, without the utmost provocation, without the most hostile invasion of their liberties and properties, resist the authority of the parent state, and lift arms against her power?"[22] Only "one common principle, and a persuasion of right," said A.M., could have brought "a people so divided" and "living most happily, and sensible of it," to "make so general an opposition to a nation which they loved, [and] expose an extended sea coast to the most formidable naval power, . . . a straggling frontier to savages and Canadians, and the habitations of the most wealthy [colonies] to the ravages of their own slaves."[23] For "the friends of the ministry" to try to "amuse us with stories of the parental affection of the mother country" and to suggest "that our indulgence, our mild benevolence has been the cause of the present disobedience of our children," wrote Janus, was, in the face of such widespread and lengthy resistance, scarcely credible.[24]

Arguing that resistance was not rebellion and decrying the idea that Britain, the land of liberty, should ever "desire to hold her empire under a forced subjection," the opponents of war condemned it as a violation of the civilized norms of familial attachment—mother against children, brother against brother—inhumane, and unjust.[25] The ministry's "measures of Blood, distress and ruin," decried Dawes, had been designed "the better to slaughter our fellow-creatures, employ our army and navy, and promote desolation in the once quiet homes of a useful and prosperous people."[26] In addition, during a debate in the House of Lords in May 1777, the Earl of Shelburne denounced the ministry for its "barbarous, unjust and tyrannical [behavior] toward their brethren and fellow subjects."[27] "You have," the Earl of Chatham charged, "made descents upon their coasts; you have burnt their towns, plundered their country, made war upon the inhabitants, confiscated their property, [and] proscribed and imprisoned their persons."[28] By "stirring up a war so destructive to common humanity; so offensive to christianity," Dawes declared, the ministry had proven themselves to be what the poet John Day denounced as "vindictive tyrants," who wrathfully, criminally, remorselessly, unjustly, and inhumanely had unleashed the "flames of vengeance, and . . . ruthless steel" against their American brethren.[29]

Conciliationist writers found proposals for the use of Indians, slaves, Russians, and Germans against Americans particularly inhumane. "Heaven forbid that slaves should ever become the masters of freemen; or that Russian ferocity should triumph over English valour in any part of the world," William Burke declared in expressing his delight that the ministry had been unable to persuade the Russian government to supply "20,000 Calmucks and Cossacks, to lay waste with fire and sword the habitations of Englishmen, and to turn one of the fairest parts of the British dominions into one of their Tartarian desarts." Although he deplored that a combination of "German penury and English prodigality" had enabled the administration to assemble a "vast army" that, with Britain's Indian allies, could go on "slaughtering, burning, and plundering," Burke denied that such were the best "means of reconciling the minds of the people to our government" and called for an end to the war, even though it would mean that German mercenaries would be deprived "of the largest part of the bloody glories they are to purchase by the slaughter of Englishmen" and that "fewer English scalps were to decorate the martial dwellings of the savage allies of our humane Ministry." To continue this inhumane conflict, he wrote, would only lead to the "Hessians . . . slaughter[ing] more men in cold blood, . . . burn[ing] more . . . towns," and producing still "more mutual rapine of English on English."[30]

Only "the certain and indubitable justice of the cause," declared an anonymous conciliationist in the spring of 1776, could possibly "authorize war." He observed, "if it cannot be determined that" the colonies "are wrong, neither can it be determined that ministry are right, and in defiance of every pervasive influence, this nation is at least divided in opinion on the matter." The writer continued, "Men who are conscious [that] they have the worst of the argument . . . decline reasoning, and have recourse to blows, and ministry, after their example, reject reasoning and assume the sword; then follow violence and rapine unrestrained, though no ways conducive to the main end and design," that end being for Britain to retain its profitable relationship with all of its colonies.[31]

IV

Those colonists who favored resistance could not have agreed more about the injustice of Britain's use of force to compel submission to parliamentary authority. Meeting on May 10, 1775, less than a month after the battles at Lexington and Concord, the Second Continental Congress, initially composed of delegates from the twelve colonies from South Carolina north to New Hampshire, found itself confronted with the joint problems of organizing and explaining colonial resistance to the forces of the imperial state. In addition to authorizing the Continental Army, with George Washington at its head, it produced a series of four state papers intended to set forth the justice of the colonial cause: a letter to the inhabitants of Great Britain, an olive-branch petition to George III, an address to the people of Ireland, and most important for our purposes here, a "Declaration by the Representatives of the United Colonies of North America . . . setting forth the Causes and Necessity of taking up ARMS."[32] Collectively, these documents supply a succinct and authoritative statement of the colonial rationale for a forceful response to British military provocations.

Deeply lamenting the "Convulsions" that were then shaking the British

Empire "to its deepest Foundations," these documents flatly contradicted metropolitan charges that the colonies had any "ambitious Designs of separating from Great Britain, . . . establishing independent States," dissolving the union that had "so long and so happily subsisted between" them, or challenging Parliament's jurisdiction over trade and other external affairs of the empire. Rather, they presented colonial actions as a necessary and appropriate response to the astonishing and "indisputable truth" that, "at this enlightened period," as the "Address to the People of Ireland" declared, "the leaders of a nation, which in every age has sacrificed hecatombs of her bravest patriots on the altar of Liberty, should presume gravely to establish an arbitrary sway over the lives, liberties, and property of their fellow-subjects in America."[33]

Taking the historical approach that had characterized colonial resistance since the mid-1760s, the writers of these documents explained that the colonists' forefathers had voluntarily emigrated from Britain without state assistance and by their "unceasing Labour" had "effected Settlements in the distant and inhospitable Wilds of America, then filled with numerous and warlike Nations of Barbarians"; had formed in their respective jurisdictions "perfect Legislatures"; and substantially contributed to the construction of a harmonious relationship with England that "in a short Time" became so mutually beneficial as to bring about an "amazing Increase of the Wealth, Strength, and Navigation of the Realm" and to enable the colonies to make major contributions to Britain's mid-eighteenth-century imperial wars. Expecting to have a "share in the Blessings of Peace, and the Emoluments of Victory and Conquest" at the end of the Seven Years' War, the colonies instead found themselves subjected to "a new System of Statutes and Regulations . . . for the[ir] Administration" that called into question their entitlement to numerous rights that they had "peaceably enjoyed" for "near two centuries." This system was the design of a new group of ministers who judged the colonies to be susceptible to "the easy Emoluments of Statutable Plunder" and who had persuaded Parliament to adopt the "pernicious Project" of taxing the colonists without their consent and thereby deprived them of their ancient "exclusive Right to dispose of" their "own Property."[34]

As the documents explained, these "meditated Innovations" had filled colonial "minds with the most painful Fears and Jealousies." For the next decade the colonies, in a vain effort to persuade metropolitan leaders to acknowledge their rights, had "incessantly and ineffectually besieged the Throne as Supplicants" and remonstrated "with Parliament in the most mild and decent Language," a strategy that they continued to follow in protesting against the Coercive Acts in 1774, when the First Continental Congress had adopted only most "temperate" and "respectful" petitions and retaliated only with the "peaceable Admonition" of breaking off all commercial intercourse with Britain. But the Crown, the writers lamented, had been "deaf to their complaints," while Parliament, "stimulated by an inordinate Passion for Power" and "blinded . . . by their intemperate Rage for unlimited Domination," had ignored colonial petitions, declared Massachusetts to be in rebellion and all the resisting colonies to be involved in "unlawful Combinations and Engagements," and despite eloquent opposition from an "illustrious" and numerous group in both houses, directed the Crown to take "the most effectual Measures to enforce due Obedience to the Laws and Authority of the Supreme Legislature," rushing through Parliament a series of other punitive and retaliatory measures.[35]

By sending "large Reinforcements of Ships and Troops" and Britain's "three most experienced generals" to Boston, the administration had clearly signaled its intention to employ the empire's military and naval resources to enforce its authority in the resisting colonies by waging "war with their fellow subjects." Acting under administration orders, General Thomas Gage had taken possession of Boston, turned it into a garrison town, and sent "a large Detachment of his Army" to make "an unprovoked Assault on the Inhabitants" of Lexington and Concord, where before being driven back into Boston by an enraged populace, they killed several colonials. Soon thereafter, Gage had declared martial law and used his "utmost Power to spread Destruction and Devastation," burning Charles Town, seizing ships, and intercepting supplies and provisions. At the same time, other British officials in America were pursuing further "refinements in parental cruelty," General Guy Carleton in Canada instigating Canadians and Indians "to deluge our settlements with the blood of innocent women and children," and officials elsewhere reportedly plotting to encourage slave uprisings.[36]

Such actions, the writers declared, had "compelled us to arm in our Defence," the colonies having been left no other means to combat such "unwarrantable Acts of Injustice and Cruelty" and to preserve their liberties and property from the ministry's efforts to reduce them "to slavery and ruin." Denying that God had ever "intended a Part of the human Race to hold an absolute Property in, and an unbounded Power over others," or for those others to become "objects of a legal Domination, never rightfully resistible, however severe and oppressive," and disavowing any interpretation of the British imperial constitution that gives "freedom to a Part" but "necessarily enslaves the Remainder of the Empire," the writers expressed certainty that those who had made the decision to use force to achieve their ends were entirely responsible for starting the war and that colonial resistance to it was just.[37]

To show how distasteful they found a fratricidal civil war, the writers offered to lay down their arms as soon as Britain ceased hostilities; removed "all Danger of their being renewed"; disavowed the ministry's "horrid design . . . to convert" the colonists "from freemen into slaves, from subjects into vassals, and from friends into enemies"; and agreed to a plan of reconciliation "on Constitutional Principles" that would restore "the Energy of mild and just Government" and the "friendly Intercourse" that "till lately" had been to the mutual advantage of all segments of the empire.[38]

V

Of course, not all North American residents perceived much justice in this defense of the colonial cause. Although they did not manage to achieve much public voice until the crisis of 1774 and 1775, many people, from the Stamp Act crisis on, had opposed resistance on a number of grounds. In various combinations these dissidents, echoing many of the themes of metropolitan coercionists and adding others, objected that resistance leaders, including the elected assemblies, were wrong on the nature of the imperial constitution; that resistance to metropolitan authority was ungrateful, undutiful, and disloyal; that the self-appointed groups—the Sons of Liberty, the committees of safety, the provisional legislatures, and the Congress—that led and enforced the resistance had no constitutional legitimacy and represented a usurped authority that repeatedly violated the rule of law and individual liberty and property by stifling dissent, persecuting and threatening the lives and destroying the property of those who challenged or defied their authority; that such massive civil resistance was the route to political and social chaos; and after Britain had resorted to force in 1775, that the colonies were too disunited, dissimilar, weak, and lacking in leadership, common interest, political and military resources, expertise, sophistication, and social capital—in other words, too provincial—to have any chance of success against the most powerful naval, military, and commercial power in the world. Yet in contrast to the situation in Britain, where the tradition of a loyal opposition permitted open and intense debate over government policy, the colonial dissidents had, unlike the advocates of resistance, neither the political leverage nor the institutional platform to give their views collective force.

As dissident protests circulated in Britain, administration spokesmen condemned the violent intimidation of, and "unexampled brutalities and cruelties" toward, individuals suspected of preferring the king's government as brutal, reprehensible, and unjust, castigating "American rebels" for their savagery in "TARRING and *feathering*" those who opposed the resistance movement, "a species of torture" they denounced as both "shocking to humanity" and a blatant departure from the rule of law.[39] Addressing "the state of America" in the House of Lords in May 30, 1777, Thomas, Lord Lyttelton succinctly summarized administration views on the behavior of the American rebels. Deploring "the anarchy that prevails there; the acts of violence, treachery, cruelty, and injustice, that are daily committed in the country, by our rebellious subjects upon their loyal and dutiful brethren, merely because they would not join in their diabolical schemes of overthrowing all just and legal government," he complained that the "laws [were being] trampled upon, the course of justice interrupted or annihilated, government dissolved, magistrates imprisoned or banished, [and] the faithful and obedient part of the people oppressed, despoiled of their property, or obliged to fly to their native land" or to British-occupied territory in order to find safety and freedom. To "all the horrors of war," Lyttelton observed, "the rebels had added the brutality of savages" without regard for justice, liberty, or common civility. For British coercionists, such repression of those who opposed resistance thus supplied additional justification for going to war to put down colonial rebellion.

VI

For the people who fell into these four camps, two of them coercionist and two conciliationist, the violence, human and fiscal costs, and length of the war operated to harden their divisions over how far to go and what strategies to use to achieve their respective objectives. Until the resistance committed the colonies to independence in late 1775 and 1776, all four camps showed a desire to keep the empire together, and victorious Americans could view the outcome of the conflict as a vindication of the justice of their cause. But the end of the war produced few visible signs among coercionists in Britain that they regretted their choice to turn to force. Indeed, many of them, including those dissident Americans who had suffered such heavy losses during the hostilities and had fled to Britain or to other British possessions, pushed strongly for its continuation—even after Cornwallis's defeat at Yorktown, while conciliationists remained persuaded that milder measures would have held the empire together.

Neither conciliationists nor coercionists can be said to have displayed particular foresight. Contrary to the conciliationsts' fears, the divorce with the former colonies did not produce a dissolution of the British Empire, nor the permanent loss of American trade, nor the destruction of the domestic economy. Contrary to the coercionists' expectations, the loosely connected coalition of dissimilar polities that came together in 1774–76 turned into a lasting union. I have long thought that British coercionists should be accorded a place among the founders of the nation that came into being as an unintended consequence of their resort to military measures. The Continental Congress's precise description of itself, in its "Declaration of the Causes and Necessity of taking up Arms," as "The Twelve United Colonies" reminds us that the United States did not exist when the colonies first came together and went to war. Before Congress could speak on behalf of these United States, it had to invent a nation by that name, which it did in the Declaration of Independence, thanks to these unwitting British founders.

Throughout the war, analysts of all persuasions addressed the knotty question that Dr. John Roebuck, a coercionist pretending impartiality, asked in the title of his pamphlet, *Whether the Guilt of the Present Civil War in America, Ought to Be Imputed to Great Britain or America.*[40] In its very articulation, this question hints that the war generated a high level of disquiet within the wider Anglophone world, and that disquiet deserves the kind of serious historical investigation that the contributors to this book give to it. From our long temporal distance and scrupulous disciplinary detachment, we can see that in a world without an impartial arbiter, the justice of wars, civil and international, depends upon the side on which a group finds itself. In the case of the American Revolution, all four sets of contemporaries regarded their behavior as just and understandable. Who are we to say otherwise? And why would we want to?

NOTES

1. In his extraordinarily important two-volume bibliographic study, appropriately entitled *The American Controversy: A Bibliographic Study of the British Pamphlets about the American Disputes, 1764–1783* (Providence: Brown University Press, 1980), Thomas Randolph Adams identifies an astonishing 1,374 separate titles, more than four times the 192 pamphlets of American origin produced in the rebelling colonies. The sheer mass of this literature, which has received only minimal historical analysis, reveals just how widely and deeply American questions stirred public debate, not only in London but also throughout the British Isles, a debate whose scope was unsuspected before Adams's work. As he points out in his introduction, pamphlets relating to the American question accounted for 30 percent of the British pamphlet press between 1763 and 1783 and 60 percent for the five parliamentary years between 1773 and 1778.
2. This division is discussed more fully in Jack P. Greene, *Evaluating Empire and Coming to Terms with Colonialism in Eighteenth Century Britain* (New York: Cambridge University Press, 2014), 84–119, 200–243.
3. *A Short and Friendly Caution to the Good People of England* (London, 1766), 8, 12–13; H. Hamersley to Horatio Sharpe, Dec. 17, 1765, in *Proceedings and Debates of the British Parliaments Respecting North America, 1754–1783,* ed. R. C. Simmons and P. D. G. Thomas, 6 vols. (White Plains, N.Y., 1982–86), 2:566.

4. *Short and Friendly Caution*, 19.
5. *The General Opposition of the Colonies to the Payment of the Stamp Duty; and the Consequences of Enforcing Obedience by Military Measures; Impartially Considered* (London, 1766), 16.
6. *The Late Occurrences in North America, and Policy of Great Britain, Considered* (London, 1766), 8–11.
7. [William Greatraks], *Applications of Some General Political Rules to the Present State of Great-Britain, Ireland and America* (London, 1766), 76–77; *Oppression. A Poem by an American, with Notes by a North Briton* (London, May 1765), 19, 21.
8. The quotations are from *General Opposition of the Colonies to the Payment of the Stamp Duty*, 5, 10, 29, 38; *Late Occurrences in North America*, 5, 7, 11, 34, 37; [Greatraks], *Applications of Some General Political Rules*, 16, 20, 84–85.
9. *Late Occurrences in North America*, 9–13.
10. *General Opposition of the Colonies to the Payment of the Stamp Duty*, 16–21, 29.
11. [Israel Mauduit], *Considerations on the American War: Addressed to the People of England* (London, 1776), 8.
12. *A Dialogue on the Principles of the Constitution and Legal Liberty, Compared with Despotism; Applied to the American Question* (London, 1776), 1.
13. *Independency the Object of Congress in America; or, An Appeal to Force* (London, 1776), 5–6.
14. *Reflections on the Present State of the American War* (London, 1776), 2.
15. Alexander Carlyle, *The Justice and Necessity of the War with Our American Colonies Examined* (London, 1777).
16. A Friend to both Countries [Charles Garth], *America Vindicated from the High Charge of Ingratitude and Rebellion* (Devizes, 1774), 30–31.
17. Janus, *The Critical Moment, on which the Salvation or Destruction of the British Empire Depends; Containing the Rise, Progress, Present State, and Natural Consequences of Our American Disputes* (London, 1776), 18; A.M., *Reflections on the American Contest, in which the Consequences of a Forced Submission and the Means of a Lasting Reconciliation Are Pointed Out* (London, 1776), 46.
18. Henry Cruger, speech, Dec. 16, 1774, in Simmons and Thomas, *Proceedings and Debates of the British Parliaments*, 5:254–55.
19. A.M., *Reflections on the American Contest*, 48–49.
20. [Mennasseh Dawes], *A Letter to Lord Chatham, Concerning the Present War of Great Britain against America* (London, 1776), 22.
21. Janus, *Critical Moment*, 36–38.
22. *The Conduct of Administration with Regard to the Colonies* (London, 1775), 22–23.
23. A.M., *Reflections on the American Contest*, 17.
24. Janus, *Critical Moment*, 36.
25. *A Letter to Dr. Tucker on His Proposal of a Separation between Great Britain and American Colonies* (London, 1774), 27.
26. [Dawes], *Letter to Lord Chatham*, 10.
27. Earl of Shelburne, speech, May 30, 1777, in *Parliamentary History of England from the Earliest Period to the Year 1803*, ed. William Cobbett et al., 36 vols. (London, 1806–20), 19:346–47.

28. Earl of Chatham, speech, May 30, 1777, ibid., 343.
29. [Dawes], *Letter to Lord Chatham,* 22, 52; Thomas Day, *The Desolation of America* (London, 1777), 23.
30. [William Burke et al.], *Letters of Valens* (London, 1777), xiv, 13–14, 36, 127.
31. *A Prospect of the Consequences of the Present Conduct of Great Britain towards America* (London, 1776), 23–24.
32. British conciliationists quickly arranged for a London printing of all of these documents in a single pamphlet: *The Declaration by the Representatives of the United Colonies of North America, Now Met in General Congress at Philadelphia, Setting Forth the Causes and Necessity of Taking up Arms* (London, 1775), 2.
33. Ibid., 9, 15–16, 25.
34. Ibid., 3–4, 6, 20, 25.
35. Ibid., 3, 4–5, 6, 20, 28.
36. Ibid., 7–8, 28–29.
37. Ibid., 3, 9. 11, 13–14, 21.
38. Ibid., 9–10, 15, 20, 26.
39. *An Appeal to the Unprejudiced; or, A Vindication of the Measures of Government, with Respect to America* (Oxford, 1777), 37; *A Full and Circumstantial Account of the Dispute between Great Britain and America* (Glasgow, 1775), 3; John Lind, *An Answer to the Declaration of the American Congress* (London, 1776), 89.
40. Dr. John Roebuck, *An Enquiry, Whether the Guilt of the Present Civil War in America, Ought to Be Imputed to Great Britain or America* (London, 1776).

PART II
Jus in Bello

5 "WHERE THE POWER OF LAW CEASES, THERE WAR BEGINS"

The British Army's Implementation of Martial Law in Boston, 1768–1776

John D. Roche

> "Should the time ever come when the law of the land shall be made to yield and truckle to military power,—what a scene of confusion would then open upon a people so jealous of their liberty?"
>
> —*A Journal of the Times,* December 6, 1768

Whig propagandists vehemently opposed the British ministry's deployment of troops to Boston in 1768 as an attempt to establish a military government. The Whigs' deep-seated fears of standing armies in peacetime led them to equate the Boston garrison's presence with martial law, tyranny, and oppression. In reality, however, Governor General Thomas Gage did not declare martial law in Massachusetts until June 12, 1775, at which time his order conformed with the principles of *jus ad bellum* and *jus in bello* found in both English domestic and international law. Furthermore, contrary to fears of a tyrannical standing army, the city's inhabitants received better treatment from the British Army after the declaration of martial law than they had prior to the commencement of hostilities, thus demonstrating Britain's commitment to just war theory and practice.

Whig opposition to standing armies in peacetime was a political legacy of the Glorious Revolution. The Bill of Rights of 1689 explicitly stated, "The raising or keeping [of] a standing army within the kingdom in time of peace, unless it be with consent of Parliament, is against law."[1] Whigs believed that unless their representatives in Parliament kept a firm bridle on the military, it would threaten their liberties with burdensome taxes and coercive power. John Trenchard, the coauthor of *Cato's Letters* (1723), demonstrated this prevailing antimilitary sentiment in two of his earlier works, *An Argument, Shewing That a*

Standing Army Is Inconsistent with a Free Government and Absolutely Destructive to the Constitution of the English Monarchy (1697) and *A Short History of Standing Armies in England* (1698). Trenchard maintained that "unhappy nations have lost that precious jewel *liberty* . . . [because] their necessities or indiscretion have permitted a standing army to be kept amongst them."[2] Whigs viewed standing armies as mercenary forces that were dangerous tools in the hands of a corrupt ministry. Britain's whiggish outlook on the military firmly entrenched itself with its American colonists, who believed the arrival of British troops in North America indicated that the government was intent upon pursuing its agenda of imperial taxation without regard to colonial interests—at bayonet point if need be.[3]

The foremost way in which American Whigs cemented their anti–standing army philosophy was through the press. These men understood the value of controlling the narrative and thus battled to win public opinion at home and abroad. While royal officials also demonstrated an appreciation of the influence of information, they never developed a platform as successful as *A Journal of the Times*. Anonymous Whig writers first printed the publication on September 28, 1768, with the arrival of the British troops in Boston Harbor and continued its run until August 1, 1769, after Governor Francis Bernard had been recalled and two of the regiments, the 64th and 65th Foot, were removed from the city. The Whig faction sent copies of this publication, masquerading as a weekly newspaper, to other colonies, where it found its way into the *New York Journal*, followed by the *Pennsylvania Chronicle*, and later appeared in other American newspapers.[4] It incessantly hammered two main grievances: first, garrison government was a direct assault upon the colonists' rights by usurping civil authority, leading to the abuse of the civilian population while simultaneously undermining the moral and material strength of the army.[5] Second, it persistently attacked the arrogance of the rapidly multiplying measures and men foisted upon the colony by Britain which threatened to bleed the colony dry.[6]

Both Governor Bernard and Lieutenant Governor Thomas Hutchinson bemoaned the maliciousness of *A Journal of the Times* as well as its effectiveness. Bernard sent Lord Hillsborough an entire letter on the topic warning him that the faction meant "to raise a general clamor against His Majesty's government in England and throughout America, as well as in Massachusetts," and by doing so "flattered themselves that they should get the navy and army removed, and again have the government and Custom House in their own hands." Bernard insisted that one of the authors must have been on the council because all of the governor's transactions with that body were "constantly perverted, misrepresented and falsified in this paper." He alluded to the Herculean task of combating such propaganda, saying, "To act about answering these falsities would be a work like that of cleaning Augeas's stable, which is to be done only by bringing in a stream strong enough to sweep away the dirt and collectors of it all together."[7]

Hutchinson was equally damning of the *Journal* while begrudgingly acknowledging its cogency. He noted its unfailing ability to "render the troops as odious as possible, and to inflame the minds of the inhabitants against them. Nobody succeeded better than the author or authors of a weekly publication, called 'The Journal of the Times,' which was managed with great art, and little truth." He further observed that "every little insignificant fact relative to the troops, which was not thought worthy of notice, or made no impression, if known, was preserved," sent to the other colonies first for publication, and then usually republished in Boston two months later, "when there was a general remembrance remaining of the fact, so as to make the aggravations more easily received." Like all great lies, the *Journal* included kernels of truth because "many false reports, which had been confuted, were mixed with true reports, and some pretended facts of an enormous nature were published." Hutchinson ruefully concluded, "This paper had a very great effect."[8]

A Journal of the Times, along with numerous other Boston newspapers, filled their pages with anti–standing army editorials and news reports condemning the arrival of troops. The writers' first goal was to convince their audience, throughout the colonies and back in England, that Boston was peaceful and therefore did not require military force to aid the civil authority. The *Boston Evening-Post* described the troops' arrival as "heavy and very threatening Grievances" and questioned the need for the Townshend duties, which would provide for the "maintenance of a large Standing Army; not for the Defence of the newly acquired Territories, but for the old Colonies, and in Time of Peace."[9] The *Boston Gazette* also played on this theme by republishing an address to the mayor of Dublin, which stated, "I cannot see how any unnecessary augmentation of the number of the army, in times of profound, universal peace, can add aught to the honour or dignity of the crown."[10] *A Journal of the Times* observed: "We now behold Boston surrounded at a time of profound peace. . . . If the people of England could but look into the town to see the utmost good order and observance of the laws."[11] The Whigs hammered away on the point that the city was "in a time of profound peace," claiming, "[Boston] has been represented as in a state subversive of all law and government, when not one instance can be produced, of the interruption of justice, in any of our courts, not so much as those held by only a single magistrate, nor even in the Courts of Admiralty."[12]

Whigs continually stressed that Boston was a peaceful and law-abiding city so that they could avail themselves of the Bill of Rights' protections against a standing army during peacetime. The problem for them was that Parliament had clearly authorized the troops with the annual Mutiny Act. To counter this factual inconsistency, the Whigs made the same constitutional argument they had since the Stamp Act: namely, that the colonial assemblies rather than Parliament were Americans' legitimate political representatives. One commentator wrote, "But the very keeping [of] a standing army, without the consent of our legislatures . . . I consider as contrary to the rights of freeborn English subjects."[13] This approach remained a standard Whig position prior to the actual outbreak of hostilities at Lexington and Concord in April 1775.

Whigs freely expressed their fears that Boston's standing army was the first step toward a military government that would deprive them of their liberties. One *Boston Evening-Post* contributor discussed the rapid expansion of Britain's military in the wake of the Seven Years' War and concluded by saying, "I am no enemy to the present military establishment, but as I conceive it may influence and endanger our liberties."[14] One month before the troops landed in Boston, the assembly sent a committee to Governor Bernard to inform him that "they [the assembly] are greatly agitated with the Expectation of a Standing Army being posted among us, and of the full Exertion of a Military Government."[15] When the assembly requested that Governor Bernard remove the troops from Boston in June 1769, he demurred, insisting that he did not have authority over them. The colonials responded by arguing that if the king's representative in the colony could not control the troops: "It is then a Power without any Check here, and therefore it is so far above absolute. An absolute Power which has the Sword constantly in its hand, may exercise a rigorous Severity whenever it pleases."[16] The Whigs in the assembly dubbed this move toward military government a "dangerous innovation" and protested "that a Standing Army is not Part of the British Constitution in any of the King's Dominions; and every Attempt to establish it as such has ever been esteemed a dangerous Innovation, and manifestly tending to enslave the People."[17] Bostonians discovered just how dangerous the military could be on the night of March 5, 1770, when troops opened fire on an angry mob, killing five people and wounding another six.[18]

In the wake of the Boston Massacre, the protests against military occupation became more vituperative. In addition to challenging the troops in Boston as an unconstitutional peacetime standing army, the colonists began to identify it as an "illegal assembly" that was far more dangerous than any riot could ever be. The *Massachusetts Gazette* claimed, "It is an unlawful Assembly of all others the most dangerous and alarming: And every Instance of its actually restraining the Liberty of any Individual, is a crime which infinitely exceeds what the Law intends by a Riot."[19] The massacre reinforced anti–standing army sentiment in neighboring colonies as well. Two weeks after the event, Whigs gathered in Newport, Rhode Island, and dedicated three of their fifteen toasts to the event. They demanded "Destruction to the Miscreants who procured the Introduction of a Standing Army in the Colonies" while idolizing the five men killed as "Martyrs to British and American Liberty" and declared that "every Town thro' this Continent deeply sympathize with the Town of Boston, and feel on Account of the Blood there cruelly and inhumanely spilt, as if it were drawn from their own Bowels."[20] The Boston Massacre brought Whig rhetoric to a fever pitch but ignored the legal reality that without a formal declaration of martial law, the army's actions supporting police functions were limited to following the orders of the local magistrates.

When the troops first arrived in Boston in 1768, Gage, then commander in chief for North America, believed that a massive demonstration of military force would not only cow the Sons of Liberty and other disaffected inhabitants of Boston but also embolden royal authorities in the city to enforce Parliament's laws. Empowering government officials in America was essential in Gage's mind because the Achilles' heel of military aid to the civil power was the latter's general unwillingness to call upon troops prior to open rebellion or the declaration of martial law. Gage wrote, "Whilst Laws are in force, I shall pay the obedience that is due to them, and in my Military Capacity confine Myself Solely to the granting [of] Such Aids to the Civil Power, as shall be required of me; but if open and declared Rebellion makes it's [*sic*] Appearance, I mean to use all the Powers lodged in my Hands to make Head against it."[21] An overwhelming military force to provide saturation policing offered the potential of solving the inherent security dilemma in the colonies—namely, that officials did not call upon the military because they felt themselves vulnerable to retaliation, yet the troops could not protect them through the enhancement of law and order because those very officials refused to authorize the military to act.[22] Despite numerous provocations between 1768 and 1770, royal officials never permitted the use of force against Bostonians. That the colonists could only point to the accidental Boston Massacre demonstrated how fastidiously Gage and the rest of the army adhered to British domestic law.

The army's failure to "awe" Bostonians into submission by "aiding the civil authority" encouraged London officials to experiment with true garrison government beginning in 1774, when they appointed Gage, now a lieutenant general, as governor general of Massachusetts to punish it for the Boston Tea Party on December 16, 1773. By combining all civil and military authority within the hands of one man, British officials expected to remove all legal impediments to the employment of military force and therefore bolster royal authority by making saturation policing effective. These hopes soon evaporated when news of the Massachusetts Government Act made the colony ungovernable starting in September 1774. Although Gage had the legal authority to use all the forces under his command, his 3,500-man city garrison was insufficient to exert political control throughout the colony. Both Hutchinson, by then the former governor, and Chief Justice Peter Oliver of the Massachusetts Superior Court agreed with this assessment. Hutchinson averred, "All legislative, as well as executive power was gone, and the danger of revolt was daily increasing. The governor retained the title of captain-general, but he had the title only."[23] Gage acknowledged the cessation of civil government by dissolving the provincial assembly in October 1774, but the delegates refused to disband and instead formed the Massachusetts Provincial Congress. Oliver also felt that closing the courts was a fatal blow, but he insisted that the provincial assembly's refusal to disband was the final straw: "Here ended the civil Government, both Form & Substance."[24] Gage cast about for ways to diffuse the crisis until the colonial secretary, Lord Dartmouth, ordered him to take military action against the colonists.

Following the Battles of Lexington and Concord, repairing the breach without either concessions or the use of force was an unrealistic goal; every royal official knew that the engagements constituted open rebellion. Brigadier General Hugh Percy succinctly wrote, "There can now surely be no doubt of their being in open Rebellion, for they fired first upon the King's Troops, as they were marching quietly along."[25] Nevertheless, Gage quixotically hoped that some diplomatic breakthrough might avert full-blown war while he waited for reinforcements.[26] As a result, he did not immediately implement martial law and continued to negotiate with the Patriots. Reinforcements—led by Major Generals William Howe, John Burgoyne, and Henry Clinton—finally arrived on May 25 and brought the city's garrison up to 6,000 men.[27] Under pressure to act from the new triumvirate, Gage finally relented and declared martial law in Massachusetts on June 12 in preparation for military operations to fortify Dorchester Heights. He explained the timing of the declaration to Lord Dartmouth: "I see no Prospect of any Offers of Accommodation and have therefore issued a Proclamation for the Exercise of the Law Martial."[28]

Once Gage accepted the necessity of confronting the rebellion with military force, he applied the tried-and-true British Army formula of decisive battle coupled with judicial punishments and pardons. The declaration, most likely written by Burgoyne, stated the army's position that "WHEREAS the infatuated multitudes . . . have at length proceeded to avowed rebellion . . . it only remains for those who are entrusted with supreme rule, as well for the punishment of the guilty, as the protection of the well-affected, to prove they do not bear the sword in vain." The declaration explicitly pointed to Lexington and Concord as the beginning of the rebellion while simultaneously laying the blame for the violence upon the colonists, stating, "a number of armed persons, to the amount of many thousands assembled on the 19th of April last, and from behind walls, and lurking holes, attacked a detachment of the King's troops, who . . . made use of their arms only in their own defence."[29] Gage employed the traditional carrot-and-stick approach: "to spare the effusion of blood . . . I do hereby offer in his Majesty's name . . . his most gracious pardon in all who shall forthwith lay down their arms, and return to the duties of peaceable subjects." The pardon was available to everyone except John Hancock and Samuel Adams because of their prominent roles in the disturbances of the past decade. Those who continued in the "present unnatural rebellion" by taking arms against the king, providing material support to those who did, or holding "secret correspondence" with those in revolt were deemed "to be rebels and traitors, and as such to be treated."[30] In other words, they should expect no quarter on the battlefield, brutal imprisonment without the status of prisoners of war, the destruction or legal confiscation of their property, and judicial execution. Although the Whigs justly excoriated the foolishness of the British ministry's policies toward Boston between 1768 and 1775, they were legally unassailable from a *jus ad bellum* and *jus in bello* perspective in British domestic as well as international law.

The first Whig claim that did not hold up to legal scrutiny was the characterization of the troops deployed to Boston as a standing army. Parliament had passed the Mutiny Act, authorizing the 1,200 troops—consisting of the 14th and 29th Regiments, two companies of the 59th Regiment, and a detachment of artillery—for a peacetime establishment.[31] Furthermore, the Whigs acknowledged George III's right to send his armies anywhere in the empire. The Massachusetts Assembly declared, "we admit, that Peace and War are in the King's Hands, and that it is an indisputable Part of the Royal Prerogative, . . . That to destine the Fleets, and march the Armies of the State to any Part of the World . . . belongs to the Crown."[32] They had no other choice than to acknowledge this power because the famous English jurist William Blackstone reaffirmed it in his work *An Analysis of the Laws of England* (1771), writing, "In FOREIGN Concerns; the KING, as the representative of the Nation, has the Right or PREROGATIVE, . . . Of proclaiming War or Peace." Blackstone also averred the king's supremacy over military forces, declaring, "He [the king] is also considered as the General of the Kingdom, and may raise Fleets and Armies, build Forts, appoint Havens, erect Beacons, prohibit the Exportation of Arms and Ammunition, and confine his Subjects within the Realm, or recall them from foreign Parts."[33] Clearly the troops in Boston were both legally raised and deployed based on the powers of Parliament and of the king.

Legal treatises dealing with rebellion and treason likewise confirmed the appropriateness of Great Britain's response. In *The Illustrious Hugo Grotius of the Law of Warre and Peace with Annotations III Parts and Memorial of the Author's Life and Death* (1655), the Dutch jurist Hugo Grotius explains the illegitimacy of rebellion: "Only the question is, whether it be lawful for private or for publique persons to make war upon them, under whose power, whether supreme or subordinate, they are. . . . But it is inquir'd, what is lawful against the Highest Power, or the Lower Powers doing what they doe by authority of the Highest. That's without controversy amongst all good men; If they command any thing contrary to naturall right or to the divine precepts, what they command is not to be done."[34]

Grotius rejects rebellion based on both natural and divine law and argues that superiors cannot force their subordinates to rebel against their masters. Attorney General and later Lord Chancellor of England Francis Bacon contends that "if any have combined to raise and stir the people to rebellion within the realm; these are high treasons, tending to the over throw of the estate of this commonwealth."[35] Grotius also likens rebellion to murder of the state, arguing, "so it is the death of a Commonwealth to be overthrown: which is, when the Civil body is dissolved."[36] Bacon insists that there are three main kinds of treason that threaten "the safety of the King's estate," which include "foreign invasion, open rebellion and sedition, and privy practice to alienate and estrange the hearts of the subjects, and to prepare them either to adhere to enemies, or to burst out into tumults and commotions of themselves."[37] Like Bacon, Edward Coke, a former solicitor general for England and Wales, also noted that English law gave wide latitude to whom the king could deem an enemy. In his work *The First Part of the Institutes of the Laws of England; or, A Commentary upon Littleton: Not the Name of the Author Only, but of the Law Itself,* he offers this definition: "'Enemies' Which is to be understood of any manner of enemies whatsoever."[38] This fungible description provides legal justification for the deployment of troops to Boston prior to the outbreak of hostilities because "the statute of 25 E. 3, *de proditionibus,* doth declare, that it is treason by the common law to adhere to the enemies of the king within the realme, or without."[39] Colonists who supported the king's enemies overseas were not immune from English law. Furthermore, those who adhered to the king's enemies were guilty of high treason and subject to an excruciating death. Blackstone lists these penalties as follows: "The PUNISHMENT of high Treason, in MALES, is generally to be, 1. Drawn. 2. Hanged.

3. Embowelled alive. 4. Beheaded. 5. Quartered. 6. The Head and Quarters to be at the King's Disposal. . . . FEMALES . . . are to be drawn, and burned alive."[40] While the Bostonian Whigs denounced King George III's tyranny, his Loyalist supporters were bewildered that the army did not even arrest, much less execute, any of the leading Patriots. The problem, of course, was with the courts; —no Boston jury would convict one of their peers of treason.

Interestingly, the status of the courts in Massachusetts was the weathervane for indicating if the colony was at war or peace. Grotius's simple definition of war, "War is the State of those that contend by Force," covers both public and private war but does not explain the origins of conflict.[41] Coke, on the other hand, insists that "when the courts of justice be open, and the judges and ministers of the same may by law protect men from wrong and violence, and distribute justice to all, it is said to be time of peace. So, when by invasion, insurrection, rebellions, or such like, the peaceable courts of justice is disturbed and stopped, so as the courts of justice be as it were shut up, *et silent leges inter arma,* then it is said to be time of warre."[42] The violent suppression of the courts that leads to a denial of justice is the key hallmark of war. The expression *et silent leges inter arma,* which roughly translates as "In times of war, the law falls silent," captures this understanding perfectly. Numerous British officials invoked this term to include Massachusetts chief justice Oliver and New Hampshire attorney general Samuel Livermore. In December 1774, after Gage's dispatches regarding the shutting of the courts reached London, Attorney General Edward Thurlow and Solicitor General Alexander Wedderburn issued their legal opinion to Lord Dartmouth "that the letters abovementioned contain the history of an open rebellion and war in the province of Massachusetts Bay." This legal opinion reinforced the king's determination to bring the colony to heel by declaring it in rebellion on February 2, 1775, followed by Parliament's confirmation one week later. Dartmouth's secret orders to Gage at the end of January noted, "I observe there is a clause [in the Massachusetts charter] that impowers the governor to use and exercise the law martial in time of actual war, invasion and *rebellion.*" Disappointed by the general's ensuing passivity, in April Dartmouth instructed him that it "will not be necessary to require the aid of the civil magistrates" and that "the conduct of the troops in a case where they are to meet open and declared rebellion must be guided and supported by a sense of the duty they owe to their King and country, and the authority of government must be maintained let the consequence be what it may." Dartmouth, following his king's lead, was eager for Gage to take the gloves off against the colonists.[43]

While George III's insistence on a military solution to the colonial problem was not wise policy, the question remains whether or not it was just. According to Grotius, there are only three acceptable justifications for war: "Defense, Recovery, [or] Revenge."[44] Since it has already been established that the king had the power to declare war, and declaring rebellion was tantamount to declaring war, clearly the king was within his royal prerogative to do so. As he put it in his oft-quoted statement to Lord North: "The New England governments are in a state of rebellion. Blows must decide whether they are to be subject to this country or independent."[45] Rebellion suppression is by its very nature a defensive war waged to protect the state from dismemberment or destruction. George III sought to recover the colony of Massachusetts by reinvigorating royal authority, and the war offered him a chance to take revenge on those who committed high treason against his authority by rebelling in the first place. When all of these factors are taken into consideration, Britain's right to go to war with its American colonies is indisputable.

Another royal prerogative of George III was his power to declare martial law during times of war. Bacon writes in his *Maxims of Law* that the Crown consists of "laws and arms, power civil and martial, with the latter whereof the law doth not intermeddle." So although the king's power rested on the dual pillars of civil and martial authority, by subverting civil authority, rebellions actually made the monarch stronger by removing the legal impediments of peacetime society. Bacon notes: "That allegiance is in vigor and force where the power of law hath a cessation, appeareth notably in time of wars, for silent leges inter arma. And yet the sovereignty and imperial power of the King is so far from being then extinguished or suspended, as contrariwise it is raised and made more absolute for then he may proceed by his supreme authority, and martial law, without observing formalities of the laws of his kingdom."[46] While Britons typically viewed martial law as an anomaly to be endured during turbulent times, its long-standing acceptance in the kingdom ensured that applying it during the American Revolution adhered to *jus in bello* principles. In *The Law of Nations* (1760), the Swiss jurist Emer de Vattel maintains that the constitution of a state determined "how and by whom the people ought to be governed; and what are the laws and duties of the governors."[47] In Vattel's view, there is no optimally balanced relationship between civil and military authority, merely a constitutional one based on tradition.

Although the declaration of martial law coupled with the Battle of Bunker Hill in June can be interpreted as a transition from garrison government to waging war, the reality was that both events in and of themselves barely affected Gage's governance of Boston. Nor did General Howe's assumption of command from Gage as commander in chief on October 10, 1775, lead to radical changes in occupation policy.[48] Howe continued Gage's focus on securing the city and providing for the army while looking for opportunities to defeat the rebels in a decisive battle. Instead, the siege of Boston after Lexington and Concord created demographic changes, logistical difficulties, and discipline challenges that forced the British Army to implement new policies.

The ongoing difficulties throughout Massachusetts caused a dramatic decrease in Boston's population while simultaneously increasing the remaining Bostonians' loyalty to the Crown. Prior to the imperial discord that led to the dissolution of civil government within the colony in the autumn of 1774, Boston's population hovered around 15,520. When the British evacuated the city on March 17, 1776, only 1,100 Loyalists sailed with them for Halifax, showing how small Massachusetts's hardcore royalist population truly was.[49] The breakdown in civilian governance—coupled with wartime conditions prevalent following Lexington, Concord, and Bunker Hill—encouraged migrations to and from the city that dramatically altered both the number and composition of the people living there. Initially Boston experienced an influx as Loyalists fled persecution in the countryside. Writing on September 12, 1774, Gage noted, "People are daily resorting to this Town for Protection, for there is no Security to any Person deemed a Friend to Government in any Part of the Country; even Places always esteemed well effected have caught the Infection." Two weeks later he echoed the same sentiments to the secretary at war, Lord Barrington, contending, "Every Man supposed averse to their [Patriots'] Measures so molest'd & oppressed, that if he can get out of the Country, which is not an Easy Matter, he takes Shelter in Boston." Yet the trickle of newly arriving Loyalists was insufficient to counterbalance the flood of Patriots from Boston that also preceded the fighting and rapidly diminished the size of the population. At the end of October 1774, Gage wrote to Dartmouth, "This [Massachusetts Provincial] Congress made an Effort to get all the Inhabitants of this Town to leave it and retire to the Country, but it was found to be an impracticable Measure; Many Individuals are gone, and others are going, thro' Fears, as they give out of being apprehended; So your Lordship will perceive some of the most Obnoxious are in the Number of those who move."[50]

As many as five thousand Bostonians left the city prior to the outbreak of hostilities, and the flight of "the most Obnoxious" Patriots as well as their sympathizers only accelerated once the shooting began. On April 29, 1775, ten days after Lexington and Concord, Lieutenant Frederick Mackenzie of the Royal Welsh Fusiliers confided to his diary, "Number of the Inhabitants having applied to the General for Permission to leave the Town, an Officer was ordered to attend at Charlestown ferry . . . to examine and receive the passes signed by the Town Major for those who have received the General's permission to go out."[51] Following the Battle of Bunker Hill, Boston looked like a ghost town to its long-term inhabitants. Justice Oliver observed that between 10,000 and 12,000 people had fled the city: "The Operation of that Battle [Bunker Hill] occasioned so great an Evacuation, that the Town was reduced to a perfect Skeleton."[52] The result of these migrations was that the British Army's task of governing the inhabitants became less arduous because it had a significantly smaller and substantially more loyal civilian population to police.

While governing this new Loyalist constituency may have been easier, providing for its health and welfare in wartime certainly was not. The first major issue that the army had to contend with was the outbreak of a deadly smallpox epidemic in July 1775. Most British soldiers in Boston had already had the disease and were therefore immune, but the New Englanders were not. Due to the physical confines of the city, quarantine efforts proved inadequate, resulting in ten to thirty deaths per day that summer.[53] The second major challenge during the siege of Boston was keeping both the troops and the inhabitants supplied with food. On August 15 Gage informed Barrington, "As we are in want of every necessary here, and the Commanding Officers of the different Regiments have wrote to their Agents for what they want; If your Lordship thinks proper this Ship may Return with them, and the sooner the better, as no Winter necessarys [*sic*] are to be got here for the Soldiers."[54] The Patriot encampments outside of Boston physically sealed off the city from resupply by land. Major Stephen Kemble, Gage's deputy adjutant general and brother-in-law, described how "from this day [April 19] the Rebels assembled in great numbers about Boston, 2,000 at least, prevented all supplies of Provision coming into Town, and used every Act of Hostility."[55] In addition to cutting the landward supply routes, Patriot privateers implemented a spotty, but effective, blockade on the high seas. Justice Oliver commented in the autumn of 1775, "Many Vessells [*sic*], which were coming from *England* & *Ireland*, with Provisions & Stores for the Army & for the Inhabitants, were captured within a few Leagues of Boston."[56] Gage alleviated his provisioning difficulties by granting civilian fishing vessels permission to leave Boston Harbor and using the transport vessels that came into port for foraging expeditions. Major Kemble commented on a typical expedition on August 15, 1775, noting, "Our Mutton fleet arrived this Evening with near two thousand Sheep and 103 Cattle taken from Gardiners, and Fishers Islands—without any sort of oposition [*sic*], not even one Shot fired."[57]

Gage's measures prevented starvation but never provided enough food to support a comfortable diet. As a result, he faced a chorus of criticism from his officers. Brigadier James Grant was one of the most outspoken detractors, arguing that Gage should violate the Prohibitory Act of 1775 to supply the city.

> I had sayd that the General not only as Commander in Chief, but as Civil Governor of the Province had sufficient Powers to throw the Harbor open to all the World for suplies wanted for the Army. That the Commissioners coud have no inspection where there was no Port & that they coud be considered as Gentln. for Safety. That the Admiral must wave his Guardianship of the Laws of Parliament with Regard to Boston & of course yield to the Necessity of the Times and to the Powers & Authority of the Civil Governor which might be strengthened if necessary by the signed Opinions of the Commander in Chief & the three Major Generals. Every Body I talk to seems to think this right, but nothing is done.[58]

Grant believed that the implementation of martial law excluded Boston from the Prohibitory Act's trade restrictions, and he resented efforts by the Royal Navy and customs commissioners to enforce them. The brigadier logically argued, "They [Admiral Samuel Graves and commissioners] cannot conceive that Law shoud give way to Necessity that in fact no Law can be in force where there is a civil War & that in cases of great Distress whatever is expedient must be right."[59] This ambiguity about the limits of martial law set the army at odds with both the navy and the few remaining civil officials in Boston in its effort to feed Bostonians and His Majesty's forces. Despite the urgency of the situation, Gage did not flout the Prohibitory Act, nor would Howe when he became commander in chief. Instead, he followed Gage's precedent of helping the inhabitants provide for themselves while using any ships available for scavenging operations. But Howe did reduce the troops' rations twice between November 26, 1775, and January 5, 1776.[60]

From April 19, 1775, until March 17, 1776, the Boston garrison found itself besieged, hungry, and the object of increasingly draconian punishments. The escalating rigor of military courts-martial increased both the number of executions and the number lashes for infractions. The rationale behind the harsher punishments was twofold. First, the officers needed to maintain the fighting ability of their soldiers during wartime by ensuring good order and discipline. Second, because the civil government had dissolved and the refugee population within Boston had become overwhelmingly Loyalist, the British Army inherited the sole responsibility for both governing and protecting the inhabitants.

The most serious challenge to the fighting efficacy of the garrison was desertion. Fortunately for the British officers, desertion from Boston became more difficult after Lexington and Concord. First, the battles increased colonial antipathy toward soldiers, thereby reducing their willingness to harbor deserters as they had in the past. Second, the outbreak of hostilities required more-robust physical security throughout the city. The rapidly increasing number of fortifications not only kept the Patriots out but also kept British soldiers in. For men still willing and able to desert, the general courts-martial attempted to dissuade them with ever-more-frequent death sentences. Only one soldier, Richard Eames, received a death sentence for desertion during the first six years of the redcoats' occupation of Boston. During the garrison's last year and a half prior to the evacuation, though, general courts-martial sentenced nine soldiers to death for desertion; two were granted clemency, but the remaining seven were executed. The British captured nine other deserters, but instead of sentencing them to death, courts-martial gave the men an average of nine hundred lashes each. Despite the garrison in Boston more than tripling, the desertion rate dramatically decreased from August 1774 until the British departure, suggesting that the sterner discipline was successful.[61]

Rampant drunkenness was the other major disciplinary issue within the garrison, which took on a greater significance in the wake of open hostilities. Widespread intoxication among the troops undermined combat readiness by fueling unruly behavior. On February 2, 1775, Lieutenant Mackenzie complained to his diary that despite the officers' strenuous efforts "to prevent Spirituous liquors from being sold to the Soldiers, Soldiers wives and others find means to dispose of the New England Rum to them in such quantities, and at so cheap a rate, that numbers of them are intoxicated daily." He insisted that "spirits of so pernicious a quality" resulted in the deaths of two soldiers from alcohol poisoning. While greed was the prime motive behind such sales, Mackenzie also noted that the "towns people encourage this excessive drinking, as when the Soldiers are in a State of intoxication they are frequently induced to desert."[62]

In addition to increasing the punishments against soldiers for their disorderly conduct—most notably desertion and assaults—when drunk, officers also targeted the soldiers' civilian suppliers. On June 21, 1775, Howe decreed, "If any Men or Women are detected selling or giving Rum to the Soldiers the former will be severely Punish'd, the Latter Dismissal with Infamy from Camp and the Soldiers found Intoxicated will have no further Allowance of Rum served out to them." By July 23, daily orders prohibited soldiers from being in civilians' huts past eight o'clock in the evening; civilians violating this order would have their hut torn down and be thrown out of Boston. This preventative measure seems to have failed. On October 14 Howe issued additional restrictions preventing army sutlers from selling alcohol to the troops and threatened to imprison "women belonging to the army [that is, camp followers]" in the provost until they could be shipped home from the city.[63]

Despite the officers' best efforts, they never curbed the prevalent binge drinking within the garrison. Brigadier Percy admitted as much when he wrote to the Swiss-born major general Frederick Haldimand on December 12, 1775, "Our Discipline is exactly the same as when you left us [the day before the Battle of Bunker Hill], which we shall begin to perceive now the Troops have got into winter quarters."[64] Percy's prediction proved prescient because amid preparations to evacuate the city on March 8, 1776, Howe issued orders to destroy all of the rum in Boston not purchased by the commissary for the voyage to Halifax. He wrote, "the General flatters himself the Soldiers will not at this Time relax in their Discipline . . . to put a Stop to Drunkeness in the Garrison, which has been too prevalent of late."[65] The officers not only struggled to keep their men in fighting shape but also wrestled with protecting the overwhelmingly Loyalist civilians from abuses by the troops.

On the one hand, Gage's declaration of martial law on June 12, 1775, merely acknowledged the de facto dissolution of royal government within Massachusetts. On the other hand, it introduced very real problems for the inhabitants of Boston, who could no longer appeal to civil government for wrongs committed against their property and persons by the army. Prior to the outbreak of hostilities, Brigadier Percy had insisted, "When the people come with complaints, I hear them with patience; and if they are just ones, I take care they shall be immediately redressed, assuring them that we are come to protect the peaceable inhabitants, not to injure them; and that as we are determined to enforce obedience to the laws in other people, we shall be ever ready and desirous to be the first to obey them ourselves."[66] The days of Patriots fraudulently accusing soldiers of crimes, as had occurred within the city between 1768 and 1770, had long passed. After Gage declared martial law, officers took accusations of crimes by their soldiers against the inhabitants and their property very seriously and did everything in their power to prevent them, albeit without much success.

In the aftermath of Lexington and Concord, Gage and Howe promulgated increasingly dire punishments for soldiers who stole or destroyed civilian property. On April 22 Mackenzie reported, "the General [Gage] expects on any future occasion, that they will behave with more discipline and in a more Soldierlike manner: and it is his most positive orders that no man quit his rank to plunder or pillage, or to enter a house unless ordered to do so, under pain of death." A week later Gage gave "strict orders that no property whatever shall be touched or damaged without orders for so doing."[67] The day after Bunker Hill, Howe warned his men still encamped on the heights of the Charlestown peninsula that, "on pain of Death no Man to be Guilty of the Shamefull and

Infamous practice of pillaging and pilfering in the Deserted Houses" in the town below. On June 26, 1775, he stressed the importance of preserving the houses there that had not been consumed by fire during the battle, threatening his troops that "any of the Soldiers Detected in future in attempting Shamefully to Purloin any part of these Buildings will assuredly be punish'd most severely, The Genl Considers such Instances of Devastation and Irregularity a Disgrace to Discipline." By July 7, from his headquarters in Boston, Gage forbade any officers or soldiers from entering houses within Boston without the owner's permission. Ten days later Howe, who still remained in Charlestown, prohibited grave robbing because "added to the meanness of such practice a pestilence from the Infection [smallpox] of the Putrify'd Bodys might reach the Camp." Howe's first orders following his replacement of Gage as commander in chief on October 12 included, "Soldiers being found Guilty of pulling down Houses, or Fences may depend on being severely punished & all Centries [*sic*] who may be detected in Conniving at or Suffering any Irregularities near their posts must not Expect Mercy for such neglect of Duty." Despite these repeated warnings, troops continued to demolish houses and fences for the firewood they needed to stay warm and cook their food. The frustration of such disobedience led Howe to resort to summary executions on December 5 by "direct[ing] the Provost to go his rounds attended by the Executioner, with orders to hang up upon the spot the first man he shall detect in the fact, without waiting for further proof by trial." Even the specter of an instant death sentence did not curtail the soldiers' looting, prompting the general to reissue the threat three days prior to evacuating Boston: "The Commander in Chief finding notwithstanding the Orders that have been given to forbid Plundering Houses have been forced open & robbed, he is therefore under a Necessity of declaring to the Troops, that the first Soldier who is caught plundering, will be hanged on the Spot."[68] Although Gage and Howe never effectively suppressed their soldiers' crimes against the inhabitants' property, they did a better job of protecting Bostonians' persons.

Gage sought to protect civilians from physical violence through a combination of policy changes and strict discipline. Beginning on October 18, 1774, he sought to avoid tumults between his soldiers and the inhabitants by advising, "Upon any Riotous Proceeding or quarrelling happening near a Centries [*sic*] post if he cannot put an End to it by his own Authority he is to call to the Guard, and Centries are to be particularly careful not to give any Molestation to the peaceable inhabitants of the Town."[69] While most sentries obediently obeyed this directive, the officers were not so meek. On the night of January 20, 1775, a drunken gambling session resulted in "a quarrel between some Officers and the town Watch," which prompted Gage to conduct a "Court of Enquiry." The court's report led to "the General being much displeased with the Conduct of his officers." Gage scolded his officers "that the attacking of the Watch of any Town in all parts of the World, must be attended with bad consequences: for as they were appointed by Law, the Law will protect them." Therefore, he decided "to make the strictest enquirey into the conduct of all Officers concerned in quarrels or Riots with the Towns people, and try them if in fault."[70] But this was not the only violence-inciting friction point within the garrisoned town. After Charlestown's ferrymen leveled accusations that officers and their men regularly assaulted and battered them, Gage declared on August 17 "that Neither Officers nor Soldiers, shall for the future presume to Strike or otherwise ill treat the ferry men, or people employ'd in the Transport Boats, but are on all Occasions to apply to the Officer Commanding the Guard, who is placed there to see that due Order is kept."[71]

Gage's and Howe's harsh proclamations were implemented in more than name alone. Starting in July 1775, courts-martial records demonstrate a dramatic increase in the number of convictions as well as the severity of the penalties for soldiers who robbed or abused civilians. Prior to July 1775, there were no general courts-martial for robbery whatsoever. Between July and December of that year, the army in Boston held the following trials for crimes against the inhabitants: twenty for robbery, two for receiving stolen goods, and one for assault on a civilian. Three of the robbers earned an acquittal. Of the remaining seventeen convicted robbers, four received death sentences, one of whom was pardoned, and the remaining thirteen received an average of six hundred lashes. The two soldiers convicted of receiving stolen property received a thousand and eight hundred lashes respectively, while the soldier who assaulted a civilian earned a thousand lashes as well.[72]

In addition to protecting the Loyalist population of Boston following the declaration of martial law, the British Army took on a multitude of other civic responsibilities to fill the vacuum left by the defunct civil government. The army issued passes to facilitate trade, ordered female camp followers to attend the sick at the hospital, required soldiers to sweep the streets, punished a female camp follower for slaughtering an army bull, issued rewards to recover the stolen seals of the province, regulated markets by requiring ship captains to obtain permits, created new graveyards when victims of battle injuries and smallpox inundated the existing ones, and established rules for cooperating with the inhabitants to fight fires. To help oversee such disparate functions, Captain Lieutenant James Urquhart was made the town major, and Captain Stephen Payne Adye became the deputy judge advocate for the soldiers and inhabitants of Boston.[73]

While the army's governance of these civilians tended to be quotidian drudgery, one distinct advantage of providing security and a modicum of comfort was the willingness of the inhabitants to help secure and defend the garrison. On October 29, 1775, Howe formed the company of the Royal North British Volunteers. The unit's officers were Captain James Anderson, 1st Lieutenant William Blair, 2nd Lieutenant P. Black, and 3rd Lieutenant J. Fleeming. Howe ordered the Royal North British Volunteers to enforce the city's curfew by "mount[ing] a Guard at Gun Fireing & Patrole the Streets within a certain District &... take into Custody all Suspicious & Disorderly Persons found in the Streets at improper Hours." On November 17 Howe commissioned Timothy Ruggles as a brigadier on the American establishment and placed him in charge of the Loyal American Associaters, consisting of three companies of Boston Loyalists who had "offered their service for the defence of the place." Last but not least, on December 7 "some Irish Merchants residing in Town, with their adherents, having offer'd their service for the defence of the place, the Commander in Chief has order'd them to be Arm'd, and directs their being form'd into a Comp^{y} to be call'd the Loyal Irish Volunteers," commanded by James Forrest, who received a commission as captain.[74] Throughout the war, most British officials assumed that mobilizing the "friends of government" would be as simple as raising the king's standard as they had done in Boston. More-astute observers, who counted just how few Loyalists within the city joined the newly created units, should have concluded that more would need to be done. If they indeed had such thoughts at this early stage in the war, British officers pushed them out of their mind while focusing on the upcoming New York campaign to decisively defeat the Continental Army and the rebellion.

In summary, despite Whig claims about the unconstitutional establishment of military government by using a peacetime standing army and martial law, the British ministry's polices toward Massachusetts between 1768 and 1775 conformed to *jus ad bellum* and *jus in bello* principles found in both international and British domestic law. King George III and Parliament designed the Coercive Acts to substantially increase the royal prerogative in Massachusetts by removing all legal impediments to Governor General Gage's implementation of garrison government, but they fell short in two key areas. Many years after the American Revolution, the Scottish antiquarian George Chalmers asked Gage if he had been "averse to taking the Government of the Massachusetts Bay. He [Gage referring to himself] desired at length that a much larger force than four weak regiments might be sent out, and the Town of Boston declared in rebellion, without which his hands would be tied up."[75] Not surprisingly, Gage's response sought to excuse his conduct as the governor general of

Massachusetts, but it was not entirely without merit. On the first count, that he had insufficient troops for the task at hand, Gage was right, though only in retrospect. Prior to taking the governorship he believed, and indeed told the king, that four regiments would be enough. The general would have been correct if Boston alone remained the problem, but since the Coercive Acts prompted the rebellion to spread to the rest of Massachusetts and throughout the other twelve colonies, his initial 3,500 troops were a mere pittance. On the second count, that the king needed to declare the colony in rebellion, Gage was incorrect because he himself held that authority as the governor general. As David Hackett Fischer has noted, Gage was temperamentally ill suited to the role of a Cromwellian Lord Protector, but when he finally resolved himself to confronting the rebellion militarily on June 12, 1775, he employed all of the British Army's standard procedures for suppressing revolts.[76] Gage offered pardons to all rebels except John Hancock and Samuel Adams, sought a decisive battle at Bunker Hill, permitted the burning of Charlestown, and prepared for future judicial punishments.

Surprisingly, when the British Army's role in Boston evolved from garrison government to martial law, the changes in the governance of the city resulted less from the removal of legal impediments than to the realities of living under siege. The mass exodus of Patriots and those concerned for their safety from the city in the wake of the fighting at Concord, Lexington, and Bunker Hill left fewer than three thousand people in Boston. Not only was the smaller population more manageable but it was also significantly more law abiding, with Loyalist refugees pouring in from the surrounding countryside seeking protection from Patriot persecution. To protect this overwhelmingly friendly population, both Gage and his successor, William Howe, punished their soldiers with ever-increasing severity to prevent robberies and assaults against the inhabitants. The army also discovered that in order to maintain its fighting effectiveness, it had to fill the void left when the civil government dissolved. Gage and Howe therefore issued a series of haphazard edicts to contend with such mundane issues as provisioning the city, regulating markets, and maintaining hygiene. While no great thought went into these efforts, the experience in Boston hinted at the value of protecting local inhabitants when Loyalists formed three separate military units to help guard the city. Unfortunately, most British officers considered the eleven-month siege they endured there an anomaly. They assumed that the Loyalist majority in New York would rally to the royal standard as soon as the army appeared—or shortly after the first major engagement provided King George III's arms with a decisive victory.

NOTES

Chapter title: Hugo Grotius, *The Rights of War and Peace,* trans. A. C. Campbell, Universal Classics Library (Washington, D.C.: M. Walter Dunne, 1901), 75.

Epigraph: Quoted in O. M. Dickerson, *Boston under Military Rule (1768–1769): As Revealed in a Journal of the Times* (Boston: Chapman and Grimes, 1936), 32.

1. "English Bill of Rights 1689: An Act Declaring the Rights and Liberties of the Subject and Settling the Succession of the Crown," *The Avalon Project: Documents in Law, History, and Diplomacy,* Yale Law School, http://avalon.law.yale.edu/17th_century/england.asp.
2. Quoted in Bernard Bailyn, *The Ideological Origins of the American Revolution,* enl. ed. (Cambridge, Mass.: Belknap Press of Harvard University Press, 1992), 62.
3. Pauline Maier, *From Resistance to Revolution: Colonial Radicals and the Development of American Opposition to Britain, 1765–1776* (New York: Knopf, 1972), 143.
4. Richard Archer, *As If an Enemy's Country: The British Occupation of Boston and the Origins of Revolution* (Oxford: Oxford University Press, 2010), 126.
5. Stephen Saunders Webb, "Army and Empire: English Garrison Government in Britian and America, 1569 to 1763," *William and Mary Quarterly,* 3rd ser., 34, no. 1 (1977); Webb, *The Governors-General: The English Army and the Definition of the Empire, 1569–1681* (Chapel Hill: Published for the Institute of Early American History and Culture, Williamsburg, Va., by the University of North Carolina Press, 1979), 4. Webb explains "garrison government" thusly:

   > Through the military government of garrison towns, the English executive bypassed the corporate structures of traditional local government and weakened the autonomy of its gentry-and-merchant ruling class. Acting as governors, royal army officers imposed the crown's military and political will directly on the cities, the centers of subject populations. Garrison government expressed the growing force of the national executive in strategic seaports, border fortresses, and political capitals in the British Isles. From Britain and Ireland, garrison government was transplanted to America. Army officers, all of them garrison veterans and many of them town governors, constituted almost nine-tenths (87.5 percent) of the 206 colonial viceroys commissioned between 1660 and 1727.

   Furthermore, while I have chosen to use the term "civilian" throughout this article to be clear to a modern audience, it is anachronistic to the eighteenth century as shown in David Avrom Bell, *The First Total War: Napoleon's Europe and the Birth of Warfare as We Know It* (Boston: Houghton Mifflin, 2007), ii. Bell cogently argues that there was no distinction such as "military" and "civilian" prior to the Napoleonic Wars and that Old Regime officers "did not draw sharp lines between their professional role as military officers and their social identity as aristocrats."
6. Dickerson, *Boston under Military Rule,* xi.
7. Quoted, ibid., x.
8. Thomas Hutchinson, *The History of the Province of Massachusetts Bay: From 1749 to 1774,* 2nd ed., ed. John Hutchinson, vol. 3 (J. Murray, 1828), 225.

9. *Boston Evening-Post,* Sept. 19, 1768.
10. *Boston-Gazette, and Country Journal,* Sept. 26, 1768.
11. Dickerson, *Boston under Military Rule,* 1.
12. *Boston-Gazette, and Country Journal,* Dec. 26, 1768; Dickerson, *Boston under Military Rule,* 66.
13. *Boston-Gazette, and Country Journal,* Jan. 29, 1770.
14. *Boston Evening-Post,* Feb. 22, 1768.
15. *Boston Post-Boy & Advertiser,* Sept. 26, 1768.
16. *Boston Weekly News-Letter,* June 15, 1769.
17. *Boston Evening-Post,* July 3, 1769.
18. Archer, *As If an Enemy's Country,* 193.
19. *Massachusetts Gazette, and the Boston Post-Boy and Advertiser,* Apr. 30, 1770.
20. *Boston Gazette, and Country Journal,* Apr. 2, 1770.
21. Thomas Gage, *The Correspondence of General Thomas Gage,* ed. Clarence Edwin Carter, 2 vols. (New Haven, Conn.: Yale University Press, 1931), 1:196.
22. British civil and military authorities frequently spoke of the ability of a large body of regular troops to "awe"—i.e., intimidate—mobs and their instigators. For example, Gov. Francis Bernard wrote to the Earl of Hillsborough on July 9, 1768, "One regiment will secure the Castle, but will not be sufficient to awe the town." Bernard sent Hillsborough another letter on October 3, 1768, saying, "My message (which was said to be very high, tho' I hope not too high for the occasion), altho' it did not disperse them, had the good effect to keep them in awe." Massachusetts [Colony] Governor, *Letters to the Ministry, from Governor Bernard, General Gage, and Commodore Hood: And Also, Memorials to the Lords of the Treasury, from the Commissioners of the Customs: With Sundry Letters and Papers Annexed to the Said Memorials,* ed. Samuel Hood Viscount Hood (Boston: Printed by Edes and Gill, 1769), 54, 93. I have dubbed the British intention of flooding Boston with troops to either deter overt resistance or to have sufficient force available to suppress any such open hostility as "saturation policing."
23. Hutchinson, *History of the Province of Massachusetts Bay,* 455.
24. Peter Oliver, *Origin & Progress of the American Rebellion: A Tory View* (Stanford, Calif.: Stanford University Press, 1961), 115.
25. Hugh Percy to Duke of Northumberland, Apr. 20, 1775, in *Letters of Hugh, Earl Percy, from Boston and New York, 1774–1776,* ed. H. P. Northumberland and C. K. Bolton (C. E. Goodspeed, 1902), 54–55.
26. John W. Shy, *A People Numerous and Armed: Reflections on the Military Struggle for American Independence,* rev. ed. (Ann Arbor: University of Michigan Press, 1990), 110; John Richard Alden, *General Gage in America: Being Principally a History of His Role in the American Revolution* (Baton Rouge: Louisiana State University Press, 1948), 252. According to Alden, Gage believed that the Second Continental Congress would adopt conciliatory measures and was hoping that the British ministry might also soften its stance.
27. Alden, *General Gage in America,* 260.
28. Gage, *Correspondence,* 1:405.

29. Oliver, *Origin & Progress of the American Rebellion,* 118. Chief Justice Oliver believed that the argument over who fired first at Lexington was irrelevant because the dissolution of the civil government represented the true beginning of the rebellion. He wrote: "Much Stress hath been laid upon, who fired the first Gun [Lexington]. This was immaterial, for as the civil Government had been resolved by the Suffolk Resolves, the military Power had a right to suppress all hostile Appearances."
30. Thomas Gage, "By His Excellency the Hon. Thomas Gage, Esq; Governor, and Commander in Chief in and over His Majesty's Province of Massachusetts-Bay, and Vice Admiral of the Same. A Proclamation" (Boston, 1775), in *The Norwich Packet and the Connecticut, Massachusetts, New-Hampshire, and Rhode-Island Weekly Advertiser,* June 19, 1775.
31. Archer, *As If an Enemy's Country,* xiv.
32. *Boston Weekly News-Letter,* June 15, 1769.
33. W. Blackstone, *An Analysis of the Laws of England* (Printed at the Clarendon Press, 1771), 17, 18.
34. Hugo Grotius, *The Illustrious Hugo Grotius of the Law of Warre and Peace: With Annotations, III Parts, and Memorials of the Author's Life and Death,* ed. Clement Barksdale (London: Printed by T. Warren, for William Lee. . . , 1655), 135–36.
35. F. Bacon, *The Works of Francis Bacon: Law Tracts. Maxims of the Law* (J. Johnson, 1803), 388.
36. Grotius, *Illustrious Hugo Grotius of the Law of Warre and Peace,* 393.
37. Bacon, *Works,* 388.
38. E. Coke et al., *The First Part of the Institutes of the Laws of England; or, A Commentary upon Littleton: Not the Name of the Author Only, but of the Law Itself. . . . : Haec Ego Grandaevus Posui Tibi, Candide Lector* (J. & W. T. Clarke, 1832), 1:L.2. C.4.Sect.111, 83.a.
39. Ibid., 2:L.3.C.7.Sect. 440, 261.b.
40. Blackstone, *Analysis of the Laws of England,* 127.
41. Grotius, *Illustrious Hugo Grotius of the Law of Warre and Peace,* 1–2.
42. Coke et al., *First Part of the Institutes of the Laws of England,* 1:249.b.
43. Oliver, *Origin & Progress of the American Rebellion,* 115; Samuel Livermore to John Wentworth, Jan. 11, 1775, *Documents of the American Revolution, 1770–1783 (Colonial Office Series),* ed. K. G. Davies, 21 vols. (1972), 9:29; Attorney and Solicitor General to Earl of Dartmouth, Dec. 13, 1774, ibid., 8:240–41; Earl of Dartmouth to Thomas Gage, Jan. 27, 1775, ibid., 9:41; Earl of Dartmouth to Thomas Gage, Apr. 15, 1775, ibid., 9:98.
44. Grotius, *Illustrious Hugo Grotius of the Law of Warre and Peace,* 176.
45. Quoted in R. Raphael and M. Raphael, *The Spirit of 74: How the American Revolution Began* (New York: New Press, 2015), 156.
46. Bacon, *Works,* 347–48.
47. Emer de Vattel, *The Law of Nations; or Principles of the Laws of Nature: Applied to the Conduct and Affairs of Nations and Sovereigns,* 2 vols. (1729), 1:16.
48. William Howe, Viscount Howe, *General Sir William Howe's Orderly Book at Charlestown, Boston and Halifax, June 17, 1775 to 1776, 26 May; to Which Is Added the Official*

Abridgment of General Howe's Correspondence with the English Government during the Siege of Boston, and Some Military Returns . . . with an Historical Introd. by Edward Everett Hale, ed. Benjamin Franklin Stevens, (Port Washington, N.Y.: Kennikat, 1970), 107.

49. For the prehostilities population, see J. H. Benton, *Early Census Making in Massachusetts, 1643–1765: With a Reproduction of the Lost Census of 1765 (Recently Found) and Documents Relating Thereto* (Charles E. Goodspeed, 1905), 74–75. For the evacuation of Boston, see Piers Mackesy, *The War for America, 1775–1783* (Cambridge, Mass.: Harvard University Press, 1964), 80; and David G. McCullough, *1776* (New York: Simon & Schuster, 2005), 97–105.
50. Gage, *Correspondence,* 1:374, 382, 2:655.
51. Frederick Mackenzie, *Diary of Frederick Mackenzie, Giving a Daily Narrative of His Military Service as an Officer of the Regiment of Royal Welch Fusiliers During the Years 1775–1781 in Massachusetts, Rhode Island and New York,* 2 vols. (Cambridge, Mass.: Harvard University Press, 1930), 1:31.
52. Oliver, *Origin & Progress of the American Rebellion,* 123–24.
53. Elizabeth A. Fenn, *Pox Americana: The Great Smallpox Epidemic of 1775–82,* ed. William B. Blythe and honoree (New York: Hill and Wang, 2001), 44–51; Jacqueline Barbara Carr, *After the Siege: A Social History of Boston, 1775–1800* (Boston: Northeastern University Press, 2005), 17.
54. Gage, *Correspondence,* 2:695.
55. Stephen Kemble, *The Kemble Papers,* 2 vols. (New York: New York Historical Society, 1884), 1:43.
56. Oliver, *Origin & Progress of the American Rebellion,* 140.
57. Kemble, *Papers,* 1:46, 55.
58. James Grant to Edward Harvey, Aug. 10, 1775, James Grant of Ballindalloch Papers, David Library of the American Revolution, Washington Crossing, Pa.
59. James Grant to Chemier, Aug. 11, 1775, ibid.
60. Howe, *General Sir William Howe's Orderly Book,* 154, 191.
61. G. W. Morgan and University of Sussex, *'A Clever Little Army': The British Garrison in Boston, 1768–1776* (University of Sussex, 2004), 104–5, 111, 138–42, 211–12.
62. Mackenzie, *Diary,* 1:6.
63. Howe, *General Sir William Howe's Orderly Book,* 11, 49–50, 111.
64. Hugh Percy to Frederick Haldimand, Dec. 14, 1775, in Northumberland and Bolton, *Letters of Hugh, Earl Percy,* 63.
65. Howe, *General Sir William Howe's Orderly Book,* 229.
66. Hugh Percy to the Worthy Independent Electors of Westminster, Aug. 10, 1774, in Northumberland and Bolton, *Letters of Hugh, Earl Percy,* 18.
67. Mackenzie, *Diary,* 1:30–31.
68. Howe, *General Sir William Howe's Orderly Book,* 3, 19–20, 36, 44, 109, 160, 237.
69. Ibid., 115.
70. Mackenzie, *Diary,* 1:4–5.
71. Howe, *General Sir William Howe's Orderly Book,* 72.
72. Morgan and the University of Sussex, *'Clever Little Army,'* 204.

73. Howe, *General Sir William Howe's Orderly Book,* 4, 23, 25, 41, 63, 97, 102, 117, 125, 127, 142.
74. Ibid., 123, 140, 161.
75. Massachusetts Historical Society, *Collections of the Massachusetts Historical Society* ([Boston]: The Society, 1858), 371.
76. David Hackett Fischer, *Paul Revere's Ride* (New York: Oxford University Press, 1994), 36–37.

6 "A CONTEST OF VIRTUE WITH VICE"

Henry Knox's Just and Honorable War for Independence

Phillip Hamilton

Was the American Revolution a "just war"? Henry Knox, the Boston bookseller who commanded George Washington's artillery and later rose to the rank of major general, certainly thought so. Knox came to this conclusion, though, not by reading the constitutional and legal treatises of such men as John Locke, Hugo Grotius, or Emer de Vattel. Rather, he decided to fight a "just war" because of an array of widely held customs and beliefs regarding liberty, self-government, and tyranny. Indeed, Knox grew to maturity in Boston in the 1760s and 1770s, where he fully internalized the community's fundamental values and traditions. Therefore, he marched off to war like many New Englanders in 1775, not to start a revolution, but to preserve basic rights and privileges to which they believed themselves entitled. He looked upon the mother country, moreover, as a nation that had abandoned all just principles and that was now sinking into an abyss of moral corruption and decay.

Once in the ranks, Knox further insisted that he would take part in the conflict only by following the accepted norms of eighteenth-century warfare. He fought according to so-called *jus in bello* principles for several reasons. In part, he was influenced by reading the many standard military texts of the age, including Marshall Saxe's *Reveries on the Art of War* and Frederick the Great's *Instructions to His Generals.* Equally important, Knox viewed the Revolutionary War as a means for the American people to prove to the world that they were worthy of self-government and individual liberties. Like the heroes of republican Rome, Americans would demonstrate to the larger world that they were a noble, virtuous, and hardy race who deserved equal treatment on the international stage of Atlantic world diplomacy. To this end, they must not make war in a barbaric fashion "like savages." Finally, given his conventional social views (best reflected by his later Federalist political leanings), he saw the war as an avenue for advancing himself above his humble origins so as to become a great man of substance and reputation. These goals, he believed, could only be achieved by acting the part of a gentleman-officer and fighting according to the civilized rules of eighteenth-century warfare.

Like many Bostonians who participated in neither politics nor the law, Henry Knox has not provided later historians with many reflections regarding exactly why he decided to fight in the Revolution. Hence, he has been largely ignored in recent decades by scholars who prefer historical figures with more active pens and addressed such issues as the law, constitutions, and colonial charters. At the same time, military historians have generally avoided Knox because he never exercised an independent command nor was he personally responsible for any great battlefield victory. His close friend Nathanael Greene, on the other hand, has attracted the attention of many serious biographers due primarily to his leadership of American forces during the southern campaign of 1780–81. Yet because Knox viewed the Revolution as a just war and fought it according to what he considered virtuous principles, it is necessary to investigate precisely how he came to adopt and live by this worldview. His modest origins, upbringing in the streets of Boston, and firm convictions likely inform us how many within New England's general population came to see the revolt against Great Britain as a just and virtuous cause.

Born on July 25, 1750, to William and Mary Campbell Knox, Henry grew up in Boston's South End on Sea Street. His father was a shipmaster and small wharf owner who struggled financially as Henry grew up. In 1759 William sailed off to the West Indies to try and recoup his fortunes; he died in 1762 without ever returning to Massachusetts. The couple had ten sons together (Henry was the seventh), but only four survived to adulthood. Their two eldest boys, John and Benjamin, became mariners and apparently died at sea. Thus, Henry grew to manhood with neither his father nor older siblings around him. His formal education proved meager. From the ages of seven to nine, he attended the Boston Latin School, but the family's straightened finances forced him to leave the same year his father departed from Boston. Yet his school years engendered in young Henry a lifelong love of learning, particularly a love of reading. He soon found employment in a bookstore owned by Nicholas Bowes and John Wharton. The job proved propitious for a number of reasons: it gave the youth a chance to earn money, to learn the bookselling trade, and to demonstrate to influential employers his innate intelligence and reliability. Perhaps most importantly, the position gave Knox access to thousands of books. A voracious yet thoughtful reader, he soon learned French, classical history, and some political science. He especially read books on military science and artillery.[1]

Knox grew toward manhood, however, in a city that had been struggling for decades. Great Britain's eighteenth-century imperial wars had repeatedly disrupted trade, curbed economic activity, and promoted higher prices and taxes. Wartime casualties, moreover, caused the number of Boston's needy widows and orphans to rise sharply. Growing competition from other North American ports, especially New York City, limited both maritime trade and the creation of new seafaring jobs linked to Atlantic commerce. Thus, Boston was, as Benjamin Carp has recently noted, "ripe for airing grievances and resentments."[2]

Despite his own family's difficulties as well as the city's economic stagnation, Knox grew intensely ambitious while working at Wharton and Bowes. During these years, he grew into a large, physically fit young man who possessed a deep baritone voice and a gregarious, engaging personality. Working in the bookstore taught him to deal with all sorts of people, from Boston's humbler citizens to those in its highest social strata. As the decade of the 1770s began, Knox therefore grew ever more determined to rise above his modest origins. He wanted not only to own his own bookstore but also to gain the respect of the city's important men as a "gentleman" of equal rank and status.

On his twenty-first birthday in 1771, Knox opened his own shop, the London Book Store. According to an announcement in the *Boston Gazette* published that same week, the store offered buyers "a large and very elegant assortment of the most modern Books in all branches of Literature, Arts, and Sciences."[3] Knox's business thrived under his direction, largely due to his energy, attention to detail, and cheerful bonhomie. Knowledgeable on many subjects, he easily struck up conversations and friendships with customers. He furthermore understood that appearances and a genteel deportment mattered in eighteenth-century society. Therefore, he always dressed in the finest suits he could afford, remaining fastidious about his appearance throughout his life. Recognizing too that many Bostonians still wished to feel connected to the larger British Empire and its cultural and political capital, he purposefully used *London* in his store's name and always stressed the breadth, sophistication, and timeliness of its catalog.[4]

In 1774 Knox married into one of Boston's most exalted families when he took Lucy Waldo Flucker as his bride. The pair had met in the shop in 1772, and an instant attraction formed that lasted their entire life together. Lucy's father was Thomas Flucker Sr., a wealthy merchant and landowner as well as Massachusetts Bay's colonial secretary, the third-highest-ranking office in the colony. Although Flucker and his wife had staunchly opposed a match between their daughter and a bookbinder from a failed maritime family, they eventually accepted the union. Before the Revolution, Knox undoubtedly hoped to use his new marital connections to enhance both his store's reputation and his own standing within Boston.

Lexington and Concord, however, changed everything. As soon as word reached the city of the bloodletting to the west, everyone knew that crucial decisions had to be made. Knox himself realized that perilous and high-stakes choices now lay before him. Having grown to maturity in Boston's streets, he had seen the imperial crisis escalate first hand. Like all boys growing up in an eighteenth-century urban environment, he had spent many days out of doors interacting with others as well as observing the momentous events around him. Because Bostonians had long governed their own affairs as well as demanded that everyone be a part of the community, Knox became a joiner and a full participant in the city's public life, during which he internalized its values, mores, and ideals.

Having grown up on Sea Street adjacent to the city's harbor, Knox initially joined the South End gang and seems to have become an active participant in its raucous Pope Day reveries, celebrating the Gunpowder Plot of 1605.[5] In 1768 Knox enrolled in Boston's Ancient & Honorable Artillery Company. Organized in 1637 for the defense of the colony, the unit was composed largely of South End mechanics and shopkeepers. During drills and other exercises, Knox learned the rudiments of artillery fire on the company's three 3-pounder guns, which apparently comprised its entire arsenal. Four years later he joined the city's elite Boston Grenadiers Company and was elected its second in command, taking the rank of second lieutenant.[6] He served the city in other ways. The same year he joined the Grenadier Company, Boston leaders chose Knox to be one of the city's clerks of the market.[7] He even participated in the more sociable aspects of Boston life. With lifelong friend Henry Jackson, Knox joined a weekly reading group, the Thursday Night Club, which likely met in one of the city's many taverns to discuss books, periodicals, literature, and politics.[8]

By the spring of 1775, members of the club had many things to ponder, especially with regard to politics and the fate of New England's long-held liberties. Knox himself had likely recalled for his fellow book-club members the Boston Massacre of March 5, 1770. Drawn into the streets that evening by the mob's loud cries and noises, the then-nineteen-year-old Knox saw the unrest in the streets escalating and actually confronted British captain Thomas Preston. As soldiers charged through the crowd with muskets ready and bayonets fixed, he grabbed Preston by the coat. Shouting to be heard above the din, he screamed, "for Gods sake take care of your Men for if they fire your life must be answerable." Soon afterward, while standing in front of Boston's Town House, Knox saw the British muskets erupt and witnessed what well-armed occupying troops, sent to impose unpopular measures, could do.[9]

Throughout the early 1770s, moreover, Knox directly experienced the consequences of the new imperial laws and regulations that the soldiers had been sent to Boston to enforce. As owner of a bookstore, he dealt with ship captains, city merchants, printers, artisans, and other booksellers on a daily basis. The London government's commercial measures had the greatest effect on these men, and it is inconceivable that in their frequent face-to-face encounters, they did not discuss such threats to their economic freedoms and livelihoods. Knox, for instance, knew John Hancock, borrowing money from him on several occasions as well as repeatedly hiring his ships, the *Lydia* and *Hayley,* to transport books from London.[10] Before Lexington and Concord, Knox also knew Paul Revere, having worked with the silversmith to sell the latter's bookplate engravings. All of the imperial measures were troubling, but none more so than the Tea Act, in which Parliament granted a trading monopoly to the East India Company and asserted the right to select the agents who would sell tea to colonial Americans. Such intrusions into their customary freedoms and the dangerous precedents they set must have been discussed, weighed, and debated over the course of Knox's daily transactions with his fellow business associates.[11]

At the same time, however, Knox heard different perspectives on the crisis from inside his own shop. The London Book Store stood just one block south of the Town House, then headquarters of the Massachusetts royal government. Therefore, Crown officials, military officers, and American Tories stopped by on a regular basis. Always friendly and desiring their business, Knox ensured that all felt welcome. One Bostonian even remembered the shop as "a great resort for the [city's] British officers and Tory ladies." Many residents, furthermore, found the king's officers to be both genteel and charming in one-on-one encounters. Even John Adams conceded that those army officers he conversed with at social occasions were "very engaging and agreeable" in their manners.[12] Knox too became fond of some of the officers he met. During the New York campaign several years later, for instance, he told his wife that Continental pickets had recently captured a "Lt. Ragg whom I knew in Boston," and they had nearly taken "[m]y friend little Barry," both members of the 52nd Regiment of the British Army. Knox particularly lamented not apprehending Barry, for "he should have been well us'd" by the Americans.[13]

Given this broad-based network of family, friends, and associates, Knox not surprisingly kept his political cards close to his vest throughout the imperial crisis. He did not join any of the city's prewar Whig associations, nor was he ever politically linked to Boston's Tories, even after his marriage into the prominent Flucker family. Knox, moreover, was an active doer throughout these years whose primary goal was to expand his business and enhance his reputation. Therefore, his prerevolutionary writings are not especially helpful or revealing; rather, they focus on tasks he had performed or that remained to be completed. Nevertheless, in the summer of 1774, soon after news of London's Coercive Acts reached Boston, Knox revealed his political opinions in correspondence to those closest to him. In late August, for example, he wrote to Henry Jackson about the crisis. His fellow Thursday Night Club member was then traveling in Nova Scotia, much to Knox's chagrin. "My dear Harry," he pleaded, "I most heartily wish to see you and very earnestly desire to converse in our social and heart[y] interesting manner." Turning to news in the city, he bluntly admitted:

> Public affairs wear a most disagreeable aspect, Mr. [Thomas] Gage [British governor general of Massachusetts] and his Co-adjustors must recede or we shall all be thrown into confusion. [I]t is impossible to say what wil[l] be the event, but under the present appearance carnage and bloodshed seem inevitable. [T]here never was any thing like the flame the last 2 Acts has produced in the Country, only erect a standard and [I] reyly[really?] believe in a fortnight there would be ten thous'd Country people flock to it and abide by the consequences.[14]

Beyond unburdening himself in writing, Knox may also have begun supporting the Whig cause more directly during this period. In February 1775 Lieutenant General Gage ordered a Patriot stockpile of seventeen cannon in Salem seized by the 64th Regiment's fusiliers. Though Gage planned the raid in great secrecy, Revere discovered it and informed Whig leaders in that port town, north of Boston. With New Englanders thus prepared, the expedition ended in a humiliating British failure. Revere told Jeremy Belknap years later that he had learned of the Salem raid from "a Gentleman who had Connections with the Tory party, but was a Whig at heart." Furthermore, this intelligence had first passed "through the then Secretary Flucker." Several historians have quite reasonably concluded that Knox, the secretary's son-in-law, was this Whig gentleman with Tory connections.[15]

By early 1775, therefore, Knox had committed himself to the Whig cause and believed that any coming conflict would be a moral and just war. Yet he reached this conclusion, not by reading books on laws and constitutions in his store, but by belonging to this large tightly knit community wedded to ancient liberties. Indeed, many New Englanders came to this conclusion and undoubtedly in this same manner. For example, Knox's soon-to-be comrade in arms, army surgeon James Thacher, wrote that spring, "Never was a cause more just, more sacred than ours; we are commanded to defend the rich inheritance bequeathed to us by our virtuous ancestors; and it is our bounden duty to transmit it uncontaminated to posterity."[16]

Knox's opinions about the righteousness of the American cause, however, did intensify as the conflict unfolded. Although he had previously written little about politics, Knox revealed his deepest-held thoughts to his wife once the war commenced. During the Revolution, the Continental Army's military operations kept Henry and Lucy Knox apart for extended periods, during which they frequently wrote to express their love and share daily activities. In these exchanges Knox painted the legitimacy of the American cause with bold, fervent, and sometimes angry strokes. The Revolution was justified first and foremost because the British people, as if members now of an entirely separate race, had completely lost their virtue and morality. On the eve of the New York campaign, for instance, he stated that the British were now members of a "Vain Nation" that "oppressed and insulted us . . . , and now like the desperate Gambler thou art about the venture thy very existence as a people upon an action in which, if beaten, then art totally lost and gone, perhaps for ever."[17] His growing outrage was also possibly a result of his burgeoning friendship with Nathanael Greene. Knox may have met the Rhode Islander before the war in his bookshop, but their relationship blossomed amid the trials and tribulations of army life and an escalating conflict. Like Knox, Greene also deeply believed in the justice and virtue of the American cause, writing to his wife, Catharine, that due to British corruption and venality, he feared "the Plains of America will be staind with Human Blood the next Campaign." Yet there "is no Alternative but Freedom or Slavery." Greene particularly blamed the king for this vile situation. George III's "boundless Ambition has plunged too [*sic*] happy Countries into an endless train of misery."[18]

By the end of 1776 after many battles, such convictions and animosities had only hardened. In early January 1777, for example, Knox wrote to Lucy characterizing the Revolution as "a Contest of Virtue with vice." He then listed Great Britain's many crimes against "the much injur'd rights of my Country," including sending "Indians to massacre the back Inhabitants, to drench their peaceful habitations with the blood of poor defenceless Women & children, Negroes to poison & assassinate their masters, & Hessians, with all their other brood of mercenaries, to desolate & lay Waste this Country, almost the only Country on earth where the Inhabitants have even the appearance of Liberty. Remember, these are the Acts of Britain, the boasted humanity of that people who calls themselves the mother Country!"[19] Later that spring Congress investigated reports of British atrocities during the 1776 campaign, whereupon members soon learned of not only the plunder of numerous civilian homes and properties but also many rapes by British and Hessian soldiers.[20]

Although Major General Sir William Howe and other British officers dismissed such charges as rebel propaganda, most Americans passionately believed them. Benjamin Franklin, for instance, bitterly attacked the British diplomat Paul Wentworth for the "Barbarities inflicted on his country" by the king's troops. After meeting with the seventy-one-year-old American in Paris, Wentworth reported to his London superiors that Franklin actually "lost his Breath in relating the burning of Towns, the neglect and ill-treatment of prisoners," and the military's "system of devastation and Cruelty" upon the innocent.[21] The same month Congress published its findings regarding British actions, Knox wrote to his wife and pointedly rejected her pleas that he resign from the army in order to better care for her and their infant daughter. He explained: "We are contending with a people cruel indeed that far from being enterprizing, far from being mark'd with scarce one Characteristick of Greatness, except a total debauch of morals be a mark of over refinedness of Manners, the consequence of ease and Luxury. Let them alone say you. I will, for I believe that God has let them alone."[22]

During the summer campaign of 1777, Knox repeatedly stressed to Lucy Britain's merciless character. Among other horrors, he imagined the couple's little daughter after she was "fully grown . . . [and] in a supplicating position from some British barbarian who is just on the eve of ravishing her!" Such scenes compelled him to stand against "their cursed tyranny" and "to lend a helping hand to rescue [her] from these most tremendous of human Miseries. These motives my dearest Girl are the only ones which keeps your affectionate Harry from you."[23] Thus, Knox and his fellow revolutionaries needed no theoretical or legal arguments to tell them that this conflict was fundamentally a just war. As with many if not most Patriots, their sentiments were, in the words of T. H. Breen, "ideas driven by immediate passions" and "amplified through fear, fury, and resentment."[24]

A final stimulant to Knox's view of the Revolution as a just war was his basic belief that the God who "orders all things for the better" had crafted this providential moment for Americans to prove their virtue and worthiness as a free people. "Such opportunities as the present do not often turn up in the course of human events," he once wrote John Adams, for "the future happiness or misery of a great proportion of the human race is at stake."[25] On the eve of the victory at Trenton when the cause was at its nadir, Knox drew strength from his conviction that the nation possessed the blessings of heaven. "America must & will rise Triumphant," he wrote Lucy. "*Much* great happiness must & will be in reserve for the virtuous part of America. Every thing goes on right, all things will work for good." Knox never lost this providential perspective, and thus he answered "the sacred calls of my Country" until the war's conclusion.[26]

As Knox believed his decision to fight the mother country to have been a fundamentally just one, he further sought to militarily defend the United States in a just and honorable manner, which could only be accomplished, he believed, by scrupulously following the established rules of eighteenth-century warfare. Knox's attitudes and actions regarding *jus in bello* stemmed from multiple sources. Reading numerous works on military science before the Revolution had led him to think of and imagine war in conventional terms. Unlike the law, Knox had a genuine passion for military texts, and throughout the war he revealed both the breadth and depth of his knowledge. As a result, he gained respect and stature among political and army leaders. John Adams, for example, requested in early 1776 that Knox provide him with a list of essential military works to be read by new junior officers in the Continental Army so that they could begin to master the intricacies of combat, drill, and discipline. In response, Knox provided his fellow Bostonian with a detailed and lengthy list, starting with "a variety of Books translated into English." At the top was "the great Marechal Saxe," French marshal Maurice de Saxe (1696–1750), and his work *Mes Reveries.* Published in 1757, the book was organized into twenty discrete chapters, each dealing with a specific topic, including artillery and small arms, marching formations, and the "Qualifications necessary for the Commander in Chief." Saxe aimed to treat war as a precise science governed by unalterable rules and laws. "Tis he," Knox explained, "who has done more toward reducing war to fix'd principles than perhaps any man of the age." In addition to Saxe, other more-focused military treatises were crucial not only for officers to read but for political leaders as well. "Mullers Artillery and Hollidays principles of Gunnery . . . and Pleydells field fortification are Books so necessary for a people struggling for Liberty and Empire, that they well merit the attention of even your respectable assembly of patriots." Underscoring the need for these essential works, Knox even urged Congress to print them at public expense. "The Cause in which we are engag'd is of such infinite moment to America," he finished, "that no costs or pains can be too great to make the Conclusion happy."[27]

During the war, moreover, Knox repeatedly referred back to his prewar readings. Three months after forwarding his list to Adams, he penned another letter to the Massachusetts delegate, this time to urge Congress to raise the pay of men and officers. Explaining that "the first emotions" for war had now "subsided," he stated that enlisted men would no longer suffer having "nothing to remit to their families;" nor were officers "vastly riveted to the honor of starving their families for the sake of being in the army." As if to seal his argument for more adequate pay, Knox concluded, "I wish you to consult Marshall Saxe on the Chapter of paying the troops."[28]

When dealing with General Washington, Knox also frequently wore his military readings on his sleeve. In late November 1777, for instance, as military operations that year finally came to a conclusion, some general officers urged the commander in chief to make one last frontal assault against British forces then entrenched around Philadelphia. Disagreeing, Knox wrote, "I believe there is not a single maxim in War that will justify a number of undisciplin'd troops attacking an equal number of disciplind troops strongly posted in redoubts and having a strong city in their rear such as Philadelphia." He then informed Washington not only that "Marshall Saxe says redoubts are the strongest and most excellent kind of Field Fortification" but also that "Charles the 12th with the best troops in the World was totally ruin'd in the attack of some redoubts at Pultowa."[29] Five days later, after Washington had agreed to end the campaign season, Knox followed up with advice regarding the coming winter encampment based on other readings. "The King of Prussia says," he asserted, "'the first object in Winter quarters is Tranquility,'" something the artillery commander clearly thought his men needed after months of hard marching and fighting.[30]

Washington respected Knox in part because he was an inspiring officer who knew how to accomplish important missions. But the commander also deeply esteemed him because of his knowledge and understanding of eighteenth-century military literature. Washington encouraged other Continental Army officers to read these same texts, explaining that there was "a great deal of useful knowledge and Instruction to be drawn" from them. As a result of the commander's advice, numerous officers obtained the key works Knox had recommended and sought to master their contents. Hessian officer Johann Ewald, for instance, noted that whenever he and his fellow Germans captured American baggage, they found that almost "every wretched knapsack . . . would be filled up with military books." Indeed, he claimed that his men had found over one hundred well-thumbed copies of Frederick the Great's *Instructions to His Generals* in pilfered enemy supplies over the course of the war.[31]

Knox and many other officers furthermore concluded that the American Revolution needed to be fought as a conventional war—conducted strictly according to eighteenth-century military customs—because of a shared past that they had all collectively experienced. While a soldier deeply committed to independence, Knox viewed the Revolution as a war to *preserve* those liberties inherited from previous generations. He was no forward-thinking radical who envisioned a more level society in social, economic, or even political terms. Rather, he believed that American society would continue to exist after the war as it had throughout his entire life, particularly in terms of its traditional class hierarchies and social structures. Therefore, he concluded that not only should the Revolution be fought in a conventional manner but also that the Continental Army should be organized along traditional lines, with rigid divisions between officers and men. This mindset certainly reflected the attitude of Washington, who insisted that an army could only function when ordinary soldiers gave "due subordination" to officers whom they considered to be "gentlemen of honor."[32]

Although no consensus existed in America regarding the specific qualities that defined a gentleman in civilian life, the need for gentlemanly officers who would be governed by the eighteenth century's martial code of honor was widely acknowledged and accepted. Such men were to display virtuous conduct and bravery in combat as well as practice humane treatment toward those who were powerless to defend themselves. By their example and qualities, they would ensure discipline in the ranks, prevent wanton destruction, and earn the respect of all mankind.[33] Like Washington, Knox also believed that he and his fellow officers were motivated to make such sacrifices by the noble ideals of preserving liberty, protecting self-government, and establishing the United States as a strong and independent republic. As a result, he always sought to promote and protect the interests of the army's officer corps.

Knox also understood, however, that most officers, including himself, were further motivated by personal ambition. While American society was hierarchical in the eighteenth century, it was not socially rigid. Rather, men of humble birth, low economic status, and modest educations could and indeed did rise in late-colonial society. Knox's own advancement testifies to this relative openness in America's social order. Yet ambition impelled him not merely to fight in the revolution but also to fight it along traditional lines. Like other men of modest origins, such as Franklin, he understood the hurdles he needed to overcome to rise into elite society. Also like Franklin, Knox further knew that one way he could overcome these obstacles was to strictly follow conventional mores and practices, though he realized that he must do so more proficiently and credibly than those born to certain advantages. Understanding that humble men in the past particularly had gained great status through military achievements, Knox conscientiously executed his soldierly duties throughout the war. He also aggressively pursued promotion whenever the opportunity presented itself and rigidly followed conventional military etiquette regarding an officer's honor and reputation. In the fall of 1775, for example, Knox knew that many in the Continental Army's general staff, including Washington, wished him to be made chief engineer, with a colonel's commission. Yet he soon learned that some in the Congress wished only to commission him a lieutenant colonel. Bristling at this check to his ambition, he stiffly told Adams, "I have the most sacred regard for the liberties of my country and am fully determined to act as far as my power in opposition to the present tyranny," but "as all honor is comparative I humbly hope that I have as good pretensions to the rank of Col. as many now in the service, the declining to confer which by the delegates not a little supriz'd me. If your respectable body should not incline to give the rank and pay of Col. I must beg to decline it, not but I will do every service in power as a Volunteer."[34] Needing Knox's talents and services, Congress commissioned him a full colonel six weeks later.

Honor and reputation, though, were intangible and fragile commodities in eighteenth-century America, and thus Knox scrupulously protected both whenever perceived threats or even slights arose. Indeed, he twice threatened to resign his commission when he observed such challenges to his newly won status and rank. In May 1777, for instance, Lucy wrote from Boston, "A french general, who stiles himself Commander in Chief of the Continental Artillery is now in Town." The French officer was Phillippe du Coudray, who had been promised by American minister Silas Deane both command of the American artillery and a major general's commission. Understanding her husband's ambitions and ambitious herself, Lucy continued: "This I am sure of, he will never suffer anyone to command him in that department. If he does, he has not that Soul which I think him possessed of."[35] Lucy Knox knew her man. On July 1 her husband wrote Hancock, then president of the Continental Congress, that if du Coudray was given command of the artillery, "I beg the favor of a permission to Retire, and that a proper certificate for that purpose be Sent me immediately."[36] Two fellow generals, Greene and John Sullivan, also threatened to resign if du Coudray was given the command. The letters infuriated Congress, which unanimously resolved that it considered the missives "an Invasion of the Liberties of the People," the officers having used threats of resignation to influence the people's representatives. Hancock wrote Washington that his generals must acknowledge "the Impropriety of the[ir] Conduct."[37] Knox angrily told Lucy that "conscious of the rectitude of my intention . . . I shall make [no] such acknowledgement whatever." Washington supported Knox, and du Coudray quietly joined the army as a volunteer. Thus, the artillery commander emerged from the controversy with his honor and reputation intact, if not enhanced, among the other officers in the American encampment.[38]

The following year Congress again nearly drove Knox to resign due to actions he believed undermined the rank and gentlemanly reputation he had worked hard to establish. In February 1778 the American legislature created the Board of Ordnance, responsible for securing arms and ammunition for the Continental Army and to which Knox would be subordinate. This arrangement, the artillery commander soon pleaded to Washington, put him in an "awkward situation," for in "all considerable Armies in Europe a General Officer has the command and direction of the Artillery and the preparation of any thing appertaining to the Ordnance."[39] Congress's actions, however, had essentially stripped Knox of this part of his command responsibility, thus he demanded modifications. By year's end, though, Congress had not acted, and the Ordnance Board operated as before. Knox told Washington that he had had enough. While he wished to serve his country, he could not do so "under such circumstances as shall reflect dishonor on me." If Congress made no alterations, he wanted "an honorable dismission by that respectable Body."[40] Once again, Washington stepped in and smoothed things out to his artillery commander's satisfaction.

Knox furthermore felt obligated to live as a gentleman of rank, honor, and status. His headquarters and lodgings were, whenever possible, in genteel and commodious homes near his artillery encampments. During the Newburgh cantonment late in the war, for example, he quartered in John Ellison's house, a sturdy Georgian-style mansion built in 1754 (and still stands today). Knox, moreover, genteelly supplied his headquarters to the best of his financial ability. In 1777 he forwarded his wife in Boston a list of essential items he needed both for himself and his staff. Although Lucy responded by castigating him for thinking she lived in "a land of plenty," she soon sent him a wagon loaded with madeira wine, port, brandy, tea, coffee, loaf sugar, pepper, and sweet meats.[41]

Knox fully realized that ambitions for his own advancement and those for the success of the new United States overlapped. Knowing his own mind and supremely confident in himself, he neither rationalized nor apologized for mingling these two goals. "I can see no reason why," he told Lucy, "individuals may not make war as ever on his own account as to assist it on account of the public."[42] Yet given the social and political worldview to which he subscribed, self-interest and the public good meant fighting the Revolution according to just, civilized, and traditional principles. "I dislike the mode of making war like Savages," he explained, "war has horrors enough which are inseparable from its nature." Therefore, "we ought [to] try every means in our power to endever to soften its rough visage."[43] Above all, such behavior would redound to the glory of the United States and further prove to the world the worthiness of a freedom-loving people. Knox even looked to republican Rome for guidance and inspiration on this point. Days after the disastrous defeat of the Continental Army at the Battle of Long Island (August 27, 1776), he claimed, "if we possess the spirit of that people whose General Character I admire, the Romans, we shall yet be a happy brave & free people."[44]

The character of a "happy brave & free people" also meant—at least in the eighteenth century—not only fighting according to the rules of civilized combat but also providing humane treatment to helpless foes in their care. Therefore, Knox once told his wife how "pleas'd" he was about the "kind treatment" American soldiers gave to British prisoners in the army's custody. He also demanded the same standard of treatment from the British. Initially, enemy officers seemed to be acting in a similar fashion toward the Americans. Indeed, Knox noted to Lucy in 1776 that Continental prisoners then "in the enemies [*sic*] hands are treated with great humanity & politeness" and that this "seems to have been in consequence of our kind treatment of their prisoners."[45]

A "happy brave & free" people in the 1700s also deserved to be treated in a genteel, respectful, and civilized manner, especially by enemy officers with whom the Americans believed themselves to be equal. At the war's outset, however, Knox realized that most Crown officers considered the Americans to be anything but their equals. The British general Lord Percy, for instance, claimed that the Continental Army was filled with "artful villains, without religion or morality."[46] Shortly before the New York campaign, Vice Admiral Lord Richard Howe's private secretary, Ambrose Serle, lampooned Washington as a "little paltry colonel of militia at the head of banditti [of] rebels."[47] Knox, therefore, was determined that he and his fellow officers would be taken seriously by the enemy and that the new republic itself would be treated with the utmost respect. To this end, he meticulously described those instances where British officers seemed to treat their Continental counterparts in an equal manner. In July 1776, for example, when the Howe brothers sought a meeting with Washington to discuss possible peace negotiations, Knox and Colonel Joseph Reed initially parleyed with the British officer conveying the admiral and general's request. Seeing the letter was addressed to "George Washington Esqr.," Reed told the enemy officer that no "George Washington Esqr." resided in the American encampment, only "General Washington." Therefore, they could not accept the message. The three officers then "went off," though Knox was careful to add, only "after having saluted & bowed to each other."[48]

The Howes tried to reopen negotiations six days later, this time sending the adjutant general of the British army, Lieutenant Colonel James Paterson, to the American garrison in New York with "a letter directed to 'George Washington Eqr &c &c.'" The colonel made it past the American pickets guarding the Manhattan shoreline whereupon he was taken to the mansion at No. 1 Broadway, where Knox himself lodged. Paterson there met with Washington, Knox, and several other American officers. Knox assiduously described the scene to his wife, emphasizing Washington's superb manners and the British messenger's abundant respect for his commander in chief. Indeed, Paterson endeavored, Knox explained, "in very elegant polite strains" to convince the general to accept and read the Howes' letter, even though it was directed to "George Washington Eqr. &c &c." "In the course of his talk, every other word" Paterson spoke "was we may please your Excellency[,] if your Excellency &c pleases. In short, no person could pay more respect than the said Adj. Gen." When the British officer explained that the "&c &c" in the letter's address "implied every thing," Washington wryly answered it could also mean "any thing." When the commander then heard that the Howes possessed great pardon powers from the king, Washington again sardonically countered, "The Americans had not offended, therefore, they needed no pardon." Knox especially noted how the general "was very handsomely dress'd and made a most elegant appearance." Perhaps best of all, Paterson "appear'd awe struck [by Washington] as if he was before something supernatural."[49] From Knox's perception, it was only the respect that the commander of a great cause deserved from an enemy junior officer. In his own report of the interview to Congress, Washington too noted the British officer's respect for his counterparts in the Continental Army, writing, "Col. Paterson behaved with the greatest Politeness & attention during the whole Business."[50]

As officers in the Continental Army strove to conduct war in a civilized manner, Knox and many others soon convinced themselves that the British military and its German allies had all but abandoned war's traditional limitations, especially as the conflict dragged on and losses mounted. They were outraged not only at the treatment of combatants and civilians during the New Jersey campaign of 1776–77 but also by other incidents that they labeled as atrocities. The killing of Lieutenant William Martin, for instance, seemed to epitomize to many Americans the escalating savagery on the part of the enemy. On May 31, 1777, a Hessian Jäger patrol surprised Lieutenant Martin and his scouting party of ten men. Outnumbered and soon surrounded, Martin supposedly cried out for quarter but was instead savagely and repeatedly bayoneted by the Germans. The cavalrymen then decapitated his corpse and left it to rot. The following morning, Knox told his wife, he had just learned that a party of Continental scouts had been "cut to pieces" by the enemy, though he did not elaborate. Soon an American patrol found Martin's body and returned it to the army's camp. A disgusted and furious Washington ordered it displayed "as an undeniable evidence of the [enemy's] brutality." The commander then sent the corpse through British lines along with a letter to General Charles Cornwallis demanding an explanation for this "spirit of wanton cruelty, that in several instances influenced the conduct of your soldiery."[51]

Five years later, attitudes among American leaders about enemy savagery had only hardened. In 1782, Loyalist soldiers serving under the king's banner had captured and hanged a New Jersey artillery captain named Joshua Huddy without any trial or judicial proceeding, supposedly for the murder of a Tory refugee.

Outraged again at yet another "instance of Barbarity by the enemy," Washington and many other high-ranking officers pledged to hang a British prisoner of equal rank in retaliation.[52] Although seventeen-year-old British captain Charles Asgill was eventually selected by lot for execution, Knox and several other officers objected. The glory and reputation of the American cause demanded that the Continental Army not lower itself by acting in such an uncivilized fashion. While Alexander Hamilton had left the military for Congress by 1782, he strenuously argued that killing Asgill would be "derogatory to our national character." Knox agreed and told Hamilton that, in his opinion, "frequent executions" by the Americans would do more harm than good. Indeed, "they will hereafter be recited to sully the purity of our cause."[53] Such concerns soon delayed the hanging, and after the French intervened to plead for mercy, Asgill was formally exchanged and returned home. As a result, the cause in Knox's eyes remained unsullied and the traditional rules of civilized warfare (at least in terms of how the Continentals practiced it) prevailed until the Revolution's conclusion.

Legal theories regarding just war were important to revolutionary writers and to the statesmen leading political efforts to resist British actions. Such ideas and concepts provided these men with clearly articulated principles and a general framework through which they could mobilize public opinion about the righteousness of the American cause. Men such as Henry Knox, steeped neither in political nor constitutional theories, nevertheless still believed in the profound justice of the American cause and in the Continental Army's civilized mode of warfare. Yet it was the deeply rooted culture of colonial self-government, individual liberties, and traditional social values that led him (and others) to such conclusions. Many participants in the war and later writers acknowledged the powerful influence exerted by inherited practices and mores upon the citizens. Washington, for example, wrote during the winter at Valley Forge that "the people at large are governed much by custom" and thus were protective of their traditional rights as well as suspicious of distant authorities. Fifty years later the Frenchmen Alexis de Tocqueville wrote in *Democracy in America* that citizens of the United States had long possessed certain "habits of the heart" crucial to "the maintenance of a democratic republic."[54] Knox's belief in the inherent virtue of the American cause continued to shape his actions throughout the conflict. Indeed, he insisted on making war strictly by *jus in bello* principles. This honorable approach, he held, would most certainly redound to his own reputation as a gentlemanly officer, thus furthering his own advancement. Practicing war in a just fashion would, above all, add to the reputation of the United States and prove to the world the civilized nobility of the newly independent American people.

NOTES

1. Francis S. Drake, *Life and Correspondence of Henry Knox* (Boston: S. G. Drake, 1873), chap. 1; North Callahan, *Henry Knox: General Washington's General* (New York: Rinehart, 1958), 16–33. On Boston's economic stagnation, see Benjamin L. Carp, *Defiance of the Patriots: The Boston Tea Party and the Making of America* (New Haven: Yale University Press, 2010), 32–33. For a recent popular biography of Henry Knox, see Mark Puls, *Henry Knox: Visionary General of the American Revolution* (New York, 2008). The best scholarly biography of Knox, though, remains Callahan, *Henry Knox.* For a recent insightful account of Knox's relationship with Washington, see Mark Thompson, "Guns of the Revolution: Henry Knox, George Washington, and the War of American Independence," in *Sons of the Father: George Washington and His Protégés,* ed. Robert M. S. McDonald (Charlottesville: University of Virginia Press, 2014), 120–48.
2. Carp, *Defiance of the Patriots,* 32–33.
3. *Boston Gazette,* 29 July 1771.
4. "Henry Knox and the London Book Store in Boston, 1771–1774," *Proceedings of the Massachusetts Historical Society,* 3rd ser., 61 (June 1928).
5. J. L. Bell, "Pope Night in Boston," *Boston 1775* (blog), 6 Nov. 2006, http://boston1775.blogspot.com/2006/11/pope-night-in-boston.html, accessed 12 Sept. 2014; Callahan, *Henry Knox,* 18. For more information on Boston's Pope Day reveries in general, see Carp, *Defiance of the Patriots,* 31–32.
6. Callahan, *Henry Knox,* 19–20.
7. *Massachusetts Gazette* and *the Boston Weekly News-Letter,* 12 Mar. 1772.
8. The Thursday Night Club is discussed in Henry Jackson to Henry Knox, 20 July 1774, Gilder Lehrman Collection, Gilder Lehrman Institute of American History, New York [hereafter GLC].
9. "Other Boston Massacre Trial Depositions," Boston Massacre Historical Society, http://www.bostonmassacre.net/trial/d-more.htm, accessed 17 Aug. 2015. Knox later testified for the prosecution, and it is clear that he believed that the British troops had acted in the wrong. Regarding Knox's actions that evening, see also Callahan, *Henry Knox,* chap. 1.
10. For Knox's interactions with Hancock and his ships, see Henry Knox Wastebook, 21 Nov., 21 Dec. 1771, July 1772, 31 May, 17 Nov., 31 Dec. 1773, Massachusetts Historical Society, Boston.
11. On Knox's work with Paul Revere, see James Rivington to Henry Knox, 17 Mar., 8, 20 Apr. 1774, GLC. On Boston's reaction to the Tea Act, see Carp, *Defiance of the Patriots,* chaps. 2–4 passim.
12. Drake, *Life and Correspondence of Henry Knox* 12; Adams quoted in Julie Flavell, *When London Was Capital of America* (New Haven, Conn.: Yale University Press, 2010), 118.
13. Henry Knox (hereafter HK) to Lucy Knox, 28 Aug. 1776, GLC.
14. HK to Henry Jackson, 29 Aug. 1774, ibid. The "co-adjustors" Knox mentions likely refers to the mandamus councilors Gage appointed to replace the old governor's council. His father-in-law, Thomas Flucker, was one of the councilors selected by

the British general, who was now also the colony's royal governor.

15. "Letter from Paul Revere to Jeremy Belknap, circa 1798," Massachusetts Historical Society Collections Online, http://www.masshist.org/database/99, accessed 21 Aug. 2015. David Hackett Fischer most recently makes this argument in *Paul Revere's Ride* (New York: Oxford University Press, 1994), 58, 382n.
16. James Thacher, *A Military Journal during the American Revolutionary War, 1775 to 1783. . .*, 2nd ed., rev. and corrected (Boston: Cottons & Barnard, 1827), 17.
17. HK to Lucy Knox, 15 Aug. 1776, GLC.
18. Nathanael Greene to Catharine Greene, [ca. 20 Dec. 1775], *The Papers of General Nathanael Greene*, ed. Richard K. Showman, vol. 1 (Chapel Hill: University of North Carolina Press, 1976), 116. The friendship between the two men probably began to flourish in the summer of 1775, when both worked on constructing fortifications around Roxbury, southwest of the besieged Boston.
19. HK to Lucy Knox, 10 Jan. 1777, GLC.
20. David Hackett Fischer, *Washington's Crossing* (New York: Oxford University Press, 2006), 178–79. Congress's report was republished in the *Pennsylvania Evening Post*, 24 Apr. 1777. See also Thacher, *Military Journal*, 72.
21. Eliga H. Gould, *Among the Powers of the Earth: The American Revolution and the Making of a New World Empire* (Cambridge, Mass.: Harvard University Press, 2012), 79–80.
22. HK to Lucy Knox, 6 Apr. 1777, GLC.
23. HK to Lucy Knox, 21 June 1777, ibid. The latter quotation is from HK to Lucy Knox, 10 Jan. 1777, ibid.
24. T. H. Breen, *American Insurgents, American Patriots* (New York: Hill and Wang, 2011), 11. Breen is also quoted in Gordon S. Wood, *The Idea of America* (New York: Penguin, 2012), 13.
25. "To John Adams from Henry Knox, 16 May 1776," *Founders Online*, National Archives, last modified 29 June 2015, http://founders.archives.gov/documents/Adams/06-04-02-0081 (from *The Adams Papers, Papers of John Adams*, vol. 4, *February–August 1776*, ed. Robert J. Taylor [Cambridge, Mass.: Harvard University Press, 1979], 189–91).
26. HK to Lucy Knox, 15, 28 Dec. 1776, GLC. Knox's phrase "orders all things for the better" is from his 15 December letter; the phrase "sacred calls of my Country" is from his letter of thirteen days later. Nathanael Greene also predicted to his wife in early December 1776 that "all things will turn out for the best" due to the divine will of Providence. Nathanael Greene to Catharine Greene, 4 Dec. 1776, *Papers of Nathanael Greene*, 365.
27. "To John Adams from Henry Knox, 16 May 1776," *Founders Online*, National Archives, last modified June 29, 2017, http://founders.archives.gov/documents/Adams/06-04-02-0081 (from *The Adams Papers, Papers of John Adams*, 4:189–91).
28. "To John Adams from Henry Knox, 21 August 1776," *Founders Online*, National Archives, last modified June 29, 2017, http://founders.archives.gov/documents/Adams/06-04-02-0225 (from *The Adams Papers, Papers of John Adams*, 4:483–85).
29. "To George Washington from Brigadier General Henry Knox, 26 November 1777," *Founders Online*, National Archives, last modified June 29, 2017, http://founders.

archives.gov/documents/Washington/03-12-02-0407 (from *The Papers of George Washington, Revolutionary War Series,* vol. 12, *26 October 1777–25 December 1777,* ed. Frank E. Grizzard Jr. and David R. Hoth [Charlottesville: University Press of Virginia, 2002], 414–17).

30. To George Washington from Brigadier General Henry Knox, 1 December 1777," *Founders Online,* National Archives, last modified June 29, 2017, http://founders.archives.gov/documents/Washington/03-12-02-0448 (from *The Papers of George Washington, Revolutionary War Series,* 12:465–66).
31. Sandra L. Powers, "Studying the Art of War: Military Books Known to American Officers and Their French Counterparts during the Second Half of the Eighteenth Century," *Journal of Military History* 70 (2006): 791 (Ewald quote); Caroline Cox, *A Proper Sense of Honor: Service and Sacrifice in George Washington's Army* (Chapel Hill: University of North Carolina Press, 2004), 44 (Washington quote).
32. Robert Middlekauff, *Washington's Revolution: The Making of America's First Leader* (New York: Alfred A. Knopf, 2015), 122. On the general issue of hierarchy in the army, see Cox, *Proper Sense of Honor,* chaps. 1–2.
33. Armstrong Starkey, "Paoli to Stony Point: Military Ethics and Weaponry during the American Revolution," *Journal of Military History* 58, no. 1 (Jan. 1994): 20.
34. "To John Adams from Henry Knox, 26 October 1775," *Founders Online,* National Archives, last modified 29 June 2015, http://founders.archives.gov/documents/Adams/06-03-02-0133 (from *The Adams Papers, Papers of John Adams,* vol. 3, *May 1775–January 1776,* ed. Robert J. Taylor [Cambridge, Mass.: Harvard University Press, 1979], 253–54).
35. Lucy Knox to Henry Knox, 18–24 May 1777, GLC.
36. HK to John Hancock, 1 July 1777, ibid..
37. "To George Washington from John Hancock, 8 July 1777," *Founders Online,* National Archives, last modified 1 Dec. 2014, http://founders.archives.gov/documents/Washington/03-10-02-0216 (from *The Papers of George Washington, Revolutionary War Series,* vol. 10, *11 June 1777–18 August 1777,* ed. Frank E. Grizzard Jr. [Charlottesville: University Press of Virginia, 2000], 227–28).
38. HK to Lucy Knox, 13 July 1777, GLC.
39. "To George Washington from Brigadier General Henry Knox, 15 June 1778," *Founders Online,* National Archives, last modified 29 June 2015, http://founders.archives.gov/documents/Washington/03-15-02-0423 (from *The Papers of George Washington, Revolutionary War Series,* vol. 15, *May–June 1778,* ed. Edward G. Lengel [Charlottesville: University of Virginia Press, 2006], 401–2).
40. "To George Washington from Brigadier General Henry Knox, 30 December 1778," ibid., last modified 29 June 2015, http://founders.archives.gov/documents/Washington/03-18-02-0594 (from *The Papers of George Washington, Revolutionary War Series,* vol. 18, ed. Edward G. Lengel [Charlottesville: University of Virginia Press, 2008], 531).
41. Lucy Knox to HK, 3–5, 19 June, 23 Aug. 1777, GLC.
42. HK to Lucy Knox, 12 Aug. 1777, ibid.
43. HK to Lucy Knox, 7 Sept. 1776, ibid.

44. Ibid.
45. Ibid.
46. Starkey, "Paoli to Stony Point," 24.
47. Quoted in Gould, *Among the Powers of the Earth,* 115.
48. HK to Lucy Knox, 15 July 1776, GLC.
49. HK to Lucy Knox, 22 July 1776, ibid.
50. "Memorandum of an Interview with Lieutenant Colonel James Paterson, 20 July 1776," *Founders Online,* National Archives, last modified 30 Dec. 2015, http://founders.archives.gov/documents/Washington/03-05-02-0295 (from *The Papers of George Washington, Revolutionary War Series,* vol. 5, *16 June 1776–12 August 1776,* ed. Philander D. Chase [Charlottesville: University Press of Virginia, 1993], 398–403).
51. HK to Lucy Knox, 1 June 1777, GLC; "From Alexander Hamilton to John Jay, 2 June 1777," *Founders Online,* National Archives, last modified 29 June 2015, http://founders.archives.gov/documents/Hamilton/01-01-02-0174 (from *The Papers of Alexander Hamilton,* vol. 1, *1768–1778,* ed. Harold C. Syrett [New York: Columbia University Press, 1961], 261–64); "From George Washington to Lieutenant General Cornwallis, 2 June 1777," ibid., last modified 29 June 2015, http://founders.archives.gov/documents/Washington/03-09-02-0588 (from *The Papers of George Washington, Revolutionary War Series,* vol. 9, *28 March 1777–10 June 1777,* ed. Philander D. Chase [Charlottesville: University Press of Virginia, 1999], 591–92).
52. "From George Washington to John Hanson, 20 April 1782," *Founders Online,* National Archives, last modified 29 June 2015, http://founders.archives.gov/documents/Washington/99-01-02-08207 (early access document).
53. "From Alexander Hamilton to Major General Henry Knox, [7 June 1782]," *Founders Online,* National Archives, last modified 29 June 2015, http://founders.archives.gov/documents/Hamilton/01-03-02-0026 [last update: 2015–06–29 (from *The Papers of Alexander Hamilton,* vol. 3, *1782–1786,* ed. Harold C. Syrett [New York: Columbia University Press, 1962], 91–93); HK to Alexander Hamilton, 24 July 1782, GLC. Knox also made it clear in his letter to Hamilton that Washington felt much the same way as him and was seeking ways out of the situation.
54. "From George Washington to Henry Laurens, 14–15 December 1777," *Founders Online,* National Archives, last modified 29 Sept. 2015, http://founders.archives.gov/documents/Washington/03-12-02-0553 (from *The Papers of George Washington, Revolutionary War Series,* 12:604–7). Tocqueville's phrase "habits of the heart" is from *Democracy in America,* bk. 1, chap. 17.

7 LIBERTY OR DEATH!

Jus in Bello and Existential Warfare in the American Revolution

Mark Edward Lender and James Kirby Martin

> Is life so dear, or peace so sweet, as to be purchased at the price of chains and slavery? Forbid it, Almighty God! I know not what course others may take; but as for me, give me liberty or give me death!
>
> Attributed to Patrick Henry, March 23, 1775

Whether Patrick Henry ever uttered the rousing words Patriots attributed to him, he certainly captured the spirit of the moment. American Whigs, their emotions fueled by more than a decade of resentments over British imperial policies and convinced that they were victims of a vast conspiracy against traditional liberties, saw the future in stark terms. Virtuous citizens had a choice: confront tyranny or see all they held dear perish. Liberty or death! There could be no middle ground. Addressing the Georgia Provincial Congress, rebel governor Archibald Bulloch put the case equally bluntly: "This is no time to talk of moderation; in the present instance it ceases to be a virtue."[1] It was in this mood that Patriots marched off to war.

Historians have long debated the nature of that war. Early on, popular enthusiasm echoed Henry and Bulloch and carried tens of thousands of Americans to rebel colors, only to see the *rage militaire* fade as the war dragged on. Patriots learned that wars are not won by zeal alone, but they are won by blood, suffering, disease, brutality, exhaustion, terror, and all the other accompanying tribulations that tormented the rebellious colonies for eight long years. Amid all of this, however, some historians have found a remarkable restraint among the combatants—a conscious desire to mitigate the worst excesses of violence. These same studies even point to the European Enlightenment doctrine of *jus in bello* as the guiding hand behind this presumed inclination toward moderation.[2]

Jus in bello was a reaction to the horrors of the Thirty Years' War (1618–48), and it sought to define acceptable and unacceptable martial behavior. While a number of Enlightenment scholars wrote on the subject, the most influential were the Dutch Hugo Grotius and the Swiss Emer de Vattel. Grotius published *De jure belli ac pacis libri tres* (*On the Law of War and Peace: Three Books*) in 1625, asserting in Book Three that natural law bound all combatants, no matter what the cause of the war, to certain standards of humane conduct. Vattel, whose *Law of Nations* (1758) stands as the most comprehensive exposition of *jus in bello*, wrote with the hope of marking the "just bounds" of war and "by the rules of justice, equity, and humanity, to moderate the exercise" of military conduct.[3] Scholars who see the influence of the Enlightenment in America naturally see *jus in bello*, and specifically Grotius and Vattel, reflected in aspects of the Patriot struggle for independence.[4]

This chapter, however, finds much of this perspective wanting, both in theory and in practice. Rather, the evidence demonstrates that the War for Independence was more reflective of the passions voiced by Henry and Bulloch—and that restraint was more the exception than the rule. Instead, revolutionary America tacitly adopted what we have called "existential warfare"—warfare in which combatants believed their very existence is in question, leading to an acceptance of violence against persons and property as preferable to defeat, which is equated with political, cultural, and even physical extinction. This meant war with few restrictions and an expectation and acceptance of ferocity and brutality, anything to avoid defeat. *Jus in bello* was present during the war, but its influence was marginal beyond Patriot and British elites; our purpose is to explain why and how this came to be.

I

The doctrine of *jus in bello* did limit military savagery in eighteenth-century Europe, where states fought primarily over limited territorial or dynastic objectives. And it is true the Enlightenment ideal, along with a related sense of military honor, played a role in curbing excesses during the War for Independence. Most senior British officers and many in the colonial elite were familiar with the *jus in bello* ideal. Translations of Grotius had been available for some time, and the first English translation of Vattel's *The Law of Nations* appeared in 1760 and apparently crossed the Atlantic soon thereafter.[5] In 1773 Washington ordered copies of both authors' works for a relative (although he may not have read Vattel himself until the 1790s), and at least one colonial governor cited Grotius in questioning the legality of capturing Indians during a formal truce.[6]

Vattel also was in evidence as the imperial crisis came to a head. John Adams noted citations to *The Law of Nations* in debates with Massachusetts governor Thomas Hutchinson, while he and Thomas Jefferson consulted Vattel in deciding points of law (especially on naval or military prize seizures) during the Revolution. Benjamin Franklin had a copy of *The Law of Nations* and indicated that members of the Continental Congress knew of the work.[7] Elite familiarity with *jus in bello,* however, was not the same as agreeing on its utility, nor was it necessarily an indication of its influence beyond Patriot military and social leaders.

Although it is difficult to assess any direct influence of Grotius and Vattel on military conduct, there were reasons beyond a philosophical ideal for avoiding excesses. Washington clearly believed that a policy of brutality toward civilians (even Tories) would alienate popular support for his army and its cause. His opponents, Lieutenant Generals Sir William Howe and Sir Henry Clinton, thought the same. With or without any notions of *jus in bello,* the sheer horror of war's miseries was enough to move some contemporaries to urge moderation and humanity in the struggle. From Congress Adams wrote his wife, Abigail, "I am obliged to hear continual accounts of the barbarities, the cruel Murders in cold blood, even the most tormenting ways of starving and freezing committed by our Enemies." A shocked Adams insisted American policy should be that of "Piety, Humanity and Honesty," even in the face of "Blasphemy, Cruelty and Villainy."[8] Citing these and other examples, historian Wayne E. Lee found restraint and the influence of *jus in bello* characteristic of key facets of the American war effort—specifically among Washington's regular troops.[9]

This conclusion seems to be generally solid. Evidence suggests that ranking officers of the regular Continental and British armies often tried to avoid needless carnage. Senior commanders on both sides knew that wanton violence, the plundering of civilians, and the mistreatment of prisoners and wounded would lead only to retaliation from opponents. Restraint had its benefits. Thus, regular officers often abided by European standards of military etiquette and honor, frequently exchanging messages under flags of truce and trying to prevent the pillage of civilian property and gratuitous harm to noncombatants. Instances of an enemy not "fighting fair" met principled objections. Washington and Howe, for example, both denounced the practice of soldiers cutting musket balls in order to inflict more damage to an opponent (although soldiers continued to do so). Lieutenant Colonel John Graves Simcoe of the Queen's American Rangers—a crack Loyalist regiment—deplored the practice of firing on sentries if no greater action was intended.[10] Another preference was to offer opponents terms of surrender rather than forcing bloody battles to the last man. There would be nasty exceptions, but senior officers, at least among the regulars, were supposed to behave as gentlemen.

Combat was harsh enough, but the incidents of restraint were quite real. After the dramatic storming of Stony Point, Brigadier General Anthony Wayne, whose command Major General Charles "No Flint" Grey had devastated at Paoli, permitted no abuse of British wounded and prisoners. As his troops marched across New Jersey in 1778 Lieutenant General Clinton, impressed with the courage of a dying militia officer who refused to disclose the location of his comrades, had the man buried with the full honors of war (a separate grave, a religious observance or formal recognition of the deceased's courage, and a musket salute). After the Battle of Monmouth, rebels returned the compliment, burying grenadier lieutenant colonel Henry Monckton, the senior British officer killed during the battle, with military honors. Also at Monmouth, Continental doctor William Read walked the bloody field, caring alike for Patriot and British wounded; he personally took charge of British wounded left behind, too injured to move, when General Clinton's army moved out. After the Patriot fiasco at Penobscot (in modern Maine), British brigadier Francis McLean treated rebel prisoners with humanity; he even provided shipping to repatriate some of them.[11] Such incidents were not uncommon and indicated that, as grim as military realties were, things could have been worse.

II

But frequently things were worse—much worse—and a case for restraint as a norm among most combatants, much less restraint with a philosophical (*jus in bello*) basis, goes too far. Convincing as they initially appear, examples of humanity and mitigated violence are too few to sustain such an argument. In reality, there are indications that the ideal of martial restraint carried less weight in any formal sense than some studies have suggested, even among rebels aware of Grotius, Vattel, and similar writers.

Significantly, there was never full agreement on what *jus in bello* precisely condoned or forbade. James Lovell, a fiery Whig congressional delegate from Massachusetts, was clear on this point. Lovell wanted Adams to consult Grotius, Vattel, and others on the technicalities of dealing with Lieutenant General John Burgoyne's Convention Army (Lovell favored breaking the convention and holding the surrendered British as prisoners of war). The congressman noted that interpretations of these authors could "support reason and common sense or destroy both." *Jus in bello* was open to all sorts of interpretation and "dispute" and was likely "to cause a vast expenditure of ink." The interest in *jus in bello* arguably was more utilitarian than theoretical; those who cited Vattel hardly focused primarily on matters of humanity. In a letter to Jefferson, who sought a legal opinion on the ownership of horses captured from Brigadier Benedict Arnold's raiders in early 1781, Edmund Randolph noted that Governor Jefferson and "the [Virginia] council probably have not access to Vattel." Obviously, Randolph did; but the gist of his note made it clear that few other Virginians possessed any *formal* knowledge of Vattel.[12] The opinion on captured horses speaks to this point, as do many specific circumstances of incidents of restraint. In a further example, during his raid in Virginia, the turncoat Arnold studiously avoided needless damage to private property and harm to noncombatants in an effort to woo Virginians back to the king. His restraint was entirely practical; theory had nothing to do with it.[13]

Among the regular troops, British observance of the "rules" of war was problematic—*or not,* depending upon how one interpreted the rules. Certainly, British regulars were wont to be hard on rebels, military and civilian, and believed they had cause. The laws of war were supposed to draw distinctions between soldiers and civilians, whenever possible sparing civilians. But *jus in bello* stressed lawful combat between the recognized armies (that is, between troops regularly raised, uniformed, organized, and officered) of sovereign states. Soldiers were distinct from civilians. Frontier warfare represented the antithesis of this position, recognizing few distinctions between soldiers and civilians. It was much the same with militia warfare, which thoroughly blurred distinctions between combatants and noncombatants. The farmer tilling his field one day could be the citizen-in-arms carrying a musket the next, then easily blend again into the civilian countryside. It was just such an "embattled farmer" who had mercilessly tomahawked a helplessly wounded redcoat near Concord Bridge. Civilians, including women and children, were prime sources of intelligence, served as messengers, and marshaled supplies for rebel forces. Dealing with hostile civilians was a constant source of apprehension and irritation for the British; how was a redcoat to know who the enemy really was? If a soldier caught a civilian in arms, what was he to do? Vattel states specifically that "the [regular] troops alone carry on the war, while the rest of the nation remain in peace. . . . [I]f the peasants of themselves commit any hostilities, the enemy shows them no mercy, but hangs them up as he would so many robbers or banditti."[14] Few British soldiers did any such thing, but no amount of restraint on the part of senior officers could prevent frustrated troops from committing atrocities.

This they did frequently, and the record of such actions belies any general influence of *jus in bello* or any other ideal of restraint. The reality was that even regular troops under senior commanders could be more than casual in attitudes toward any "rules" of humane warfare. In 1776 General Howe's army plundered its way across New Jersey; there were frequent documented instances of rape, and British officers did little to restrain their men. In early 1778 a British foraging expedition under Lieutenant Colonel Charles Mawhood surprised a New Jersey militia detachment at Hancock's Bridge, bayoneting the helpless militia rather than asking for surrender. Mawhood then further threatened to "attack the militia wearing arms, burn their houses, and reduce them, their unfortunate wives, and their children to beggary and distress." New Jersey militia colonel Elijah Hand, seizing the chance for a propaganda coup, quickly retorted, "Your threat to burn and destroy, induces me to imagine that I am reading the orders of a barbarous Attila, and not of a gentleman, brave, generous, and polished."[15] Two years later Clinton's retreating army swept through the state like locusts; while an enraged Clinton offered generous rewards for information on looters and arsonists, no soldier informed on a comrade or camp follower. In June 1780 British troops, infuriated by swarms of sniping militia, who were plainly local residents, burned most of the village of Connecticut Farms, New Jersey, and much of nearby Springfield.[16] Admiral George Rodney's conquest of Saint Eustatius (1781) led to a systematic pillaging of private and public property that almost led to parliamentary calls for his prosecution. The admiral claimed that he was a mere military man with no knowledge of *The Law of Nations*.[17]

This list could go on ad infinitum. Thus, if ideals of humanity in war sought to spare civilians the worst cruelties of martial abuse, there is plenty of reason to question how commonly such notions prevailed among British regulars—at least beyond the thinking or intentions of senior commanders. Certainly, angry redcoats, and especially Loyalist troops, fully believed local Whig rebels deserved to feel the hard hand of war. No listing of "humane" examples of martial conduct can obscure the reality that the War for Independence was often a desperately brutal affair in which warfare as actually *practiced* often had only a tenuous connection to any philosophical ideal of restraint, no matter what the intentions of senior officials may have been.

III

The reasons for the disparity between the ideal and the actual are not hard to find. If senior commanders of the regular armies were the most likely to urge moderation in war—and they were—this point is fatal to any argument for a pervasive *popular* acceptance of *jus in bello,* for most of the fighting over the eight years of conflict did not involve regulars, or did so only marginally. Howard H. Peckham's meticulous compilation of Revolutionary engagements and casualties makes this point abundantly clear. Peckham counted 1,546 land and naval actions between 1775 and 1783. Of the 1,331 land actions, only 60 were primarily engagements between the regular armies; the rest were fights (not necessarily small) between Patriots and Loyalists or Native Americans (sometimes both), with regulars playing only peripheral roles if any at all. Moreover, Peckham's count was conservative. This is the implication of David Munn's more detailed compilation of New Jersey battles and skirmishes. Munn verified more than 600 military and naval engagements in New Jersey or off its immediate coasts. Of these, only 14 pitted the regular armies against one another.[18] The clear implication of the Peckham and Munn studies is that most combat was local and took place without senior British or Continental officers on the scene.

The vast majority of these engagements occurred in a widely dispersed number of "military frontiers."[19] These were the regions in which neither side had established firm military control and in which residents lived in a perpetual state of insecurity. Raids, pillaging, murder, and all manner of violence was a constant possibility. Much of the southern backcountry was such a frontier, as were the eastern shores of Virginia and Maryland; so too were the New Jersey counties fronting British-occupied New York City and its environs, along with the New Jersey and Pennsylvania regions around the British garrison in Philadelphia. The frontier marking Indian-white contact was volatile on an arc running from western New England through the Middle Colonies into the Deep South and west into Trans-Appalachia.[20] Thus, these military frontiers encompassed an enormous span of territory too vast for either of the regular armies to pretend to control. Absent regular officers to urge or enforce restraint (if they were so minded—and as we have seen, they frequently were not), the military frontiers were rife with exactly the sort of combat that most lent itself to unrestrained mayhem. The dark divide between *jus in bello* and the reality of war became most obvious in these regions.

The farther one got from the main armies of Washington, Howe, and Clinton, the more frightful the violence became. This pattern was certainly apparent in conflicts between Loyalists and Patriots; the sheer number of frightful incidents makes it difficult to sustain an argument for military restraint as the prevailing norm among the broadest spectrum of combatants.

This reality was painfully obvious in the South. Prompt Whig action against Tories or would-be Tories in 1775 generally held the backcountry Carolinas and Georgia for the rebel cause until the British invasions of 1778 and 1780. Inhumanity was common, remorse generally scarce. Again, a few examples must illustrate the broader trend. In late 1775 a Georgia Patriot mob confronted Loyalist Thomas Brown, insisting that he support the rebel cause. When he resisted, Whigs fractured his skull with a rifle butt, tarred his legs and held them over a fire, then cut off his hair, scalped him, and left him for dead. The Patriot Georgia Council of Safety, as historian John Buchanan has pointed out, considered the matter something of a lark. "The said Thomas Brown is now a little remarkable, wears his hair very short, and a handkerchief around his head in order that his intellect . . . may not be affected." The council would regret its levity. Brown—"Burntfoot" Brown ever after—lost two toes but recovered to become a talented guerrilla commander and scourge of Patriots for the rest of the war.[21] In early 1777 at Morristown, New Jersey, Patriots hanged two Tories and would have executed dozens of others had those men not "volunteered" for the Continental Army. A year later Pastor Nicholas Collin of Penn's Neck in southwestern New Jersey lamented the calamitous state of affairs: "Everywhere distrust, fear, hatred, and abominable selfishness were met with. Parents and children, brothers and sisters, wife and husband were enemies to one another."[22] After the Battle of Kings Mountain, South Carolina (1780), Patriots sentenced more than thirty surrendered Loyalists to death after drumhead courts-martial. They hanged nine of them—some in front of their relatives—before senior officers said enough.[23] In Monmouth County, New Jersey, Loyalist raids from British-occupied Sandy Hook and Staten Island drove regional Patriots to extreme measures. Under militia general "Black David" Forman (whose malevolent nom de guerre said it all), they organized as the Association for Retaliation. The Retaliators were an extralegal militia organization—actually vigilantes—who terrorized regional Loyalists; their conduct appalled the Patriot state government.[24] This list could go on with example piled on example demonstrating war at its least humane, with all concerned fighting to win at all costs.

If anything, fighting between rebels and Indians was even more ferocious. Warfare on the Indian frontiers was frightening to all but the most hardened combatants and civilians, white or Indian. "Facing east," Native Americans viewed the advance of the colonial farming frontier with alarm; white settlers too often meant dispossession. Tribes negotiated with colonists when they could but fought when they thought they must to defend rights to traditional hunting grounds and indeed their very ways of life. These well-founded fears of white expansion led most western tribes to ally with the British—alliances of rational self-interest rather than any love of King George. "Facing west," white immigrants to the frontiers emerged from the French and Indian War traumatized by Indian warfare. There were few large battles, but frequent, sudden, and ferocious raids kept frontier society, and often beyond, encased in fear. Historian Peter Silver has argued convincingly that the terror was such as to help unify often "fractious" settler communities and imbue them with a sense of victimhood and deep-seated resentments against not only Native Americans but also easterners (especially Quakers) who failed to appreciate their anxieties. Patrick Griffin has extended this argument, asserting that white fears hardened into a racist conception of the "Indians as innately inhuman, irredeemable," and beyond any hope of attaining any civilized state as Europeans understood it.[25] Hatreds were venomous on both sides of the frontier.

The Native American frontiers of New York, Pennsylvania, the South, and the Trans-Appalachian West saw instances of stunning brutality. As with Tory-Patriot conflicts, a brief résumé of Indian-Patriot clashes makes for grim reading. Along the southern frontier, the Cherokees, smarting from defeat in the Anglo-Cherokee War of 1758–61, declared for the British cause. It brought them only grief. In a 1776 campaign Carolina and Virginia troops devastated fifty Cherokee towns and forced the Indians to cede some of their oldest homelands. Defeat also caused an embittered split between Cherokees who sued for peace and those who wanted to fight on, many of whom left for lands in modern Tennessee—from which they would continue their resistance.[26]

Although most frontier warfare consisted of raids on isolated settlements and individual farms, some actions were larger—and devastating. Some of the most destructive were often joint Indian-Loyalist operations, and several examples tell the tale. In July 1778 Loyalist ranger John Butler and some 400 Tories and perhaps 500 Senecas and Cayugas under Cornplanter struck the militia garrison of Forty Fort in the Wyoming Valley of Pennsylvania (near modern Wilkes-Barre). In a tactical masterpiece, the attack virtually annihilated the ineptly led militia. Tales of slaughter in battle and the subsequent torture of prisoners spread across the rebellious colonies, probably exaggerated but with a grisly basis in fact. Hessian captain Johann Ewald reported a conversation with one of Butler's rangers who fought at Wyoming Valley. The ranger supposedly claimed "two whole brigades massacred [this was an exaggeration], of which the greater part were scalped half dead, and in such misery lost their lives." The eyewitness continued that he had "worked so hard with my tomahawk and scalping knife that my arms were bloody above the elbows." Exaggerated tales or not, Patriots believed the worst and decried the "Wyoming Valley Massacre."[27] This did nothing to moderate rebel attitudes toward the Indians and Loyalists.

There was more of the same. On November 11, 1778, Walter Butler (son of John, who was absent with rheumatism) and Joseph Brant descended on the central New York village of Cherry Valley. They failed to carry a stockaded fort, but militia and nearly fifty civilians caught outside fell to musket shot, tomahawk, and scalping knife. Butler and Brant were unable to restrain the bloodshed. The raiders withdrew after burning most of the village, driving off livestock, and cutting up a militia sally from the fort. The Iroquois broadcast the fate of Cherry Valley as a warning to Patriots to stop attacking Indian settlements.[28]

But Brant was not done. A year later he led Indians and Loyalists in a raid on Peenpack (also called Minisink, now Port Jervis), New York, in the upper Delaware Valley. Brant ordered the village destroyed but made sure that women and children were unharmed; the aftermath, however, was less sanguine. When militia gave chase, the raiders trapped them on a hilltop near the Delaware River and finally overran them, killing most. The survivors, their commander, Colonel John Hathorn, reported, were terrified of the "bloody monsters" and expected "nothing . . . but the hatchet, spear, and scalping knife. The tremendous yells and whoops, all the fiends in the confines of the Infernal Regions with one united cry, could not exceed it. Add to this the cries and petitions of the wounded around me not to leave them, was beyond parallel or idea. My heart bleeds for the unfortunate wounded who fell into their hands." Indeed, most of the wounded were slaughtered. Of 170 militia engaged, only 30 men escaped.[29] In proportion to the numbers involved, the Battle of Minisink was one of the worst Patriot defeats of the war and left the region traumatized. At least through mid-1779, imperial forces appeared to be winning the war on the northern frontiers.

The situation was less clear along the western frontiers of Virginia and Pennsylvania. In Detroit, Quebec lieutenant governor Henry Hamilton supported Shawnee, Delaware, Wyandot, and other tribal assaults against colonial settlers. The Indians fought in hopes of driving encroaching Euro-American settlers from traditional Native American homelands, mostly in modern Kentucky, Ohio, and western Pennsylvania. The British understood these raids would unavoidably kill civilians, although Hamilton officially (and probably sincerely) discouraged harm to women, children, and other innocents. Nevertheless, the offer of scalp bounties earned the lieutenant governor the epithet "Hair-Buyer." It was a conflict of small-scale raids, ambushes, and terror. Patriot authorities could do little to protect western communities until the Virginia expedition of George Rogers Clark temporarily—and *only* temporarily—stabilized the frontier in 1778.

Patriots were in a quandary. As desperate pleas for help from the frontiers reached the East, Washington lacked the strength to respond. Military priorities kept the Continental Army focused on Clinton's redcoats; meanwhile local defense, the general insisted, must rest with militia. In 1779, however, when relative calm in the East finally allowed Washington to act, he did so with harsh determination. The rebel commander in chief had little thought of crushing the Iroquois forever, but he wanted to land a shattering blow. Assigning the command to Major General John Sullivan, he issued blunt orders: "The immediate objects [of the expedition] are the total destruction and devastation of their settlements and the capture of as many prisoners of every age and sex as possible. It will be essential to ruin their crops now in the ground and prevent their planting more." Washington stressed that the Iroquois "country may not be merely overrun but destroyed."[30]

These were among the grimmest orders Washington ever issued. On June 18 Sullivan's Continentals marched from Easton, Pennsylvania, into Iroquois country in New York.[31] Most fighting comprised a series of skirmishes, which were vicious enough. Patriot soldiers skinned dead Indians to make leggings, and Iroquois tortured and killed Continental prisoners. On August 29 Sullivan shattered an attempt by Brant's Iroquois and Tories under Sir John Johnson and the Butlers to stand at Newtown (modern Elmira), New York. Thereafter, Patriot troops spent the following month devastating Indian villages and crops, assuring the inability of the Iroquois to feed themselves over the coming winter. The beleaguered Indians had no choice but to fall back to northwestern New York and depend on British rations and shelter, mostly at Fort Niagara. Nevertheless, many starved or froze to death. It was war against the entire Indian population and their ability to sustain themselves economically and socially (and thus militarily). It was war as another American general understood it a century later—indeed, it was fitting that one of the honored speakers at the centennial celebration of the Sullivan Expedition was none other than General William Tecumseh Sherman. His remarks were to the point: Sullivan's job was cruel, but he did what he had to do.[32]

The Mohawk and Schoharie Valleys of New York featured scenes of unforgiving civil war involving Indians, Loyalists, and regular troops. The valleys were major sources of grain supplies for the Continental Army, and British policy aimed at devastating the regions in order to starve the rebel military. In 1780, the year after Sullivan's desolation of the Iroquois heartland, vengeful Iroquois again struck hard in the Mohawk Valley, often in conjunction with Loyalists. Some raiding parties were large, with 400 to 500 troops. These forces were bad enough, but small-scale operations, sometimes with a dozen or fewer men, made terror the order of the day. Historian Isabel Kelsay has noted the ability of "three or four skulking warriors and their constant burnings and scalpings and taking into captivity, and the terrible uncertainty that hovered over everything and everybody," to keep regional Patriots perpetually on edge. By late 1780 entire villages were deserted and some 1,200 Mohawk Valley farms abandoned.[33]

The Schoharie region suffered similarly. In October 1780 Sir John Johnson, son of deceased British superintendent of Indian affairs Sir William Johnson, led up to 1,500 Indians, Tories, and a small redcoat detachment on a six-day raid into the valley. Although they failed to overrun any fortified positions, the raiders burned out virtually all rebel properties before withdrawing. Patriots quickly retaliated by torching Loyalist homesteads, leaving much of the valley a scorched wasteland.[34] By the end of the year, the entire region west of Schenectady—less than twenty miles northwest of Albany—was essentially lost to the Patriots. At war's end Patriot and Loyalist depredations had cost the Mohawk and Schoharie Valleys some 7,000 people killed, captured, exiled, or driven from their homes in fear and destitution. Surveying the events that engulfed this region and the New York frontiers generally, James Kirby Martin has concluded that the realities of the strife "neutered the philosophical canon of just, humane warfare as called for in the writings of Vattel and other European commentators."[35] Indeed, it is impossible to conclude otherwise.

Matters were equally bloody in the South. In an egregious instance of cruelty, on November 3, 1781, less than a month after the British capitulation at Yorktown, the Patriot defenders of Gowen's Fort in western South Carolina surrendered to a combined force of Cherokees (some of whom had remained hostile) and Loyalists under Tory captain William Bates. "Bloody Bill" Bates had promised quarter, but when the Patriots grounded arms, he ordered the slaughter of men, women, and children. Only a fortunate few, including a woman scalped and left for dead, escaped. The massacre was part of the broader pattern of brutality that characterized the war beyond the purview of the regular armies.

This war-to-the-knife reached a disgraceful crescendo in the Trans-Appalachia. The region already had seen its share of war. Clark's expedition had staked a Virginia claim to much of the area with a minimum of violence. Still there were some vicious incidents. On August 24, 1781, near Laughery Creek on the Ohio River (close to present Aurora, Indiana), a party of Indians and Loyalists intercepted Pennsylvania militia on the way to reinforce Clark. The Indians killed many Patriots outright and then murdered those taken prisoner. Pennsylvanians may have had the Laughery Creek incident in mind—they certainly had boiling resentments over losses at the hands of other Indian attacks—when they perpetrated a beastly massacre. On March 7, 1782, militia under Colonel David Williamson attacked a village of Christian Lenape Indians at Gnadenhutten, a Moravian mission on the Muskingum River in modern Ohio. Having captured ninety-six Moravian Lenape, the militia voted to kill them, doing so in cold blood the next day. Williamson's men murdered twenty-eight men, twenty-nine women, and thirty-nine children with mallet blows and scalping. The massacre was so grisly that even some Patriots were revolted; outrage is too slight a word to describe Native American reactions.

Three months later an Indian force defeated 480 Virginia militia near present-day Sandusky, Ohio. They captured Colonel William Crawford, a friend of Washington's, and in retaliation for Gnadenhutten, they tortured and burned him at the stake.[36] The news left Washington stunned, and his reaction is worth quoting at length: "I am particularly affected with the disastrous fate of Colo. Crawford: no other than the extremest Tortures which could be inflicted by Savages could, I think, have been expected, by those who were unhappy eno' to fall into their Hands; especially under the present Exasperation of their Minds for the treatment given their Moravian friends [at Gnadenhutten]. For this reason, no person should at this Time, suffer himself to fall alive into the hands of the Indians."[37]

To summarize: Although American and British elites, including senior military figures, did seek to moderate war-related violence, knowledge of and adherence to the ideals of *jus in bello* became more tenuous as the distance from the regular armies increased. At times there was little enough restraint even when combatants were primarily regular troops, no matter what senior officers or political leaders may have intended. Most engagements, however, were smaller-scale affairs removed from the major theaters of war—"military frontiers" in the West and in disputed territories in the East and South—where violence was endemic and often ferocious. Notions of *jus in bello* meant little among the Native Americans, militia, Loyalists, and independent settlers who confronted one another, frequently in desperate circumstances. We have cited many examples of common and often horrific violence, and they were not "cherry picked"—we could have cited many more. When aggregated examples form a clear trend, and that trend of evidence remains consistent, we can plausibly argue that it represents reality. That reality hardly fit a general pattern of restraint during the War for Independence or spoke to any significant influence of *jus in bello*.

IV

Given this dark picture of warfare during the Revolution, it remains to explain the reasons for this pervasive and persistent ruthlessness in a war fought (at least on one side) in the name of freedom and liberty. These reasons were historical and ideological and combined to form what we have termed "existential warfare." As explained, this was conflict in which combatants believed they were fighting for their very existence and accepted an all-or-nothing brand of war, one that knew few rules other than survival and saw brutality against enemies as preferable to devastating defeat.

We have noted that much of what the Revolutionary generation witnessed in battle had its origins in colonial frontier warfare. The colonial American military experience made few distinctions between soldiers and civilians; it was society versus society, and *everyone* was a target. Indeed, the New England war against the Pequot Indians during the 1630s was virtually a war of deliberate annihilation. John Grenier has convincingly argued that English settlers quickly adopted the brutal tactics of the European wars of religion—what he calls "extirpative" warfare—in campaigns against the Indians. In waging extirpative warfare, colonists "accepted, legitimized, and encouraged attacks upon and the destruction of noncombatants, villages, and agricultural resources . . . in shocking violent campaigns to achieve their goals of conquest."[38] *Jus in bello* counted for nothing. French and Native American attacks on British settlers repeatedly targeted civilians. A strike on German Flatts in the Mohawk Valley in 1757 is a prime example: the assault destroyed the village, killed civilians, and took prisoner surviving women and children. White civilians were not defenseless and fought back as families, ad hoc groups, or township militia. As in the War for Independence, elements of *jus in bello,* or at least gentlemanly honor, were present between the regular armies (as at Louisburg in 1758) but *not* on the New England or Virginia frontiers. Even General Louis-Joseph de Montcalm was unable to prevent Indian allies from attacking the surrendered garrisons—including civilians—of Forts Oswego and William Henry.[39] This, then, was the cruel legacy of colonial warfare.

There was a measure of restraint between the formal armies and the senior commanders, and there were times when *jus in bello* tacitly—because few Americans or British expressly cited Grotius—governed military behavior.[40] But frontier warfare observed few such niceties. It was the war Americans knew, and it coexisted with those of the regular armies. This brand of fighting carried unbroken into the Revolution. Patriots and Indians continued to view each other as existential threats. Native American leaders made no apologies for raids against civilian targets or for killing wounded Patriots. Rebel victory would have been (and *was*) disastrous for the tribal nations, and the Indians knew it.

It is nothing new to note that the War for Independence was a civil war between Americans, but we need to stress that Patriots and Loyalists, like Patriots and Indians, also saw their struggles in existential terms. Revenge and reprisal were commonplace, visited on both sides by combatants who could not conceive of a tolerable life or even survival at the hands of a victorious enemy.

There was an ideological dimension to such feelings. As historian Ruma Chopra has explained, for Loyalists, the rebellion was incomprehensible—"unnatural" in the view of New York City Tories—a revolt against the proper order of society and something profoundly troubling psychologically.[41] There were many motives for loyalism, but it is enough to note that whatever reasons tied them to the empire, Loyalists generally shared a dismay of the Revolution at a deeply emotional level. They saw the rebellion as an existential threat to society as they knew it, to their physical safety, and to their future in America. (They too were right.)

Tories dreaded independence as a precursor to tyranny by fanatical Patriots (sort of turning republicanism on its head). Many had good reason to think in these terms, having lost everything to Patriot confiscations, forced exile, and terror. They were subjected (as General Burgoyne put it) to "the *completest System of Tyranny*" ever devised, including "arbitrary imprisonment, confiscation of property, persecution and torture, unprecedented in the inquisition of the Romish church."[42] With nothing to lose, Tories responded accordingly. In his raids Loyalist commander William Tryon, the last royal governor of New York, frankly waged a war of "desolation" on rebel towns. In 1781, during Arnold's raid on New London, Connecticut, unrepentant Loyalist troops were heavily involved in the sacking and torching of the town.[43] The Tory world had come apart, and they sensibly concluded that only a British military victory could put it back together. Those who bore arms for the king wasted little sympathy on Patriot opponents, and many fought with the desperation of people who feared losing everything of value in their lives.

Ideology also fueled Patriot violence; indeed, many Americans shared an ideological predilection to extremism. Republican ideology fostered an almost paranoiac worldview. Its phobic suspicions of tyrannical plots against liberty, fears of "slavery," and insistence on militant virtue were hardly predisposed to restraint. Rather, republicanism encouraged existential warfare. "Give me liberty or give me death" was no plea for restraint; nor was Bulloch's dismissal of moderation. One can reasonably conclude that such rallying cries—or Thomas Paine's dictum "Tyranny, like Hell, is not easily conquered"—suggested doing whatever was necessary to win. Certainly, as all of the examples cited have indicated, rebels were not squeamish about the often violent tactics they adopted to avoid defeat. To fight for liberty was not to grant it to enemies; to fight for democracy was not to practice it. Win the war, *then* fully establish a polity. This was the thrust of T. H. Breen's *American Insurgents.* Breen makes clear that rebel Whigs did whatever they had to do to consolidate control at the local level and that Patriot elites often had little control over local tactics.[44] Violence or threats of violence were the norm.

V

The War for Independence represented a violent era. No one really knows how many Loyalists died fighting or of disease during the war, but the number was not small. In addition, thousands of surviving Loyalists wanted nothing to do with an America governed by victorious rebels. Historian Maya Jasanoff has estimated that some 60,000 of them chose to abandon America after independence, including 15,000 former slaves. This is probably a conservative estimate. Even so, 60,000 was no small migration; proportionately, it represented five times the number of French driven into exile during the French Revolution.[45] Some exiles were voluntary, but it is difficult to imagine such a large exodus taking place in an atmosphere of restraint among the victors. Most Loyalists, having endured as much as they could during the war, were justifiably unconvinced that they faced a secure or peaceable future in the new republic. Their memories were of violence, terror, disillusion, and death—they knew what and why they were fleeing.

The Loyalists had lost a war fought with the bitterness of desperation, one in which fears of defeat frequently overrode the moderation and restraint characterizing the ideals of *jus in bello.* Any notions of *jus in bello* had only marginal influence during the Revolution—it meant little in theory and just as little in reality. Indeed, our review of the fighting across the colonies suggests that the Revolution actually *exacerbated* the level of human devastation and that the War for Independence often reflected "a contagion of violence."[46] Combatants had waged an existential war—exactly the kind Grotius, Vattel, Samuel Pufendorf, and other Enlightenment writers had hoped to discourage. *Jus in bello* was in part a reaction to a previous age of ideological war, the unrestrained mayhem of Catholic-versus-Protestant convulsions that had devastated much of Europe. To a significant extent, the War for Independence was a revival of ideological warfare, with self-perpetuating cycles of revenge and reprisal. While some Americans and British, as well as a number of Indian, combatants willingly embraced moderation during the conflict, their restraint could not contain the brutality borne of a heritage of frontier warfare and the ideological predispositions to violence inherent in Patriot republicanism and Loyalist abhorrence of an "unnatural rebellion."[47]

In the fifth century Thucydides wrote of the civil conflict in Corcyra during the Peloponnesian War, and his understanding of that bitter struggle, in which mercy gave way to carnage, was every bit as applicable to what happened in America during the War for Independence: "In their struggle for ascendancy nothing was barred; terrible indeed were the actions to which they committed themselves, and in taking revenge they went further still. Here they were deterred neither by claims of justice nor by the interests of the state."[48] As with the ancient Greeks, Patriots, Loyalists, Native Americans, and many British combatants saw little middle ground in their war, and they fought accordingly. Thus we end where we began—with "Liberty or Death!"—and the desperate and inhumane consequences of an existential struggle for victory.

NOTES

1. "Speech of His Excellency Archibald Bulloch . . . to the [Georgia] Provincial Congress . . . June 5, 1776," in *American Archives,* ed. Peter Force, ser. 4, vol. 6 (Washington, D.C.: M. St. Clair and Peter Force, 1846), 718.
2. On the notion of viewing the War for Independence as a limited war denoted by martial restraint and in various ways tied to Enlightenment thinking, see for example Walter Millis, *Arms and Men: A Study of American Military History* (New Brunswick, N.J.: Rutgers University Press, 1981); and Wayne E. Lee, *Crowds and Soldiers in Revolutionary North Carolina: The Culture of Violence in Riot and War* (Gainesville: University Press of Florida, 2001). Stephen Conway claims that colonists fortunate enough to reside in regions controlled by British forces were generally safer and better off than those living in hotly contested war zones. See *The American Revolutionary War* (London: I. B. Tauris, 2013), 130–31. This conclusion assumes a high level of British humanity toward American rebels that much evidence to the contrary would challenge. In terms of an evolving early American military tradition inconsistent with notions of martial restraint, see for example, John Ferling, *A Wilderness of Miseries: War and Warriors in Early America* (Westport, Conn.: Greenwood Press, 1980); and John Grenier, *The First Way of War: American War Making on the Frontier, 1607–1814* (New York: Cambridge University Press, 2005).
3. Hugo Grotius, *De jure belli ac pacis libri tres* [On the Law of War and Peace: Three Books], trans. and ed. A. C. Campbell (1625; Kitchener, Ont.: Batoche Books, 2001), https://socserv2.socsci.mcmaster.ca/econ/ugcm/3ll3/grotius/Law2.pdf; Emer de Vattel, *The Law of Nations, or, Principles of the Law of Nature, Applied to the Conduct and Affairs of Nations and Sovereigns, with Three Early Essays on the Origin and Nature of Natural Law and on Luxury,* ed. Béla Kapossy and Richard Whatmore (1797; Indianapolis: Liberty Fund, 2008), bk. 3, chap. 1, sec. 3, oll.libertyfund.org/titles/vattel-the-law-of-nations-lf-ed, accessed 14 July 2015.
4. For example, see the early sections of both Reginald C. Stuart, *War and American Thought: From the Revolution to the Monroe Doctrine* (Kent, Ohio: Kent State University Press, 1982), and John Fabian Witt, *The Laws of War in American History: Lincoln's Code* (New York: Free Press, 2012). For a more nuanced discussion, see Wayne E. Lee's thoughtful *Barbarians and Brothers: Anglo-American Warfare, 1500–1805* (New York: Oxford University Press, 2011), 169–208.

5. Vattel, *Law of Nations* (2008), xxi.
6. Lee, *Barbarians and Brothers,* 189–90; George Washington to Robert Cary & Co., 6 Oct. 1773, *The Papers of George Washington Digital Edition*, ed. Theodore J. Crackel [hereafter *PGWde*], *Colonial Series,* 9:344, http://rotunda.upress.virginia.edu/founders/default.xqy?keys=GEWN-print-02-09-02-0268, accessed 7 Aug. 2017; Reuters, "George Washington's Library Book Returned 221 Years Late," 20 May 2010, http://www.reuters.com/article/2010/05/20/us-library-washington-idUSTRE64J4EG20100520, accessed 14 July 2015; Lee, *Barbarians and Brothers,* 189–90.
7. For example, "Reply of the House to Hutchinson's First Message," 26 Jan. 1773, *The Adams Papers,* ed. Robert J. Taylor et al., 18 vols. (Cambridge, Mass.: Harvard University Press, 1977–2016), 1:315–31; "Reply of the House to Hutchinson's Second Message," 2 Mar. 1773, ibid., 331–46; James Lovell to John Adams, 1 Jan. 1778, ibid., 13:379–81; "To John Adams from Jean Henri David Uhl, 1 July 1782," *Founders Online,* National Archives, last modified 29 June 2017, http://founders.archives.gov/documents/Adams/06-13-02-0087-0001; Edmund Randolph to Thomas Jefferson, with a memorandum by Jefferson, 9 Feb. 1781, *The Papers of Thomas Jefferson*, ed. Julian P.Boyd, vol. 4 (Princeton, N.J.: Princeton University Press, 1951), 571–72 (hereafter *PTJ*). On Franklin, see Albert de Lapradelle, introduction to Emer de Vattel, *The Law of Nations* [Le droit des gens], trans. Charles G. Fenwick (1758; Washington, D.C.: Carnegie Institution of Washington, 1916), 3.
8. John Adams to Abigail Adams, 17 Feb. 1777, *Adams Family Correspondence,* ed. Lyman Butterfield, 2 vols. (Cambridge, Mass.: Belknap Press of Harvard University Press, 1963), 2:163.
9. Lee, *Barbarians and Brothers,* 169–208.
10. Daniel M. Sivilich, "Ammunition in Colonial America: Musket Balls and Their Uses" (unpublished MS, Monmouth Battlefield State Park, Freehold, N.J., 2012), 81–82, 92–93; J[ohn] G[raves] Simcoe, *Simcoe's Military Journal: A History of the Operations of a Partisan Corps, Called the Queen's Rangers, Commanded by Lieut. Col. J. G. Simcoe, during the War of the American Revolution* (1787; reprint, New York: Bartlett and Welford, 1844), 173.
11. "Reminiscences of Read," in *A Documentary History of the American Revolution,* ed. Robert W. Gibbes (New York: D. Appleton, 1857), 256–57; Michael M. Greenberg, *The Court-Martial of Paul Revere: A Son of Liberty & America's Forgotten Military Disaster* (Lebanon, N.H.: University Press of New England, 2014), 145–47.
12. James Lovell to John Adams, 1 Jan. 1778, *Adams Papers,* 13:379–81; Edmund Randolph to Thomas Jefferson, with a memorandum by Jefferson, 9 Feb. 1781, *PTJ,* 571–72.
13. Mark Edward Lender and James Kirby Martin, "A Traitor's Epiphany: Benedict Arnold in Virginia and the Quest for Reconciliation," *Virginia Magazine of History and Biography* 125 (2017): 314–57.
14. Vattel, *Law of Nations* (2008), bk. 3, chap 15, sec. 226, p. 613.
15. Mawhood and Hand quoted in W[illiam] H[enry] Carpenter and T[imothy] S[hay] Arthur, *The History of New Jersey from Its Earliest Settlement to the Present Time* (Philadelphia: Claxton, Remsen & Haffelfinger, 1874), 198–99. On sexual violence against

civilian women, see Holger Hoock, "*Jus in Bello,* Rape and the British Army in the American Revolutionary War," *Journal of Military Ethics* 14 (Apr. 2015): 74–97; and Linda Grant DePauw, *Fortunes of War: New Jersey Women and the American Revolution* (Trenton: New Jersey Historical Commission, 1975), 18–20.

16. Thomas Fleming, *The Battle of Springfield* (Trenton: New Jersey Historical Commission, 1975), 26–27. Connecticut farms and Springfield were hardly unique in their misery. On 27 and 28 June 1778 in British-occupied Monmouth Court House, New Jersey, rebel homes and other structures went up in flames while Tory properties were spared the torch. Mark Edward Lender and Garry Wheeler Stone, *Fatal Sunday: George Washington, the Monmouth Campaign, and the Politics of Battle* (Norman: University of Oklahoma Press, 2016), chap. 6.

17. Andrew Jackson O'Shaughnessy, *The Empire Divided: The American Revolution and the British Caribbean* (Philadelphia: University of Pennsylvania Press, 2000), 218.

18. Howard H. Peckham, ed., *The Toll of Independence: Engagements and Battle Casualties of the American Revolution* (Chicago: University of Chicago Press, 1974), 130; David C. Munn, ed., *Battles and Skirmishes of the American Revolution in New Jersey* (Trenton, N.J.: Bureau of Geology and Topography, Dept. of Environmental Protection, 1976).

19. Michael S. Adelberg deserves credit for the term. See "Destitute of Almost Everything to Support Life: The Acquisition and Loss of Wealth in Revolutionary Monmouth County, New Jersey," in *The American Revolution in New Jersey: Where the Battlefront Meets the Home Front,* ed. James J. Gigantino II (New Brunswick, N.J.: Rutgers University Press, 2015), 110.

20. Military frontiers could shift. During the British occupation of Philadelphia, the surrounding Pennsylvania counties and the Delaware River counties of New Jersey endured foraging sweeps by both armies and the turmoil of clashes between local Whigs and Tories. With the British departure in 1778, however, relative tranquility returned once Whigs reestablished control on both sides of the Delaware.

21. John Buchanan, *The Road to Guilford Courthouse: The American Revolution in the Carolinas* (New York: John Wiley & Sons, 1997), 95–96; Georgia Council of Safety quoted in ibid., 96.

22. "The Reverend Nicholas Collin on the Ravages of War," in *New Jersey in the American Revolution, 1763–1783: A Documentary History,* ed. Larry R. Gerlach (Trenton: New Jersey Historical Commission, 1975), 303.

23. Lyman Copeland Draper, *King's Mountain and Its Heroes: History of the Battle of King's Mountain, October 7th, 1780, and the Events Which Led to It* (Cincinnati: P. G. Thomson, 1881), 332–43.

24. Michael S. Adelberg, *The American Revolution in Monmouth County: The Theater of Spoil and Destruction* (Charleston, S.C.: History Press, 2010), 121–43.

25. Peter Silver, *Our Savage Neighbors: How Indian Warfare Transformed Early America* (New York: W. W. Norton, 2007); Patrick Griffin, *American Leviathan: Empire, Nation, and Revolutionary Frontier* (New York: Hill and Wang, 2007), 171.

26. William L. Anderson and Ruth Y. Wetmore, "Cherokee: The Revolutionary War, Cherokee Defeat, and Additional Land Cessions," *Encyclopedia of North Carolina*

(Chapel Hill: University of North Carolina Press, 2006), *NCPedia,* 1 Jan. 2006, http://ncpedia.org/cherokee/revolutionarywar.

27. Johann Ewald, *Diary of the American War: A Hessian Journal,* trans. and ed. Joseph P. Tustin (New Haven, Conn.: Yale University Press, 1979), 166–67.

28. Joseph T. Glatthaar and James Kirby Martin, *Forgotten Allies: The Oneida Indians and the American Revolution* (New York: Hill and Wang, 2006), 130–37; Harold E. Selesky, ed., *Encyclopedia of the American Revolution,* 2nd ed., vol. 2 (Detroit: Thomson Gale, 2006), 726–27.

29. John Hathorn to [Gov. George Clinton] [Col. John Hathorn's Official Report], 27 July 1779, Draper Manuscript Collection, Wisconsin Historical Society, http://albertwisner-montage.auto-graphics.com/#search/itemDetails/entities%2F6275, accessed 7 Aug. 2017; Selesky, *Encyclopedia of the American Revolution,* 726–27.

30. George Washignton to John Sullivan, 31 May 1779, *PGWde, Revolutionary War Series,* 20:716–17, http://rotunda.upress.virginia.edu/founders/default.xqy?keys=GEWN-print-03-20-02-0661, accessed 7 Aug. 2017.

31. Sullivan was augmented to 6,000 troops when a contingent under Brig. Gen. James Clinton (no relation to Sir Henry) subsequently joined him. Oneida, Tuscarora, and Mahican scouts accompanied the Patriots as well. Farther west, a smaller party under Col. Daniel Broadhead, rebel commandant at Pittsburgh, moved against the tribes in northwestern Pennsylvania. In terms of enemy numbers, the Indians had never faced such a formidable challenge.

32. "Address by General William T. Sherman," *Journals of the Military Expedition of Major General John Sullivan against the Six Nations of Indians in 1779 with Records of the Centennial Celebrations,* ed. Frederick Cook (Auburn, N.Y.: Knapp, Peck, & Thomson, printers, 1887), 439–40.

33. Isabel Kelsay, *Joseph Brant: Man of Two Worlds* (Syracuse, N.Y.: Syracuse University Press, 1984), 246, 301.

34. Earle Thomas, "Johnson, Sir John," *Dictionary of Canadian Biography,* vol. 6 (1821–35), University of Toronto/Université Laval, 2003–, http://www.biographi.ca/en/bio/johnson_john_6E.html; Selesky, *Encyclopedia of the American Revolution,* 301.

35. For a detailed discussion of warfare on the New York frontiers and its relation to the ideal of *jus in bello,* see James Kirby Martin, "A Contagion of Violence: The Ideal of Jus in Bello Versus the Reality of Fighting on the New York Frontier during the Revolutionary War," *Journal of Military Ethics* 14 (Apr. 2015): 57–73.

36. Peckham, *Toll of Independence,* 94–96; Ted Franklin Belue, "Crawford's Sandusky Expedition," in *The American Revolution, 1775–1783: An Encyclopedia,* ed. Richard L. Blanco, vol. 1 (New York: Garland, 1993), 416–20.

37. George Washington to William Irvine, 6 Aug. 1782, *The Writings of George Washington from the Original Manuscript Sources,* ed. John C. Fitzpatrick, 39 vols. (Washington, D.C.: U.S. Government Printing Office, 1931–44), 24:474.

38. Grenier, *First Way of War,* 10.

39. Howard H. Peckham, *The Colonial Wars, 1689–1762* (Chicago: University of Chicago Press, 1964), 158–59, 162–63.

40. This is not to argue that colonial officials were unaware of Grotius; some were and

were concerned to observe the rules of war as Grotius propounded them. See Lee, *Barbarians and Brothers,* 189–90. There is little, however, to support a broad appreciation of *jus in bello* in colonial America.

41. Ruma Chopra, *Unnatural Rebellion: Loyalists in New York City during the Revolution* (Charlottesville: University of Virginia Press, 2011).
42. *The Case and Claim of the American Loyalists Impartially Stated and Considered* ([London]: Printed by Order of their Agents, [1783]), 9.
43. Paul David Nelson, *William Tryon and the Course of Empire: A Life in British Imperial Service* (Chapel Hill: University of North Carolina Press, 1990).
44. T. H. Breen, *American Insurgents, American Patriots: The Revolution of the People* (New York: Hill and Wang, 2010), 16–20.
45. Maya Jasanoff, *Liberty's Exiles: American Loyalists in the Revolutionary World* (New York: Alfred A. Knopf, 2011).
46. See Martin, "Contagion of Violence," 59–60.
47. The role of religion in existential warfare is beyond the immediate ken of this article, but the relationship invites further investigation. There are two initial questions in this regard. First, to what extent did Patriots consider their cause a "holy war"? John D. Carlson, citing some impressive scholarship, thinks that most rebels did not. Yet some Patriots certainly *did,* and how widespread this belief may have been begs clarification. Second, if some Patriots believed that they were engaged in a crusade—that God was on their side—how might this conviction have justified the measures they employed in waging their crusade? Finally, if, as Carlson further suggests, religious fervor blended with republican ideology in sustaining faith in the Revolution, to what extent did this conflation of religion and ideology fuel belief that almost any military measures were acceptable to secure victory? Carlson does not raise questions of existential warfare, but we believe his article implicitly suggests a religious dimension to the matter. See John D. Carlson, "A Just or Holy War of Independence? The Revolution's Legacy for Religion, Violence, and American Exceptionalism," in *From Jeremiad to Jihad: Religion, Violence, & America,* ed. John D. Carlson and Jonathan H. Ebel (Berkeley: University of California Press, 2012), 208.
48. Thucydides, *History of the Peloponnesian War,* trans. Rex Warner (New York: Penguin, 1972), 243–44.

8 "DISREPUTABLE AMONG CIVILIZED NATIONS"

Destroying Homes during the Revolutionary War

Benjamin L. Carp

Sometime in May 1779, Benjamin Franklin and the Marquis de Lafayette were designing prints for a schoolbook to illustrate British cruelties. The first seven of these all dealt with the burning or bombardment of "defenseless Places": Charlestown, Massachusetts; Falmouth, Maine; Norfolk, Virginia; New Bedford, Massachusetts; Esopus (or Kingston), New York; Bristol, Rhode Island; and Stonington, Connecticut.[1] Had Franklin waited a few years, he could have added Georgetown, South Carolina; Springfield, New Jersey; New London, Connecticut; and dozens of other American towns. Naturally, he did not mention that Norfolk was largely burned by Virginia and North Carolina militiamen or that American partisans had deliberately and strategically burned dozens of towns among the Iroquois, Shawnees, Delawares, and Cherokees.

Reflecting on a fire that destroyed a sixth of New York City, John Joseph Henry, a Pennsylvania judge, wrote in 1811: "It may be well, that a nation, in the heat and turbulence of war, should endeavor to promote its interests, by propagating reports of its own innocency and prowess, and accusing its enemy of flagrant enormity and dastardliness. . . . [B]ut when peace comes, let us, in God's name, do justice, to them and ourselves. Baseness and villainy are the growth of all climes, and of all nations."[2] While he was prisoner aboard a ship anchored three miles south of Governor's Island, Henry had witnessed the fire on September 21, 1776. Although Americans successfully propagated the narrative that the inferno was an accident (or the work of the occupying British forces), Henry insisted to the end of his days that some fellow Americans, "the most low and vile of persons," had done the deed.[3]

Franklin's proposed illustrations and Henry's memoir illustrate why it has been so difficult for historians to assess the wartime conduct of combatants during the Revolutionary War. From the very beginning, print and rumor shaped the way participants viewed wartime actions. After two centuries of

Whiggish history and a late nineteenth-century rapprochement between Great Britain and the United States—both of which discouraged an emphasis on the most grisly theaters of the conflict—historians have only recently begun to reassess the Revolution's atrocities. Americans' wartime actions shaped the policies—and, indeed, the character—of the new nation, yet chroniclers have not always taken the ethical conduct of the war as their central concern.[4]

This chapter examines the destruction of towns, cities, and Indian settlements during the Revolutionary War as a subset of *jus in bello.* Although receiving very little attention from historians, these actions caused widespread economic, environmental, and geographic upheaval and revealed much about contemporary social attitudes, political beliefs, and strategic goals. Property destruction might seem less atrocious than the mistreatment of noncombatants and prisoners, but contemporaries took it seriously. From the Declaration of Independence onward, they often mentioned "death" and "desolation" in the same breath.

The destruction of civilian buildings during the American Revolution was widespread, and three factors shaped the way that observers weighed the justice of such conduct. First, many officers, politicians, and elite observers demonstrated an understanding of the "laws of war"; however, these were ambiguous enough that they could not stand alone as a guide for officers and soldiers. Second, even if we could affirm that combatants understood the laws of war, the theaters of combat—and the structures that guided them—were sufficiently diffuse that many armed men took the liberty to disobey. Historians have shown that senior commanders on both sides of the conflict wanted to avoid atrocities but that subordinates, stragglers, deserters, and allies did not always adhere to these policies. Finally, even though violations of the laws of war might be sporadic, the repercussions in public opinion might well be widespread, rendering an imperfectly just war into a one-sided memory of the other side's injustice. The British and Americans hoped to triumph politically by portraying themselves as being more virtuous than their enemies while disavowing or minimizing any actions that might impugn their own reputation. Thus, scholars must contend with the tensions that resulted from the diffusion of authority and the obfuscations of propaganda if they are to properly understand the wartime conduct of the Revolution and "do justice" to its history.

Destruction and the Laws of War

Just war theorists had drawn a rather blurry line between what was considered moderate, justifiable conduct and inexcusable barbarity. With regard to property destruction in particular, Emer de Vattel writes, "The . . . destruction of towns . . .

[is] odious and detested on all occasions, when evidently practised without necessity, or without urgent reasons," but it might be excused in cases of "punishment."[5] Thus, commanders might feel free to justify the destruction of a town and attribute it to "necessity," chastisement, or "urgent reasons." Furthermore, as Wayne E. Lee has highlighted, Anglo-American tradition gave commanders license to ignore restraint when the enemy was composed of rebels or barbarians. Since the Revolutionary War was—it should be emphasized—both a civil war and a war between Indians and whites, this gave combatants ample opportunity to characterize their enemies as deserving of harsh treatment.[6]

Destruction often accompanied pillaging, or the appropriation of civilian property, which also had a widespread effect on civilians during the American Revolution. Contemporaries often interpreted the military practice of foraging as pillaging.[7] Although it was easier for a logistically deprived army to justify plunder than outright destruction, this mattered little to victims. Some records of damage claims, in fact, fail to distinguish between the two.[8] Because the laws of war were ambiguous and porous, articulated beliefs about restraint rarely matched the experiences of homeowners and residents.

British Destructive Campaigns

The diffuse nature of the Revolutionary War and its command structures disrupted the implementation of just war policies. Although elite leaders on both sides of the conflict referred to Enlightenment ideas of "humanity" as a guide for wartime conduct, such constraints imperfectly shaped actions on the ground. Moreover, commanders generally paired their "humane" impulses with practical considerations, such as the fear of reprisal and the desire to maintain discipline.[9] For these leaders, strategy and military ethics might reinforce one another, but they faced the additional challenge of inculcating these ideas among their subordinates.

The British wrestled with two competing strategic goals during the Revolution: forcing the Americans to submit, and reconciling Americans to their allegiance. The former might necessitate destroying towns to overawe and chastise the colonists; the latter encouraged restraint for ideological as well as pragmatic reasons.[10] Thus, on the eve of Lexington and Concord, one British official wrote: "It is in our power to harass, lay Waste, & Depopulate America, to destroy the Towns, settlements & provisions & consequently to Reduce their Boasted numbers in a few Months by Famine & Misery. But all considerations of humanity out of the question that would prove a very unprofitable as well as ineffectuall method of conducting the War." This strategist recognized that women and children would more quickly fall victim to devastation and famine. Such suffering would drive enraged, homeless, and armed widowers into the countryside. Nevertheless, he believed that laying waste to a few New England estates would be effective.[11]

It was not long before British forces had the opportunity to destroy civilian homes. They shelled and destroyed Charlestown, Massachusetts, during the Battle of Bunker Hill on June 17, 1775. The town had around four hundred houses, and its residents lost £117,982 5s. 2d. worth of property.[12] A few months later, Vice Admiral Samuel Graves sent Lieutenant Henry Mowat aboard the HMS *Canceaux* with three other vessels "to lay waste burn and destroy such Seaport Towns as are accessible to his Majesty's Ships." Mowat demanded that the people of Falmouth surrender their arms and ammunition. Upon their refusal, his four vessels bombarded the town on October 18, 1775, before he sent a landing party to torch the remaining houses and stores. By the time Mowat was finished, his men had burned three-fourths of the town's buildings, with total damage estimated at £55,000. Fear swept up and down the American seaboard; vulnerable New England towns hastily organized coastal defenses and traded dreadful rumors.[13]

British officers disagreed about the ethics and efficacy of destroying homes. After Major General John Vaughan burned the town of Esopus, New York, in 1777, Major General James Robertson wrote that he accepted the destruction of mills, stores, and shipping useful to the enemy, but "burning houses . . . gives the people a notion that we despair of possessing" North America, which then led them to support the rebels.[14] Captain Frederick Mackenzie argued the opposite in 1778: "Very few parts of America know, as yet, what the horrors of War are, and if their houses, farms, and other property was destroyed and laid waste, their resentment would turn upon Congress, and their numerous other rulers."[15] In this disagreement lies the conundrum the British faced. If they burned enough houses, Mackenzie believed, it would convince Americans that Congress could not protect them, and the resulting dissension would weaken the rebellion. On the other hand, as Robertson argued, even small amounts of destruction might drive Americans into the arms of the Whig government. Yet despite these doubts, Stephen Conway has argued that as frustration mounted and victory proved elusive, "the number and vehemence of the hard-liners increased." The influence of more conciliatory or restrained officers was ultimately too limited to overshadow the outrages that Americans experienced locally.[16]

British commanders may have hesitated to pursue a wholehearted policy of destruction, yet there were more than enough officers and soldiers (sometimes ill disciplined) who were inclined to destroy houses, whether out of vengeance, frustration, or hardline attitudes. Conway states that many field-grade officers condoned or overlooked acts of plundering and marauding in part out of solicitude for their men. Their actions created enough devastation to galvanize some Americans into supporting the Whigs and to cause depoliticization and despair in particularly chaotic regions, but devastating British raids were never enough to crush the Americans' war effort completely.[17] Some British allies—German mercenaries, Native Americans, and blacks—participated in destructive actions that particularly enraged American Whigs. During the New York campaign of 1776, the Hessians had such a dreaded reputation for plunder and ruin that, according to Ambrose Serle, Americans "almost run away at the name." In 1779–80 a self-emancipated black river pilot named Colonel Tye led a band of raiders and marauders throughout Monmouth County, New Jersey. Yet His Majesty's troops did more than enough destructive work without Americans having to apply ethnic labels to their enemies. Newspapers and rumors floridly described and thoroughly decried the actions of British soldiers and their allies.[18] Both during and after the war, Whig leaders were successfully able to claim that the British had engaged in wanton destruction that violated the laws of war.

The Americans' Destructive Campaigns

Yet the Americans were hardly blameless in this regard. The diffusion of their command structure played an even greater role in soldiers resorting to destruction. Because the states (who raised their own regiments) retained significant power, neither George Washington nor the Continental Congress had as much centralized authority over Whig forces as the British generals and admirals had over theirs. Most importantly, the Continental Army was only half the story: well over a third of Patriots in arms served in state regiments or the militia.[19] In the militia and (to a lesser degree) in the Continental Army, self-governance was a cherished value among the rank and file, which sometimes led soldiers to push back against their instructions.[20] The militia answered mostly to their own local communities, not necessarily to the wider world's understandings of military ethics, and thus were the first to slip the bonds of restraint or retaliate for real or imagined offenses.[21] Michael McDonnell notes that its officers often "ignored laws or evaded them."[22] From Pennsylvania to South Carolina, many American militiamen took up arms in hopes of plunder.[23] Finally, militiamen played a particularly active role in campaigns against the Native Americans, who suffered extensive devastation.[24]

The diffusion of authority on the American side yielded a muddled array of Whig statements about wartime conduct. In late 1775 John Adams, even as he contemplated destructive campaigns against Nova Scotia, wrote, "the late conduct [of the British], in burning towns, so disgracefull to the English name and character, would justify anything, but similar barbarity." He urged: "Let us preserve our temper, our wisdom, our humanity and civility, though our enemies are every day renouncing theirs. But let us omit nothing necessary for the security of our cause."[25] Adams paid obeisance to the ideals of "humanity and civility," but he also concluded that it might be "necessary" to fight fire with fire.

From their very first venture, Whig forces attempted to levy destructive campaigns beyond the densely settled areas in the thirteen colonies. As Americans besieged Quebec in 1775–76, they set fire to the suburbs and some ships, fired red-hot shot into the town, and sent a fireship to burn the Lower Town and the ships docked there in the hopes of storming the town during the confusion. After their retreat, they attempted to burn Montreal, did burn the fort and provisions at Saint-Jean, and also destroyed or ransacked several houses and churches.[26] James Willing's men burned plantations along the Mississippi River below Natchez in 1778. Rebels on the Pennsylvania frontier torched property as part of their ongoing land disputes with rival white settlers. Massachusetts privateers raided the Nova Scotia coast.[27] Throughout the war, Whigs expressed a willingness to conduct more such campaigns. While Esek Hopkins and Samuel Nicholas assured the inhabitants of New Providence, Bahamas, in 1776 that they did not intend to harm civilian property, a 1778 expedition under John P. Rathburne was more serious about burning Nassau. Americans named their ships *Reprisal, Retaliation,* and *Revenge.* Commodore John Paul Jones launched a "revenge raid" on the Cumberland town of Whitehaven in England in April 1778; although his men only succeeded in burning one boat, the damage might have been more extensive. Furthermore, the English had not suffered from a naval invasion of this sort since 1667, so Jones's raid had significant psychological repercussions.[28]

The British burning of the towns of Fairfield and Norwalk, Connecticut, and Bedford, New York, in 1779 inspired a wave of desire for vengeance among American Whigs. James Lovell cried in a letter to Franklin: "Will no one under a Commission from these United States retaliate on the Coasts of England for the Burning of our beautiful Fairfield? A single Privateer might I think show, there, a striking Sample of the Species of War now carried on by Britain against America."[29] Within days William Henry Drayton moved that the Marine Committee determine the most effective means to execute a policy of "burning and destroying the towns belonging to the enemy in Great Britain and the West Indies."[30] A letter (perhaps unsent) specified Bristol, Liverpool, Glasgow, Edinburgh, and London as targets, or "the first objects of national retaliating resentment"—a bold statement of this sort naturally required the burning of Great Britain's most populous and important cities. The letter suggested using "a few desperate determined Men, under the promise of handsome rewards . . . well acquainted with . . . the large Towns in England & Scotland."[31] Congress wrote to its ministers in France complaining of the burning of towns in Virginia and Connecticut as well as other ravages in Georgia and South Carolina. "It becomes . . . a common cause of all nations to punish a people who so daringly violate the rights of humanity" and "those laws which are held sacred among civilized nations." Congress then instructed them to "employ Incendiaries to set fire to the Capital of the British Dominions, particularly the royal Palace, and to such other Towns in Great Britain as may be most expedient." Nor was this operation to be clandestine: a manifesto was to avow that the act had been done by congressional order, declaring that Americans "are determined at all times to meet their enemies in whatever kind of war they shall chuse to carry on, whether it be of civilized or of savage nations."[32]

These resolutions led directly to another mission by Commodore Jones. Earlier in 1779, Franklin had written to him to be wary of violating the laws of war. Jones was to display proper conduct toward prisoners despite "the more barbarous Usage by the English in many Places towards the Americans." Franklin mentioned that "the English have wantonly burnt many defenceless Towns in America" but ordered, "you are not to follow this Example, unless where a Reasonable Ransom is refused." Even in such a case, he noted, Jones ought to give timely warning so that the sick, aged, women, and children might evacuate before initiating a bombardment or burning.[33] Franklin later wrote that Jones "would have endeavour'd to put some considerable Towns to a high Ransom or have burnt them"; if it had not been for contrary winds, he would have attempted Leith and Edinburgh. Furthermore, Franklin wrote, "the late Provocations by the burning of Fairfield and other Towns . . . have at length demolish'd all my Moderation" and hinted strongly that his instructions for future expeditions would not include the temperate attitude of his earlier letter.[34]

A second series of town fires in different regions of North America sponsored a new wave of vengeful murmuring in 1781 within the Continental Congress. In September Congress learned of the cannonading of Georgetown, South Carolina, and Brigadier Benedict Arnold's burning of New London, Connecticut.[35] A committee noted these and previous town burnings, resolving to order "the demolition of cities and villages in the Kingdom of Great Britain so as fully to retaliate." The motion expressed the belief that such retaliation was "fully justified by the laws of self defence and sound policy" and hastened to emphasize "that we are not moved by any light and hasty suggestions of anger or revenge." Officers were also empowered to put to death anyone (presumably including soldiers and officers) captured in the act of burning an American town—either by throwing them in the flames or by other means. The committee recommended a manifesto that called British burnings "inconsistent with the dignity of the United States . . . and with the respect due to the benevolent rules by which civilized nations have tempered the severities and evils of war." Since Congress acknowledged that the destruction of British towns might be out of their power, they thought it would be "more consonant to the spirit of justice and humanity" that the "instruments for these incendiary purposes should be the objects of vengeance [rather] than the remote and unoffending inhabitants" of British towns. Congress resolved, therefore, that British officers in captivity would pay for fiery destruction with their lives.[36]

Had Lord Cornwallis's surrender at Yorktown not thwarted the British war effort, the Whigs might have carried out such threats. Although Washington and other moderate leaders had striven mightily to keep more radical and disobedient soldiers largely in check, every atrocity led the warring parties closer to a disastrous cycle of fiery reprisals. The laws of war had been heated by torch and carcass almost to the point of explosion. Each side emphasized its opponents' villainy as justification for its own harsh acts; they also each had rank-and-file soldiers acting independently, though sometimes with their officers' support. As a result, the Revolutionary War years were scorched with bitterness.

The southern theater, in particular, degenerated into a war of retaliation. Destruction among plantations was extensive on two different fronts: coastal raiding by the British, and inland partisan marauding waged by both sides, the unintended outcome of a failed British strategy.[37] As early as the summer of 1776, the Georgia militia began this destructive cycle with raids on East Florida.[38] The British, under Brigadier Augustine Prévost, burned their way through Georgia and South Carolina in 1779, inviting reprisals on Loyalist property, while an expedition under Commodore George Collier and Major General Edward Mathew struck at Portsmouth, Virginia.[39] By late 1779, British policy focused on returning the South to British allegiance through "pacification." Savannah fell to the British, and the Franco-American attempt to retake that city involved a destructive bombardment. Charles-Henri, comte d'Estaing later claimed to be horrified that Major General Benjamin Lincoln would not allow the women and children to evacuate during the barrage.[40] The long British siege of Charleston also involved destruction of property in the vicinity, culminating with a horrific powder-magazine explosion on May 15, 1780, that Hessian officers attributed to British incompetence and perhaps Whig malfeasance.[41] British raiding in the Chesapeake also continued, with Arnold, Major

John Graves Simcoe, and Major General William Philips wreaking havoc on Richmond and the James River valley.[42]

British conquest of the interior proved much more difficult. Out of frustration, Cornwallis wrote to Lieutenant Colonel Nisbet Balfour, "I have given orders that all inhabitants of this province [South Carolina] who have subscribed and have taken part in this revolt, should be punished with the greatest rigour, and also those that will not turn out, that they may be imprisoned, and their whole property taken from them and destroyed."[43] The British unleashed Colonel Banastre Tarleton, Major John Wemyss, Major Patrick Ferguson, and Lieutenant Colonel John Harris Cruger on the property of Whig supporters, which inspired Brigadier General Thomas Sumter, Lieutenant Colonel Elijah Clarke, and Colonel Andrew Pickens to plunder and burn enemy plantations in return.[44] Other commanders professed to disavow this sort of fighting. When a party of Whigs burnt some houses along the Little Pee Dee River, Brigadier General Francis Marion assured Major General Horatio Gates that "there is not one house Burnt by my Orders, or by any of my People. It is what I detest to Distress poor Women & Children."[45] Nevertheless, the extent of destruction in the Carolinas was undeniable, and it was perpetrated by all sides.

Destruction of Indian settlements was also particularly widespread. This was not a radical new development but a continuation of devastating campaigns along the outer edges of Anglo-American settlement. Connecticut settlers, for instance, had razed the village of Teedyuscung on April 19, 1763; years later Captain John Butler led his British and Indian allies to destroy more than a thousand dwellings during the Wyoming Valley "Massacre" of 1778. In retaliation, Whig soldiers, first under Colonel Thomas Hartley and then under Major General John Sullivan, Brigadier General James Clinton, and Colonel Daniel Brodhead, burned dozens of towns in 1778 and 1779. Washington urged his commanders not to listen to any overture of peace from the Iroquois "before the total ruin of their settlements is effected," after which the officers could "endeavour to draw further advantages from their fears." The commander in chief explained that such severe chastisement would ensure "our future security." In response, parties of British and Indian fighters burned hundreds of towns in 1780 and 1781. During the Revolution, Americans wrought devastation upon the Cherokee, Iroquois, Delaware, Shawnee, and Miami Indians that caused starvation, displacement, and forced migration on a massive scale. In doing so they justified these actions by arguing that they needed to retaliate for Indian attacks. Yet it has also long been clear to historians that whites burned out the Native Americans with the intention of occupying their land. Indians were the "other," which allowed white Americans to commit atrocities they never would have committed against other whites. The war between Patriot and Loyalist combatants was bad, but these acts of destruction against Native Americans reached new depths of atrocity, increasingly rooted in indiscriminate racism. White Americans repeatedly burned towns, not just villages of enemy Indians but also those that were neutral or friendly toward the Whig cause. The attack on Gnadenhutten in 1782 was perhaps the most senseless example.[46]

Indian leaders such as Joseph Brant burned white settlements in defense of native lands or to advance British war aims. During the Cherry Valley raid of 1778, Indians allied with the British also burned the homes of Loyalists, explaining that otherwise the Whigs would do it themselves.[47] The Patriots' goals during their own destructive campaigns, meanwhile, were clear. As Drayton wrote to South Carolina military officers, "make smooth work as you go—that is, you cut up every Indian corn-field, and burn every Indian town . . . that the nation be extirpated, and the lands become the property of the public."[48] American commanders certainly tried to be thorough. Brigadier General Andrew Williamson reported to Drayton, "I have now burnt down every town, and destroyed all the corn, from the Cherokee line to the middle settlements."[49] By the end of the war, Sullivan, Colonel Goose Van Schaick, Brigadier General George Rogers Clark, Colonel Benjamin Logan, Brigadier General Griffith Rutherford, Colonel William Christian, Colonel Arthur Campbell, and Colonel John Sevier could make similar boasts. In 1790 the Seneca leader Cornplanter told Washington that the Six Nations' name for him was "town destroyer; and to this day, when that name is heard, our women look behind them and turn pale, and our children cling close to the necks of their mothers." The president rather blithely replied, "it is my desire, and the desire of the United States, that all the miseries of the late war should be forgotten, and buried forever." He hoped for "mutual friendship and justice" in the future.[50] Americans, like the British, engaged in destructive acts at various points during the war—and threatened to do even worse.

Propaganda

These actions show how imperfectly the laws of war were obeyed and applied in Revolutionary North America. A gap opened up between intention and observed behavior, and propagandists rushed to fill the void. Each side was eager to minimize or conceal its own actions while playing up its enemies' violations. The war was waged, therefore, not just on the battlefields and in the homes of civilians but also in the theater of public opinion. As both sides fought to prove that their cause was more just, its propagandists sought to shape the truth in ways that sometimes bore a tenuous relationship to events on the ground.

Partisans of the United States succeeded in minimizing the Americans' harsher treatment of Loyalists, Indians, and ordinary civilians during the war. There are two reasons for this: first, the British never developed a communications network in North America that was effective as that of the rebels, and second, the United States emerged victorious from the conflict, giving it more leverage to define the war afterward.[51] Since many Americans also had a strong interest in resuming relationships with Great Britain, many writers minimized the destructive actions of the British. Ultimately, much of the history of destroyed homes is buried in claims records and plays little role in the national histories of the Revolutionary War.

We often assume that propaganda is the product of dishonest state actors foisting misinformation upon the people. Yet we can also define "propaganda" broadly and free it from its customary opprobrium, thinking of it instead as deliberate persuasion with the intent to influence public opinion.[52] As William B. Warner helps demonstrate, such a definition allows us to see oral communication (with its "fluidity, authenticity, and local intensities") and print (with its "fixity, authority, spatial reach, and public anonymity") as overlapping and mutually reinforcing.[53] Recent scholars have found that American networks of persuasion during the war were decentralized, allowing ideas and information to spread horizontally, from the bottom up, or from peripheries to the center. Such networks often gained strength when forced to accommodate distance and diversity.[54]

The propagation of information never worked perfectly, of course: the direct experience of war was often brutal and depoliticizing, and the long-distance mobilization fostered by political leaders and their networks could not always overcome a person's proximity to events.[55] Efforts to influence public opinion were most effective when paired with recruitment efforts and the hostile actions of armed men, and in this way the Americans' endeavors to politicize followers ultimately triumphed.[56] As Andrew J. O'Shaughnessy writes, the presence of British forces alienated colonials' affections, even those who might at one time have been disposed toward loyalty. Atrocities attributed to the British "were recounted in the revolutionary press and helped perpetuate the image of a hostile foreign presence."[57] As Philip M. Taylor writes, propaganda "works most effectively when words and deeds (the propaganda and the policy) are synchronous, but the 'propaganda of the deed' is in itself a powerful persuader." The destruction of towns can "send powerful messages that form part of the persuasive process."[58]

The intertwining of fiery words and fiery deeds recurred throughout the war. As early as January 1776, Washington wrote, "A few more of such flaming arguments as were exhibited at *Falmouth* and *Norfolk,* added to the sound doctrine and unanswerable reasoning contained in the pamphlet 'Common Sense,' will not leave numbers at a loss to decide upon the propriety of a separation."[59] Ironically, it was Whig militiamen who had destroyed the majority of Norfolk (the sixth-largest city in the thirteen colonies), though this fact was suppressed for sixty years.[60] British lieutenant John Dalrymple predicted correctly that Patriot propagandists would take "the Inhumanity of the Action off their Shoulders" and place it "upon our own."[61] Samuel Adams, looking for southern support, was undaunted: "The burning of Norfolk & the Hostilities committed in North Carolina have kindled the Resentment of our Southern Brethern who once thought their Eastern Friends hot headed & rash; now indeed the Tone is alterd & it is said that the Coolness & Moderation of the one is necessary to allay the heat of the other."[62] The resulting Declaration of Independence complained that King George III had "burnt our towns," in addition to its other grievances.

Going forward, both Britons and Americans understood that they opened themselves up to criticism on the basis of natural law if the "candid world" (another phrase from the Declaration of Independence) perceived them as carrying on excessive destruction. Americans in particular hoped that proper military conduct would demonstrate to other nations that they were the rightful heirs of civilized European notions of natural rights, not villainous rebels or a motley collection of woodland savages.[63]

Thus, Benjamin Franklin and Robert Morris of the Committee of Secret Correspondence denied Whig capability for the destruction of New York City in 1776 (though John Joseph Henry, and most British partisans, believed otherwise). They sought to "convince all the World we had no desire to burn Towns or destroy Citys but that we left such Meritorious works to grace the History of our Enemies."[64] By contrast, six weeks later, Whig troops unambiguously set fire to the courthouse and other buildings in White Plains, New York, on November 5; Washington court-martialed Major Jonathan Williams Austin for this action. The New York Committee of Safety complained to both the general and the Continental Congress, and they urged that arson be made a capital crime. "If the army is not seasonably [*sic,* reasonably] restrained from such acts of barbarity," committee member Pierre Van Cortlandt wrote, "the consequence must be fatal to the cause of a people whose exalted glory it is, to be advocates for the rights of mankind, against the tyranny and oppression of lawless power."[65] Colonials condemned this particular act of arson by the Continental Army in 1776 but foisted the blame for others onto the British.

American Whigs, meanwhile, continued to take offense with every British act of destruction, and their channels of communication (especially newspapers) helped spread their outrage to the public. The circulation of atrocity stories was an essential part of their propaganda effort throughout the war. The rebels hoped to convince the world that they were justified in defending themselves against a tyrannical power that violated the laws of war; they also hoped to convince the "apolitical majority" of Americans to share in their views.[66] Wartime propaganda invoked shared norms to shame enemy combatants into proper conduct. Racial fears were also part of this effort: propagandists drew upon—and invigorated—whites' longstanding paranoia about Indian raids and slave uprisings. Gregory Dowd demonstrates the ways that rumors, for instance, are the products of a collaborative process of identity information—a process intensified by war. Similarly, Robert G. Parkinson chronicles the wartime development of a racially based "common cause appeal," wherein newspapers helped develop "the first construction of what it meant to be an American."[67]

The breast-beating of the *New Jersey Gazette* in 1778 was typical: "Some have the effrontery to say, that the British officers by no means countenance or allow of burning. Did not the wanton burning of Charleston [Massachusetts] and Kingston in Esopus [New York], besides many other instances, sufficiently evince the contrary, their conduct in Freehold [New Jersey] I think may—the officers having been seen to exult at the sight of the flames, and heard to declare that they never could conquer America until they burnt every rebel's house, and murdered man, woman, and child."[68] A few months earlier Henry Laurens wrote, "Great Britain[,] now convinced of the impossibility of subduing these United States, is endeavouring to distress them by such extravagant Acts in predatory War as will Stain the annals of history with marks of Infamy & disgrace upon that once Magnanimous people." He mentioned specifically the burning of houses, furniture, and provisions, leaving women and children exposed to the elements. Adding an ethnic cast to his diatribe, Laurens noted that the British had "improved upon the lessons learned from their Indian Consorts."[69] Richard Henry Lee also concluded that the British had "carried on a low, pitiful, and disgraceful kind of War" by vengefully burning the houses of several individuals. "Yet all this Militates against themselves," he declared, "by keeping up an inflamable Indignation in the Country towards them."[70] Such indignation derailed American negotiations with the Carlisle commissioners, as Drayton (who had previously ordered officers to "burn every Indian town") called British destructive policies "an outrage upon humanity."[71] Arguments over the conduct of the Revolutionary War remained a sticking point throughout the conflict.

During negotiations over the Treaty of Paris, any attempts to claim repayment of debts or compensation for seizure of Loyalist property were met with

American reminders of the towns the British had burned.[72] Yet soon after the war, some Americans (particularly among the elite) were eager to tamp down inflammatory recollections of wartime devastation in order to resume diplomatic and commercial relations with Great Britain. In 1784 Alexander Hamilton appealed to "the common interests of humanity" in the treatment of Loyalists, rather than "a prolongation of the calamities of war," especially since, he noted, "the world has its eye upon America." Native Americans, of course, benefited little from such negotiations, and for them the devastation continued.[73] Anglo-Americans probably understood that they could not spend too much time discussing the burning of towns, lest their own actions be laid at their feet. In the view of many, it was better to struggle for security, expansion, and diplomatic integrity in a world of hostile powers, at least until the War of 1812 again raised the specter of burning towns—including Washington, D.C.

Conclusion

The tensions that surround Revolutionary War devastation suggest an important paradox. The Enlightenment and practical considerations may have inculcated values of restraint in Anglo-American professional armies, however difficult these may have been to enforce. But the British armed forces faced an internal conflict over strategy, wherein any sporadic acts of destruction negated whatever conciliatory policies the commanders might pursue. The Continental Army showed a great deal of restraint (toward other white settlers), yet they also marched alongside state militias with a strong tradition of self-governance and a poorer track record when it came to just conduct in warfare. On both sides, while leaders hoped for ethical restraint, they faced an imperfect embrace of their ideals. And because of wartime propaganda and their victorious postwar commemoration, Americans have since read tales of British atrocities, their own high ideals, and pitched battles rather than the messy reality of fiery deeds. Perhaps the lesson Americans learned was one echoed in the Federalists' response to the French Revolution (and white Americans' response to the Haitian Revolution): too much freedom gave way to licentiousness. Following this logic, the Revolutionary Whigs could not simultaneously honor the nation's Enlightenment ideals and its localist, democratic impulses. The result would be either an unrestrained American soldiery, with its attendant atrocities, or a more disciplined and centralized army, with its attendant hierarchies. For all these reasons, a democratic nation would struggle to do justice to its enemies.[74]

NOTES

Chapter title: John Adams to Abigail Adams, July 7, 1775, *Founders Online,* National Archives, last modified June 29, 2017, http://founders.archives.gov/documents/Adams/04-01-02-0160 (from *The Adams Papers, Adams Family Correspondence,* vol. 1, *December 1761–May 1776,* ed. Lyman H. Butterfield [Cambridge, Mass.: Harvard University Press, 1963], 241–43).

1. "Franklin and Lafayette's List of Prints to Illustrate British Cruelties," in *The Papers of Benjamin Franklin,* ed. Barbara B. Oberg et al., 41 vols. to date (New Haven, Conn.: Yale University Press, 1959–) [hereafter cited as *PBF*], 29:590–91. For another interpretation, see Robert G. Parkinson, *The Common Cause: Creating Race and Nation in the American Revolution* (Chapel Hill: University of North Carolina Press, 2016), 400–407.
2. John Joseph Henry, "Arnold's Campaign against Quebec," in *An Accurate and Interesting Account of the Hardships and Sufferings of that Band of Heroes who Traversed the Wilderness in the Campaign against Quebec* (Lancaster, Pa.: William Greer, 1812), 186.
3. Ibid., 185. See also Benjamin L. Carp, "The Night the Yankees Burned Broadway: The New York City Fire of 1776," *Early American Studies* 4, no. 2 (Fall 2006): 471–511.
4. See, however, Armstrong Starkey, "Paoli to Stony Point: Military Ethics and Weaponry during the American Revolution," *Journal of Military History* 58, no. 1 (January 1994): 7–27; Colin G. Calloway, *The American Revolution in Indian Country: Crisis and Diversity in Native American Communities* (Cambridge: Cambridge University Press, 1995); Edwin G. Burrows, *Forgotten Patriots: The Untold Story of American Prisoners during the Revolutionary War* (New York: Basic Books, 2008); James Kirby Martin, "A Contagion of Violence: The Ideal of *Just In Bello* versus the Realities of Fighting on the New York Frontier during the Revolutionary War," *Journal of Military Ethics* 14, no. 1 (Apr. 2015): 57–73; Holger Hoock, "*Jus in Bello,* Rape and the British Army in the American Revolutionary War," *Journal of Military Ethics* 14, no. 1 (Apr. 2015): 74–97; and Hoock, *Scars of Independence: America's Violent Birth* (New York: Crown, 2017).
5. Emer de Vattel, *The Law of Nations, or Principles of the Law of Nature Applied to the Conduct and Affairs of Nations and Sovereigns,* trans. from French (Philadelphia: P. H. Nicklin and T. Johnson, 1829), bk. 3, chap. 9, p. 435. Hugo Grotius's injunctions were similarly open to multiple interpretations. See Hugo Grotius, *The Rights of War and Peace, including the Law of Nature and of Nations,* trans. A. C. Campbell (London: M. Walter Dunne; reprint, Westport, Conn.: Hyperion, 1979), 332–33, 365–68. See also James Turner Johnson, *Ideology, Reason, and the Limitation of War: Religious and Secular Concepts, 1200–1740* (Princeton, N.J.: Princeton University Press, 1975), chap. 4.
6. Wayne E. Lee, *Barbarians and Brothers: Anglo-American Warfare, 1500–1865* (New York: Oxford University Press, 2011).
7. George L. Coil, "War Crimes of the American Revolution," *Military Law Review* 82 (Fall 1978): 178.
8. Inventories of Damages by the British and Americans in New Jersey, 1776–82, Records of the Legislature, New Jersey State Archives, Trenton.

9. Wayne E. Lee, *Crowds and Soldiers in Revolutionary North Carolina: The Culture of Violence in Riot and War* (Gainesville: University Press of Florida, 2001), chap. 4.
10. Stephen Conway, "To Subdue America: British Army Officers and the Conduct of the Revolutionary War," *William and Mary Quarterly,* 3rd ser., 43, no. 3 (July 1986): 381–407.
11. "Reflections on the Means Necessary to Reduce the Americans," Mar. 1775, Liverpool Papers, Additional MSS 38374, f. 111, British Library, London.
12. Richard Frothingham Jr., *History of the Siege of Boston, and of the Battles of Lexington, Concord, and Bunker Hill,* 2nd ed. (Boston: Charles C. Little and James Brown, 1851), 201–3.
13. Vice Adm. Samuel Graves to Lt. Henry Mowat, Oct. 6, 1775, in *Naval Documents of the American Revolution,* ed. William Bell Clark, vol. 2 (Washington, D.C.: U.S. Government Printing Office, 1966), 324–26; Donald A. Yerxa, "The Burning of Falmouth, 1775: A Case Study in British Imperial Pacification," *Maine Historical Society Quarterly* 3 (1975): 119–60.
14. James Robertson to Jeffrey Amherst, Oct. 27, 1777, U 1350 079/19, Amherst Papers, Kent Archives Office, Maidstone, quoted in Conway, "To Subdue America," 390.
15. *Diary of Frederick Mackenzie: Giving a Daily Narrative of His Military Service as an Officer of the Regiment of Royal Welch Fusiliers during the Years 1775–1781 in Massachusetts Rhode Island and New York,* 2 vols. (Cambridge, Mass.: Harvard University Press, 1930), 1:298–99.
16. Conway, "To Subdue America," 397–98 (quote, 398).
17. Stephen Conway, "'The great mischief Complain'd of': Reflections on the Misconduct of British Soldiers in the Revolutionary War," *William and Mary Quarterly,* 3rd ser., 47, no. 3 (July 1990): 370–90; Gregory T. Knouff, *The Soldiers' Revolution: Pennsylvanians in Arms and the Forging of Early American Identity* (University Park: Pennsylvania State University Press, 2004), 148–53; Sung Bok Kim, "The Limits of Politicization in the American Revolution: The Experience of Westchester County, New York," *Journal of American History* 80, no. 3 (Dec. 1993): 868–89.
18. Harry M. Ward, *Between the Lines: Banditti of the American Revolution* (Westport, Conn.: Praeger, 2002), 4 (Serle quote), 58, 61–67; Graham Russell Hodges, *Root and Branch: African Americans in New York and East Jersey, 1613–1863* (Chapel Hill: University of North Carolina Press, 1999), 151–53; Rodney Atwood, *The Hessians: Mercenaries from Hessen-Kassel in the American Revolution* (Cambridge: Cambridge University Press, 1980), chap. 8; Calloway, *American Revolution in Indian Country,* 292–98; Sylvia R. Frey, *Water from the Rock: Black Resistance in a Revolutionary Age* (Princeton, N.J.: Princeton University Press, 1991), chap. 2, esp. 59, 69, 73; Lee, *Crowds and Soldiers,* 143–44, 197–98, 200; Parkinson, *Common Cause,* esp. chap. 4, 472–73, 497–98, 502.
19. Francis B. Heitman gives a very rough figure of about 38.5 percent. *Historical Register of Officers of the Continental Army during the War of the Revolution, April, 1775, to December, 1783,* rev. ed. (Washington, D.C.: Rare Book Shop, 1914), 691. Walter Sargent finds that 61.5 percent of Massachusetts soldiers served in provincial or militia units. "The Massachusetts Rank and File of 1777," in *War and Society in the*

American Revolution: Mobilization and Home Fronts, ed. John Resch and Walter Sargent (DeKalb: Northern Illinois University Press, 2007), 55.

20. Ricardo A. Herrera, *For Liberty and the Republic: The American Citizen as Soldier, 1775–1861* (New York: New York University Press, 2015), esp. chap. 3; John A. Ruddiman, "'A record in the hands of thousands': Power and Persuasion in the Orderly Books of the Continental Army," *William and Mary Quarterly,* 3rd ser., 67, no. 4 (Oct. 2010): 747–74.
21. Lee, *Crowds and Soldiers,* 148–58, 194–208; Mark V. Kwasny, *Washington's Partisan War, 1775–1783* (Kent, Ohio: Kent State University Press, 1996), 28, 50, 160, 257–58, 309, 326, 331–37. See also Knouff, *Soldiers' Revolution,* xix–xxi, 78–85.
22. Michael A. McDonnell, *The Politics of War: Race, Class, and Conflict in Revolutionary Virginia* (Chapel Hill: University of North Carolina Press, 2007), 505.
23. Ward, *Between the Lines,* 1–8; Hoock, *Scars of Independence,* chap. 4.
24. Calloway, *American Revolution in Indian Country,* 46–56.
25. John Adams to Joseph Ward, Nov. 14, 1775, in *Letters of Delegates to Congress, 1774–1789,* ed. Paul H. Smith et al., 25 vols. (Washington, D.C.: Library of Congress, 1976–2000) [hereafter *LDC*], 2:344; John Adams, proposals for an expedition to Nova Scotia, [Nov. 2–10, 1775], ibid., 286–88.
26. Guy Carleton to William Tryon, May 17, 1776, CO 5/1107, transcripts of records from The National Archives, Public Record Office, Library of Congress, Washington, D.C.; Gustave Lanctot, *Canada and the American Revolution,* trans. Margaret M. Cameron (Toronto: Clarke, Irwin, 1967), 105, 129, 133, 137–38, 145–47, 152.
27. J. Leitch Wright Jr., *Florida in the American Revolution* (Gainesville: University Press of Florida, 1975), 46–53; Knouff, *Soldiers' Revolution,* 216–18; John D. Faibisy, "Privateering and Piracy: The Effects of New England Raiding upon Nova Scotia during the American Revolution, 1775–1783" (Ph.D. diss., University of Massachusetts, 1972).
28. Gardner W. Allen, *A Naval History of the American Revolution,* 2 vols. (New York: Russell and Russell, 1962), 1:95–100, 139, 230, 266, 273, 292–95, 337–38, 342–48, 362, 595–96; Louis C. Kleber, "Jones Raids Britain," *History Today* 19, no. 4 (Apr. 1969): 277–82; Stephen Webbe, "Revenge Raid on Whitehaven," *MHQ: The Quarterly Journal of Military History* 12, no. 3 (2000): 20–27. On "vengeance," see also chapter 10 below.
29. James Lovell for the Committee for Foreign Affairs to Benjamin Franklin, July 16, 1779, *PBF* 30:110. See also Committee for Foreign Affairs [Richard Lee and James Lovell] to American Commissioners [Benjamin Franklin, Silas Deane, and Arthur Lee], Oct. 31, 1777, ibid., 25:135.
30. *Journals of the Continental Congress, 1774–1789,* ed. Worthington Chauncey Ford et al., 34 vols. (Washington, D.C.: Government Printing Office, 1904–37) [hereafter *JCC*], 14:851–53.
31. Marine Committee to Benjamin Franklin, [after July 19, 1779], *LDC,* 13:262.
32. *JCC,* 14:915–16. On the fears inspired in Baltimore and Annapolis by the burning of Suffolk and Portsmouth, see Maryland delegates to George Washington, May 23, 1779, *LDC,* 12:515–16.

33. Benjamin Franklin's instructions to John Paul Jones, [Apr. 28, 1779], *PBF,* 29:387.
34. Benjamin Franklin to James Lovell, Oct. 17, 1779, ibid., 30:547–48.
35. See Mark Mayo Boatner III, *Encyclopedia of the American Revolution* (New York: David McKay, 1966), 420, 787–88.
36. *JCC,* 21:977–78 ("fully justified"), 1017 ("light and hasty suggestions"), 1018 ("demolition of cities"), 1029–30 ("inconsistent," "more consonant," "instruments"). See also Arthur Middleton's draft resolves, [Sept.? 1781], *LDC,* 18:89–91.
37. John Shy, "British Strategy for Pacifying the Southern Colonies, 1778–1781," in *The Southern Experience in the American Revolution,* ed. Jeffrey J. Crow and Larry E. Tise (Chapel Hill: University of North Carolina Press, 1978), 155–73.
38. Frey, *Water from the Rock,* 83.
39. Piers Mackesy, *The War for America, 1775–1783* (Cambridge, Mass.: Harvard University Press, 1964), 267–70; Frey, *Water from the Rock,* 88–94, 150–51.
40. Alexander A. Lawrence, *Storm over Savannah: The Story of the Count d'Estaing and the Siege of the Town in 1779* (Athens: University of Georgia Press, 1979), 76–84; Augustine Prévost to Count D'Estaing, Oct. 6, 1779, CO 5/182, The National Archives, Public Record Office, London; Benjamin Lincoln and Count d'Estaing to Prévost, Oct. 6, 1779, ibid.; David B. Mattern, *Benjamin Lincoln and the American Revolution* (Columbia: University of South Carolina Press, 1995), chap. 5; Prévost to Lord George Germain, Nov. 1, 1779, in *Documents of the American Revolution, 1770–1783 (Colonial Office Series),* ed. K. G. Davies (Dublin: Irish Academic Press, 1985), 17:241–50.
41. Bernhard A. Uhlendorf, ed. and trans., *The Siege of Charleston: With an Account of the Province of South Carolina: Diaries and Letters of Hessian Officers from the von Jungkenn Papers in the William L. Clements Library* (Ann Arbor: University of Michigan Press, 1938), 89–91; Bruce E. Burgoyne, ed. and trans., *Diaries of Two Ansbach Jaegers* (Bowie, Md.: Heritage Books, 1997), 150–51; John Peebles, *John Peebles' American War: The Diary of a Scottish Grenadier, 1776–1782,* ed. Ira D. Gruber (Mechanicsburg, Pa.: Stackpole Books, 1998), 374; Lachlan McIntosh, "Journal of the Siege of Charlestown, 1780," in *Lachlan McIntosh Papers in the University of Georgia Libraries,* ed. Lilla Mills Hawes (Athens: University of Georgia Press, 1968), 121–22; George Fenwick Jones, ed., "The 1780 Siege of Charleston as Experienced by a Hessian Officer," *South Carolina Historical Magazine* 88 (Apr. 1987): 69; David Ramsay, *History of South-Carolina, from Its First Settlement in 1670, to the Year 1808,* 2 vols. (Charleston, S.C.: David Longworth, 1809), 1:330–31; William Moultrie, *Memoirs of the American Revolution. . . ,* 2 vols. (New York: David Longworth, 1802), 2:109–12; Carl P. Borick, *A Gallant Defense: The Siege of Charleston, 1780* (Columbia: University of South Carolina Press, 2003).
42. Frey, *Water from the Rock,* 149–58, 167, 210–11; Ward, *Between the Lines,* chap. 9.
43. Lord Cornwallis to Nisbet Balfour, Aug. 1, 1780, Cornwallis Papers, The National Archives, Public Record Office, 30/11/98/10, quoted in Frey, *Water from the Rock,* 129.
44. See various essays in Ronald Hoffman, Thad W. Tate, and Peter J. Albert, eds., *An Uncivil War: The Southern Backcountry during the American Revolution* (Charlottesville: University Press of Virginia, 1985); Frey, *Water from the Rock,* 98–104, 129–37;

John Buchanan, *The Road to Guilford Courthouse: The American Revolution in the Carolinas* (New York: John Wiley and Sons, 1997), 103, 120–21, 124, 132, 182–85, 188, 191, 200–201, 222, 242–51, 280, 301, 304, 333, 343–44, 363; John S. Pancake, *This Destructive War: The British Campaign in the Carolinas, 1780–1782* (University: University of Alabama Press, 1985), 14–17, 31, 34, 36, 81–89, 200–201, 206–7; Jerome J. Nadelhaft, *The Disorders of War: The Revolution in South Carolina* (Orono: University of Maine at Orono Press, 1981), 57, 61, 64–66, 68, 73, 75–76, 80, 85; Ward, *Between the Lines,* 205, chap. 14.

45. Francis Marion to Horatio Gates, Oct. 4, 1780, in Walter Clark, ed., *The State Records of North Carolina,* vol. 14 (Winston, N.C.: M. I. and J. C. Stewart, 1896), 666. See also Lee, *Crowds and Soldiers,* 200.

46. George Washington to John Sullivan, May 31, 1779, in *Papers of George Washington: Revolutionary War Series,* ed. Philander D. Chase et al., 24 vols. (Charlottesville: University Press of Virginia, 1985–2016) [hereafter *PGW:RWS*], 20:716–19. See also Frederick J. Stefon, "The Wyoming Valley," in *Beyond Philadelphia: The American Revolution in the Pennsylvania Hinterland,* ed. John B. Frantz and William Pencak (University Park: Pennsylvania State University Press, 1998), 133–52; Gregory T. Knouff, "Soldiers and Violence on the Pennsylvania Frontier," ibid., 171–93; Joseph R. Fischer, *A Well-Executed Failure: The Sullivan Campaign against the Iroquois July–September 1779* (Columbia: University of South Carolina Press, 1997); Barbara Graymont, *The Iroquois in the American Revolution* (Syracuse, N.Y.: Syracuse University Press, 1976); Randolph C. Downes, *Council Fires on the Upper Ohio: A Narrative of Indian Affairs in the Upper Ohio Valley until 1795* (Pittsburgh: University of Pittsburgh Press, 1969); William R. Nester, *The Frontier War for American Independence* (Mechanicsburg, Pa.: Stackpole Books, 2004); John Bakeless, *Background to Glory: The Life of George Rogers Clark* (Lincoln: University of Nebraska Press, 1992); Calloway, *American Revolution in Indian Country;* Tom Hatley, *The Dividing Path: Cherokees and South Carolinians through the Era of the Revolution* (New York: Oxford University Press, 1993); James H. O'Donnell, *The Southern Indians and the American Revolution* (Knoxville: University of Tennessee Press, 1972); Max M. Mintz, *Seeds of Empire: The American Revolutionary Conquest of the Iroquois* (New York: New York University Press, 1999); Samuel Cole Williams, *Tennessee during the Revolutionary War* (1944; reprint, Knoxville: University of Tennessee Press, 1974); Barbara Alice Mann, *George Washington's War on Native America* (Westport, Conn.: Praeger, 2005); R. Douglas Hurt, *The Ohio Frontier: Crucible of the Old Northwest, 1720–1830* (Bloomington: Indiana University Press, 1996); Rob Harper, "Looking the Other Way: The Gnadenhutten Massacre and the Contextual Interpretation of Violence," *William and Mary Quarterly,* 3rd ser., 64, no. 3 (July 2007): 621–44; and chapter 7 above.

47. Graymont, *Iroquois in the American Revolution,* 187–88.

48. William Henry Drayton to Francis Salvador, July 24, 1776, in *A Documentary History of the American Revolution,* ed. Robert W. Gibbes, vol. 2 (New York, 1857), 29. See also Edward J. Cashin, "'But Brothers, It Is Our Land We Are Talking About': Winners and Losers in the Georgia Backcountry," in Hoffman, Tate, and Albert, *Uncivil War,* 251–52.

49. Andrew Williamson to Drayton, Aug. 22, 1776, in Gibbes, *Documentary History,* 2:32. See also Edward J. Cashin, *The King's Ranger: Thomas Brown and the American Revolution on the Southern Frontier* (Athens: University of Georgia Press, 1989), 52.
50. Speech of Cornplanter, Half-Town, and Great-Tree, Dec. 1, 1790, in *American State Papers: Documents, Legislative and Executive, of the Congress of the United States,* ed. Walter Lowrie and Matthew St. Clair Clarke, vol. 4, *Indian Affairs* (Washington, D.C.: Gales and Seaton, 1832), 1:140; George Washington's reply, Dec. 29, 1790, ibid., 142.
51. Philip G. Davidson, *Propaganda and the American Revolution, 1763–1783* (Chapel Hill: University of North Carolina Press, 1941), 365–75, 402–4. There are several excellent studies of the Revolutionary Era press, propaganda, persuasion, and public opinion, though not all of these works discuss the war years. See Arthur M. Schlesinger, *Prelude to Independence: The Newspaper War on Britain, 1764–1776* (New York: Knopf, 1958); Carl Berger, *Broadsides and Bayonets: The Propaganda War of the American Revolution* (Philadelphia: University of Pennsylvania Press, 1961); Bernard Bailyn, *The Ideological Origins of the American Revolution* (Cambridge, Mass.: Harvard University Press, 1967); Eric Foner, *Tom Paine and Revolutionary America,* rev. ed. (New York: Oxford University Press, 2005); Bernard Bailyn and John B. Hench, eds., *The Press and the American Revolution* (Worcester, Mass.: American Antiquarian Society, 1980); Michael Warner, *Letters of the Republic: Publication and the Public Sphere in Eighteenth-Century America* (Cambridge, Mass.: Harvard University Press, 1990); Jeffrey L. Pasley, *"Tyranny of Printers": Newspaper Politics in the Early American Republic* (Charlottesville: University Press of Virginia, 2001); Trish Loughran, *The Republic in Print: Print Culture in the Age of U.S. Nation Building, 1770–1870* (New York: Columbia University Press, 2007); Troy O. Bickham, *Making Headlines: The American Revolution as Seen through the British Press* (DeKalb: Northern Illinois University Press, 2009); Marcus Daniel, *Scandal and Civility: Journalism and the Birth of American Democracy* (New York: Oxford University Press, 2009); Konstantin Dierks, *In My Power: Letter Writing and Communications in Early America* (Philadelphia: University of Pennsylvania Press, 2011); Carol Sue Humphrey, *The American Revolution and the Press: The Promise of Independence* (Evanston, Ill.: Northwestern University Press, 2013); William B. Warner, *Protocols of Liberty: Communication Innovation and the American Revolution* (Chicago: University of Chicago Press, 2013); Russ Castronovo, *Propaganda 1776: Secrets, Leaks, and Revolutionary Communications in Early America* (New York: Oxford University Press, 2014); Gregory Evans Dowd, *Groundless: Rumors, Legends, and Hoaxes on the Early American Frontier* (Baltimore: Johns Hopkins University Press, 2015); and Parkinson, *Common Cause.*
52. For this definition, see Philip M. Taylor, *Munitions of the Mind: A History of Propaganda from the Ancient World to the Present Era,* 3rd ed. (1990; 1995; Manchester, U.K.: Manchester University Press, 2003), introduction.
53. Warner, *Protocols of Liberty,* 26.
54. Castronovo, *Propaganda 1776,* 179; Loughran, *Republic in Print,* 44–58; Warner, *Protocols of Liberty,* 19, 24; Barbara Clark Smith, *The Freedoms We Lost: Consent and Resistance in Revolutionary America* (New York: New Press, 2010), 87. See also

Pauline Maier, *From Resistance to Revolution: Colonial Radicals and the Development of American Opposition to Britain, 1765–1776* (New York: Alfred A. Knopf, 1972; reprint, New York; Vintage Books, 1974), ii; David Hackett Fischer, *Paul Revere's Ride* (New York: Oxford University Press, 1994), 301.

55. Sung Bok Kim, "Limits of Politicization."

56. John W. Shy, "The Military Conflict Considered as a Revolutionary War," in *A People Numerous and Armed: Reflections on the Military Struggle for American Independence* (Ann Arbor: University of Michigan Press, 1990), 213–44.

57. Andrew Jackson O'Shaughnessy, *The Men Who Lost America: British Leadership, the American Revolution, and the Fate of Empire* (New Haven, Conn.: Yale University Press, 2013), 11, 116 (quote), 117, 354.

58. Taylor, *Munitions of the Mind,* 1, 4, 8 (quotes), 9. For the origins of modern "propaganda by the deed," see John Merriman, *The Dynamite Club: How a Bombing in Fin-de-Siècle Paris Ignited the Age of Modern Terror* (Boston: Houghton Mifflin Harcourt, 2009), 62–63, 207. I am grateful to Steven P. Remy for this suggestion.

59. George Washington to Joseph Reed, Jan. 31, 1776, in *American Archives. . . ,* ed. Peter Force, 4th ser., vol. 4 (Washington, D.C.: M. St. Clair Clarke and Peter Force, 1843), 899–900.

60. Carp, "Night the Yankees Burned Broadway," 499–500.

61. Lt. John Dalrymple to recipient, CO 5/40, f. 126, quoted in Robert L. Scribner and Brent Tarter, "Friday, 1 December 1775–Saturday, 20 January 1776: An Introductory Note," in *Revolutionary Virginia: The Road to Independence,* comp. William J. Van Schreeven, ed. Robert L. Scribner, vol. 5, *The Clash of Arms and the Fourth Convention, 1775–1776: A Documentary Record* (Charlottesville: University Press of Virginia, 1979), 17. See also ibid., 18–19, 24n89.

62. Samuel Adams to Samuel Cooper, Apr. 30, 1776, *LDC,* 3:602.

63. Eliga H. Gould, *Among the Powers of the Earth: The American Revolution and the Making of a New World Empire* (Cambridge, Mass.: Harvard University Press, 2012), 113–19.

64. Committee of Secret Correspondence [Benjamin Franklin and Robert Morris] to Silas Deane, Oct. 1, 1776, *PBF,* 22:641–42. See also Thomas Jefferson's comments ten years later about the French historian François Soulés's *Historie des troubles de l'Amérique Anglaise* (1785), in *The Papers of Thomas Jefferson,* vol. 10, *June 1786 to December 1786,* ed. Julian P. Boyd (Princeton, N.J.: Princeton University Press, 1954), 370, 375n12.

65. *Journals of the Provincial Congress, Provincial Convention, Committee of Safety and Council of Safety of the State of New-York, 1775–1777,* vol. 1 (Albany, N.Y.: Thurlow Weed, 1842), 723–24, 729. See also Pierre Van Cortlandt to George Washington, [ca. Dec. 2, 1776], in *PGW:RWS,* 7:254–55.

66. Shy, "Military Conflict," 242.

67. Parkinson, *Common Cause,* passim, esp. 8–9 (quote, 665); Dowd, *Groundless,* 4. See also Knouff, *Soldiers' Revolution,* 153–54, chap. 5; Woody Holton, *Forced Founders: Indians, Debtors, Slaves, and the Making of the American Revolution in Virginia* (Chapel Hill: University of North Carolina Press, 1999), chap. 5; and Peter Silver, *Our Savage*

Neighbors: How Indian War Transformed Early America (New York: Norton, 2008), chap. 8.

68. *New Jersey Gazette,* Aug. 5, 1778, quoted in Lee, *Crowds and Soldiers,* 311n20.
69. Henry Laurens to David Espy and others, May 17, 1778, *LDC,* 9:693.
70. Richard Henry Lee and James Lovell to the Commissioners at Paris, May 15, 1778, *LDC,* 9:670–71. See also Leonard J. Sadosky, *Revolutionary Negotiations: Indians, Empires, and Diplomats in the Founding of America* (Charlottesville: University of Virginia Press, 2009), chap. 3; and Parkinson, *Common Cause,* 384–99.
71. William Henry Drayton to the Carlisle Commissioners, Oct. 24, 1778, *LDC,* 11:109.
72. Benjamin Franklin to Richard Oswald, Nov. 26, 1782, *PBF,* 38:350–56; Benjamin Franklin to Jonathan Shipley, Mar. 17, 1783, ibid., 39:348–50.
73. [Alexander Hamilton], "Second Letter from Phocion, [April 1784]," *Founders Online,* National Archives, last modified June 29, 2017, http://founders.archives.gov/documents/Hamilton/01-03-02-0347 (from *The Papers of Alexander Hamilton,* vol. 3, *1782–1786,* ed. Harold C. Syrett [New York: Columbia University Press, 1962], 530–58). See also Robert M. Calhoon with Timothy M. Barnes, "The Reintegration of the Loyalists and the Disaffected," in *Tory Insurgents: The Loyalist Perception and Other Essays,* ed. Robert M. Calhoon, Timothy Barnes, and Robert S. Davis, rev. ed. (Columbia: University of South Carolina Press, 2010), 350–69; and Maya Jasanoff, *Liberty's Exiles: American Loyalists in the Revolutionary World* (New York: Knopf, 2011), 317–34.
74. Geoffrey Best, *Humanity in Warfare* (New York: Columbia University Press, 1980), chap. 1; Alfred F. Young, *The Shoemaker and the Tea Party: Memory and the American Revolution* (Boston: Beacon Press, 1999); Peter S. Onuf, "American Exceptionalism and National Identity," *American Political Thought* 1, no. 1 (Spring 2012): 77–100.

9 "TO ANNOY REBELS, OR OTHER ENEMIES IN ARMS AGAINST US"

The Limits of Legitimate Violence against Civilians during the American Revolution

William P. Tatum III

On September 2, 1776, Major General Sir William Howe, the British commander in chief in North America, convened a general court-martial at Newtown, Long Island, to try six soldiers for crimes they allegedly committed against civilian inhabitants. Four of these soldiers—Private John Kelly of the 27th Regiment of Foot and Privates John Scoffield, Henry Swaffield, and Thomas Ingram of the 28th Regiment of Foot—stood accused of "pillage and plundering and destroying the property of His majesty's Subjects," while the other two soldiers—Privates John Dunn and John Lusty of the 57th—were charged with raping Elizabeth Johnstone, "an Inhabitant of Long Island." After hearing testimony from a relatively lengthy line of witnesses, the thirteen officers serving as judges handed down mixed verdicts. The court found Scoffield, Swaffield, and Ingram innocent of all charges and released the soldiers to their duty. The judges convicted Kelly, Dunn, and Lusty, sentencing Kelly to receive one thousand lashes with the cat-o'-nine-tails, the whip reserved exclusively for formal corporal punishment in the army, and Dunn and Lusty "to suffer Death, by being hanged by the neck untill they are Dead."[1]

On the surface, one might see the results of these trials as sending a severe yet evenhanded message to soldiers regarding the perils of attacking the civilian population. Scholars examining the British soldiers' conduct during the American Revolution, however, have taken these trials and others as evidence that the British Army lacked a firm commitment to conventional standards of *jus in bello* doctrine. Historians Stephen Conway, Sharon Block, and Holger Hoock have established plundering (property crime) and rape as the key military-on-civilian crimes for understanding the army's commitment to protecting noncombatants. Focusing primarily on plundering, Conway concluded that divisions within the officer corps exacerbated soldiers' ill treatment of civilians and contributed to a generally low record of maintaining conventional protections, due to many officers casting a blind eye toward marauders.[2] Block's work has focused on documenting and understanding rape within the context of contemporary power relations without direct comment on *jus in bello* practices.[3] Hoock alone has weighed in on the British Army and *jus in bello,* claiming that "the inconsistency of British responses to rape . . . supported American allegations that the British violated *jus in bello.*" Observing, in company with Block, a seeming shortfall of general court-martial trials in relation to the projected frequency with which British soldiers raped American civilians, Hoock has concluded that "the importance of choice and prosecutorial discretion on the part of individual British officers" explains the relatively small number of soldiers punished in response to widespread sexual assaults committed on American women. In effect, officers chose not to prosecute soldiers for rape and thereby consciously breached *jus in bello* doctrine.[4]

Aside from a number of evidentiary issues within Hoock's work, there remains the larger question of whether we are asking the right question in considering the relationship between the British Army's conduct of the American Revolution and *jus in bello* doctrine.[5] Hoock and other historians have generally assumed that British military justice was informed, on some level, by the writings and principles of Hugo Grotius and Emer de Vattel.[6] Yet little evidence has come to light that British officers read these authors' treatises or consciously followed their philosophical arguments. Historian Ira Gruber's exhaustive survey of the personal libraries of forty-two British officers who served during the eighteenth century turned up only three with copies of Grotius's *De jure belli ac pacis* (all of whom served long before the American Revolution) and no copies of Vattel's treatise.[7] Conway's survey of officers' correspondence and diaries likewise failed to reveal any references to either theoretician: instead, he argues that "instinctive reactions rather than . . . a reasoned analysis" informed the British prosecution of the war.[8]

In the absence of any firm indications of Grotius's or Vattel's philosophy at work among the British officer corps, the search for a *jus in bello* connection inevitably shifts to the military justice system, which will be the focus of this chapter. The Mutiny Act and the Articles of War, updated annually, provided the sole formal codes of conduct for the eighteenth-century British Army and the operation of military justice. Neither code made official reference to Grotius or Vattel, though overtones of the former's philosophy are evident in sections of the Articles of War. Instead, these offered guidance and directives that were firmly rooted in the governmental crisis following the Glorious Revolution (the Mutiny Act) and medieval military law (the Articles of War). In both cases the key focus lay with maintaining discipline and control over the military, rather than with the moral implications of warfare. While Conway's division of the officer corps into conciliationists and hardliners carries with it certain moral implications, institutionally and operationally, British officers were far more concerned with maintaining control over their subordinates than with protecting civilians and adhering to *jus in bello* doctrine. As general courts-martial testimony demonstrates, the military justice system did respond directly to civilian complaints when and where it was possible to do so. Shortfalls in institutional capacity and the overwhelming focus on maintaining internal discipline over policing civil-military relations provide a better explanation for the army's poor record of protecting civilians than any endemic intentional policy of devastation, particularly in regard to rape.[9]

Despite having undergone a decades-long process of consolidation and rationalization by the 1770s, the official codes and procedures defining and guiding military justice provided only limited clarity for officers in the field during the American Revolution. The basis of this institutional cognitive dissonance lay in the markedly different origins and focuses of the fundamental legal codes. The Mutiny Act, initially devised to fill the void created by King James II's abdication in 1689, focused on ensuring civilian control over the army. It contained no specific protections for civilians in war zones and deferred to the Articles of War for most points of procedure on the execution of military justice.[10] The origins of the latter regulations, in turn, can be traced back to medieval military codes issued by English kings on a short-term basis for military expeditions, thus reflecting fundamental philosophical origins that far antedated even Grotius's writings.[11] The formal title of these regulations—*Rules and Articles for the Better Government of His Majesty's Horse and Foot Guards, and all other His Majesty's Forces*—ably demonstrates their focus on internal discipline and control. Most of the multiarticle sections of this code focus on enumerating crimes and outlining procedures to be followed in prosecuting offenses.

Nevertheless, the Articles of War did contain limited protections for noncombatants. Any officer or soldier who attacked English subjects or their property would be surrendered to the local civil authority, and any officer discovered providing protection for such miscreants would be instantly cashiered.[12] Likewise, any officer or soldier who assaulted civilians supplying the army "employed in Foreign Parts" would suffer immediate capital punishment. Finally, any military personnel who maligned or destroyed "any Property whatsoever belonging to any of Our Subjects" would be punished by the verdict of a regimental or general court-martial. This last injunction, however, contained an important loophole: soldiers could, with the local commander in chief's authorization, devastate property "to annoy Rebels, or other Enemies in Arms against

Us."[13] Although British generals seldom permitted such actions, this article nevertheless echoed Grotius by formalizing the idea that rebels were beyond the protection of military law. As a result, officers had a sound institutional basis for ignoring the complaints of any civilians who appeared to be in active rebellion against the Crown.[14] Neither the Mutiny Act nor the Articles of War provided any commentary or guidance on the justness of war.

Furthermore, the Mutiny Act and the Articles of War established a formal military justice process that was at best unwieldy during active military operations. The difficulties in holding trials at least exacerbated the problems that Block and Hoock have documented for prosecuting rapists and provide a more nuanced explanation for the shortfall in official court proceedings than officers' discretion alone. Military courts followed a two-tier structure consisting of regimental and general courts-martial. The differences between the cases heard by each type of court depended upon the variety of punishment that could be brought against the offender: regimental courts addressed "all offences . . . not extending against life or limb," with capital crimes going to general courts.[15] Regimental courts consisted of between three and five judges, depending on the number of officers available, reached a verdict by a majority vote of the judges, and generated written proceedings. The commanding officer would review these records, after which he would authorize execution of the sentence, mitigate it, or pardon the offender.[16] Regimental court-martial proceedings have generally failed to survive in public archives, largely due to the absence of any requirement for officers to preserve them. In contrast, general courts-martial consisted of thirteen officers acting as judges. An additional officer served as the deputy judge advocate, who would administer official oaths to the judges, guide the prosecution and defense, and prepare written proceedings for transmission to the commander in chief for his review, who in turn would send copies to the Judge Advocate General's Office in Whitehall, England. The Articles of War required the regimental commander to apply for a warrant from the commander in chief to hold a general court-martial, which, if granted, included relatively exhaustive instructions on preparing the written proceedings. The commander in chief reviewed all general court-martial trials and could order the judges to revise the proceedings only once if he found them unsatisfactory. If after this change the general still deemed the trial conducted inappropriately or the sentence too light, he could void the proceedings entirely, releasing the offender, who could not be retried.[17]

Although general courts-martial have become a favorite source for modern historians due to the high level of detail preserved in the record, the logistical burden of holding them, reflected in the requirement to secure a warrant, meant that relatively few such courts sat. Whenever possible, officers sought to address offenses at regimental courts and often preferred the fundamental level of martial law: summary justice. The printed commission that formally set each officer's rank and status within the command hierarchy charged the bearer with "Exercising and Well disciplining both the inferior Officers and Soldiers" under his command.[18] Influential contemporary military theorist Captain Bennett Cuthbertson emphasized the importance of summary justice, arguing that nothing trivialized courts-martial in the eyes of common soldiers more than trying offenses "for which an Officer (by his own authority) might have inflicted a punishment, sufficiently adequate, and as severe a one, as a Court-martial may chuse to do."[19] Military authorities intended summary justice to be meted out on the spot at the time of the infraction. It is possible, and perhaps even probable, that some officers may have punished less-aggravated instances of plundering or physical assaults against civilians on the spot, particularly when the realities of active operations did not allow the time to convene a court-martial. Unfortunately for historians, regulations did not require officers to record instances in which they exercised this disciplinary power. As a result, we are largely blind to the frequency and specific contexts of summary justice, particularly with regards to protecting noncombatants.

Commanding generals certainly encouraged summary justice as a means of addressing crimes against civilians while the army was on the march. When British transports arrived off Sandy Hook in June 1776 to begin the New York campaign, General Howe, commander in chief in North America, issued an order warning that "any person belonging to the Army or Transports, found guilty of plundering, or any Soldier Straggling from his Platoon, will be Executed on the Spot." On October 31 of the same year, Howe issued an additional standing order "to the Provost Martial for Executing upon the Spot, any Soldier, Seaman, or follower of the Army, found Guilty of Plundering or Marauding" and would issue similar orders during the following year.[20] With origins stretching back to the Middle Ages, provost marshals were a fixture of the British military establishment by George I's accession. References to these officials appear in military records throughout the empire, wherever the army was present in force.[21] As prolific military-guidebook writer Thomas Simes observed, the provost marshal "secure[d] deserters, spies, and all other criminals: he goes round the encampment, garrison, and its environs: hinders the soldiers from pillaging, indicts offenders, executes the sentence pronounced, and regulates the markets, weights and measures.[22] Though it dates prior to the American Revolution, Corporal William Todd of the 30th Regiment of Foot recorded a vivid impression of a provost marshal's actions in France in 1758 suggestive of instances that likely occurred in the subsequent conflict. In his diary entry for June 6, Todd relates that the captain of the provost guard had received "orders to Hang any Man he Catches out of the Line." That same day Grenadier William Cross of Todd's regiment heard a disturbance in the forest outside of the army's encampment and went to investigate, interrupting another soldier in the act of raping a French woman. While Cross's sudden appearance scared away the would-be rapist, the woman's cries had alerted the provost marshal, "who came up to the place, & took William Cross, & Hang'd him up in one of the trees without any more to do." As Todd further observed, the only report made of the incident was the provost marshal delivering Cross's regimental coat to his commanding officer in order to collect a reward.[23] The combination of active provost marshals, a top–down emphasis on summary justice in general, and the difficulties of holding courts-martial under field conditions provide an important logistical qualification to officers' prosecutorial discretion as an explanation for the relative dearth of general court-martial trials for rape.

Though lacking as a statistically significant source for understanding the relative levels of plundering and rape, general court-martial proceedings nevertheless reveal much about the British Army's institutional capacity for policing military-on-civilian crime. Such offenses went beyond the intentions of the framers of military justice, who as observed above directed that any military personnel offending civilians criminally would be surrendered to the civil authority. The absence thereof in America during the Revolution meant that a system designed for internal policing inevitably took on a tasking (in this case, external policing) for which it was not intended. The following analysis will focus on the key elements of detection of the crime, apprehension of the suspect, trial proceedings, and punishment to evaluate how effectively the military justice system's capacity matched the challenge of punishing plundering and rape. The table below tabulates the general courts-martial trial sample, representing twenty-six surviving proceedings against soldiers charged with plundering and rape held between September 1776 and June 1779.

The British Army relied on a variety of means to detect crimes, ranging from pickets stationed to guard the military perimeter to attentive officers and complaints from aggrieved parties. During the Philadelphia campaign in 1777, Captain Patrick Ferguson's pickets succeeded in capturing several parties of looters attempting to reenter British lines. In testimony given at the court-martial of Privates Abraham Pike, William Huston, and John Smith on August 30, Ferguson observed that his men had apprehended so many prisoners that he could not unequivocally identify the three men in question, except Huston. The captain was certain that three men of the 23rd were taken up attempting to pass through the lines with a horse, some poultry, and a "spying glass."[24] In the subsequent trial of Drummer William King of the 27th Regiment of Foot, Ferguson testified that his soldiers had arrested King as he came through their lines festooned with "seven or eight canteens and earthern jars, containing whisky."[25] When Private William Johnstone of the 43rd Regiment of Foot attempted to pass through the 1st Battalion of Light Infantry's lines on August 27, Lieutenant Colonel Robert Abercromby arrested him. Two hours later "a countryman named Taylor" arrived with a note from headquarters instructing Abercromby to arrest a member of the battalion who had robbed the civilian, who identified the contents of the bundle Johnstone was carrying as his property.[26]

In other instances, particularly observant officers played the role of military police in tracking down miscreants. When Captain Nicholas Parker of the 27th Regiment of Foot discovered that Private John Kelly of the same regiment had been absent from their camp on Long Island for three hours in September 1776, he went in search of the soldier with a file of men. They discovered Kelly more

GENERAL COURT-MARTIAL TRIALS FOR PLUNDERING AND RAPE, 1776–1779

TRIAL DATE	LOCATION	DEFENDANT	UNIT	CHARGE	VERDICT, SENTENCE
Sept. 1776	Long Island, N.Y.	Pvt. John Kelly	27th Regt. of Foot	Plundering John Lawrence	Guilty, 1,000 lashes
Sept. 1776	Long Island, N.Y.	Pvt. John Scoffield	28th Regt. of Foot	Plundering Garret Boerum	Acquitted
Sept. 1776	Long Island, N.Y.	Pvt. Henry Swaffield	28th Regt. of Foot	Plundering Garret Boerum	Acquitted
Sept. 1776	Long Island, N.Y.	Pvt. Thomas Ingram	28th Regt. of Foot	Plundering Garret Boerum	Acquitted
Sept. 1776	Long Island, N.Y.	Pvt. John Dunn	57th Regt. of Foot	Rape of Elizabeth Johnstone	Guilty, death by hanging
Sept. 1776	Long Island, N.Y.	Pvt. John Lusty	57th Regt. of Foot	Rape of Elizabeth Johnstone	Guilty, death by hanging
Aug. 1777	Head of Elk, Md.	Pvt. William Johnstone	43rd Regt. of Foot	Plundering Taylor	Acquitted
Aug. 1777	Head of Elk, Md.	Pvt. Abraham Pike	23rd Regt. of Foot	Plundering	Guilty, 1,000 lashes
Aug. 1777	Head of Elk, Md.	Pvt. William Huston	23rd Regt. of Foot	Plundering	Guilty, 1,000 lashes
Aug. 1777	Head of Elk, Md.	Pvt. John Smith	23rd Regt. of Foot	Plundering	Guilty, 1,000 lashes
Aug. 1777	Head of Elk, Md.	Drum. William King	27th Regt. of Foot	Plundering	Acquitted
Sept. 1777	Germantown, Pa.	Pvt. John Walton	46th Regt. of Foot	Plundering Isaac Pemberton	Guilty, 600 lashes
Sept. 1777	Germantown, Pa.	Pvt. John Connell	46th Regt. of Foot	Plundering Isaac Pemberton	Acquitted

than a mile outside of camp, carrying a bundle of loot, with additional items secreted in his pockets and wrapped around him underneath his coat. Local inhabitant John Lawrence arrived shortly thereafter, identifying his possessions among Kelly's plunder.[27] In September 1777 at Germantown, Pennsylvania, Lieutenant Edward Chandler of the 46th Regiment of Foot paused upon hearing a noise coming from an unoccupied house and arrested Privates John Walton and John Connell of his own regiment as they exited the structure.[28] Earlier that year, during the advance on Philadelphia, Brigade Major William Brown heard "a noise of People screaming and crying out in a house" and immediately proceeded to the location with another officer and a detachment of dragoons to investigate.[29]

Finally, military authorities detected and apprehended offending soldiers by quickly responding to complaints from their civilian victims. Surgeon Donald McIntire and Volunteer Terence Kern of the 43rd Regiment of Foot apprehended Privates John Dunn and John Lusty of the 57th when their victim,

TRIAL DATE	LOCATION	DEFENDANT	UNIT	CHARGE	VERDICT, SENTENCE
Sept. 1777	Germantown, Pa.	Pvt. Benjamin Allen	2nd Regt. of Foot Guards	Plundering Charles Hey	Guilty, death by hanging, recommended for mercy
Sept. 1777	Germantown, Pa.	Pvt. Thomas Jones	49th Regt. of Foot	Plundering Charles Hey	Guilty, 1,000 lashes
Sept. 1777	Germantown, Pa.	Pvt. George McCulloch	49th Regt. of Foot	Plundering Charles Hey	Guilty, death by hanging
Dec. 1777	Philadelphia, Pa.	Pvt. Murdock McLeod	42nd Regt. of Foot	Plundering	Acquitted
Dec. 1777	Philadelphia, Pa.	Sgt. William Richards	2nd Regt. of Foot Guards	Plundering	Acquitted
Dec. 1777	Derby, Pa.	Cpl. Bartholomew Judge	63rd Regt. of Foot	Plundering John Horne	Guilty, reduced, 1,000 lashes
Dec. 1777	Derby, Pa.	Pvt. Daniel McBride	63rd Regt. of Foot	Plundering John Horne	Acquitted
Dec. 1777	Derby, Pa.	Pvt. Francis Boyce	63rd Regt. of Foot	Plundering John Horne	Guilty, 500 lashes
Dec. 1777	Derby, Pa.	Pvt. John Noland	63rd Regt. of Foot	Plundering John Horne	Acquitted
Dec. 1777	Derby, Pa.	Pvt. Henry Smith	63rd Regt. of Foot	Plundering John Horne	Guilty, 500 lashes
Dec. 1777	Derby, Pa.	Pvt. John Henderson	42nd Regt. of Foot	Plundering John Horne	Guilty, 1,000 lashes
July 1778	Brooklyn, N.Y.	Pvt. Bartholomew McDonough	1st Btn, Delancey's Brigade	Rape of Phebe Coe	Guilty, death
June 1779	Stoney Point, N.Y.	Sgt. John Boswell	Vols. of Ireland	Rape of Elizabeth Loundberry	Guilty, death

Elizabeth Johnstone, approached the two officers as they were walking by her home.[30] When Private Bartholomew McDonough of the 1st Battalion, Delancey's Brigade raped Phoebe Coe in Brooklyn, New York, during the summer of 1778, Coe's slave Mingo conveyed a message to an unidentified British officer in the nearby camp. Although the officer dispatched a patrol of soldiers to the house, the men arrived too late to apprehend McDonough in the act, later arresting him on witness testimony.[31] No less an authority than General Howe dispatched his orderly sergeant and a Hessian sergeant to investigate reports of looting at Charles Hey's house in Germantown, Pennsylvania, in September 1777; the men apprehended Privates Benjamin Allen, Thomas Jones, and George McCulloch in the act.[32] Lieutenant Edward Chandler of the 46th Regiment of Foot distinguished himself a second time in December 1777 by accompanying Quaker John Horne back to his house at Derby, Pennsylvania, after Horne lodged a complaint about soldiers looting.[33]

In stopping soldiers wandering through checkpoints, investigating suspicious circumstances, and responding to civilian complaints, officers followed the same protocols that applied in cases of disorder within the ranks. Many of these examples of detection and apprehension could reflect concern over military discipline rather than with noncombatants' well-being. As Conway has established, the British officer corps fell along a spectrum of feeling between those who adopted a conciliatory attitude toward Americans and others who preferred a hardline, scorched-earth policy. While Conway aligned these extremes toward Grotius and Vattel, evidence has not come to light that either author directly influenced British officers. General court-martial data is inevitably weighted toward those commanders who took action, regardless of their reasons for doing so. Little evidence exists for officers turning a purposefully blind eye toward excesses, and at least one significant purported primary source for such behavior has been debunked. Both Conway and Hoock have referred to a letter written by Francis, Lord Rawdon describing a purported rash of rapes on Staten Island, New York, in 1776, making this source a cornerstone for arguments that officers effectively condoned rape. As historian Don Hagist has revealed, no documentation exists to support Lord Rawdon's claims that a "girl cannot step into the bushes to pluck a rose without running the most imminent risk [of] being ravished" and that daily courts-martial were held to punish the rapists.[34] While rape almost certainly occurred more frequently than the surviving general courts-martial record would lead one to believe, congressional investigations and reports in the rebel press were far from reliable indicators of officers casting a blind eye toward incidents of this capital crime. Though Conway's and Hoock's arguments that some officers disregarded civilian complaints cannot be entirely invalidated, these arguments are more likely applicable to plundering than to rape. The sort of passing approval given to plunder by Article 16 of Section XIV of the Articles of War was never extended to sexual assault. If some officers were inclined to permit such crimes to go unpunished, those decisions would be far from a wholesale incrimination of the army or its military justice system, nor would they suggest a conscious policy of devastation.

The successful detection and apprehension of military offenders led to formal trials in at least some circumstances, though not exclusively general court-martial trials. British orderly books throughout the war feature references to regimental courts-martial for plundering and theft, though no references have yet been located to regimental proceedings against soldiers accused of assault or rape in America. No records from the plundering trials survive at the regimental level. Those for regimental courts-martial held in Ireland during this period include references to several trials for soldiers who assaulted civilians, at the victim's request, raising the possibility that something comparable may have occurred in America during the Revolution.[35] Nevertheless, general court-martial trials provide the most detailed data for evaluating how seriously the officer corps applied the procedures of military justice to determining the guilt or innocence of the accused. In instances of rape and plundering, courts-martial judges invested significant time and effort into arriving at their verdict.

As Block and Hoock have observed, rape cases proved especially difficult on the evidentiary grounds of establishing that a crime had in fact occurred. Military judges' adoption of the questions employed in civilian courts in this regard should not be simply taken at face value.[36] Despite efforts by various authors, including Stephen Payne Adye, there was effectively no exchange of judicial procedure between civilian and military courts.[37] Army officers received no instruction in civilian law, and their exposure to military law remained confined to the guidance offered with warrants for holding general courts-martial and reading the Articles of War. Military judges asking the same questions of rape victims used in civilian trials constituted a rare example of judicial convergence and an extra effort by army officers, who could have just as easily handed the offenders over to the provost marshal for execution. In the three rape trials sampled, judges sought to establish that the perpetrators had penetrated their victims, that they "emitted" within them, and that the victims had resisted to their utmost ability. Failure to establish all three variables cast the veracity of the allegation into question. For example, the judges in Sergeant John Boswell's 1779 trial were particularly concerned with establishing why his victim, Elizabeth Loundberry, had kept a child in her arms during the entire rape episode—doing so limited her ability to fight back and could have suggested that she was not an entirely unwilling victim. Loundberry answered that she had "kept the child in hopes of exciting the prisoners compassion," which appropriately moved the court in her favor.[38] In Elizabeth Johnstone's case, the court was concerned to establish that the widow was "in that violent agitation of spirits, that a modest woman might be supposed to be in, after being treated in such a manner." While one of the arresting officers testified that he did not believe she had been because "she told her story very plain, but . . . was crying whilst she told it," his colleague confirmed that Johnstone "seemed to be in the greatest distress and confusion, and exclaimed much" when they met her.[39] In Coe's case, the defendant, Private McDonough, attempted to generate doubt over the action by asking the widow why she had only reported her daughter's rape at first and not her own as well. Coe replied that, not being sworn to give testimony at the time, she "thought it a shocking thing to tell of" and believed that her daughter's circumstance would ensure severe punishment for him.[40] The court's determination to establish the facts of the crime and to follow civilian court procedures in the absence of any guidelines from the Articles of War demonstrated their dedication to sincerely executing proper justice.

Instances of plundering were relatively easier to prove since the presence of contraband or unusual goods in a soldier's possession was both evidence of a crime and of guilt. The key challenge for the court was establishing the defendant's presence on or near the scene of pillaging with plunder in his possession. Given the circumstances under which many marauders were captured, correctly identifying them was far from a foregone conclusion. When Brigade Major Brown caught Private Murdock McLeod of the 42nd Regiment fleeing from a plundered house, it was well after sunset. In his resultant testimony, Brown could not "speak positively to his face" when asked by the court if McLeod was the man he had captured. Luckily, the private had given his name to Brown at the time. Likewise, Captain Michael Hamerton of the 55th, who accompanied Brown in capturing McLeod, was unable to identify the man by sight, having to depend on examining the plunder the soldier had with him when captured.[41] As observed above, Ferguson had difficulty identifying the three soldiers from the 23rd Regiment accused of plunder, while Lieutenant Chandler arrived too late at John Horne's house to observe any troops looting. Identification in that case rested with Horne and one apprentice, the former unsure that Private Daniel McBride was present, and the latter being the sole testimony against Private John Henderson for having stolen flour, for which the soldier received a thousand lashes.[42] The absence of witness testimony enabled some soldiers to escape apprehension and trial: Horne deposed that there had been "a great many" soldiers plundering his house besides the six accused, while the two most vociferous plunderers of Charley Hey's house in Germantown managed to escape with loot before Howe's orderly sergeant arrived.[43] Nevertheless, the care taken to record witness testimony to both the events and the plunder itself reflect the proper application of standard court-martial procedure.

A final indicator of the seriousness with which military authorities approached crimes against civilians comes from the defenses made by the accused. In each instance, the defendants offered detailed, somewhat plausible stories explaining how they were not culpable, suggesting that they took the trials and their judges' willingness to punish them seriously. Dunn deposed that he and Lusty had simply gone away looking for cider and had heard a cry for help from Johnstone's house on their way back to camp. Despite Lusty warning him, Dunn decided to investigate, finding the widow in a distraught state. She supposedly told him that other soldiers had violated her and offered him a book as a gift.[44] In Coe's case, McDonough attempted to throw blame on a fellow soldier, Private Laurence Dunnavon of the 1st Battalion, Delancey's Brigade, claiming that Dunnavon had bragged about the rape at the quarter guard. He called Dunnavon and McKie (the other two soldiers with him at Coe house) to testify, neither of whom would support his claims.[45] Sergeant Boswell, when charged with raping Elizabeth Loundberry, claimed that he had left his camp to look for a frying pan and was walking back when two men in Loundberry's front yard called out that gentlemen were coming to arrest him. He attempted to bolster his defense by decrying the absence of officers from the Volunteers of Ireland and the 24th Regiment of Foot who would have acted as character witnesses.[46] While it is difficult to infer circumstantial evidence from these records, such as judges' attitudes going into the trial or the manner in which defendants delivered their statements, theoretically these arguments could have at least thrown doubt on a victim's story, particularly if hardliner officers were serving on the court. The verdicts and recommendations for maximum sentences demonstrate that such doubts did not influence the ultimate decisions.

Accused soldiers in plundering cases also offered lengthy defenses designed to throw doubt on the charge. John Kelly, William Johnstone, and Murdock McLeod were each apprehended carrying bundles of plundered goods that they claimed to have received from other soldiers: Kelly stated that the items he possessed had been "pickt up near a barn, where some soldiers had been plundering," Johnstone said his bundle had been tossed to him by a grenadier he encountered on the road, while McLeod claimed to have received his package from two Hessians fleeing a house.[47] The presence of civilian victims, both in reporting crimes to the military authorities and in testifying at trials, was an essential component for refuting these defenses and guaranteeing conviction, as reflected in the table above. The arrival of inhabitants who identified their belongings in Kelly's and Taylor's hands sealed both men's fates.[48] In other cases, catching soldiers in the act of plundering provided the necessary evidence. In the example of Allen's, Jones's, and McCulloch's trial for plundering Charles Hey's house, McCulloch having been apprehended while wearing one of Hey's shirts effectively guaranteed a verdict against all of them despite the absence of loot in the other prisoners' hands when the authorities arrived.[49] Private John Walton of the 46th Regiment presented the most straightforward example, being apprehended by an officer when leaving the Pemberton house in Germantown with "a Case containing 4 green handled knives and forks, a band box and a bottle about half full of some sort of cordial."[50] Of all the sampled trials, that of the six men of the 63rd accused of plundering Horne's house in Derby, Pennsylvania, in December 1777 provided the least amount of detailed evidence. It seems probable that Judge, Boyce, Smith, and Henderson received punishment to provide an example for the other soldiers who managed to escape from the scene.

The final metric for appraising the military justice system's engagement with soldier-on-civilian crime is punishment. The capital sentences entered against the three convicted rapists seemed, on the surface, to make an unequivocally firm statement on the army's view of sexual assault. But as historian Judith Van Buskirk has documented, General Howe pardoned Elizabeth Johnstone's rapists in general orders, purportedly "at the intercession of the injured party."[51] Similarly, Lieutenant General Henry Clinton's orders for the Rhode Island garrison on December 24, 1776, included a pardon for Private John Dowling of the 22nd Regiment of Foot, sentenced to death for committing a rape, due to "intercession having been made by the injured party."[52] While potentially intended as an instructive example of mercy to send a message to the army in general, such pardons may well have effectively nullified the best intentions of general court-martial judges: any rapist could expect to escape punishment as long as his victim could be said to intervene on his behalf.

The punishments meted out in plundering cases offered a more mixed message. Of the twenty-three trials sampled, ten resulted in acquittals, while General Howe further remitted punishment in three cases in which he found it "inadequate" to the crime. These remissions could be taken as an indication that the courts-martial judges were evincing too much sympathy for the defendants.[53] The case of Private William Johnstone of the 43rd Regiment of Foot provides a pointed example. In his general orders for August 30, 1777, Howe directed the officers serving as judges for that trial to immediately revise their proceedings, expressing his displeasure with the court's findings. This seemed to have had little effect, for in general orders on September 2, the commander in chief expressed his disapproval of Johnstone's acquittal, though he still ordered the soldier to return to his regiment: voiding the trial proceedings would have had the same effect, and Howe could not order a second revision.[54] A week later, in the general orders for September 9, Howe directed Private Andrew Lauder of the 10th Regiment of Foot, "guilty of the Crime of marauding, and detected with Plunder upon him," to be immediately executed and warned that he was "determined for the future to show no mercy to any Man guilty of that Crime."[55]

The sentences for soldiers convicted of plundering that met with Howe's approval were mostly charged with violating Article 21, Section XIV, of the Articles of War, the same section that permitted license in destroying rebel property in Article 16. Article 21 stated that any officer or soldier who went "in Search of Plunder" should "suffer Death, or such other Punishment as by a Court-martial shall be inflicted."[56] John Kelly provided the single exception among the sample: the court judged him to have violated Article 13, Section XIV, which forbade soldiers from any misbehavior before the enemy, including running away, by speaking "words inducing others to do the like" and plundering, with a similar punishment of death or whatever other sentence a court-martial passed.[57] The choice of the specific article and section that a defendant violated rested with the officer bringing the charge, probably advised by the judge advocate general. Nevertheless, the fact that both articles of Section XIV authorized death and only two men were executed is telling. Both violators were involved in the pillaging of the Hey house, which was an extensive and brutal example of marauding witnessed by General Howe's orderly sergeant firsthand. Private Benjamin Allen of the 2nd Regiment of Foot Guards and Privates Thomas Jones and George McCulloch of the 49th Regiment were the soldiers involved. As noted above, McCulloch had the audacity to immediately put on a shirt he stole from Hey, though McCulloch claimed that he had found the shirt earlier at the waterside while washing his issue clothing.[58] By stealing and immediately donning plundered apparel, McCulloch certainly singled himself out as a fitting example for discouraging similar actions among the soldiers at large. Allen likely earned his capital sentence by joining McCulloch in demanding Hey's money.[59] The remaining corporal punishments were in standard keeping with the British punishment structure at the court-martial level, and probably reflect the endemic nature of plundering: offenses were so widespread that executing every convicted defendant was not a realistic option.[60]

The acquittals in this sample reflect the fact that an accusation of plundering civilian property without official sanction required a formal investigation. Both Johnstone and McLeod were brought to trial having been found under suspicious circumstances with civilian goods—extremely weak evidence, even for the period. While Johnstone's case obviously garnered Howe's suspicion, McLeod's account of having been near the house from which a great outcry issued, which prompted Brigade Major Brown to investigate, and having seen two Hessians running from it, who tossed the bundle to him must have been convincing. Drummer King, Private Connell, and Sergeant Major William Richards had likewise been taken under suspicious circumstances: King as discussed above, Connell in the vicinity of the house that his comrade Walton plundered in Germantown, and Richards having ordered two soldiers to carry away loot found by the pickets. The court-martial judges were unable to establish that King's liquor was plundered rather than purchased, that Connell had actually been in the house plundering (he had no items on him), and that Richards appeared to be acting properly to send suspicious material to his commander for orders.[61] Privates John Scoffield, Henry Swaffield, and Thomas Ingram of the 28th Regiment had been apprehended by loyal civilians while searching a house for arms: the civilians' testimony detailed the lengths to which the prisoners went to avoid damaging property while carrying out their orders to find contraband arms and powder.[62] McBride and Noland, two of the six men from the 63rd accused of plundering Horne's house in Derby, were likely acquitted due to scanty evidence and as an example of mercy to balance out the corporal punishment ordered for their four compatriots. Overall, the acquittals served to emphasize the army's commitment to following procedure, which required a formal investigation and trial even when the defendant's guilt was not clear from the beginning.

The general courts-martial cases considered here seem, on the surface, to indicate that the British military justice system did contain the capacity to police and punish offenses against civilians in a manner that matched Vattel's approach to *jus in bello.* A less optimistic reading, however, would suggest that these cases simply reflect instances where soldier-against-civilian crimes could be mainstreamed relatively easily into the existing process. The key for this successful inclusion rested with detection and apprehension of the suspects combined with officers' willingness to prosecute rather than casting a blind eye toward military miscreants. Identifying a crime in progress and catching the offender were not forgone conclusions in all cases: the relatively small numbers of officers and provost-marshal patrols versus the total number of soldiers and the wide area of operations did not make detection a certainty. Officers could easily ignore reports of plunder and rape from local civilians or accept soldiers' explanations for why they were in possession of contraband. Perhaps most importantly of all in regard to both Block's and Hoock's arguments concerning rape, summary justice provided officers and the provost marshal with a means of punishing soldiers that did not generate a paper trail. As a result, historians remain largely blinded to the realities of enforcement outside of those instances chronicled in general courts-martial. Unfortunately, that surviving material also fails to provide the level of detail required to discern between a systemic concern over the ethical treatment of noncombatants and a more simple focus on maintaining internal discipline.

Ultimately, the most significant point to come out of any consideration of *jus in bello,* military justice, and the American Revolution is that the British Army's disciplinary apparatus was not specifically designed to provide the level of protection for civilians that Vattel's philosophy demanded. The military justice system as constituted through the Mutiny Act and the Articles of War acted on a presupposition of a civil authority that would police and punish crimes committed by soldiers against civilians. Thus there was no formal precedent or procedure for maintaining noncombatant protections, particularly in the context of a civil war. The only portion of the official codes that addressed treatment of civilians during hostilities provided a qualified encouragement for the destruction of civilian property that some officers could have interpreted as grounds for not prosecuting plundering soldiers. The structure of the military justice process was ill suited for trying offenders in the field, at least at the court-martial level. In the absence of a modern judge advocate general's corps of trained lawyers and judges, the British military justice system relied disproportionately on regular officers for staffing. As a result, when courts-martial did sit in judgment over offenders, personal attitudes took on a defining role in the process, granting officers who subscribed to a vision closer to that of Grotius than of Vattel with the opportunity to stop or derail the judicial process. Even if the institutional capacity had existed to guarantee civilian security through the military justice system, the underlying themes of the Mutiny Act and the Articles of War clearly placed maintaining order within the army as a higher priority. As a result, *jus in bello* played a tangential role at best in the British Army's prosecution of the war.

NOTES

1. The National Archives of Great Britain [hereafter TNA], War Office [hereafter WO] 71/82, 405–25.
2. Stephen Conway, "British Army Officers and the American War for Independence," *William and Mary Quarterly,* 3rd ser., 41, no. 2 (1984): 265–76; Stephen Conway, "'The Great Mischief Complain'd Of': Reflections on the Misconduct of British Soldiers in the Revolutionary War," *William and Mary Quarterly,* 3rd ser., 47, no. 3 (1990): 370–90; Stephen Conway, "To Subdue America: British Army Officers and the Conduct of the Revolutionary War," *William and Mary Quarterly,* 3rd ser., 43, no. 3 (1986): 381–407.
3. Sharon Block, "Rape in the American Revolution: Process, Reaction, and Public Re-Creation," in *Sexual Violence in Conflict Zones: From the Ancient World to the Era of Human Rights,* ed. Elizabeth D. Heineman (Philadelphia: University of Pennsylvania Press, 2011); Sharon Block, *Rape and Sexual Power in Early America* (Chapel Hill: University of North Carolina Press, 2006); Sharon Block, "Rape without Women: Print Culture and the Politicization of Rape, 1765–1815," *Journal of American History* 89, no. 3 (2002): 849–68.
4. Holger Hoock, "Jus in Bello, Rape, and the British Army in the American Revolutionary War," *Journal of Military Ethics* 14, no. 1 (Jan. 2, 2015): 74–76.
5. Ibid., 79–80; Block, *Rape and Sexual Power in Early America,* 126–27. Both Block and Hoock have acknowledged the problems of a fragmentary primary-source base and the difficulties that rape victims faced in bringing their assailants to trial. Both also rely largely on rebel propaganda to support their claims that significantly more rapes occurred than went to trial. Hoock is especially aggressive on this point but fails to offer any comment on the probable bias contained with the congressional reports and one letter from George Washington, upon which so much of his argument relies. Neither manifest a detailed understanding of the military justice process. Further, Hoock employs Conway's analysis of British officers' writings without any consideration of the challenging circumstances of operating within a hostile civilian population, where testimony from purported victims could not be taken at face value.
6. Conway, "To Subdue America," 396–97; Hoock, "Jus in Bello, Rape, and the British Army in the American Revolutionary War"; J. Daryl Charles, "Framing the Issues in Moral Terms I: Applying Just War Tradition," *The Ashgate Research Companion to Military Ethics,* ed. James Turner Johnson and Eric D. Patterson (Burlington, Vt.: Ashgate, 2015), 125; James Turner Johnson, "Enforcing and Strengthening Noncombatant Immunity," ibid., 308; Johnson, "Maintaining the Protection of Non-Combatants," *Journal of Peace Research* 37, no. 4 (July 2000): 421–48.
7. Ira D. Gruber, *Books and the British Army in the Age of the American Revolution* (Chapel Hill: University of North Carolina Press and the Society of the Cincinnati, 2010), 100, 130, 135.
8. Conway, "To Subdue America," 395–96.
9. Well-documented instances of formal devastation did occur during the war, but these were orchestrated from the top of the command hierarchy down under specific circumstances, as Benjamin Carp ably covers in chapter 8 above.

10. *An Act for punishing Mutiny and Desertion; and for the better Payment of the Army and their Quarters* (London: Printed by Charles Eyre and William Strahan, printers to the King's most Excellent Majesty, 1774). The Mutiny Act's protections for civilians applied within the British Isles and focused on issues involving quartering, impressing of carts and carriages, and forced enlistments.
11. While contemporary military theorists, particularly Stephen Payne Adye, have maintained that courts-martial descended from the medieval court of chivalry, G. D. Squibb has conclusively demonstrated that this line of descent does not hold up under close scrutiny. Squibb, *The High Court of Chivalry: A Study of the Civil Law in England* (Oxford: Clarendon, 1959), 2–3, 8; Stephen Payne Adye, *A Treatise on Courts Martial* (New York: H. Gaine, 1769), 34–35.
12. Sec. XI, Art. 1, *Rules and Articles for the Better Government of His Majesty's Horse and Foot Guards, And All Other His Majesty's Forces in Great Britain and Ireland, and Dominions beyond the Seas, and Foreign Parts* (London: Printed by Charles Eyre and William Strahan, printers to the King's most Excellent Majesty, 1774) [hereafter cited as Articles of War (1774)], 166. This protection only applied in areas where British civilian law was in effect, which did not include the thirteen colonies of North America after the king's proclamation of rebellion on 23 August 1775.
13. Sec. XIV, Arts. 11, 16, ibid., 177, 179.
14. Hugo Grotius, *The Law of War and Peace*, ed. Louise Ropes Loomis (New York: Published for the Classics Club by Walter J. Black, 1949).
15. "Orders and Articles of Warr composed and Corrected by the Advice of the Duke of Albemarle, Captain-General of His Majesty's Armyes," 9 Apr. 1666, in *Military Forces of the Crown; Their Administration and Government,* comp. and ed. Charles M. Clode, 2 vols. (London: John Murray, 1869), 1:447. These regulations constituted the foundation for the structure and function of the British military justice system, upon which subsequent developments in the eighteenth century rested. They also contain the clearest descriptions of the jurisdictions of the varieties of courts-martial.
16. Articles of War (1774), 193.
17. Ibid., 184–91. Judge Adv. Gen. Edward Hughes in 1715 developed the standard form for the deputation, which would remain in use throughout the eighteenth century. For examples, see deputation to John Beaver to serve as deputy judge advocate for Gibraltar in 1715, TNA WO71/14, 71–73; deputations for courts-martial held in the Brigade of Guards in the summer of 1722, ibid., 309–12; deputations for courts-martial for 23 Apr. 1757, Henry Bouquet, *The Papers of Col. Henry Bouquet,* ed. Donald H Kent and Sylvester K Stevens (Harrisburg: Department of Public Instruction, Pennsylvania Historical Commission, 1941), 11–14; and deputations for courts-martial for some time in the period 1764–70, TNA WO72/6.
18. Commission to William Robertson as Ensign in the 63rd Regiment of Foot, 24 Nov. 1775, National Archives of Scotland (hereafter NAS) General Deposit (hereafter GD) 132/819. See also Commission to William Robertson Gent, as Lieutenant in the 55th Regiment of Foot, 18 Dec. 1777, ibid., GD132/821; and Sir Andrew Agnew's commission as Cornet in the Royal North British Dragoons (Scots Greys), 11 May 1705, ibid., GD154/612.

19. Bennett Cuthbertson, *A System for the Compleat Interior Management and Œconomy of a Battalion of Infantry* (Dublin: Printed by Boulter Grierson, 1768), 120. As an indication of Cuthbertson's influence on the British Army, Ira Gruber observes that more than 900 officers subscribed to underwriting the printing of Cuthbertson's book, many of whom went on to hold important commands in the British Army during the American Revolution. Gruber, *Books and the British Army,* 33.
20. Stephen Kemble, *The Kemble Papers,* vol. 1 (New York: New-York Historical Society, 1893), 383, 399, 480–81.
21. Duke of Cumberland's order book during the campaign of 1746, Jan. 28–July 7, NAS GD1/322/1, 3–4, 12, 27; General Orders, 18 July 1777, Orderly Book of Capt. Murdoch MacLaine's Grenadier Company at Halifax, 1777, GD174/2107; Trial of Murphy the Marshal, Keeper of the Savoy, 11 Apr. 1716, Horse Guards, TNA WO71/14, 96–99; Orders, 14 Sept. 1783, American War of Independence Orderly Book, Campbell of Balliveolan Papers, NAS GD13/94, 3.
22. Thomas Simes, *The Military Instructor* (London: Millan, 1779), 82.
23. William Todd, *The Journal of Corporal Todd, 1745–1762,* ed. Andrew Cormack and Alan Jones (London: Sutton Publishing for the Army Records Society, 2001), 46–47.
24. TNA WO71/84, 201.
25. Ibid., 202–3.
26. Ibid., 197–98.
27. TNA WO71/82, 406–7.
28. TNA WO71/84, 318, 323.
29. TNA WO71/85, 151, 153.
30. TNA WO71/82, 419.
31. TNA WO71/86, 203–4.
32. TNA WO71/84, 330–31.
33. TNA WO71/85, 192.
34. Hoock, "Jus in Bello, Rape and the British Army in the American Revolutionary War," 78; Conway, "To Subdue America," 394; Don N. Hagist, "Rawdon's Ruse," *Journal of the American Revolution,* last modified July 23, 2014, accessed Aug. 19, 2016, https://allthingsliberty.com/2014/07/rawdons-ruse/.
35. For examples of regimental proceedings referenced in orderly books, see A. R. Newsome, "A British Orderly Book, 1780–1781," *North Carolina Historical Review* 9, no. 2 (Apr. 1932): 163–86; and Orderly Book of the 37th Regiment of Foot, 1780–81, Eyre Coote Papers, William L. Clements Library, University of Michigan, Ann Arbor. For Irish regimental courts-martial, see HL/PO/JO/10/7/544, House of Lords Record Office, London. Records survive for the 1st, 2nd, 3rd, and 4th Regiments of Horse; the 8th, 12th, 13th, and 18th Regiments of Light Dragoons; the 9th Regiment of Dragoons; and the 3rd, 11th, 36th, 67th, and 68th Regiments of Foot. Article 5 of Section IX of the Articles of War required commanding officers to "see Justice done" to any officer or soldier under their command who aggrieved civilians if the victims complained to the commanding officer. *Rules and Articles for the Better Government of His Majesty's Horse and Foot Guards, and All Other His Majesty's Forces in Great Britain and Ireland, and Dominions beyond the Seas, and Foreign Parts* (London, 1771)

[hereafter cited as Article of War (1771)], 164.

36. Block, *Rape and Sexual Power in Early America,* 126.
37. Adye, *Treatise on Courts Martial.* Adye attempts to meld civilian and military practice together in an effort to legitimize courts-martial in the civil authority's eyes. While his treatise was reprinted numerous times, it in no way reflects the official procedures that the Judge Advocate General's Office enforced army-wide.
38. TNA WO71/88, 526.
39. TNA WO71/82, 418–19.
40. TNA WO71/86, 202.
41. TNA WO71/85, 151–52.
42. Ibid., 192–93.
43. Trial of Cpl. Bartholomew Judge, Pvt. Daniel McBride, Pvt. Francis Boyce, Pvt. John Noland, Pvt. Henry Smith, and Pvt. John Henderson, ibid., 192; trial of Pvt. Benjamin Allen, Pvt. Thomas Jones, and Pvt. George McCulloch, ibid., WO71/84, 327.
44. TNA WO71/82, 423–25.
45. TNA WO71/86, 204–6.
46. TNA WO71/88, 527–28.
47. TNA WO71/82, 409; WO71/84, 199; WO71/85.
48. The court finding Johnstone innocent despite being in possession of identified stolen property likely explains Howe's direction to the judges to revise their proceedings and his public expression of disapproval in general orders when the court returned the same verdict.
49. TNA WO71/84, 327, 330.
50. Ibid., 319.
51. Judith L Van Buskirk, *Generous Enemies: Patriots and Loyalists in Revolutionary New York* (Philadelphia: University of Pennsylvania Press, 2002), 25. Van Buskirk quotes from the diary entry of Lt. John Peebles of the 42nd Regiment of Foot for 30 September 1776.
52. General Orders, Rhode Island, TNA WO36/2. Both examples of intercession by the victims strike this author as suspicious, potentially hinting at politics behind the scenes, including the possibility of officers pressuring the victims in order to spare their men, who constituted valuable investments of training time.
53. Trials of Pvts. Abraham Pike, William Huston, and John Smith of the 23rd Regiment of Foot, in Kemble, *Papers,* 483.
54. Ibid., 482–83.
55. Ibid., 491.
56. Articles of War (1771), 180–81.
57. Ibid., 177.
58. TNA WO71/84, 331.
59. Ibid., 327.
60. For more details on the British Army's approach to corporal punishment, see Sylvia R. Frey, "Courts and Cats: British Military Justice in the Eighteenth Century," *Military Affairs* 43, no. 1 (1979): 5–11.
61. TNA WO71/84, 202–4; WO71/84, 317–25; WO71/85, 182–84.
62. TNA WO71/82, 410–13.

10 "ELATED WITH VICTORY, AND REEKING WITH REVENGE"

The Yorktown Prisoners and the Laws of War in Revolutionary America

T. Cole Jones

Charles, Earl Cornwallis, graduate of the prestigious military school at Turin, veteran of two wars, and victor of nearly every battle in which he had fought, despaired. He had good reason. In early October 1781, a combined Franco-American force under the command of General George Washington was methodically approaching his positions at Yorktown and Gloucester Point on either side of the York River in the Virginia tidewater. With a French fleet blocking his escape by sea, the siege proceeded in quintessential European fashion. Despite the heat and mosquito-borne illnesses of early autumn, Washington's forces advanced steadily, digging saps and parallels to bring their guns within range of Cornwallis's fortifications. Washington was in his element, personally observing and directing the placement of his artillery. On October 9, the general had the honor, and no doubt the pleasure, of putting "the match to the first gun." The entire American line erupted in flame and smoke. The barrage was relentless. According to Continental Army surgeon James Thacher, "the whole peninsula trembles under the incessant thunderings of our infernal machines." Defiant to the end, the British troops endured the bombardment for eight days before Cornwallis sent his American counterpart word that he wished "to settle terms for the surrender of the posts of York and Gloucester." Washington, animated by "an ardent desire to spare the further effusion of blood," acquiesced. Cornwallis's American campaigns were over.[1]

In the conventional narrative of the American Revolution, Cornwallis's capitulation at Yorktown leads directly to the ratification of the Treaty of Paris, ending the war and formally establishing American independence. Yet for the nearly seven thousand British and Germanic soldiers who surrendered there, the struggle had just begun. This chapter analyzes their experience in captivity within the context of the contemporary laws of war. Washington tried to uphold European standards by treating Cornwallis, his officers, and men equitably, according to their military rank and social station. By granting magnanimous terms for their surrender, the general hoped to demonstrate the new nation's commitment to European norms for the conduct of war and thus its suitability for membership in the international community as an independent state. Only by upholding European conventions, Washington believed, could the United States shed the stain of rebellion and secure its sovereignty on the world stage.

His logic, however, proved unconvincing to the revolutionary leadership in the Continental Congress and in the individual states. Unlike in the European wars Washington aspired to emulate, in which monarchs and the generals who served them set military policies regardless of their subjects' input, in the American republic, public opinion could not be so easily ignored. To the congressmen and their constituents alike, Cornwallis seemed like an underserving subject for Washington's benevolence. The brutality with which his army had waged the southern campaigns of 1780 and 1781 was infamous. In the opinion of the Loyalist newspaper *Royal Gazette,* revolutionary Americans after Yorktown were "elated with victory, and reeking with revenge."[2]

Over the coming months, Congress violated Washington's terms by refusing to exchange Cornwallis's troops, consigning them instead to an arduous captivity in the Virginia, Maryland, and Pennsylvania backcountry. With its powers derived from the consent of the governed and unable to levy taxes, Congress had few other options. Once in the custody of state officials that had neither the inclination nor the means to provide for them, these men suffered chronic food shortages, retaliatory policies, and the caprice and cruelty of their captors, all guaranteeing that they would spend the remainder of the war in misery, losing as many as a third of their number to disease and malnutrition. The Yorktown prisoners' ordeal reveals that the regulation of wartime violence, which was so central to European monarchical military culture, was unsustainable in the new nation. After six years of sanguinary civil warfare, the laws of war had little purchase among the populace.

In the decades before armies clashed on the Yorktown peninsula, it was Anglophilia rather than independence that gripped most colonial Americans. Scholars such as John Murrin, T. H. Breen, and Richard Bushman have noted the paradoxical tendency of eighteenth-century Americans to self-consciously model themselves on their British counterparts. This trend was especially pronounced among the privileged colonial elite. From the tea they drank to the clothes they wore to the houses they built, elite Americans aspired to be British. It is little wonder then that when war came to the colonies in 1775, the leaders of the resistance movement looked across the Atlantic for martial inspiration. While some prominent revolutionaries like Washington had gained experience serving alongside British regulars during the Seven Years' War (1756–63), most elite Americans were amateurs at arms. To combat their inexperience, revolutionary America's political leaders consulted the works of Enlightenment scholars of the laws of war. From its inception, Congress kept a well-stocked library of legal volumes, including those by Hugo Grotius, Samuel Pufendorf, and Jean-Jacques Burlamaqui, but the delegates appear to have favored Swiss jurist Emer de Vattel's 1758 treatise *The Law of Nations.*[3]

Although he covered the legal justifications for going to war, known as *jus ad bello,* Vattel devoted the majority of his study of war to the legal restraint of its conduct: *jus in bello.* For Vattel, war was the prerogative of the state. It was waged by organized and disciplined armies, not by the population at large. In book 3 of *The Law of Nations,* entitled "Of War," Vattel laid out the rules by which European armies should conduct themselves. In a just war, what Vattel called "a regular war," "certain rules, either prescribed by the law of nature, or adopted by custom, are observed" by combatants on both sides. These rules were aimed at limiting the destructive power of warfare and protecting noncombatants and enemy prisoners. Moderation and restraint should characterize every facet of warfare, from preventing plundering to upholding surrender agreements, he argued. On the issue of prisoners of war, Vattel was clear: "On an enemy's submitting and laying down his arms, we cannot with justice take away his life." Unlike the seemingly unrestrained violence of the seventeenth-century religious wars, Vattel was pleased by "the humanity with which most nations in Europe carry on their wars at present."[4]

Much to Washington's chagrin, the strategic and operational conditions of the Revolutionary War, as well as deficiencies in men and materiel, precluded the type of warfare of maneuver and siege commonly practiced in Europe. Consequently, the general had few opportunities to implement Vattel's laws in person. With the exception of his Christmas 1776 coup de main at Trenton, which yielded more than nine hundred prisoners, Washington's forces had rarely captured many enemy soldiers. That all changed at Yorktown. Cornwallis's exposed position on the peninsula presented Washington with the opportunity, for the first time in his long military career, to not only conduct a conventional European-style campaign but also to demonstrate American humanity and military proficiency on a grand scale.

Given Cornwallis's tactical predicament—he was surrounded and subject to cannonade by land and sea—Washington could have demanded his unconditional surrender; instead the American general promised him that "the same honors will be granted to the surrendering army as were granted to the garrison of Charlestown." They could expect "the benevolent treatment of prisoners which is invariably observed by the Americans." On this last point, Washington was not being entirely truthful. He knew that Congress had nullified the Convention of Saratoga, the surrender agreement that had promised to permit the British army captured at Saratoga in 1777 to return to England on parole. With the tide of public opinion against the convention, Congress resolved in January 1778 to abrogate the treaty on the mere pretense of British infraction. Instead of swift repatriation, those enemy soldiers would remain in captivity for the duration of the war. Washington must have known that the terms he proffered Cornwallis would be equally unpopular. Nevertheless, he believed that the magnitude of his current victory, as well as the presence of his French allies, would induce Congress to uphold the deal.[5]

This promise must have been cold comfort to Cornwallis, but he had little other choice but to accept the terms. His men would become prisoners of war, but the officers were "indulged in retaining their side arms and the officers and soldiers may preserve their baggage and effects." More importantly for the common soldiers, they were to be "supplied with the same rations of provisions as are allotted to the soldiers in the service of America," the cost of which was to be reimbursed by the British treasury. As soon as convenient, the soldiers would march to internment "in Virginia, Maryland or Pennsylvania," while the bulk of the officers were "permitted to go on parole" to England or New York. Cornwallis himself could sail for New York, there to be paroled to England as soon as convenient. Only one junior officer for each group of fifty soldiers was required "to reside near their respective regiments, to visit them frequently and be witness of their treatment." Although the garrison was not granted the full honors of war—they could not surrender with their flags flying—the American general did allow the British dragoons to parade "with their swords drawn, trumpets sounding," out of respect for their hard-fought defense of Gloucester. These terms were as generous as the troops could hope for under the circumstances. One of Cornwallis's Hessian soldiers, Stephan Popp, recorded the feelings of his comrades: "We were all glad and happy that this siege had finally come to an end and that it had turned out to be such a reasonable truce."[6]

At four o'clock in the afternoon on October 19, 1781, roughly seven thousand British and Hessian troops filed out of their entrenchments to surrender. Flanked on either side of the road by French and American soldiers, Cornwallis's army marched to an open field outside the siege lines and laid down their arms in defeat. No taunts or shouts of joy could be heard from the ranks of the victorious allies; a "universal silence and order prevailed." To Hessian captain Johann Ewald, it was a "melancholy parade." Surgeon Thacher noted that "many of the soldiers manifested a sullen temper, throwing their arms on the pile with violence, as if determined to render them useless." While the soldiers surrendered their weapons, Brigadier Charles O'Hara, standing in for Cornwallis, who was "pretending indisposition" according to Thacher, offered the earl's sword to his fellow European officer, Lieutenant General Jean-Baptiste Donatien de Vimeur, comte de Rochambeau. In deference to his allies, Rochambeau motioned to Washington, who in turn instructed O'Hara to give the sword to Major General Benjamin Lincoln, the man who had surrendered Charleston the year before. By allowing Lincoln to accept the surrender, Washington symbolically wiped away the shame of Charleston—the conquered had become the conqueror.[7]

Although they held their American captors beneath contempt, Cornwallis's troops took comfort from the presence of the French army and the strict accordance to European custom during the ritual of surrender. Captain Ewald observed that "after the troops were surrendered into captivity, every officer was greeted by the French generals and officers with the greatest courtesy. . . . One scarcely knew whether he was among his friends or foes." Similarly, British captain Samuel Graham remembered that he received "much courtesy from the French" officers, who offered him generous loans as well as hospitality. In the evening after the surrender, the French officers lavishly entertained their British and German counterparts, excluding their American allies. Ewald thought "that the French officers preferred the company of the English, Ansbach, and Hessian officers to that of their own allies," who were clearly bothered by the camaraderie among the Europeans.[8]

The Americans were in no mood to fraternize with their erstwhile foes, and Washington knew it. That past July, one of his officers had informed the general that the militiamen from the southern states were "a People who having Experienced no inconsiderable portion of British Barbarism, are become keen for revenge and appear properly determined." Ewald seconded this assessment. As he phrased it, "the American officer, like his soldier, hates his foes more than we do." The root of the animosity was clear. The British had "practiced the most abominable enormities" that "spread terror and desolation throughout the Southern states," according to Thacher. The French priest abbé Claude Robin feared for the British prisoners, who "had to bear a great deal from the Americans, who seemed resolved to take ample vengeance for the robberies and murders that had been perpetrated in their habitations." Robin's concerns were well founded. An American militia colonel who had been a prisoner of the British encouraged his comrades to vent their anger on the prisoners. "Boys, retaliate," he commanded. "These are the very men that plundered our men, and used them so badly." To ease tensions, Washington prudently sequestered the captured troops, preventing any widespread ill treatment, but the prisoners knew all too well that the Americans yearned to "steal or plunder or otherwise abuse us as is their usual practice." The European-style siege and surrender ceremony belied the fact that this was no longer a limited conflict constrained by the laws of war—it was a war of vengeance.[9]

When news of the victory reached Congress, the members' exuberance was quickly subsumed by concern over the generous terms Washington had granted Cornwallis. Congressman Elias Boudinot, a man who had seen British atrocities firsthand while serving as commissary general of prisoners, feared the terms were "rather too favourable." Although the articles of capitulation were no more generous than those "allowed to our People at Charles Town," Washington had failed to account for the fact that Lieutenant General Sir Henry Clinton had violated those terms by revoking the garrison's paroles and confining many American soldiers on board disease-ridden prison hulks in Charleston Harbor. From the British perspective, Clinton's actions were entirely consistent with European *jus in bello.* The Americans, after all, were rebels in arms and thus outside of the international community; simply forgoing mass executions was a sign of mercy. To outraged Americans, however, the decision to renege on the Charleston surrender agreement was just the latest example of British perfidy and barbarism. From the outset of hostilities, the British had denied American combatants the protections of prisoner-of-war status, and thousands had perished in their hands. Few in Congress felt that Washington's generosity would have a corrective effect on the enemy's policy.[10]

Instead of lenient paroles and ample rations, Americans of all social orders yearned to exact retribution for years of abuse. As one outraged citizen argued in his petition to Congress, "Providence has thrown into our hands a numerous army" that should be used to revenge the mistreatment of American prisoners at "the expence, if it be necessary, of the[ir] lives." He pressed the delegates to embrace "retaliated confinement as a measure just in its principles." Many in Congress concurred. Harshly confining the Yorktown prisoners would placate their outraged constituents and demonstrate to the world that the United States was unafraid to invoke the *lex talionis:* the law of retaliation.[11]

Washington knew well the role of retaliation in contemporary European warfare and feared its consequences. Under the principles of *jus in bello,* violations of the rules by one belligerent party could be met with a proportional reprisal by the other. The mere hint of retaliation was often enough to induce good behavior. Regrettably, that had not been the case in America. Threats of congressional retaliation had fallen on deaf ears among the British high command. With popular enthusiasm for revenge on the rise, Washington worried that this time Congress would be in earnest. In his opinion, rather than demonstrating American strength, retaliating on defenseless enemy prisoners would "be to the eternal disgrace of the Nation." But the decision was not his to make. "Congress have [retaliation] under consideration," he told one of his generals, "and we must await their determinations." While Washington waited, Boudinot, the newly elected president of Congress, gathered a committee to investigate "the motives which led to the several Articles of the Capitulation."[12]

Conspicuously absent from Boudinot's committee, the delegates from South Carolina, whose state had suffered the most at the hands of Cornwallis's troops, were particularly incensed. In a letter to Aedanus Burke, Arthur Middleton fumed, "It is d[amne]d hard that rascals should be parol'd" when they "deserve[d] hanging." Middleton urged Burke to "remember the Sufferings of our fellow men" and embrace "retaliation." For him, that "alone is the only magic rod which converts cruelty into mercy and effects wonders." Unwilling to publicly question the wisdom of Washington's decision so soon after a resounding victory, Boudinot's committee resolved to convey "the thanks of the United States in Congress assembled" to both him and General Rochambeau "for the wisdom and prudence manifested in the capitulation." Less publicly, some members continued to "think no treatment could have been too severe for the Garrison." In the opinion of South Carolina delegate John Mathews, Cornwallis deserved to have his "neck stretched, as some small sacrifice to the manes of the numbers whose necks he has stretched."[13]

The revolutionary press agreed with the irate congressmen. One Whig writer questioned why the "inhuman Earl Cornwallis" and his men should be allowed "to riot upon the fat of the land . . . , let loose upon parole to corrupt and intimate our citizens" when had he been victorious, Cornwallis would have held American prisoners "upon half an allowance of stinking pork and musty bred in barns and churches . . . , kicked and cursed by every ensign in the British army." Even before his capture, newspapers across the continent had launched a concerted attack on Cornwallis's character and reputation. The *Pennsylvania Packet* named him "the British Cerberus," a reference to the three-headed hound that guarded the gates of the underworld in Greek mythology. His "bloody-mindedness" had induced the British general to commit crimes so "heinous, that old Beelzebub himself would blush." The author anticipated with glee "the moment when terrible vengeance from heaven may come hurling down upon" him. A columnist for the *Independent Chronicle* thought all Americans should be "astonished at the generous terms granted to Cornwallis and his army" in light of "the innumerable acts of barbarity, with which the Britons have stained themselves and the nation in the American war." In the opinion of the *Freeman's Journal*, Washington had done nothing less than grant "mild terms to Satan's firstborn son." Allowing Cornwallis to return to England on parole while American prisoners daily died in British prison hulks and jails was a "virtue too sublime" under the circumstances. To wrathful revolutionaries everywhere, Yorktown looked like the ideal moment to enact "ample retaliation."[14]

Despite the generosity of the articles of capitulation, retaliation was exactly what the British prisoners feared, and many seized the first opportunity to escape their would-be tormentors. One such prisoner, Sergeant Roger Lamb, had escaped from American captivity before. Rather than starve in another prison camp, Lamb "determined to attempt [his] escape to New York." Fortunately for him, confusion reigned in the aftermath of the siege, creating an ideal opportunity to run. One American officer colorfully described the "Scene of Confusion" in the days following the surrender: "British officers, and French Sailors, Soldiers, Marines, fatiguemen, boatmen, British Merchants, American Speculators, Jews & Infidels.—Negroes, British Misses, Soldiers trolls with a song etc. So be-mixed, be-Hurried, be-knave'd, be-frighted & be-Devil'd, that nothing Short of the Pen or the Pencil of Hogarth, could Possibly do them Justice to Delineate or Describe." Capitalizing on his captors' disorganization, Lamb managed to "elude the French and American sentinels" and make good his escape—for the time being.[15]

Those less-daring prisoners prepared themselves to march into American captivity. The articles of capitulation stipulated that the men be confined in the interior parts of Virginia, Maryland, or Pennsylvania, but the last was already burdened with the Saratoga prisoners who Congress resolutely refused to release. As an example, Lancaster alone had over fourteen hundred prisoners, "exclusive of women & children," to feed and house. Pleading with the Executive Council of Pennsylvania to remove the captives, a group of "burgesses and inhabitants" of the town claimed that the county was "exceedingly drained of Provisions for some years past" by all of the prisoners. Furthermore, "a most contagious Disorder [had] raged for some time" that "proved fatal to very many" of the internees. In short, Pennsylvania simply could not take any more enemy captives. Cognizant of this problem, Washington gave orders for the Yorktown prisoners to be divided into two sections: half would go to Winchester, Virginia, and the other half to Fort Frederick, Maryland. For the moment, Congress voted to pass on retaliation, but it also neglected to forward any supplies for the starving prisoners. Washington had made promises that Congress's coffers simply could not keep.[16]

In the absence of any congressional assistance, the prisoners' care and supervision fell by necessity to Virginia. Setting out for their respective places of confinement on the morning of October 21, the prisoners were escorted by members of the Virginia militia, who were none too thrilled about their assignment. The task of feeding the men was equally vexing to Virginia's governor, Thomas Nelson. To solve the problem, he empowered militia general Robert Lawson to impress supplies, as a military necessity, from the local inhabitants when the need arose. Apparently, Lawson's definition of "necessity" differed from that of the prisoners. Private Johann Conrad Döhla, of the von Seybothen regiment of Ansbach-Bayreuth troops, complained of having "very little food to divide and eat." The rations he did receive were insufficient for men expected to march all day and camp in the open, exposed to the elements. Those prisoners with hard currency could supplement their diets by patronizing the merchants and sutlers who flocked to the column to sell their goods, but most of the prisoners had to subsist on "Indian bread," which Döhla found "very unfamiliar." Thankfully, the Virginia militia guards, who "were all from the upper parts of the state, called backswoodsmen," turned a blind eye to the prisoners' creative procurement of provisions from the tidewater plantations along their line of march. Captain Samuel Graham remembered that the guards "did not scruple also to let us make free with a turnip field." Discipline was lax, and desertion rampant.[17]

For men already exhausted by a taxing summer campaign and an arduous siege, the trek into the Virginia backcountry was grueling. Their earlier trials had not prepared them for the "miserable marching" on a diet of "poor provisions." Hessian prisoner Stephan Popp reported covering "18 to 20" miles a day, often in the rain. Compounding their predicament, the weather turned colder as the prisoners approached the Shenandoah River in early November. Fording the river in their only dry suit of clothing, the soldiers thought they "would freeze to death" when they emerged dripping and shivering on the opposite bank. In Döhla's opinion, constant marching in cold, wet clothes "caused all sorts of sickness" among the prisoners. Exhaustion and hunger slowed the pace of the column's progress, and the sick and injured began to lag behind. Frustrated, the guards fired on a party of British stragglers, "which resulted in one English prisoner being killed and three men wounded."[18]

To the prisoners' dismay and indignation, when the first contingent reached Winchester on November 5, they discovered their quarters in complete disarray. Stephan Popp and his comrades "were amazed when we saw" the "old tumbledown barracks." Lieutenant Johann Prechtel from Ansbach-Bayreuth was shocked that the buildings "were truly very poorly put together" and "not half adequate for quartering the troops." Döhla described the structures as "numerous wretched huts built of wood and clay, most of which have no roofs or poor roofs, no cots, [and] only poor fireplaces." Snow, rain, and biting wind coursed through the halls. Each room was crowded with between "twenty or thirty men" who "did not have room enough to stand." The prisoners, "locked in like dogs," had little choice but to make due with quarters that Döhla called "worse than the pig stalls and doghouses are in Germany."[19]

Despite orders from Governor Nelson for the purpose, the barracks at Winchester had not been adequately repaired or prepared for the prisoners. The local commissary of prisoners, Colonel Joseph Holmes, informed the governor in late October that the site could hold only eight hundred men. Furthermore, he could not persuade the town's craftsmen to build any other structures because the governor had still not paid them for building the initial barracks last year. If the prisoners wanted shelter, they would have to build it themselves, Holmes regretted to report. Resigned, the prisoners tried to repair their quarters as best they could, but tools and materials were in short supply. No one in town would so much as spare a hammer to help them build huts. Under the circumstances, Commissary Holmes had no alternative but to order more than a thousand prisoners to make camp in the open without tents. It was not long before snow blanketed the ground, covering the men as they slept. British private John Robert Shaw recalled that at Winchester "we suffered much: our houses had no covering to shelter us from the inclemency of the weather; and we were exposed to cold, hunger and want of clothing; and all manner of ill treatment, insult and abuse."[20]

The paucity of provisions in Winchester was even more dispiriting to the prisoners than their shoddy quarters. Because local farmers refused to trade their produce for promises of future remuneration, Commissary Holmes had not been able to establish a sufficient store of food at the barracks. The demoralized and downtrodden men pleaded with their American captors for foodstuffs that simply did not exist. Rations "were meted out to us very sparingly and of poor quality," Döhla griped. "We received absolutely no bread except for an occasional uncooked Indian bread." Merchants in town were more than pleased to accept the prisoners' hard currency for goods at drastically inflated prices, but all shunned Congress's paper money; those without solid coin went hungry. Such treatment was clearly a *jus in bello* violation, but few Americans felt any compunction about the captives' distressed situation. The Yorktown prisoners were not only a burdensome intrusion for the inhabitants of the Virginia backcountry but also the living embodiment of British depravity and cruelty, the very men who had burned and pillaged their way across the South. They would receive no aid from their new neighbors. Instead of the full rations and commodious quarters they were promised in the surrender agreement, Popp and his fellow prisoners endured "hunger and cold . . . in abundance."[21]

The prisoners' hunger pangs stemmed not just from the avarice and anger of the locals but also from a fundamental disagreement between Congress and the government of Virginia. Years of printing unbacked currency had resulted in extensive inflation, and despite significant loans from France and other allied European powers, Congress was broke. Completely incapable of providing for the prisoners' needs, the delegates looked to Virginia to take responsibility. Having already supplied the Saratoga prisoners for years, Virginia's governor and Board of War were in no mood to be cooperative. The commissioner of the board, William Davies, was determined to protect the state's financial future. He told Commissary Holmes that "it is the particular duty of Major Forsyth the continental commissary of provisions to make the necessary purchases and procure the proper supplies for the prisoners at Winchester." He further declared that he would "always be much averse to adopt any step that will have a tendency to throw the burthun [*sic*] of supplying these men on Virginia." In a letter to Congress's quartermaster general, Timothy Pickering, Virginia major Richard Claiborne was even more explicit: the "government [of Virginia] decline advancing any thing farther for the Continent." The prisoners could expect little help from state authorities.[22]

Virginia's intransigence meant that the prisoners had to survive on next to nothing. Men sold anything they had, including the coats off their backs, to local farmers in exchange for food. They had little option. As Döhla described on December 7, "the issue of rations is much behind schedule and we already were twenty days behind in our issue of flour, which was a bad situation." Exposure and malnutrition weakened the prisoners' immune systems, and predictably disease flourished. Lieutenant Prechtel noted the presence "of consumption in the barracks," which claimed the life of one of his grenadiers. Döhla reported that "the wife of musketeer [Georg] Meichel" and "Private [Johann Georg] Korn had also perished." Commissary Holmes knew that something had to be done or few of the prisoners would be left to see the spring.[23]

Frustrated by the apparent lack of preparation on the part of the American commissaries and by the townspeople's indifference to their soldiers' misery, British officers began to take matters into their own hands. Captain Graham, the senior British officer at the barracks, fired off a barrage of letters to anyone he thought might help his men. One of these arrived at the nearby home of Daniel Morgan, the American victor of the Battle of Cowpens (1781). Although the general had resigned his commission, Graham hoped that he would use his influence with Washington and Congress to relieve "the distresses of the Soldiers." In the meantime, the captain appealed to Holmes for permission to quarter his men in one of the town's five churches. Given the rapidly accumulating snow, the American commissary saw no reason to deny this request. "Accordingly, 500 men were brought in [to the church], and the huts thus emptied were distributed among the other prisoners." For the first time since they left their entrenchments at Yorktown, the men all had shelter, dilapidated and cramped though it was.[24]

When Morgan learned of Graham's intentions, he was furious at the British officer's temerity. To quarter Cornwallis's soldiers in a house of God was sacrilegious and disrespectful to the memories of those Americans who had perished at their hands. In a stern letter of reproach, he told the captain that "Col. Holmes had no Right to bring them to town, thay [*sic*] were ordered to the Barrack[s], and thare [*sic*] thay ought to have continued." Citing his own experience in British captivity during the Canadian campaign, Morgan claimed, "I have been a prisoner as well as thay, and was kept in close goale [*sic*] five month and twelve days; six and thirty officers and there [*sic*] servts in one room, so that when we lay down upon our straw we covered the whole floore [*sic*]." Considering the British treatment of American prisoners, the general thought that Graham's men had "nothing to grumble at." Morgan, confident that his actions would meet with Washington's "approbation," ordered all of the prisoners back to the barracks. All Graham could do was continue his letter-writing campaign, which to his dismay "had but little effect." According to one American officer, by Christmas 1781, "the prisoners at Winchester [were] in a calamitous situation."[25]

Initially, Maryland seemed far more receptive to the second contingent of Yorktown prisoners than Virginia had been to the first. Unlike that state's government, which had shirked its responsibility to the captives, the State Council of Maryland appointed merchant George Murdock as a commissary, with instructions to "forward a sufficient Quantity of Supplies" for "at least 2000" men. The council was less forthcoming with instructions for where to house the prisoners. In his orders to the Continental commissary general of prisoners, Abraham Skinner, Washington had suggested that the men be confined at Fort Frederick, a Seven Years' War–era stone fortification in western Maryland that had been used to confine some of the Saratoga prisoners. The fort, however, was in ruins. Skinner apprised the general that "the barracks at Fort Frederick was [*sic*] insufficient for the reception of the prisoners—indeed they are almost totally destroyed and cannot be repaired." In his opinion as head commissary, the best option was to confine the men in the stone barracks within the town of Frederick itself. In order to prepare the barracks for habitation, Skinner ordered a stockade erected around the buildings and a supply of "beef & flour for about Six Weeks" put into storage. With the prisoners on their way, the council soon realized that the fort's accommodations alone would be "insufficient to hold the Prisoners," authorizing Colonel Philip Thomas to appropriate "the Poor's House, Logged Gaol and every other empty House proper for Barracks." If these buildings were still not sufficient to comfortably house the prisoners, Thomas had permission to "take Possession of any such Buildings which you may deem necessary."[26]

Thomas and Murdock's orders were far more detailed than those Holmes had received in Winchester, but the two men were incapable of fully executing the council's commands. The townspeople, who had lived among British prisoners since December 1777, were overwhelmed by the additional captives. The Saratoga prisoners had already stripped the area of cattle and grain and had damaged most of the public buildings in Frederick. According to one resident, the neighborhood was "continually plundered, owing as it is thought in great measure to the prisoners & Guards being so badly supplied with provisions." Compounding the problem, the town had provided numerous soldiers to serve in the American southern army, many of whom had fallen in action against Cornwallis's troops. Thus, the spirit of resentment ran high in Frederick. Sergeant Lamb, who had been recaptured during his escape attempt after the siege and brought to the Maryland town, recalled being "used in the most cruel manner" by his guards, who were constantly "rejoicing in my distress." Explaining the "reason of the bad usage" he received, Lamb claimed that "this town had suffered much by the deaths of several young men, who had been killed during the war," which was the "source of general inveteracy to all British prisoners." As one townsman put it, "I hope the time not far of[f] that we shall return" British abuses "measure for measure." Murdock and Thomas could count on little assistance from the local inhabitants, who yearned for vengeance and restitution.[27]

Just as at Winchester, when the first Yorktown prisoners arrived at Frederick on November 4, they were appalled by their accommodations and provisions. According to Lamb, "our place of confinement was a most deplorable situation. Forty or fifty British soldiers crowded together in a small room." The men "huddled" together for warmth "as the winter was remarkably cold." The contingent's commander, Captain Eyre Coote, was deeply concerned for his men's health. He informed his superiors in New York that "when the whole arrive, our numbers here will amount to near Two Thousand men, & very sickly." The prisoners "suffer[ed] extremely for want of Blankets." Worse yet, Coote feared that his troops would not be "supplyed with Provisions in the Winter, as there is no magazine here," the men having already gone "two or three days without meat."

Officials in Maryland had done their best to acquire provisions, but there were simply none to be had. Commissary Thomas Price had purchased cattle from neighboring Virginia, but the sellers, looking "to rid that State of the Trouble of maintaining them through the Winter," had sent him a herd that was "intirely [*sic*] unfit for Slaughter." At a loss for what to do, the Maryland council was forced to admit that there were "many Difficulties and Impediments in providing for the British Prisoners. . . . [W]e are totally unprepared for their Reception."[28]

Frigid and starving, the prisoners soon became restive. When guards ordered one group to cut wood for their fires, the prisoners refused. Unwilling to brook revolt, the Americans leveled their bayonets and charged at them. The guard's commander, Captain Montjoy Bayley, explained to Coote that his men had "been under the disagreeable necessity of making use of Violents [*sic*] to keep the prisoners in order." Coote did not see it that way. As he protested to Commissary General Skinner, "there has been three soldiers wounded by the Militia with Bayonets, and I am induced to believe those men did not deserve that Treatment." Predictably, this protest availed him nothing. Maryland's commissary of prisoners, Colonel Moses Rawlings, informed him that not only would the guards not be prosecuted but also the prisoners should expect equally harsh treatment in the future. The colonel was resolute in his determination "to punish [the prisoners] Agreeable to Offences." American troops could and would use force when necessary to control the restless captives. Nevertheless, Rawlings knew that violence alone would not solve his problem. The prisoners' situation was unsustainable. If fresh provisions did not arrive soon, he would have a full-scale rebellion on his hands.[29]

While the prisoners struggled to survive the increasingly deplorable conditions of their confinement, the governments of Virginia and Maryland took steps to rid themselves of the captives. In mid-December 1781, the Council of Maryland sent word to Congress's superintendent of finance, Robert Morris, "that from the exhausted Situation of this State, it is not within the Compass of our Abilities to subsist the Prisoners quartered upon us, without your Assistance." If Congress could not produce £20,000 in hard currency, the prisoners would have to be moved. The Virginia House of Delegates was even more determined to see their allotted prisoners leave. It resolved "that provisions ought not to be impressed for the support of the British prisoners after the first day of January [1782]." Without impressments, the captives could not possibly be fed, even at a bare subsistence level. The Virginia house further resolved to inform Congress "of the inability of this country in the present exhausted state of its treasury to furnish" the prisoners at all; the sooner they departed, the better.[30]

Running out of options, Congress resolved to relocate the prisoners. Morris, acting on behalf of Congress, responded to Virginia's ultimatum by proposing to transport the men "from Winchester to Frederick [Maryland]." The delegates followed up on Morris's suggestion by resolving to send half of the Yorktown prisoners to Frederick and half to Lancaster and York in Pennsylvania, where they would be confined alongside the remaining Saratoga prisoners. Once settled in these locations, the office of the secretary at war, which had been established by Congress in February 1781, would take responsibility for their maintenance. In order to placate the Council of Maryland, Secretary at War Benjamin Lincoln promised that only the German prisoners, who as rented soldiers had no vested interest in British victory and from experience proved less of a security risk than their comrades, would be housed in Maryland. Congress hoped that lenient treatment and lax confinement would induce many Hessians to desert and join the revolutionary cause. The same could not be said for the British prisoners. "Convinced that a strict hand will be necessary over the British," Lincoln ordered them to be "closely confined under Continental Guards" at Lancaster. The move was slated to take place in January 1782 as soon as adequate wagons and guards could be assembled. This was hardly the "benevolent treatment of Prisoners" that Washington had promised and that the principles of *jus in bello* prescribed.[31]

The prospect of a second winter march so soon after their arrival in Winchester greatly distressed the prisoners in Virginia. Commissary Holmes had finally succeeded in securing shelter for the remaining men, and he regretted "the hardship & difficulty" they would "encounter on the March" due to the "extreme coldness of the season." They were "almost as naked as the hour they were born, & not an ounce of animal food" was to be had for them. Without adequate provisions and clothing, how could they be expected to make another winter march? As he confessed to Colonel James Wood, "it seems to shock the feelings of humanity to drive out of a warm habitation a poor creature stark naked in such a season." Holmes's appeal on humanitarian grounds had little traction with Virginia's governor, who could not wait to see the prisoners depart. Consequently, on January 27, 1782, the Winchester contingent marched out amid the worst snowstorm they had yet encountered. Lieutenant Prechtel reported that during the march, "three English private soldiers froze to death" because they had "to camp in the woods on the snow." Popp left this vivid account of the agonizing march to Frederick:

> The first day we made a march of 12 miles, and then camped out in the open snow. We did make large fires, but still could not keep warm,

> because of the great cold. The snow was up to our knees where we had to remain over night. The sharp wind continued all night without letup, so that we believed we would all freeze. Besides, we were poorly clothed. . . . [M]any had sold their uniforms and everything else out of poverty, just to stave off hunger. . . . [M]any had wrapped their feet in plain rags. But they had to march along too, so it wasn't long before their feet were exposed and were completely frozen.[32]

The British prisoners, despised by the militia guards who had been habituated to think of all British soldiers as barbarians, had to contend with constant abuse as well as nature's trials during the march. According to Private Shaw, "the cruelty of this new guard exceeded anything we had yet seen; their conduct was indeed shameful and altogether incompatible with the profession of either soldiers or christians [*sic*]; they drove us like so many bullocks to the slaughter." He claimed that the captain of the guard "broke his broad sword by cutting and slashing the prisoners, who were too much weekend by hunger and former ill treatment to keep up in the march." Another American officer, who Shaw derided for his lowly birth, stabbed one of the prisoners in the back. Far from behaving like gentlemen of sensibility, the American officers' behavior "was a disgrace" even for men more suited to "chimney corner" than to military command. Shaw and his comrades' only consolation was the hope that Pennsylvania would bring better rations, superior quarters, and speedy release "from such cruel bondage."[33]

Arrived at their new prison camps in early February 1782, both the German and British prisoners were profoundly distressed to discover that the conditions of their confinement were not much improved. Popp observed that "as far as our quarters were concerned they were all much in ruins." He and thirty-nine of his fellows were "too thickly quartered" in the barracks and "always bumping [one] another." Private Koch's entire company shared one room in a "poorhouse" that "was so small that no one could lie down." All were covered with "vermin" that were "so numerous we could hardly bear it." Döhla remembered that "frequent epidemics occurred, and bugs and lice in great numbers appeared in our tattered clothing." Things were much the same at Lancaster and York, where "the soldiers of lord Cornwallis's army were closely confined in their pen," according to Lamb. Captain Graham described the barracks at Lancaster as "surrounded by a high stockade, and strictly guarded." While the German prisoners in Lancaster were eventually allowed to hire their labor to local farmers and thus escape the cramped barracks, the British were closely confined and forbidden to leave the stockade for any purpose. The men's sole hope for release was that Congress would agree to exchange them for the American captives in New York. In this too, they would be disappointed.[34]

Soon after he received word of the capitulation terms at Yorktown, General Clinton reached out to Washington "to treat for the Exchange" of Cornwallis and his army. Although the two commanders had never before been able to reach an agreement on a general cartel, Clinton was confident that the time was ripe for a large-scale exchange. Many of the American senior officers captured at Charleston remained unexchanged, and Washington had earlier expressed concern for the American sailors held in New York. Clinton was particularly anxious to exchange Cornwallis, both to prevent the earl from being recalled from his parole at the capricious whim of Congress and to forestall any claim that he was inattentive to his case because of personal enmity. Cornwallis had informed Clinton that Washington was willing to exchange him for a former president of the Continental Congress, Henry Laurens, who had been captured while en route to France in September 1780. Instead of treating the diplomat as a prisoner of war, British authorities had locked the South Carolinian in the Tower of London on charges of treason. Exchanging Laurens for Cornwallis, though technically unorthodox since the American did not hold military rank, was not without precedent and was in keeping with *jus in bello* principles. Clinton was happy to acquiesce to the swap, but he was also willing to exchange Cornwallis by composition—that is, to trade several American officers of lesser rank for the British general—a practice that was commonplace in European warfare. Washington responded with assurances of his intention to appoint commissioners who were "fully authorized to treat [for] the Exchange of Lord Cornwallis and the Honble [*sic*] Mr Laurens," but he could give no "assurance His Lordship should be exchanged for Mr Laurens" because the matter rested with Congress, which, as it turns out, had other plans.[35]

Just as they had opposed the generous terms of the capitulation of Yorktown, so too did the South Carolina congressional delegates object to exchanging Cornwallis on any terms whatsoever. In a series of notes he made in preparation for a speech before Congress, Arthur Middleton enumerated the many disadvantages he saw to liberating the British general. Some of his reasons had to do with Cornwallis's military acumen and Middleton's concern that he would return to America determined "to retrieve lost Honor." But the South Carolinian's principal objection centered on the manner in which Cornwallis had waged the war in the South. To Middleton, the earl was "a Barbarian. An Infringer [of] Capitulations, sacred." Releasing Cornwallis would deny the people of South Carolina their longed-for vengeance. He knew his constituents; he knew their anger, and their thirst for revenge; and he knew that it would "affect the people [of the] South to see a Beast let Loose." In Middleton's estimation Cornwallis's "nonexchange [was the] only mode of retaliating for his misdeeds and corrects the mild but impolitic Capitulation of York Town."[36]

Middleton was not alone in his determination to prevent the earl's release. On February 18, 1782, Congress passed a secret resolution "prohibiting the exchange of Lieut[t] General Lord Cornwallis." Washington was puzzled by this decision, knowing that the British would never agree to a cartel that specifically excluded Cornwallis. In a letter of protest to Congress's new president, John Hanson, Washington confessed feeling "so exceedingly embarrassed by the operation of the Secret Resolve." To detain Cornwallis when he could so easily be exchanged would seem like "conduct so apparently strange" to the American prisoners who expected imminent release. Moreover, the British could claim a "breac[h] of faith" on the part of Congress and thus justifiably renege on their obligation to provide reimbursement for the prisoners' provisions. The general believed that the resolution would "operate against the public interest" in the long run.[37]

Confident of failure, Washington nonetheless proceeded with exchange negotiations. He instructed Commissary Skinner that when meeting with the British commissary, he would have "to wave the exchange of Lord Cornwallis" for the time being "in as delicate a manner as possible." Predictably, Skinner's efforts were of little avail. He apologized to Washington that British commissary Joshua Loring "refuse[d] to Exchange the whole of our Officers without reserving a certain Number of them, equal to the Value of His Lordship." If a straightforward swap for Laurens was impossible, surely Congress would trade one disgraced general, now comfortably on parole in England, for several long-confined American junior officers, Loring reasoned; forgoing the exchange was simply not in America's best interest militarily. Persuaded by the British logic, Washington pleaded with Congress to reverse its decision on Cornwallis. As he later explained to John Laurens, whose father still occupied a cell in the Tower of London, "*I am sorry to inform you,* that upon my arrival at Philadelphia, and for a long time after I had been there, I experienced the greatest *disinclination in Congress to the exchange of Lord Cornwallis; upon any terms.*" Mindful of his subordinate position to the civilian authority but deeply concerned for both his own reputation and that of the infant nation he served, not to mention the welfare of his officers in British hands, Washington continued to press for an exchange that encompassed the earl.[38]

For Congress, preventing Cornwallis's exchange was a symbolic gesture of retaliation for his conduct of the war in the South. Unsurprisingly, Southern delegates were particularly keen to block the exchange of a man they viewed as "remarkably cruel and barbarous." Because Cornwallis was "an Officer whose foot steps have been stained by the blood of innocent Citizens," North Carolina delegate Hugh Williamson believed that Congress was under no obligation to agree to the exchange. Summarizing their position, Middleton argued that Cornwallis "ought not to be exchanged by composition at this time, not from any apprehensions of his influence or superior abilities; but because they look upon him not in the light of a British general, but a barbarian" who had "infringed every rule of war established among civilized nations."[39]

After several extended debates, Congress eventually consented to the exchange, though not before tying Cornwallis's release to several perquisites to which the British were unlikely to agree. Washington could exchange the earl by composition only if the British first released Henry Laurens on parole and then reimbursed Congress for the expenses incurred by feeding the Saratoga prisoners since October 1777. The delegates were well aware that Parliament would never agree to pay the more than £200,000 they demanded. When Washington's commissioners, Gouverneur Morris and Major General Henry Knox, met with their British counterparts at Elizabethtown, New Jersey, in late March 1782, they did so with their hands tied. Negotiations continued for weeks but amounted to naught. The men of Cornwallis's army would never be exchanged.[40]

But Congress could not afford to hold the prisoners without British reimbursement for their expenses. Once it became clear that Clinton's replacement as commander in chief, General Sir Guy Carleton, would not pay for the prisoners' upkeep, Congress resolved, in breach of *jus in bello* principles, to sell the German prisoners into indentured servitude and to reduce the British prisoners' rations. In early May 1782 Robert Morris convened a meeting of senior revolutionaries, including Secretary at War Lincoln and General Knox, to determine what to do with the Yorktown prisoners. After some debate, all present agreed that "the Hessian and other foreign Prisoners should be Sold, the British close confined and put to short allowance." Congress officially approved Morris's plan in early June. To the enraged American populace that Congress represented, these retaliatory measures were entirely justified. As one Pennsylvania farmer admonished his countrymen that summer, "Say not that the capitulations can save any of them from being retaliated upon" because Americans were "justified, before God and man, in inflicting a dreadful punishment upon . . . those whom the chance of war hath put in our power."[41]

With congressional authorization, American recruiters soon entered the Hessian barracks eager to fill their quotas of men from among the well-disciplined Germans. Telling the prisoners that the government could no longer afford to house or feed them, the American officers gave the Germans the choice of either enlisting into the Continental Army for a term of three years or paying a fine of eighty Spanish dollars, an enormous sum for men who had not received their pay in months. If they could not pay and refused to enlist, they could indenture themselves to local farmers or craftsmen who would remunerate Congress for the use of their labor. One Hessian sergeant claimed that "the prisoners were mistreated in order to make them enlist." Another group of Hessians informed their commander in New York that they were in "extreme despair" because the Americans had sent them a "barbarous proposition" to either pay up or indenture themselves. Congress's resolve, which effectively transformed "free soldiers" into slaves, "completely stunned" them. To the Hessians, it seemed as if the Americans were determined to treat them "not like prisoners of war to a Christian Nation, but like wretches fallen into the hands of Barbarians." According to Secretary Lincoln, few among them accepted the offer to enlist; most preferred indentured servitude to the betrayal of their commanders and comrades.[42]

While no doubt draconian, at least the Germans had a choice; British prisoners were rounded up and closely confined in jails, dungeons, and camps throughout Pennsylvania. On July 11, 1782, Congress ordered the secretary at war to "have all the British prisoners of war closely confined, and to stop all issues of provision to the women and children who are with them." The soldiers' rations were reduced again. Predictably, the jails soon became scenes of agony, anguish, and despair. Hessian adjutant general Major Carl Leopold Baurmeister claimed that "instead of twenty men per room, thirty men were packed together, which makes the condition of these people even worse. Eight hundred and eighty-two English prisoners in Philadelphia endured their misery within even narrower confines." In October, a group of British prisoners begged General Knox to "consider our Masaurable Satuation." The men had "no Cloaths But is all moste Nacat for want [of] Cloathing and the coald weather is Coming on and we have No Releaf Heare." Knox could do nothing to help them without disobeying Congress. Pitying the deplorable confinement of the "wretched creatures," Baumeister decried the Americans' "unreasonably revengeful" policy as "contrary . . . to the law of nations." As an aristocratic European officer, the major could not comprehend what Congress and the American people knew all too well: Vattel and his laws had no place in a war of vengeance. For the past seven years, the revolutionaries had endured innumerable *jus in bello* violations, and they were no longer afraid to return the favor.[43]

The Yorktown prisoners' nineteen-month ordeal finally came to an end when they received word in early May 1783 that the United States had ratified the preliminary articles of peace with Great Britain. Despite some opposition to ratification on the grounds that the prisoners should be held as security for British compliance with the treaty, on April 15 Congress authorized Washington to "inform the Commander in Chief of the British forces in America that the U.S. are ready to liberate . . . all prisoners of war." The expense of holding the captives outweighed any political advantage that would be gained by further detaining them. When news of their impending release reached the men in Frederick, they were exuberant. They threw a raucous party in their barracks to celebrate their liberation and to honor their king. Their toasts of "Hyroh [*sic*] for the King George! God save the King George" elicited the ire of their guards. The American commander "sent in a large patrol and ordered it to beat [the prisoners] and arrest them." Four prisoners were fatally wounded in the altercation.[44]

The death of their comrades could not dampen the remaining prisoners' enthusiasm. Private Döhla was elated by "the joyful news and long-wished-for and passionately awaited order, to begin our departure march." On May 13, 1783, he and the German prisoners "marched out of the barracks at Frederick, having spent a year and three and one-half months here, wretchedly, very often hungry and thirsty." Popp was just happy that he and his friends "had lived to see the day of our release." Many of his fellows had not.[45]

Although gaps in the archival record preclude any definitive accounting of the surviving Yorktown captives, Secretary Lincoln estimated that there were approximately 6,000 enemy prisoners, including women, children, and the Saratoga troops, remaining in American hands at war's end. He neglected to note how many had perished on his watch, but surviving sources paint a grim picture. Of the eighty-nine members of Döhla's Von Quesnoy company of Ansbach-Bayreuth troops captured at Yorktown, seventy-three were liberated that spring. Only five of Döhla's comrades were listed as deserters (5.6 percent), while eleven died during captivity (12.4 percent). From the Hessian Von Bose Regiment's returns, of the 365 common soldiers who surrendered at Yorktown, 104 men deserted (28.5 percent), while 33 (9 percent) perished in American custody. The Hessian mortality rate, while low when compared to the startling mortality of American sailors on board British prison ships in New York Harbor (upward of 60 percent), was much higher than that of either the American sailors confined in landlocked English prisons (5 percent) or of civilian prisoners in the late eighteenth-century Netherlands (4 percent). Yet compared to their British counterparts, the Hessians were relatively healthy. For much of their captivity, these prisoners enjoyed the freedom to move about the countryside, procure extra provisions, and even work for wages. These privileges, which Congress granted in the hopes of inducing the Germans to abandon their British employers, shielded many of them from the deprivation and disease of the camps.[46]

Cornwallis's British troops were not so fortunate. From a sampling of the muster rolls of the 43rd Regiment of Foot, fourteen of the thirty-six men of Captain Cameron's company died during their imprisonment after Yorktown (38.8 percent). The soldiers of Major Ferguson's company were even more unhealthy. Of the fifty-four enlisted men, noncommissioned officers, and musicians in his company, twenty-five perished while in captivity (46.3 percent). Captain Thorne's company had a mortality rate of 29.4 percent, while Lieutenant Colonel Marsh's company suffered 41.4 percent losses. The statistics for the 80th Regiment of Foot are similar. Of the forty-eight privates in Captain Arbuthnot's company, fifteen died in American captivity (31.3 percent). Captain Cumine's company of the same regiment lost fifteen of their forty-seven men during the same period (31.9 percent). The soldiers of Major Gordon's company were comparatively healthy: only ten of their forty-seven succumbed while in American hands (21.3 percent). If the experiences of these two regiments are indicative of their comrades in other corps, the overall mortality rate for British Yorktown prisoners was 34 percent—one out of every three men captured did not survive their imprisonment. To put these numbers in perspective, the mortality rate of Union prisoners of war at the notorious Confederate prison at Andersonville, Georgia, was 28 percent. By the standards of eighteenth-century European warfare, these statistics were truly "shocking to humanity."[47]

With the Treaty of Paris ratified and the British Army withdrawn from American shores, Washington retired as a soldier, though not before congratulating his civilian superiors in Congress on "the confirmation of our Independence and Sovereignty." He was "pleased with the opportunity afforded the United States of becoming a respectable Nation." Victory achieved, America could now take its seat at the international table. Yet Washington knew that in attaining that victory, Americans had not lived up to the rigorous standards of *jus in bello* that were markers of respectability in Europe. Yorktown had presented the general, and the new nation he served, with the opportunity to perform national legitimacy through adherence to the laws of war, but Congress had squandered it. The delegates recognized that their constituents, outraged by years of British violations of the laws of war, disapproved of the articles of capitulation's generous terms. By refusing to exchange the men while also incapable of supplying them, Congress committed the Yorktown prisoners to the custody of a vindictive populace. The results were predictably gruesome. Though soon forgotten in a cloud of nationalism and mythmaking, their story warns of the limitations of law in the face of the power of vengeance. It is a sobering lesson for our times.[48]

NOTES

1. Edward G. Lengel, *General George Washington: A Military Life* (New York: Random House, 2005), 329–44. For the effects of disease on Cornwallis's garrison and the conduct of the siege, see J. R. McNeil, *Mosquito Empires: Ecology and War in the Greater Caribbean, 1620–1914* (Cambridge: Cambridge University Press, 2010); James Thacher, *Military Journal of the American Revolution* (Hartford, Conn.: Hurlbut, Williams, 1862), 283, 286; Cornwallis to Washington, York in Virginia, Oct. 17, 1781, in *The Cornwallis Papers: The Campaigns of 1780 and 1781 in the Southern Theatre of the American Revolutionary War*, 6 vols., ed. Ian Saberton (East Sussex, Eng.: Naval and Military Press, 2010), 6:112; Washington to Cornwallis, Camp before York, Oct. 17, 1781, ibid., 113. For more-detailed narratives of the siege, see Dan L. Morrill, *Southern Campaigns of the American Revolution* (Baltimore: Nautical and Aviation Publishing, 1993), 171–84; and John D. Grainger, *The Battle of Yorktown, 1781: A Reassessment* (Woodbridge, Suffolk: Boydell and Brewer, 2005), 93–149. For a useful narrative history of the Yorktown prisoners' captivity, see James Linwood Carpenter Jr., "The Yorktown Prisoners: A Narrative Account of the Disposition of the British Army which Capitulated at Yorktown, October 19, 1781" (M.A. thesis, College of William and Mary, 1950).
2. For the conventional narrative, see John Ferling, *Almost a Miracle: The American Victory in the War of Independence* (Oxford: Oxford University Press, 2007), 523–62. On Washington's insistence on upholding European customs of war in order to secure national legitimacy at home and abroad, see Eliga Gould, *Among the Powers of the Earth: The American Revolution and the Making of a New World Empire* (Cambridge, Mass.: Harvard University Press, 2012), 114–16; *Royal Gazette*, Mar. 30, 1782.
3. On "Anglicization," see John M. Murrin, "A Roof without Walls: The Dilemma of American National Identity," in *Beyond Confederation: Origins of the Constitution and American National Identity*, ed. Richard Beeman, Stephen Botein, and Edward C. Carter II (Chapel Hill: University of North Carolina Press, 1987), 333–48; Stanely N. Katz and John M. Murrin, eds., *Colonial America: Essays in Politics and Social Development* (New York: Knopf, 1983); T. H. Breen, "An Empire of Goods: The Anglicization of Colonial America, 1690–1776," *Journal of British Studies* 25 (1986): 467–99; and Richard Bushman, *The Refinement of America: Persons, Houses, Cities* (New York: Vintage Books, 1992). For an overview of the scholarly debates about Anglicization and early American military culture, see Geoffrey Plank, "A Medieval Response to a Wilderness Need: Anglicizing Warfare in Colonial America," in *Anglicizing America: Empire, Revolution, Republic*, ed. Ignacio Gallup-Diaz, Andrew Shankman, and David J. Silverman (Philadelphia: University of Pennsylvania Press, 2015). On the relative lack of martial spirit in the colonies, I agree with John Morgan Dederer, *War in America to 1775: Before Yankee Doodle* (New York: New York University Press, 1990), 22. For an account that stresses the militancy of early America, see John Ferling, *A Wilderness of Miseries: War and Warriors in Early America* (Westport, Conn.: Greenwood Press, 1980). For a list of Congress's library, see Record Group 360, Papers of the Continental Congress, M247, item 183, 2:31, National Archives,

Washington, D.C. [hereafter cited as PCC]. According to Eliga H. Gould, Vattel "enjoyed near canonical status in Britain and the colonies." Gould, "Zones of Law, Zones of Violence: The Legal Geography of the British Atlantic, circa 1772," *William and Mary Quarterly*, 3rd ser., 60, no. 3 (July 2003): 477. See also "To James Madison from William Bradford, 17 October 1774," *Founders Online*, National Archives, last modified June 29, 2017, http://founders.archives.gov/documents/Madison/01-01-02-0036.

4. Emer de Vattel, *The Law of Nations; or, Principles of the Law of Nature Applied to the Conduct and Affairs of Nations and Sovereigns*, bk. 3, http://www.constitution.org/vattel/vattel_03.htm (accessed Aug. 10, 2017); For works on the laws of war in the eighteenth century, see Geoffrey Best, *Humanity in Warfare* (New York: Columbia University Press, 1980), 25–36; Geoffrey Parker, "Early Modern Europe," in *The Laws of War: Constraints on Warfare in the Western World*, ed. Michael Howard, George J. Andreopoulous, and Mark. R. Shulman (New Haven, Conn.: Yale University Press, 1994); Stephen C. Neff, *War and the Law of Nations: A General History* (Cambridge: Cambridge University Press, 2005). For the laws of war in the American context, see John Fabian Witt, *Lincoln's Code: The Laws of War in American History* (New York: Free Press, 2012). For Washington's concern that his troops observe European *jus in bello* principles in order to uphold their "reputation," see "From George Washington to Benjamin Lincoln, 29 October 1781," *Founders Online*, National Archives, last modified June 29, 2017, http://founders.archives.gov/documents/Washington/99-01-02-07318.
5. Washington to Cornwallis, Camp before York, Oct. 18, 1781, *Cornwallis Papers*, 6:114. On the Convention of Saratoga and Congress's decision to nullify it, see T. Cole Jones, *Captives of Liberty: Enemy Prisoners and the Violence of the American Revolution* (Philadelphia: University of Pennsylvania Press, forthcoming), chap. 4.
6. Washington to Cornwallis, Camp before York, Oct. 18, 1781, *Cornwallis Papers*, 6:114; Articles of Capitulation, Oct. 19, 1781, ibid., 119. Popp was a corporal at the time of his capture at Yorktown. Stephan Popp, *A Hessian Soldier in the American Revolution: The Diary of Stephan Popp*, trans. Reinhart J. Pope (Racine, Wisc.: private printing, 1953), 25.
7. There is some dispute about the total number of prisoners who surrendered at Yorktown. Thomas Durie, the deputy commissary of prisoners with Washington's army, made a "General Return of Officers and Privates Taken Prisoner" on October 19. He claimed that there were 7, 171 men taken exclusive of the naval prisoners, who according to the Articles of Capitulation were prisoners of the French. Another return by Durie enclosed in Washington's letter to Congress of October 27, 1781, lists 6,935 "land" prisoners and 2,000 seamen who were turned over to the French. The list also claims there were eighty "followers of the army." See "[Diary entry: 20 October 1781]," n1, *Founders Online*, National Archives, last modified June 29, 2017, http://founders.archives.gov/documents/Washington/01-03-02-0007-0006-0014; Thacher, *Military Journal*, 289, 290; Johann Ewald, *Diary of the American War: A Hessian Journal*, trans. and ed. Joseph P. Tustin (New Haven, Conn.: Yale University Press, 1979), 339.

8. Ewald, *Diary,* 342; Samuel Graham, *Memoir of General Graham . . . ,* ed. James J. Graham (Edinburgh: R. & R. Clark, 1862), 64–65.
9. "To George Washington from Marinus Willett, 6 July 1781," *Founders Online,* National Archives, last modified June 29, 2017, http://founders.archives.gov/documents/Washington/99-01-02-06310; Ewald, *Diary,* 342; Thacher, *Military Journal,* 292; Abbé Claude Robin, *New Travels through North-America . . .* (Philadelphia: Robert Bell, 1783), 65; "The Journal of Colonel Daniel Trabue," in *Colonial Men and Times . . . ,* ed. Lillie DuPuy VanCulin Harper (Philadelphia: Innes & Sons, 1916), 115; Johann Conrad Döhla, *A Hessian Diary of the American Revolution,* trans. Bruce E. Burgoyne (Norman: University of Oklahoma Press, 1990), 178.
10. Boudinot to William Livingston, Philadelphia, Oct. 24, 1781, in *Letters of Delegates to Congress, 1774–1789,* 25 vols., ed. Paul H. Smith, et al. (Washington, D.C.: Library of Congress, 1976–2000), 18:163 [hereafter cited as *LDC*]. For British perspectives on the treatment of American prisoners, see Edwin Burrows, *Forgotten Patriots: The Untold Story of American Prisoners during the Revolutionary War* (New York: Basic Books, 2008), chap. 2.
11. In his petition to Congress, Connecticut governor Jonathan Trumbull summarized the sentiments of several of his constituents, who demanded retaliation for the mistreatment of a friend in a British prison. The petition, with Trumbull's cover letter, was forwarded to Boudinot. Jonathan Trumbull to the President of Congress, Lebanon, Conn., Apr. 24, 1782, PCC, item 66, 2:224. See also ibid., 228, 232.
12. "From George Washington to Nathanael Greene, 15 December 1781," *Founders Online,* National Archives, last modified June 29, 2017, http://founders.archives.gov/documents/Washington/99-01-02-07535. Tench Tilghman, Washington's aide who had brought Congress news of the capitulation, was questioned about the generous terms of surrender by the committee, which was composed of Edmund Randolph, Elias Boudinot, and Daniel Carroll. "To George Washington from Tench Tilghman, 27 October 1781," ibid., http://founders.archives.gov/documents/Washington/99-01-02-07303. The ostensible task of the committee, which apparently also included James Mitchell Varnum, was to determine the most appropriate mode of thanking Washington and Rochambeau for their "illustrious work." *Journals of the Continental Congress, 1774–1789,* 34 vols., ed. Worthington C. Ford et al. (Washington, D.C., 1904–37), 21:1071–72 [hereafter cited as *JCC*].
13. Middleton to Burke, [Nov. ? 1781], *LDC,* 18:221; *JCC,* 21:1080; "To George Washington from Tench Tilghman, 27 October 1781," *Founders Online;* John Mathews to Nathanael Greene, Philadelphia, Oct. 22, 1781, *LDC,* 18:154.
14. *Newport Mercury,* Dec. 1, 1781; *Pennsylvania Packet,* Sept. 6, 1781; *Independent Chronicle,* Nov. 29, 1781; *Freeman's Journal,* Nov. 7, 1781. At least one columnist argued that generosity, rather than vengeance, should characterize the American response to "the barbarous Cornwallis." In his words, Americans should "scorn to follow his base example by exercising cruelty to your enemies when in your power; but by shewing mercy to the unfortunate, demonstrate to the world that you are the brave, the generous, true songs of liberty." *Connecticut Gazette,* Dec. 7, 1781.
15. According to Justus Eggert, an enlisted soldier in a Ansbach-Bayreuth regiment

captured at Yorktown, the prisoners expected retaliation for their depredations in the South and were surprised by their initial generous treatment. *Memoir des Corporal Justus Eggertt vom Bayreuther Regiment, Brandenburg-Ansbach-Bayreuth,* quoted in Daniel Krebs, "Approaching the Enemy: German Captives in the American War of Independence, 1776–1783" (Ph.D. diss., Emory University, 2007), 353; Roger Lamb, *A British Soldier's Story: Roger Lamb's Narrative of the American Revolution,* ed. Don N. Hagist (Baraboo, Wisc.: Ballindalloch, 2004), 93; Journal of Lt. Enos Reeves, Nov. 4, 1781, York, Va., Box 1, Enos Reeves Papers, Duke University Special Collections, Durham, N.C.; William Feltman, *The Journal of Lieut. William Feltman, of the First Pennsylvania Regiment, 1781–82 . . .* (Philadelphia: Henry Carey Baird, 1853), 22.

16. "Petition and Memorial of the burgesses and inhabitants of the borough of Lancaster to the President & Supreme Executive Council of the Commonwealth of Pennsylvania," July 14, 1781, Box 7, Jasper Yeates Papers, Collection 740, ser. 2, Historical Society of Pennsylvania, Philadelphia; "From George Washington to Abraham Skinner, 25 October 1781," *Founders Online,* National Archives, last modified June 29, 2017, http://founders.archives.gov/documents/Washington/99-01-02-07272. On Thursday October 25, 1781, Arthur Middleton of South Carolina made a motion in Congress to detain the Yorktown prisoners as an act of retaliation, preventing the officers from leaving on their paroles to New York. His motion was defeated on the floor by a vote of 19 to 5. *JCC,* 21:1073–74.

17. The militia guard was commanded by the commanding general of the state militia of Virginia, Robert Lawson. Militia officer St. George Tucker recorded that he was relieved to be "excus'd from this disagreeable Jaunt." "St. George Tucker's Journal of the Siege of Yorktown, 1781," ed. Edward M. Riley, *William and Mary Quarterly,* 3rd ser., 5, no. 3 (July 1948): 394; Carpenter, "Yorktown Prisoners," 7; Döhla, *Hessian Diary,* 183; Graham, *Memoir,* 66.

18. Popp, *Hessian Soldier,* 30; Döhla, *Hessian Diary,* 184, 188.

19. Popp, *Hessian Soldier,* 31; Johann Ernst Prechtel, *A Hessian Officer's Diary of the American Revolution,* trans. and ed. Bruce E. Burgoyne (Bowie, Md.: Heritage Books, 2008), 230–31; Döhla, *Hessian Diary,* 189.

20. Holmes to Nelson, Winchester, Va., Oct. 26, 1781, *Calendar of Virginia State Papers and Other Manuscripts . . . ,* 11 vols., ed. William Pitt Palmer, Sherwin McRae, and Raleigh Edward Colston (Richmond, Va.: R. F. Walker, 1875), 2:569–70 [hereafter cited as *CVSP*]. Commissary Holmes claimed that the townspeople would not provide him with tools or assistance because "no person here will Trust the Public with a shilling's worth, and paper money has no Kind of circulation in this side [of] the blue ridge." Holmes to Col. William Davies, Winchester, Va., Nov., 6, 1781, ibid., 579; John Robert Shaw, *John Robert Shaw: An Autobiography of Thirty Years, 1777–1807,* ed. Oressa M. Teagarden and Jeanne L. Crabtree (Athens: Ohio University Press, 1992), 45.

21. Döhla, *Hessian Diary,* 190; Popp, *Hessian Soldier,* 31.

22. Davies to Holmes, Dec. 17, 1781, Virginia Board of War Letterbook, misc. reel 632, Library of Virginia, Richmond; "Extract from Major Claiborne's letter of Decr 23d

1781. Dated at Richmond," enclosed in "To George Washington from Timothy Pickering, 17 January 1782," *Founders Online,* National Archives, last modified June 29, 2017, http://founders.archives.gov/documents/Washington/99-01-02-07699. For Congress's distressed financial situation in 1781, see E. Wayne Carp, *To Starve the Army at Pleasure: Continental Army Administration and American Political Culture, 1775–1783* (Chapel Hill: University of North Carolina Press, 1984), chap. 7.

23. Döhla, *Hessian Diary,* 192–93; Prechtel, *Hessian Officer's Diary,* 233.
24. Samuel Graham to Daniel Morgan, Winchester, Va., Nov. 22, 1781, enclosed in "To George Washington from Daniel Morgan, 25 November 1781," *Founders Online,* National Archives, last modified June 29, 2017, http://founders.archives.gov/documents/Washington/99-01-02-07445; Graham, *Memoir,* 68.
25. Morgan to Graham, Saratoga, Va., Nov. 28, 1781, transcribed in Graham, *Memoir,* 69; "To George Washington from Daniel Morgan, 25 November 1781," *Founders Online.* Washington thanked Morgan for "the trouble you had taken with the prisoners of War" but gently chided him for overstepping his bounds. "From George Washington to Daniel Morgan, 12 December 1781," *Founders Online,* National Archives, last modified June 29, 2017, http://founders.archives.gov/documents/Washington/99-01-02-07522; "Extract from Major Claiborne's letter of Decr 23d 1781. Dated at Richmond," enclosed in "To George Washington from Timothy Pickering, 17 January 1782," ibid., http://founders.archives.gov/documents/Washington/99-01-02-07699.
26. Council of Maryland to George Murdock, Nov. 2, 1781, in *Archives of Maryland,* 99 vols. (Baltimore: Maryland Historical Society, 1883–2000), 45:659; "From George Washington to Abraham Skinner, 25 October 1781," *Founders Online,* National Archives, last modified June 29, 2017, http://founders.archives.gov/documents/Washington/99-01-02-07272; "To George Washington from Abraham Skinner, 23 November 1781," ibid., http://founders.archives.gov/documents/Washington/99-01-02-07439; Council of Maryland to Col. Philip Thomas, Nov. 2, 1781, in *Archives of Maryland,* 45:659–60.
27. Andrew Krug, "'Such a Banditty You Never See Collected!': Frederick Town and the American Revolution," *Maryland Historical Magazine* 95 (2000): 15; Baker Johnson to Gov. Thomas Lee, Feb. 17, 1780, in *Archives of Maryland,* 47:74; Lamb, *British Soldier's Story,* 97–99; Fielder Gannt to Gov. Thomas Lee, Feb. 1, 1780, in *Archives of Maryland,* 47:46.
28. Lamb, *British Soldier's Story,* 97; Coote to Adj. Gen. Oliver De Lancey, Fredrick Town, Md., Nov. 4, 1781, Sir Eyre Coote Papers, William L. Clements Library, University of Michigan, Ann Arbor; Thomas Price to Governor Lee, Nov. 23, 1781, in *Archives of Maryland,* 47:555; Council of Maryland to Col. Philip Thomas, Nov. 10, 1781, ibid., 45:665.
29. Captain Bayley to Coote, Frederick Town, Md., Dec. 1, 1781, Coote Papers; Coote to Abraham Skinner, Frederick, Md., Dec. 2, 1781, ibid. Rawlings told Washington that he "inform'd the Officers this morning that unless their men behav'd better than they have done hitherto, that we should Continue to punish them Agreeable to Offences." "To George Washington from Moses Rawlings, 2 December 1781,"

Founders Online, National Archives, last modified June 29, 2017, http://founders.archives.gov/documents/Washington/99-01-02-07474.

30. Council of Maryland to Robert Morris, Dec. 14, 1781, in *Archives of Maryland,* 48:24; "Instruction to Virginia Delegates, 29 November 1781," *Founders Online,* National Archives, last modified June 29, 2017, http://founders.archives.gov/documents/Madison/01-03-02-0158.
31. "Instruction to Virginia Delegates, 29 November 1781," n.1, *Founders Online; JCC,* 21:1164. For background on the formation of the office of secretary at war, see Lucille E. Horgan, *Forged in War: The Continental Congress and the Origin of Military Supply* (Westport, Conn.: Greenwood Press, 2002) 44–48; Benjamin Lincoln to the County Lieutenant of Frederick, Va., Dec. 12, 1781, *CVSP,* 2:653; "From George Washington to Moses Rawlings, 12 December 1781," *Founders Online,* National Archives, last modified June 29, 2017, http://founders.archives.gov/documents/Washington/99-01-02-07523; "From George Washington to Charles Cornwallis, 18 October 1781," ibid., http://founders.archives.gov/documents/Washington/99-01-02-07192. For more information on Congress's policy of treating German prisoners more generously than British captives, see Daniel Krebs, *A Generous and Merciful Enemy: Life for German Prisoners of War during the American Revolution* (Norman: University of Oklahoma Press, 2013), 7–8, 143–55.
32. Holmes to Wood, Winchester, Va., Jan. 24, 1782, in_"As Others Saw Us," *Tyler's Quarterly Historical and Genealogical Magazine* 3, no. 1, (July 1921), 13; Prechtel, *Hessian Officer's Diary,* 234–35; Popp, *Hessian Soldier,* 31–32.
33. Shaw, *John Robert Shaw,* 46.
34. Popp, *Hessian Soldier,* 33; Koch, *Battle of Guilford Courthouse,* 24; Döhla, *Hessian Diary,* 201; Lamb, *British Soldier's Story,* 100–101; Graham, *Memoir,* 73.
35. "To George Washington from Henry Clinton, 24 November 1781," *Founders Online,* National Archives, last modified June 29, 2017, http://founders.archives.gov/documents/Washington/99-01-02-07441. On Washington's concern for American maritime prisoners in New York, see "From George Washington to Henry Clinton, 25 January 1781," ibid., http://founders.archives.gov/documents/Washington/99-01-02-04646; "To George Washington from Henry Clinton, 11 February 1782," ibid., http://founders.archives.gov/documents/Washington/99-01-02-07813; and "From George Washington to Henry Clinton, 26 February 1782," ibid., http://founders.archives.gov/documents/Washington/99-01-02-07874.
36. Arthur Middleton's notes for a speech in Congress, Feb. [23?], 1782, *LDC,* 18:355, 357.
37. "From George Washington to John Hanson, 20 February 1782," *Founders Online,* National Archives, last modified June 29, 2017, http://founders.archives.gov/documents/Washington/99-01-02-07848. For the actual resolve that authorized Washington to engage in negotiations for a general cartel of exchange but was not to be "construed to authorize the exchange of Lieutenant General Cornwallis by composition," see *JCC,* 22:76–77.
38. "From George Washington to Abraham Skinner, 5 December 1781," *Founders Online,* National Archives, last modified June 29, 2017, http://founders.archives.gov/

documents/Washington/99-01-02-07495; "To George Washington from Abraham Skinner, 18 February 1782," ibid., http://founders.archives.gov/documents/Washington/99-01-02-07842; "From George Washington to John Laurens, 22 April 1782," ibid., http://founders.archives.gov/documents/Washington/99-01-02-08231.

39. PCC, item 19, 3:457; *JCC,* 22:93-94.

40. *JCC,* 22: 95; "From George Washington to Henry Knox, 11 March 1782," *Founders Online,* National Archives, last modified June 29, 2017, http://founders.archives.gov/documents/Washington/99-01-02-07950. In the end, Lord Cornwallis's exchange was only arranged as part of the preliminary articles of peace in early January 1783. The British released Henry Laurens in March 1782, and Benjamin Franklin, acting independently in France, agreed to absolve Cornwallis's parole that June. Yet Congress did not officially agree to negotiate for the earl's exchange as part of the peace negotiations until November 26, 1782. Even then some delegates, such as Hugh Williamson, John Rutledge, and James Duane, opposed the measure on the grounds that "Cornwallis had rendered himself so execrable by his barbarities." "Notes on Debates, 22 November 1782," ibid., http://founders.archives.gov/documents/Madison/01-05-02-0132. See also "Franklin: Discharge of Cornwallis from His Parole, 9 June 1782," ibid., http://founders.archives.gov/documents/Franklin/01-37-02-0282; *JCC,* 23:754; *Correspondence of Charles, First Marquis Cornwallis,* 3 vols., ed. Charles Ross (London: John Murray, 1859), 1:135–36; and Joseph J. Casino, "Elizabethtown 1782: The Prisoners-of-War Negotiations and the Pawns of War," *New Jersey History* 102, nos. 1–2 (1984): 1–35, esp. 12–18.

41. Robert Morris, *The Papers of Robert Morris, 1781–1784,* 9 vols., ed. James E. Ferguson (Pittsburgh: University of Pittsburgh Press, 1973–), 5:90; *JCC,* 22:321; extract of a letter from a farmer in Juniata County to a correspondent in Philadelphia, Aug. 14, 1782, *Pennsylvania Packet,* Aug. 22, 1782. The editor of the *Pennsylvania Gazette* argued on pragmatic, as well as ideological, grounds to prevent the exchange of Cornwallis's troops. See *Pennsylvania Gazette,* Sept. 4, 1782.

42. *JCC,* 22:316–17; Morris, *Papers,* 5:557; Krebs, "Approaching the Enemy," 395; Hesse-Hanau sergeant Vaupel quoted ibid., 401; prisoners of the Regiment von Knyphausen to Colonel von Borck, quoted ibid., 399–400; "Translation of a Letter from Hessian Prisoners of War of the Regt. De Knyphausen in the Gaol at Philadelphia, July 28, 1782," British Headquarters Papers, David Library of the American Revolution, microfilm, reel 24; Benjamin Lincoln to the President of Congress, Philadelphia, Sept. 13, 1782, PCC, item 149, 2:171.

43. *JCC,* 22:382; Carl Leopold Baurmeister, *Revolution in America: Confidential Letters and Journals, 1776–1784 of Adjutant General Major Baurmeister of the Hessian Forces,* trans. and ed. Bernahard A. Uhlendorf (New Brunswick, N.J.: Rutgers University Press, 1957), 518, 530, 569; Petition of Sergeant Samuel Caswell and six other prisoners to Henry Knox, Oct. 9, 1782, Henry Knox Papers, roll 10, frame 43, Massachusetts Historical Society, Boston.

44. *JCC,* 24:251–52; Martha W. Dixon, "Divided Authority: The American Management of Prisoners in the Revolutionary War" (Ph.D. diss., University of Utah, 1977), 302–5; Döhla, *Hessian Diary,* 221.

45. Döhla, *Hessian Diary,* 221, 222; Popp, *Hessian Soldier,* 33.
46. "Agreement for Liberating British Prisoners, 19 April 1783," *Founders Online,* National Archives, last modified June 29, 2017, http://founders.archives.gov/documents/Washington/99-01-02-11108; Krebs, *Generous and Merciful Enemy,* 248, table 8; Krebs, "Approaching the Enemy," 412. For the mortality rates on board British prison ships in New York, see Burrows, *Forgotten Patriots,* 200. For the mortality rate at British prisons in England, see Paul Gilje, *Liberty on the Waterfront: American Maritime Culture in the Age of Revolution* (Philadelphia: University of Pennsylvania Press, 2004), 119. For the calculations of the yearly mortality rate in Dutch prisons between 1781 and 1800, see Pieter Spierenburg, *The Prison Experience: Disciplinary Institutions and Their Inmates in Early Modern Europe* (New Brunswick, N.J.: Rutgers University Press, 1991), 191.
47. Muster rolls of Capt. Duncan Cameron, Maj. David Ferguson, Capt. William Thorne, and Lt. Col. James Marsh's companies of the 43rd Regiment of Foot, June 1781–June 1783, WO 12/5562, The National Archives of the United Kingdom, London; muster rolls of Capt. Alexander Arbuthnot, Capt. George Cumine, and Maj. James Gordon's companies of the 80th Regiment of Foot, June 1781–June 1783, WO 12/8454, ibid. The official mortality rate for Andersonville Prison was 28.1 percent, but some historians argue that it was higher. E.g., Robert Scott Davis estimates that 31.5 percent is more realistic. Robert Scott Davis, *Ghosts and Shadows of Andersonville: Essays on the Secret Social Histories of America's Deadliest Prison* (Macon, Ga.: Mercer University Press, 2006), 30.
48. "From George Washington to United States Congress, 23 December 1783," *Founders Online,* National Archives, last modified June 29, 2017, http://founders.archives.gov/documents/Washington/99-01-02-12223.

PART III
Jus post Bellum

11 "THE CAUSE OF GOD, OF HUMAN NATURE AND POSTERITY"

John Jay and Justice in the American Revolution

Jonathan Den Hartog

The waning months of 1776 were an inauspicious time for the cause of American independence. After defeats on Long Island and Manhattan, George Washington and the Continental Army had retreated into New Jersey, closely pursued by the British under Lieutenant General Charles Cornwallis.[1] With lower New York occupied, Patriot leaders in the state worried about the fate of their cause. In those dark days of November and December, the New York Convention worked to rally support. One effort came through a pamphlet, *An Address of the Convention of the Representatives of the State of New-York to Their Constituents.* Although published corporately, the *Address* was really the production of a prominent New York Patriot, John Jay.

Jay laid out the stakes for his readers. He acknowledged British success: "Taking advantage of that critical moment, when our forces were almost disbanded, they have penetrated into Jersey, and marched a considerable distance without being attacked." Further, Patriot zeal was draining from the state as the British offered a general amnesty to all who would swear a loyalty oath, or "false suggestions, artful misrepresentations, and insidious promises of protection." Against these temptations, Jay pointed to higher stakes, even invoking the Most High in his appeals. "At this important period, when the freedom and happiness, or the slavery and misery, of the present and future generations of Americans is to be determined on a solemn appeal to the Supreme Ruler of all Events," he insisted that New Yorkers must carry on the fight. To undergird that effort, Jay spent much of the pamphlet reminding his readers why America had declared its independence. Ultimately, he wanted them to remember that "we fight not for conquest, but only for security; that our cause is the cause of God, of human nature and posterity." In short, Jay believed the fight for independence to be just—a just war. Thus, the *Address* was not merely a motivational piece but a reminder of the just principles that had propelled the colonies to independence.

Secure in the knowledge of the basic justice of their cause, Americans could call upon divine aid and then put their full effort into fighting.[2]

In thinking about the American Revolution and the ideas of just war, Jay, as a prominent statesman and articulate leader, deserves careful attention. Born in 1745, Jay grew up in Rye, New York. He attended King's College (1760–64), and after graduation he was admitted to the New York bar and became an active and successful lawyer. Jay's early rise in New York society was marked by his marrying into the prominent family of Patriot statesmen William Livingston, whose daughter Sarah he wed in 1774. These family connections drew him into the imperial conflict, where he gravitated to the Patriot cause and was elected to the First and Second Continental Congresses. Jay did not sign the Declaration of Independence because Patriot leaders had recalled him to New York. Serving in the state's convention when news of the Declaration reached them, he led the body in endorsing independence. The convention quickly afterward appointed Jay the first chief justice of the New York Supreme Court, a post he retained for the next two years while providing material support for the Revolution. In 1778 New York sent him back to Congress, where the next year he served as president. At the end of 1779, Congress appointed him as a diplomat to the Spanish Court to help further America's standing abroad. When the British indicated a willingness to discuss peace, Congress sent Jay to Paris to negotiate alongside John Adams and Benjamin Franklin. Thus, the New Yorker was an active participant in the whole movement for independence.[3]

Examining a figure like Jay in the period of the American Revolution allows us to look at the intersection of a specific individual with broader, theoretical concerns. Without rehearsing the entire philosophy of just war theory, it is important to acknowledge the challenge of applying its clear, normative claims and principles to the confused, complex world of lived reality. This becomes quite relevant when dealing with the American Revolution. Historians and theologians have expressed grave concerns about the ethics of the Revolution and of its qualifications as a just war.[4]

Before any ethical evaluations of the American Revolution can be made, however, historical analysis is necessary. A full accounting that gathers available historical data through which to produce interpretation and evaluation must precede judgments on the justness of the Revolution. Even then, such an evaluation is an act of moral interpretation rather than a simple result of assembling historical data. The historian examining the past is well situated to recognize its moral complexities and to identify the ethical reflections of historical actors. Thus, one way of understanding historical complexities is through grounding examination in a small group or an individual—in this case John Jay.[5] Jay articulated political principles clearly and effectively in a way that spoke to many Americans. His distinctive position of leadership gave him many opportunities to speak to and for his countrymen. From that elite position, he clearly expressed several ways in which Americans in his day could see the Revolutionary War as just. The historical labor of tracing Jay's thought can prepare the way for subsequent theoretical or ethical analysis.

Jay's behavior as a statesman during the Revolution demonstrated attention to important aspects of just war theory, even though he did not couch his concerns in its traditional or expected language. Jay showed aversion to parting from Great Britain, supporting war and independence as a last resort. In defending the American cause, he effectively presented justifications of fighting for independence, including religious reasons, to support a *jus ad bellum* claim. In supporting the war effort, Jay demonstrated that *jus in bello* did not rule out a full-orbed struggle against Great Britain. He also made a special appeal for virtue during wartime, a distinctive approach to defining just conduct in war. Finally, Jay remained persistently concerned about concluding the conflict with a just resolution (*jus post bellum*).[6] He expressed this in his diplomacy and in his longstanding concern for a constitutional settlement that would ensure justice on the state and national level. By securing liberty and justice, the American Revolution would demonstrate its just character to a watching world.

Jay and War as Last Resort

Participating in the Continental Congress, Jay took a moderate stance. He had been very willing to protest British mistreatment of the colonies as a violation of the "rights of Englishmen," but he viewed separation as another matter entirely. Thus, Jay could offer forceful denunciations of royal policy within a framework of British constitutionalism. In the First Congress, he drafted an *Address to the People of Great Britain,* which highlighted a customary constitutional appeal. Jay began by claiming shared status as Englishmen, describing his fellow colonists as "we . . . whose forefathers participated in all the rights, the liberties, and the constitution, you so justly boast, and who have carefully conveyed the same fair inheritance to us, guarantied by the plighted faith of government and the most solemn compacts with British Sovereigns." Thus, Jay could declare, "*Know then,* That we consider ourselves, and do insist, that we are and ought to be, as free as our fellow-subjects in Britain, and that no power on earth has a right to take our property from us without our consent; That we claim all the benefits secured to the subject by the English constitution." He went on to catalog the perceived offenses that the colonists had endured, including the Stamp Act, the Declaratory Act, the Quebec Act, the Tea Act, and the recent Intolerable Acts, which suspended Massachusetts's colonial government and closed Boston Harbor. To Jay (and the Congress), these acts revealed a ministerial plot to place the colonies in "slavery" since the conclusion of the French and Indian War (1754–63). In the face of this, colonial resistance was necessary: nothing less than "the overruling principles of self-preservation"—that is, basic self-defense—led them to resistance. Jay hoped an appeal to the British people would justly sway public opinion. To do so, his pamphlet rejected rumors of American desires for independence. "Be assured that these are not facts, but calumnies," he insisted. Instead, Jay hoped for rectifying problems and restoring harmony. "Permit us to be as free as yourselves, and we shall ever esteem a union with you to be our greatest glory and our greatest happiness, we shall ever be ready to contribute all in our power to the welfare of the Empire." Thus, the stance that Jay—and Congress—was taking still hoped for a restoration of amity.[7]

Even as the First Congress approved the *Address to the People of Great Britain* in 1774 and subsequently disbanded, events would take the lead, with Massachusetts at center stage. There, Governor General Thomas Gage's attempt to arrest Patriot leaders and seize militia supplies would lead to the Battles of Lexington and Concord (April 19, 1775) as well as the subsequent Battle of Bunker Hill (June 17, 1775). With actual fighting breaking out, many more Americans began to contemplate a break from Great Britain.[8] Against this backdrop, and now with an army in the field, the Second Continental Congress met in 1775 to decide which direction to take. In such a setting, Jay continued to oppose a break with England; he actively pursued peace.

This stance was present in his contribution to drafting the Olive Branch Petition. Even as Congress in May and June 1775 prepared defensive measures, the body called for a conciliatory address to King George III. Jay joined John Dickinson, Franklin, Thomas Johnson, and John Rutledge on the committee to draft the petition. Jay and Dickinson were closely allied in seeking some rapprochement with Britain. As the committee worked, Jay even penned his own draft, which revealed a deep desire to avoid war. He denied an American wish to go to war and reasserted loyalty both to Crown and country. Colonial resistance was rooted in a plea "for Justice & to request only that Portion of Liberty to which God and the Constitution have given them Right"—a significant mix of religion, British constitutionalism, and self-defense. In the end, the committee endorsed Dickinson's final version of the Olive Branch Petition, and Jay strongly advocated for it in debate.[9]

Jay's hope to avoid war continued even after Congress authorized the Olive Branch. He called for a second conciliatory petition as a follow-up, a move

Congress did not approve. As late as December 1775, Jay was arguing against independence. He drew upon the recently printed *Journal of Congress* to show that the body was not committed to a separation, calling rumors to the contrary "false Reports, wicked Slanders and insidious Misrepresentations" meant to destroy continental unity. Thus, it was nothing less than an "ungenerous & groundless Charge" that the Americans were "aiming at Independence, or a total Separation from G. Britain." Jay concluded, "to charge the Congress with aiming at a separation of these Colonies from great Britain is to charge them falsely and without a single Spark of Evidence to support the Accusation." While many congressional delegates considered independence as the only option, Jay continued to work for reconciliation. He was making every effort to avoid hostilities, which he saw as a measure of last resort. In this way, Jay was pursuing actions in line with just war theory.[10]

Jay and the Justification of War as Self-Defense against Tyranny

Despite Jay's best efforts to avoid armed conflict, attitudes in the colonies were shifting. His willingness to consider other possibilities was evident in the early days of 1776, when he wrote to his brother James, "tho We desire Reconciliation, [we] are well prepared for contrary Measures. This is an unnatural Quarrel, & God only knows why the British Empire should be torn to pieces by unjust Attempts to subjugate us."[11] This statement demonstrates Jay's balanced perspective. While he still desired peace, he was increasingly willing to contemplate alternatives. Significantly, his contention that British efforts at domination were *unjust* would lay the groundwork for a defense of the American Revolution as a *just* response. Jay's perspective in Congress darkened still further when news arrived that, rather than gravely considering the Olive Branch Petition, George III had refused even to hear it. When legitimate appeals to the monarch based in loyalty and a shared British constitutional heritage had failed, and after news arrived that a British and Hessian mercenary army was assembling for service in America, Jay concluded that the king had crossed a line and had lost his claim to rightful authority. He thus participated in a Congress in early 1776 that inched toward independence as it issued orders to the colonies to form their own governments and prepare their defenses.[12]

Jay would remain in Philadelphia until May 1776, when family illness and the needs of New York's Patriot movement called him back there. Thus, he was not present for the debate over independence. In fact, the remaining New York delegation received no direction from their convention about the matter, making them the only colony to abstain from voting in favor of independence on July 2. Still, when news of the congressional declaration reached the New York Convention, Jay acceded and put his full effort toward its support.[13]

In the renamed New York Provincial Congress, Jay headed the committee dealing with responding to the Declaration and drafted the response, which the New York Congress unanimously approved. This resolution endorsed the reasoning of the Declaration of Independence, asserting "that the Reasons assigned by the Continental Congress for declaring the United Colonies free and independent States are cogent and conclusive."[14] Thus, Jay looked—as many Americans likewise did—at the center section of the Declaration, the indictment of George III. It was the deeds of the king, not the surrounding philosophical claims, that had driven Americans to independence.[15] Next, the New York resolution demonstrated the resignation to independence felt by Jay and moderate Patriots. "While we lament the cruel necessity which has rendered that measure [independence] unavoidable," it declared, "we approve the same, and will, at the risk of our lives and fortunes, join with the other Colonies in supporting it."[16] Just as New York now supported independence and endorsed its delegates to Congress in doing the same, so Jay swung decidedly behind the Patriot cause.

In the next two years, Jay would have several opportunities to advocate for the American perspective, repeatedly presenting a justification for American independence as self-defense against slavery. This argument was most on display in Jay's *Address of the Convention of the Representatives of the State of New-York*. Published in December 1776, a principal argument in the *Address* was the need for Americans to fight based on the justice of their cause. This note sounds from the first page, where Jay declared:

> You and all men were created free, and authorized to establish civil government, for the preservation of your rights against oppression, and the security of that freedom which God hath given you, against the rapacious hand of tyranny and lawless power. It is therefore not only necessary to the well-being of society, but the duty of every man, to oppose and repel all those, by whatever name or title distinguished, who prostitute the powers of government to destroy the happiness and freedom of the people over whom they may be appointed to rule.[17]

This was a justification of armed revolt. The British had turned oppressive, trampled on American freedom, and created tyranny and "lawless power" (force without right). Such actions justified the overthrow of an alleged ruler, who had himself lost the justification for his rule.

In Jay's narrative the British grab for power was a departure from an original condition of peace. "During the space of between one and two hundred years, every man sat under his own vine and his own fig-tree, and there was none to make him afraid. That the people of Britain never claimed a right to dispose of us, and every thing belonged to us according to their will and pleasure, until the reign of the present King of that Island." In contrast to the vision of safety and liberty called up by Micah 4:4, the present ministry—and indeed the monarch—had innovated away from the arrangement. To enforce such "abominable" claims, "they have invaded our country by sea and land." The Revolution was thus justifiable as literal self-defense against foreign invasion.[18]

This theme of self-defense carries through an extended passage in which Jay argues that, despite claims of the occupying army, the British were not really in favor of peace, only submission:

> If there be one single idea of peace in his [the king's] mind, Why does he order your cities to be burnt, your country desolated, your brethren to starve and languish and die in prisons? If any thing was intended besides destruction, devastation, and bloodshed, Why are the Mercenaries of Germany transported near four thousand miles, to plunder your houses; to ravish your wives and daughters; to strip your infant children; to expose whole families, naked miserable and forlorn, to want, to hunger, to inclement skies and wretched deaths? . . . Why like the Demons of old, is their wrath to be expiated only by human sacrifices? Why do they excite the savages of the wilderness to murder our inhabitants and exercise cruelties unheard of among civilized nations?[19]

Through this emotional rhetoric, Jay was driving home the point that war, initiated by King George, was bringing these horrors upon Americans. The idea that these actions were outside the bounds of a conflict suggest that Jay was operating with specific *in bello* expectations. With this destruction, with these violations of a code of war, the American war was truly one of self-defense.

The colonies were fighting in self-defense against a monarch who had lost the right to any claim of obedience. First, George III led a nation with "designs against us wicked, unjust, cruel, contrary to the laws of God and man, pursued with implacable, unrelenting vengeance, and in a manner barbarous, and opposed to the usage of civilized nations." The unjust character of the king and of his country had stripped him of legitimacy to rule in America. Second, his actions had added up to nothing less than an abdication: "That he declared you to be out of his protection. That he absolved you from all allegiance. That he made war upon you, and instead of your King became your enemy and destroyer. By his consent, by his own act, you became independent of his crown."[20] Just as in the Glorious Revolution, when James II's abdication had opened to Parliament the choice of selecting new rulers in William and Mary, so George's abdication opened the right for independence for the American colonies. This argument also recalled the Declaration of Independence, which charged that the king had "abdicated Government here, by declaring us out of his Protection and waging War against us." George's actions had removed from him any right to rule: he had chosen to abandon his role as a rightful king deserving obedience.

Jay put a finer point on his specific claims against the king a year later, when he addressed the state's grand jury. As New York's chief justice, Jay revealed that his argument against George III had a particularly constitutional bent. He observed that "the infatuated Sovereign of Britain" had destroyed "our former constitutions" and made "unwarrantable attempts, *to bind us in all cases whatever.*"[21] The king's lawlessness had demonstrated that he was no longer a "nursing father" to the American colonies—thus, he was no longer king.[22] This position received further reinforcement as he had destroyed "former constitutions," both specific colonial charters and the British Common Law constitution that had been operative for more than a century.[23] Always concerned with laws and constitutions, Jay saw this as a definitive stroke. The monarch himself had broken the charters, leaving the colonies no choice but to establish a new, independent government. As a result of these violations, George III's rule had become an example of force without right, of "arbitrary and violent domination." Not surprisingly, such arbitrary rule brought "anarchy, confusion, and licentiousness." The actions of the king and of the British had violated all known standards of justice. They would "unjustly determine, by violence and force, to execute designs which were reprobated by every principle of humanity, equity, gratitude, and policy."[24] General lawlessness followed royal lawlessness, and thus the interest of law, justice, and constitutionality rested with the American side.

Among these general political and constitutional claims, Jay added a strongly religious argument, a distinctive claim that characterized his early writings about the American Revolution. Not only did he affirm that liberty is a "heavenly gift," but he also saw religious rights as worth fighting for and defending. Jay justified his position by pointing to British aggression against faith and the churches. "No regard for religion or virtue remains among them," he claimed. "Your very churches bear witness to their impiety. Your churches are used without hesitation, as goals [jails], as stables, and as houses of sport and theatrical exhibitions." Such actions revealed British soldiers as "deaf to the calls of humanity, dead to every sentiment of religion and void of all regard for the temples of the Lord of Hosts."[25] This approach partook of a type of Protestant resistance theory. More than just defense of life, property, or constitutions, defense of churches and faith was itself justification for armed resistance.[26] Because Jay believed that religion gave positive endorsement of independence, he actively looked for divine aid. Believing that God *did* favor the American cause, he could pass on that confidence to his countrymen: "A revolution which, in the whole course of its rise and progress, is distinguished by so many marks of the Divine favour and interposition, that no doubt can remain of its being finally accomplished."[27] Such confidence in Jay led not to arrogance but to a steely commitment to doing his duty and pointing the country—justified in its independence and war—on the right course forward.[28]

Justice and Virtue during the Revolution

Having concluded that independence and war were justified, Jay turned all his efforts to supporting them. He demonstrated a wholehearted dedication to the success of the cause. If a war was just, then it deserved to be prosecuted until won. Jay provided active, logistical support for the Patriot effort in New York. One measure of this commitment was his communication with military commanders, including Major General Philip Schuyler, Major General Arthur St. Clair, and others.[29] Most significant was his increasing correspondence with Commander in Chief Washington.[30] Jay also endorsed spying as justifiable. In fact, he helped direct a spy ring that kept tabs on British movements in occupied southern New York.[31] Such actions were justified conduct during wartime.

Still, for Jay, just conduct in war meant more than simply fighting and winning. He also demonstrated two specific *jus in bello* concerns: protecting property and respecting debts. Jay objected to unregulated impressment of private property, even by American forces. "It is the undoubted Right & unalienable Priviledge of a Freeman not to be divested, or interrupted in the innocent use, of Life Liberty or Property," he insisted. He recognized the need for the army to supply itself but objected to the Quartermaster Corps simply seizing property under the umbrella of "necessity." Instead, Jay called for some legislation to protect New Yorkers' property. This principle was subsequently enacted into New York law, which empowered justices of the peace to oversee military requisitions. In this instance Jay was concerned about property as a piece of *jus in bello.*[32]

Jay also demonstrated a concern for the country's credit (understood as both financial standing and reputation). As president of Congress in 1779, he had to respond to questions about the confederation's finances, with elements of taxes, debt, and currency stability all swirling. In this context, Jay penned the *Circular Letter from Congress to Their Constituents.* In it he realized the necessity of repaying American debts contracted for independence. For him, a just nation needed to respect its credit, nothing less than a matter of just conduct during war. For Jay, "violating our national faith [regarding debts], or omitting to pursue the measures necessary to preserve it" would be both "baseness and bad policy." Rather, "knowing the value of national character, and impressed with a due sense of the immutable laws of justice and honour, it is impossible that America should think without horror of such an execrable deed." Such strong words showed his commitment to just standards and to the integrity of America's credit, built upon reputation and character. In order to support the confidence Jay had, he called on Americans to renew their patriotism and follow through on the obligations laid upon them by Congress. "To keep your battalions full, to encourage loans, and to assess your taxes with prudence, collect them with firmness, and pay them with punctuality, is all that will be requisite on your part."[33] To follow the path of virtue required normal activity, and Jay believed that he could expect American citizens to follow through on their commitment to just dealings.

Finally, Jay's reflections on *jus in bello* added a final, distinctive dimension: a concern for individual and corporate virtue as a form of just conduct. Jay would link the decline of virtue in the late colonial period with the coming of the Revolution. In 1776 he speculated that "we should still have enjoyed the blessings of peace and plenty, if we had not forgotten the source from which those blessings flowed, and permitted our country to be contaminated by the many shameful vices which have prevailed among us." Still, if virtue was the goal, the war could prove very useful, for it could bring purification and the reestablishment of virtue. Thus, Jay would intuit a blessing from the conflict: "It seems as tho' Providence were determined to use them [the British] as instruments to punish the guilt of this country, and bring us back to a sense of duty to our Creator." The path to right conduct and success lay in a religiously motivated return to virtue. Jay promised that "if we turn from our sins, he [God] will turn from his anger. Then will our arms be crowned with success and the pride and power of our enemies . . . will vanish away. Let us do our duty and victory will be our reward. Let a general reformation of manners take place." He then listed examples, such as taking care of widows and orphans rather than taking advantage of them, and standing firm rather than fleeing to safety in another state. He concluded, "Let universal charity, public spirit and private virtue, be inculcated, encouraged and practiced." This approach would lead to honorable conduct during the war and ultimately to success. Thus, Jay was concerned not only with a just prosecution of the war but also with justice from the country that was fighting it, both individually and collectively. His emphasis on the public significance of virtue was significant, given his public prominence, and he helped publicize this concern.[34]

Jus post Bellum Concerns in Diplomacy, Law, and Constitutionalism

Even as the war continued, Jay turned his thoughts to the future of his state and the nation after a successful break with Britain, thereby embodying a concern for a just and legal settlement to the war (*jus post bellum*). He understood implicitly that a just conclusion would go far in vindicating the break. Logically, the separation from Britain would only make sense if the result was better than what had been left behind. Although a formal category of *jus post bellum* had not been defined in Jay's day, a legal and diplomatic standard did exist for the proper conclusion of warfare, which he worked conscientiously to enact in his diplomacy. Still, Jay's motives suggest important principles that have been adopted by subsequent just war thinkers. As Mark Allman and Tobias Winright observe: "The goal of a just war must be to establish social, political, and economic conditions that are more stable, more just, and less prone to chaos than what existed prior to the fighting. . . . The goal . . . is not simply the cessation of violence, but political, economic, social, and ecological conditions that allow citizens to flourish." Jay's efforts to craft a postbellum settlement inspired both diplomatic activity and a concern for reestablishing constitutional government that stretched for years after the British surrender at Yorktown.[35]

Jay pursued a diplomatic course to secure both American independence and a just postwar settlement. Under orders from Congress, he served as the first U.S. minister to the Spanish Court, where he was tasked with raising financial support for the war effort.[36] From there, Congress sent him to Paris to negotiate, alongside Franklin and John Adams, the final peace treaty with Britain. Jay sought to end the War for Independence well and preserve just relations between the United States, France, and Great Britain, thereby laying the groundwork for successful postwar international relations.[37]

In these negotiations Jay was informed by the larger literature of international law, the laws of nations (*jus gentium*) expressed as both formal principles and the rules governing diplomacy. Although built on the writings of Hugo Grotius—especially his *De jure belli ac pacis*—in the eighteenth century, it was Emer de Vattel's thought regarding international relations that helped shape Jay's principles.[38] The New Yorker's legal training equipped and inspired him with the motivation to master the legalities of international relations. Jay noted Vattel's international influence even as he scoffed at the Spanish Court's willful ignorance of the Swiss jurist's works.[39] For Vattel, diplomatic negotiations are designed to achieve a just, even if imperfect, settlement of competing claims. Discussions between states are predicated on the principle of state sovereignty, which empower nations and their diplomatic representatives to make agreements within a range of options. Thus, Jay was aware of the standards of international law in his day and desired to use the diplomatic forms to achieve a just and peaceful resolution of the war.[40]

Jay's actions in Paris demonstrated his desire to achieve justice, a commitment to right behavior as a path to an upright outcome. In his cooperative dealings with Franklin and Adams, he often led the way toward the negotiating strategies that the ambassadors would adopt. These demands were present in at least two places. One concerned the issue of diplomatic credentials. The initial credentials brought by the British delegation did not meet international standards and instead were based on a format used within the British Empire. Despite the advice of the comte de Vergennes, the French foreign minister, to accept them, Jay advised Franklin and the rest of the delegation to refuse them and to demand that the credentials recognize the United States as a sovereign, separate entity.[41] After the American protest, the British later produced corrected credentials. In this way, the Americans achieved equal legal status as negotiators with the British, as both sides representing equal sovereign entities.

Once negotiations began, Jay came to conclude—using his judgment as an ambassador in the middle of the action—that justice in concluding the war would be better served by making a separate peace with Great Britain rather than waiting and following the lead of France, whose officials desired American independence but not American success as a strong North American power. Even though these actions cut against the express instructions of Congress, the ambassadors decided to act unilaterally, with Jay sending a representative, William Vaughan, as an unofficial messenger to London. Jay later asserted, "though we were determined faithfully to fulfill our Treaty and Engagements with this Court [France], *yet it was a different thing to be guided by their or our Construction of it.*"[42] In short, the Americans had fulfilled the letter of the treaty with France—persevering until independence had been gained—though achieving it via unanticipated means.

In the peace treaty with Great Britain, Jay also sought a just resolution after the conflict that enabled a positive, if imperfect, conclusion to the war. Several theorists have emphasized the significance of reconciliation between states and between individuals at the conclusion of hostilities, and Jay's work represented efforts at normalizing relations.[43] The treaty recognized private interests and empowered creditors on either side to recover all legitimate debts (4th Article). It also called upon Congress to "earnestly recommend it to the Legislatures of their respective States to provide for the Restitution of all Estates, Rights, and Properties which have been confiscated belonging to real British Subjects" (5th Article). Property for the losing side would not be threatened, nor would future prosecutions be made for wartime decisions (6th Article). Prisoners were to be released, and British military withdrawals were to occur without undue destruction or, significantly for southerners, with "carrying away any Negroes or other Property of the American Inhabitants" (7th Article). Finally, fishing "rights" and "liberties" were delineated (3rd Article). Although not satisfying either the Americans or the British fully, the treaty secured most interests and laid the groundwork for future resolutions of issues. A rough, imperfect justice had been secured diplomatically.[44]

Jay's second postwar concern, the establishments of effective laws and constitutions as structures for future national flourishing, showed up very shortly after independence. Thus, his *Charge to the New York Grand Jury* in 1777 served as an initial report on the issue of just constitutionalism. The state convention had named Jay the first chief justice under the independent government. Jay welcomed this position, not only because of his legal background but also because he valued the way law and constitutions structured society. The pursuit of justice in the new society would be just as pressing as it had been under British rule. As such, Chief Justice Jay used his grand jury charge not simply to instruct on technical matters of the law but also to discuss larger matters and to teach his audience about law, constitutions, and citizenship in a free republic.

The initial report was a positive one. Whereas Jay had justified independence in part because of George III's destruction of "our former constitutions," he now rejoiced that the upheaval actually "enabled us to erect more elegible systems of government on their ruins." He continued, "Whoever compares our present with our former constitution, will find abundant reason to rejoice in the exchange, and readily admit, that all the calamities, incident to this war, will be amply compensated by the many blessings flowing from this glorious revolution." Through the darkness of the revolutionary struggle, Jay hoped that he saw glimpses of a brighter future, one built on a better constitutional system. This better system arose, he believed, because "the Americans are the first people whom Heaven has favoured with an opportunity of deliberating upon and choosing the forms of government under which they should live." In short, this constitutional endeavor was a divine gift that should not be treated lightly. In deliberating upon government, Jay believed that Americans were not dependent on "violence or accidental circumstances" but could instead employ "the guidance of reason and experience" to craft a constitutional settlement.[45]

Jay noted the "general satisfaction" that the New York Constitution had produced and then went on to enumerate many compelling elements of it. He started by noting that "the highest respect has been paid to those great and equal rights of human nature, which should forever remain inviolate in every society," considering the state constitution to be in line with the principles of the American Revolution. In this, he connected "rights" with "human nature"—that is, humans derive their rights from their natural character as humans. Next, Jay praised the separation of powers present in the constitution. The "disposition of the legislative, executive, and judicial powers of government" allowed for justice to be more easily done. Informed by the works of Montesquieu, New York's framers had crafted a document that would "promise permanence to the constitution, and give energy and impartiality to the distribution of justice."[46] The result would be that "your live[s], your liberties, your property, will be at the disposal only of your Creator and yourselves." This represented simultaneously the halting of the abusive powers of British rule and the restoration for every individual to sit under his own "vine and fig tree." Jay continued that the state constitution protected "the rights of conscience and private judgment"—that is, it upheld religious liberty, allowing free expression of faith, in contrast to the partial Anglican establishment that had prevailed in New York prior to the Revolution.[47] Finally, Jay praised the equal, impartial protection under law provided by the constitution.[48] If New York's citizens continued to uphold their duties as responsible republicans, they would certainly improve on the constitution from before independence—a definite *jus post bello* conclusion.

If the narrative stopped there, that result would have been easily proven. But Jay delivered those words only one year into independence. The coming years—especially those after peace—would paint a darker picture, again raising questions about the justness of the Revolution. Jay was in a prime position to monitor these developments as secretary of foreign affairs for Congress. Having the responsibility to follow through with ensuring the elements of the peace treaty with Britain that he had helped write as well as maintaining proper relations with other European nations—especially those that had loaned money to the new republic—he found the new states resisting and even violating the peace treaty. The Confederation government refused to stop them, even as it was unable to raise money to dispose of its own justly contracted debts. Jay bemoaned this fact to John Adams, observing, "there has not been a single Day since it [the peace treaty] took effect, on which it has not been violated in America, by one or other of the States."[49] Congressional weakness came into full view when it was unable to force the states to do what was required of them under international treaty or to uphold national credit.

The failure of the United States to keep its word promised repercussions in foreign affairs. Even worse, from Jay's perspective, was the moral and even divine judgments that threatened such abridgments. As he informed Washington:

> It is too true that the Treaty has been violated. . . . I am uneasy and apprehensive; more so than during the War. *Then* we had a fixed Object, and though the Means and Time of obtaining it were often problematical yet I did firmly believe we should ultimately succeed, because I was convinced that Justice was with us. The Case is now altered; we are going and doing wrong, and therefore I look forward to Evils and Calamities, but without being able to guess at the Instrument, Nature, or measure of them.[50]

Political matters were still a question of justice. Whereas Jay had been confident that the cause of the War for Independence had been just, he was now convinced of American wrongdoing, of injustice on the international stage. Believing that the world operated according to moral laws, he feared the results of violating them. Wrongdoing would lead to definite punishments, either naturally or providentially. To avoid natural consequences and divine judgments, a government able to enforce its treaty obligations and to act justly was necessary.

This search for a permanent just settlement after the war would propel Jay forward in his seeking a new national constitution in the late 1780s. He monitored developments and provided incisive analysis to other leaders throughout the country. Given Jay's preference for a stronger national government, New York did not appoint him to the Constitutional Convention. Nonetheless, he approved of the convention's result. He observed to Adams, "I think it much better than the one we have, and therefore that we shall be Gainers by the Exchange, especially as there is Reason to hope that Experience and the good Sense of the People will correct what may prove to be inexpedient in it." If imperfect, it offered a great improvement. Given this promise, Jay had to decide how to work to achieve ratification of the proposed constitution as a means of securing the revolutionary settlement.[51]

In his writing and activity, Jay connected ratification to the American Revolution. In "Federalist No. 2" he viewed the revolutionary struggle as creating a new nation. He described the Americans as "by their joint counsels, arms, and efforts, fighting side by side throughout a long and bloody war, [to] have nobly established their general liberty and independence." The war had forged a "band of brethren, united to each other by the strongest ties."[52] Jay believed that the revolutionaries understood the value of both "Liberty" and "Union," and he claimed that the new constitution guaranteed both.

Similarly, in his widely read *Address to the People of the State of New-York, on the Subject of the Constitution,* Jay framed the push for the constitution in light of the revolutionary experience. The controversy began "when the King of Great-Britain, misguided by men who did not merit his confidence, asserted the unjust claim of binding us, in all cases whatsoever, and prepared to obtain our submission by force." In the face of that threat, the American colonies were forced to recognize the value of union. Jay approved of that sentiment: "That Union was the child of wisdom—Heaven blessed it, and it wrought out our political salvation." But with the return of peace, "evils, like the worst of weeds," have entered into American politics. It thus was incumbent on Americans to reflect on political structures, so he recommended the new constitution as a recommitment to political union and a guarantee of liberty. It would ensure the just relations between states and between the United States and other countries. He concluded with a challenge to secure the reputation of the "cause of freedom" and preserve republican forms of self-government.[53]

Beyond his published writings, Jay would actively work to ensure ratification, most centrally at the New York Ratification Convention. There, he offered a voice of reason in defense of the constitution and did so in a convention initially biased against it. Through Jay's canny leadership, he maneuvered the convention not only to ratify the new constitution but also to do so without conditions.[54] Jay would see the ratified U.S. Constitution as the capstone of the Revolution, the final guarantee of justice after the war.

Conclusions

With this survey, we can draw conclusions about John Jay, the American Revolution, and the concept of just war. Jay's leadership and activities mean that he deserves significant attention as one close to the center of the politics of the American Revolution. Because of the positions he held and the contributions he made, Jay provided both symbolic leadership and important guidance for the course of independence. It is true that he spoke primarily in categories of justice, not "just war" explicitly, but in his words and actions, he showed a significant concern for justice in America's national doings. Thus, Jay laid out an extended case for the just character of American resistance and independence. By holding out against separation for as long as possible—until finally rejected by George III—Jay demonstrated that the war was a last resort. He also justified the conflict as the route of self-defense forced upon the Americans by the British, who had rejected an earlier constitutional arrangement and now sought to bring the colonists to heel by force. During the war, Jay endorsed fighting but protected property and so sought a just conduct of the war. He especially emphasized virtue as a significant feature of just American conduct. During and after the war, he served U.S. diplomacy to secure peaceful and just international relations according to expectations of international law. Further, he pursued a constitutional settlement, both in New York and in the nation. Constitutional government would secure the just and secure functioning of the American republic, for which independence had been declared. Jay's constitutional pursuit demonstrated what he had been after all along: the liberty of self-government under law. Through working to ensure this constitutional, settled liberty after the Revolution, Jay helped retroactively justify the entire conflict.

From these historical observations, we can strive to make philosophical and ethical judgments. In this endeavor, I am rightfully cautious, aware that I am moving beyond historical grounds to draw normative conclusions. I acknowledge that Jay did not speak for the entire war, nor was his outlook the only one that shaped the American cause.[55] Still, as a prominent, significant, and vocal leader, he worked to conduct the war in a just manner. In his restraints on evil during the war and pursuit of an equitable peace and constitutional government after the fighting ceased, he labored to defend and further the just conduct and resolution of the American Revolution. His thought and actions demonstrate the possibility of a just motive to war (*jus ad bellum*), just conduct during the war (*jus in bello*), and a just settlement after the war (*jus post bellum*). Jay's sustained involvement in the American Revolution demonstrates the great concerns the founding leaders had to ensure that the War for Independence was, in fact, a just war.

NOTES

1. For the background to these events, see David Hackett Fischer, *Washington's Crossing* (New York: Oxford University Press, 2004), 66–181.
2. John Jay, *An Address of the Convention of the Representatives of the State of New-York to Their Constituents* (Fish-Kill, N.Y.: S. Loudon, 1776), 3, 13, 16.
3. For Jay on nation building, see Jonathan Den Hartog, *Patriotism and Piety: Federalist Politics and Religious Struggle in the New American Nation* (Charlottesville: University of Virginia Press, 2015), 21–44. General biographies include Frank Monaghan, *John Jay: Defender of Liberty against Kings and Peoples, Author of the Constitution & Governor of New York, President of the Continental Congress, Co-author of the Federalist, Negotiator of the Peace of 1783 & the Jay Treaty of 1794, First Chief Justice of the United States* (Indianapolis: Bobbs-Merrill, 1935); and Walter Stahr, *John Jay: Founding*

Father (New York: Hambledon and London, 2005). Also valuable is Milton Klein, "John Jay and the Revolution," *New York History* 81 (Jan. 2000): 19–30.

4. For historians using theological and biblical categories, see Nathan Hatch, George Marsden, and Mark Noll, *The Search for Christian America* (Colorado Springs: Helmers and Howard, 1989), 70–106; and John Fea, *Was America Founded as a Christian Nation? An Historical Introduction* (Louisville, Ky.: Westminster/John Knox Press, 2011), 108–33. Even in an endorsement of the American Revolution, Wayne Grudem is very circumspect in his argumentation. Grudem, *Politics according to the Bible: A Comprehensive Resource for Understanding Modern Political Issues in Light of Scripture* (Grand Rapids, Mich.: Zondervan, 2010), 87–91. For a contrasting religio-political argument, see John Keown, "America's War for Independence: Just or Unjust?" *Journal of Catholic Social Thought* 6, no. 2 (2009): 277–304.
5. For a complementary perspective using a similar approach, see chapter 6 above.
6. It should be noted that the concept of *jus post bellum* was less articulated in the eighteenth century than it has become in more recent thought about just wars. Yet Jay still maintained an abiding concern for a just and lawful conclusion to the American Revolution.
7. John Jay, *The Selected Papers of John Jay*, 4 vols. (to date), ed. Elizabeth Nuxoll et al. (Charlottesville: University of Virginia Press, 2010–15) [cited hereafter as SPJJ], 1:100–101, 106, 107.
8. For the best narrative of Lexington and Concord, see David Hackett Fischer, *Paul Revere's Ride* (New York: Oxford University Press, 1994). The situation after Lexington and Concord truly marked the shift documented in Pauline Maier, *From Resistance to Revolution: Colonial Radicals and the Development of American Opposition to Britain, 1765–1776* (New York: W. W. Norton, 1972, 1991).
9. SPJJ, 1:119–20, 123. On Dickinson, see Jane Calvert, *Quaker Constitutionalism and the Political Thought of John Dickinson* (New York: Cambridge University Press, 2009).
10. SPJJ, 1:174, 175, 177. There is no record that Jay published his catalog, but that he even drafted it demonstrated his thinking—and what he hoped to pass on to his countrymen—in very late 1775.
11. Jay to James Jay, 4 Jan. 1776, ibid., 195.
12. Edmund Morgan, *The Birth of the Republic, 1763–1789,* 4th ed. (Chicago: University of Chicago Press, 2013), 68–76. Cf. Benjamin Irvin, *Clothed in Robes of Sovereignty: The Continental Congress and the People Out of Doors* (New York: Oxford University Press, 2011).
13. For background, see SPJJ, 1:237–38, 265–66.
14. Ibid., 266.
15. On the declaration, see Pauline Maier, *American Scripture: Making the Declaration of Independence* (New York: Alfred A. Knopf, 1997), 97–123.
16. SPJJ, 1:266.
17. Jay, *Address of the Convention,* 3.
18. Ibid., 5. For the use of the vine-and-fig-tree metaphor during the American Revolution, see Daniel L. Dreisbach, *Reading the Bible with the Founding Fathers* (New York: Oxford University Press, 2017), 211–28.

19. Ibid., 8–9. For specific examples of burning cities, see chapter 8 above. Further, as Jay was writing this from New York, a state divided between British and Patriot occupations, he was well aware of depredations then occurring.
20. Jay, *Address of the Convention,* 11, 16.
21. John Jay, *The Charge Delivered by the Honourable John Jay, Esq.; Chief Justice of the State of New-York, to the Grand Jury, at the Supreme Court, Held in Kingston, in Ulster County, September 9, 1777* (Kingston, N.Y.: John Holt, 1777), 6.
22. The reference is to Isaiah 49:23. Cf. Benjamin Lewis Price, *Nursing Fathers: American Colonists' Conception of English Protestant Kingship, 1688–1776* (Lanham, Md.: Lexington Books, 1999).
23. On Common Law constitutionalism, see James Stoner, *Common Law and Liberal Theory: Coke, Hobbes, and the Origins of American Constitutionalism* (Lawrence: University Press of Kansas, 1992).
24. Jay, *Charge Delivered,* 5, 7.
25. Jay, *Address of the Convention,* 9, 11.
26. For Protestant political thought, see chapter 2 above. For further elaboration on Protestant resistance, see John Witte Jr., *The Reformation of Rights: Law, Religion, and Human Rights in Early Modern Calvinism* (New York: Cambridge University Press, 2007), 81–142. On religious motivations for the American Revolution, see Thomas Kidd, *God of Liberty* (New York: Basic Books, 2010); James Bell, *A War of Religion: Dissenters, Anglicans, and the American Revolution* (New York: Palgrave Macmillan, 2008); and Glenn Moots, *Politics Reformed: The Anglo-American Legacy of Covenant Theology* (Columbia: University of Missouri Press, 2010).
27. Jay, *Charge Delivered,* 6.
28. For Jay and religious belief during the Revolution and in the new nation, see Jonathan Den Hartog, "John Jay and the 'Great Plan of Providence,'" in *The Forgotten Founders on Church and State,* ed. Daniel L. Dreisbach, Mark D. Hall, and Jeffry H. Morrison (Notre Dame, Ind.: Notre Dame University Press, 2009), 145–70.
29. For example, see SPJJ, 1:436–44, 450–53, 460–64, 466–67.
30. Among many, see Jay to George Washington, 21 Apr. 1779, ibid., 616–17.
31. For details, see ibid., 347–50.
32. Ibid., 502–3. Cf. Jay to William Livingston, 22 Mar. 1777, ibid., 388–90.
33. Ibid., 668, 669, 675.
34. Jay, *Address of the Convention,* 4, 5, 10, 11. For a discussion of virtue, justice, and religion in the American Revolution, see Kidd, *God of Liberty,* 97–114. In advocating for virtue from a leadership position, Jay sounded similar to Samuel Adams. Ira Stoll, *Samuel Adams: A Life* (New York: Free Press, 2009).
35. Mark Allman and Tobias Winright, *After the Smoke Clears: The Just War Tradition and Post War Justice* (Maryknoll, N.Y.: Orbis Books, 2010), 14, 15. For elaboration on these points, see ibid., 90–100, 143–63. Other recent discussions of the *jus post bellum* concept include Carsten Stahn and Jann K. Kleffner, eds., *Jus Post Bellum: Towards a Law of Transition from Conflict to Peace* (New York: Cambridge University Press, 2008); Eric Patterson, *Ending Wars Well: Just War Theory in Post-Conflict* (New Haven, Conn.: Yale University Press, 2012); Larry May, *After*

War Ends: A Philosophical Perspective (New York: Cambridge University Press, 2012); and Larry May and Andrew T. Forcehimes, eds., *Morality, Jus Post Bellum, and International Law* (New York: Cambridge University Press 2012), esp. 1–10, 204–56.

36. For Jay in Spain, see SPJJ, vol. 2.
37. On Jay's role in the peace negotiations, see Richard B. Morris, *The Peacemakers: The Great Powers and American Independence* (New York: Harper & Row, 1965); and, more recently, Jack Rakove, *Revolutionaries: A New History of the Invention of America* (Boston: Houghton Mifflin Harcourt, 2010), 242–89.
38. On Vattel, see chapters 1 and 3 above. For peacemaking, see especially Vattel, *The Law of Nations* (Indianapolis: Liberty Fund, 2008), bk. 4, chaps. 1–3.
39. Jay to Gouverneur Morris, 28 Sept. 1781, in SPJJ, 2:574–76.
40. For the ideas of this paragraph, I am grateful for conversations with Benjamin Lyons, who is doing extensive research on Jay's diplomacy and use of *Law of Nations.* See Benjamin Lyons, "The Law of Nations in the Diplomacy of the American Revolution" (Ph.D. diss., Columbia University, 2016).
41. For Jay's reasoning on taking this strong stance, see John Jay, memo to Vergennes (unsent), c. 11 Sept. 1782, in SPJJ, 3:121–42.
42. Jay to Secretary for Foreign Affairs Robert R. Livingston, 17 Nov. 1782, in SPJJ, 3:244.
43. Allman and Winright, *After the Smoke Clears,* 14–15, 102–16. Cf. May and Forcehimes, *Morality, Jus Post Bellum, and International Law,* 32–48, 113–38.
44. For the treaty, see Hunter Miller, ed., *Treaties and Other International Acts of the United States of America,* 2 vols. (Washington, D.C.: U.S. Government Printing Office, 1931–48), 2:151–56.
45. Jay, *Charge Delivered,* 6, 8.
46. On Montesquieu, see Paul Carrese, *Democracy in Moderation: Montesquieu, Tocqueville, and Sustainable Liberalism* (New York: Cambridge University Press, 2016).
47. Jay, *Charge Delivered,* 9. On "conscience and private judgment," see Nicholas Miller, *The Religious Roots of the First Amendment* (New York: Oxford University Press, 2012).
48. Jay, *Charge Delivered,* 11.
49. Jay to John Adams, 1 Nov. 1786, in SPJJ, 4:435–38.
50. Jay to George Washington, 27 June 1786, in SPJJ, 4:354–56.
51. Jay to John Adams, 16 Oct. 1787, in SPJJ, 4:568–70. On Jay's compelling rhetorical strategies, see Robert Ferguson, "The Forgotten Publius," in *Reading the Early Republic* (Cambridge, Mass.: Harvard University Press, 2004), 151–71. Some treatment of Jay and the Constitution can be found in John Kaminski, "Shall we have a king? John Jay and the Politics of Union," *New York History* 81 (Jan. 2000): 31–58. Jay also features prominently in larger studies, such as Richard Morris, *Witnesses at the Creation: Hamilton, Madison, Jay, and the Constitution* (New York: Holt, Rinehart, and Winston, 1985); and Joseph Ellis, *The Quartet: Orchestrating the Second American Revolution, 1783–1789* (New York: Alfred A. Knopf, 2015).
52. Jay, "Federalist No. 2," in *The Federalist Papers,* ed. Clinton Rossiter and introduced

by Charles Kesler (New York: Signet Classics, 2003), 32–33.

53. Jay, *An Address to the People of the State of New-York, On the Subject of the Constitution* (New York: Samuel and John Loudon, 1788), 4, 5, 16, 18, 19.

54. Monaghan, *John Jay,* 286–93; Linda Grant De Pauw, *The Eleventh Pillar: New York State and the Federal Constitution* (Ithaca, N.Y.: Cornell University Press, 1966), 91–117; and Pauline Maier, *Ratification: The People Debate the Constitution* (New York: Simon and Schuster, 2010), 320–44.

55. One can think of unjust elements, such as the burning of noncombatant Iroquois settlements in New York. Cf. Alan Taylor, *The Divided Ground: Indians, Settlers, and the Northern Borderland of the American Revolution* (New York: Alfred A. Knopf, 2006), 77–108.

12 AN END TO EMPIRE?

British Strategy in the American Revolution and in Making Peace with the United States

William Anthony Hay

Sir John Harington captured an important dynamic in writing that "treason doth never prosper, what's the reason? Why if it prosper, None dare call it treason."[1] Much the same applies to rebellion. Successfully overthrowing legally constituted authority, either by replacing its ruler or making good a separate-polity independence, turned rebellion into a different kind of struggle. Rebels became rivals, even when on different terms than a foreign foe. Conceptions of just war—regarding both the legitimacy of a conflict (*jus ad bellum*) and the rules for waging it legitimately (*jus in bello*)—are applied differently from a revolt against lawful authority. Chapters in parts I and II of this book directly engage the challenges of suppressing a revolt versus waging war against rival states. This chapter explores instead how British policy, rooted in particular understandings of just war, changed over the course of the struggle. As Britain's experience during the American Revolution demonstrates, practical considerations shaped how soldiers and statesmen applied various principles. The determination to uphold the just claims of sovereignty against rebellion that George III and his ministers shared with much of the British public gave way to pragmatic efforts at salvaging what they could as the military situation deteriorated.

After losing the prolonged struggle to suppress a colonial revolt that had escalated into a global conflict that threatened the foundations of its power, Britain accepted American independence and made peace with the Treaty of Paris (1783). What might have seemed a humiliating concession reflected a subtle, though dramatic shift. Fears that losing mainland American colonies vital to the larger imperial system would damage Britain's position as a great power beyond repair reinforced the determination to suppress revolt. Mutual dependence within the British Atlantic world—especially the reliance upon American provisions and timber by rich plantation colonies in the Caribbean that generated vital earnings—pointed to a domino effect as other dependencies would follow the thirteen colonies out of the empire. Indeed, concern over weak imperial ties had prompted the centralizing reforms that sparked colonial resistance. The pressures of war, however, brought a gradual reassessment of British policy. French, and later Spanish, entry into the war from 1778 diverted London's attention from America. When defeat at Yorktown in 1781 made recovering the colonies impossible, Britain looked to divide its opponents while rebuilding ties with the new nation that might, paradoxically, secure it commercial advantage from conceding American independence.

Britain and its colonies' fundamentally incompatible views of sovereignty underlay successive conflicts over taxation and commercial regulation. The very nature of government required that *some* person or group have final authority. The English legal definition of sovereignty that evolved over the century after the English Civil War (1642–49), Charles II's restoration in 1660, and then the Glorious Revolution of 1688 differed sharply from colonial understandings. Sovereign power in Britain rested with a parliament comprised of the king, the House of Lords Spiritual and Temporal, and the House of Commons, a formulation otherwise described as the Crown-in-Parliament. Citing Sir Edward Coke, William Blackstone insisted that parliamentary jurisdiction had no external bounds or limits. Conquest and subsequent occupation had subjected territories to English law at various times, thus rendering any local assemblies subordinate to Parliament.[2] The first volume of Blackstone's legal commentaries, published in 1766 amid American reactions to the Stamp Act crisis (1765), reinforced views already widely held in Britain. Alan Ramsay, a writer and artist with court ties, insisted that "*sovereignty* admits of no degrees, it is always *supreme* and to level it, is in effect to destroy it." In Britain, Ramsay continued, that supreme power rested with Parliament. He described overseas possessions as provinces integral to the kingdom and under its sovereignty rather than as colonies, a term Ramsay argued implied some degree of independence.[3]

Dissenting voices in Britain rejected parliamentary sovereignty in a debate that lasted into the 1770s. The doctrine prevailed by then partly because its critics never agreed themselves on the location and nature of sovereignty. Jacobites looking to Sir Robert Filmer, radical Whigs invoking arguments from John Locke and James Tyrrell, or a later generation epitomized by Richard Price each argued from divergent premises of divine right and either limited or general popular sovereignty, thus precluding consensus. More importantly, they all operated on the political margins and lacked significant elite or popular support. The men who set policy, especially in Lord North's administration, along with their spokesmen and political followers accepted parliamentary sovereignty as a guiding principle.[4] British critics of the Stamp Act, Townshend duties, and reforms tightening metropolitan control over the colonies made their case on the prudence or justice of the measures rather than Parliament's power to adopt them. While Edmund Burke argued that without asserting a universal principle of jurisdiction, British authority would "vanish into an empty name," he also distinguished the claims of sovereignty from their practical use.

The Declaratory Act of 1766, which accompanied the Rockingham administration's repeal of the Stamp Act, affirmed parliamentary sovereignty. Lords Chatham and Shelburne distinguished internal taxation of the colonies from other legislation, but neither denied that parliamentary statutes applied throughout the empire. Chatham's view on giving the colonies privileges that Ireland long had enjoyed took subordination for granted. Urging conciliation in 1775 on grounds that fighting over taxation served no national interest, Henry Seymour Conway still declared Parliament's supremacy over the colonies "of the essence of our relationship to them."[5] Despite other differences on policy toward America, ministers, their opponents, and the British establishment took parliamentary sovereignty as a given.

Colonists across the British Atlantic world, however, interpreted their legal relationship with Parliament very differently. As Jack Greene rightly notes, the extraordinary agency dominant settler populations had exercised in creating the polities that governed them, and the growth of those polities over the seventeenth century, framed a conception of the imperial constitution that granted local assemblies extensive power over the own affairs. The expansion of representative government, from New England to Barbados, took root through practice as a vital part of colonial identity. Far from depending upon Parliament for their existence, colonists insisted that their assemblies enjoyed rights and privileges that could not be abridged. Strengthening metropolitan control during the 1760s violated colonial understanding of the imperial constitution.[6] Along with usage and custom in the colonies themselves, appeals to royal charters that predated the Georgian consensus on parliamentary sovereignty and the persistence of seventeenth-century arguments for royal prerogative as a bulwark against threats to liberties from parliamentary factions provided justification for American resistance.[7] Benjamin Franklin tapped an important concern when he complained in 1767 that "every man in England seems to consider himself as a piece of a sovereign over America; seems to jostle himself into the throne, and talks of OUR *subjects in the same colonies.*"[8]

Lord Hillsborough, responsible as colonial secretary for American policy, considered upholding Parliament's supremacy over the colonies as "essential to the existence of the empire." Giving up such a "great constitutional point" by conceding assemblies the "rights of national legislatures" over policy and taxation would render them effectively independent. Allowing the colonies to legislate for themselves would create *imperium in imperio,* which Hillsborough dismissed as "polytheism in politics." His arguments tapped wider British sentiments expressed in both pamphlets and parliamentary speeches.[9] Even where compromise or concession on particular issues might be possible, parliamentary supremacy remained a sticking point. Positions hardened. British concessions aimed only at dampening tensions and blunting challenges to sovereignty.

Ministers and officials treated colonial unrest largely as a law-and-order matter until the Boston Tea Party in 1773. Violent protest fit their experience with plebeian resistance at home. Even rioting had an accepted, if unwelcome, place in the Anglophone Atlantic world.[10] Defying lawful authority differed from its usurpation by rebels in this instance. The Stamp Act riots and other colonial protests resembled the 1769 Spitalfield Riots by striking silk weavers more than they resembled the Jacobite risings. Lord Barrington, the minister overseeing the army, likened American commotions to "such as we see almost every day in our own country." Troops could suppress riots there as they did at home. While law may be without efficacy for a time, he wrote, the arrival of legal force would enable magistrates to do their duty and thereby secure future obedience.[11] The army's job encompassed helping civilian authorities uphold order and enforce laws, though soldiers disliked a service that rendered them liable to prosecution and thus operated under rules different from fighting rebels or a foreign foe. Authority, including the decision to call for troops, rested with magistrates; commanders acting on their own initiative could be liable to prosecution. The same rules operated in the colonies, along with the shared distrust of standing armies as a threat to liberty.[12]

America had little experience with large detachments of regulars before the Seven Years' War (1756–63). Friction grew when commanders realized the colonial governors neither could nor would provide the support they expected. Civilians resented demands for transport, labor, and supplies to facilitate military operations. Reports of tensions shaded the outlook of ministers and officials who reviewed them in London.[13] Introducing a substantial peacetime garrison to be funded by colonial taxation marked an innovation unwelcome in American. Opposition grew with the Stamp Act and measures against smuggling. Relations between military commanders and civil officials brought continued friction over supplies and barracks. The Stamp Act crisis made explicit the army's policing role in more settled parts of the colonies, but magistrates and even governors hesitated to use force against riotous civilians.[14] As commander in chief of the army in North America, Lieutenant General Thomas Gage struggled to preserve order in an escalating cycle of confrontation in which each incident emboldened further defiance. Boston's civil government had "ceased in an instant" during the uproar over the Stamp Act, when Governor Francis Bernard found himself without "the least authority to oppose or quiet the mob," whose violent protest the wider public condoned, if not supported.[15]

The problem became more acute as magistrates, especially in Massachusetts, hesitated to enforce laws against community sentiment. British officers complained that the rules of military aid to civil authority sharply limited their ability to act. Soldiers became targets for harassment, which created further confrontations. Gage concluded by 1768 that colonists "mean to go on step by step till they throw off all subjugation."[16] As he urged Barrington, "quash this spirit at a blow, without too much regard to expense, and it will prove economy in the end." While agreeing that "riotous Englishmen in New England must be treated as their fellows in old England," Barrington saw that the least reversal to British troops in a clash with colonists "would be fatal there & all over the continent." Better that "Massachusetts remained in rebellion uncontrolled for years than that we made a fruitless attempt to control them."[17]

The Boston Tea Party and its aftermath made it impossible to evade action. Resistance backed by organized groups defying the Crown forced the question of who governed the colonies. Lord North's administration, backed by Parliament and much of British public opinion, determined that the issue could be resolved only by compelling Massachusetts to submit unequivocally. Asked for a legal opinion by Colonial Secretary Lord Dartmouth, the attorney and solicitor general described the crowd's destruction of tea as high treason in levying war against the king.[18] Rebellion in Massachusetts, North argued, involved the people of that province rejecting the government established by the king and Parliament and opposing it by force of arms. "The moment that they acknowledge that government and meet in assembly under it," North told the House of Commons, "the rebellion is at an end."[19] His words in 1774 distinguished breaking laws and evading taxes from organized resistance to lawful authority's just claims. Upholding those claims now mattered more than the policies that had fueled tensions between the colonies and Britain. Taxes or regulations might be dropped; sovereignty remained non-negotiable. Hans Stanley, who supported measures against rebellious colonists, "wanted nothing but the Americans to submit." Amnesty and conciliation might then follow, though some rebels ought to be made examples of as a warning against future defiance. Lord George Germain, soon to replace Lord Dartmouth as colonial secretary, observed that those who favored the 1766 Declaratory Act, asserting Parliament's legislative authority over the American colonies, ought logically to support subduing America.[20] One step followed from the other.

North responded to the challenge with legislation punishing Massachusetts for the destruction of tea in Boston Harbor and strengthening the power of governors against disorder. Crafted on the advice of Gage and his predecessor, Lieutenant General Sir Jeffrey Amherst, and drawing upon experience since 1766, the Coercive Acts sought to compel submission to Parliament's authority while securing restitution for the damage. Working through Parliament emphasized the need to submit while allowing ministers to do more than royal prerogative alone could accomplish.[21] Gage's appointment as governor aimed to facilitate the restoration of lawful authority by combing civil authority with command over the king's troops. He would have both the power and the means to prevent mob violence from interfering with officials or intimidating citizens inclined to cooperate. Dartmouth hoped that Gage's appointment would break the deadlock that persistent defiance had created in Massachusetts.[22] "Everybody seems in earnest," Gage wrote from London to a subordinate. The colonists "had at length tired out their strongest friends among the parliamentary opposition."[23]

When he arrived in Boston, Gage reported that, while the "violent party seemed to break and people fall off from them," no steps had been taken to comply with the Boston Port Act.[24] Events quickly shattered hopes that merchants open to reconciliation would prevail over their restive neighbors. Attempts to bring the Boston Town Meeting to pay compensation for the tea and abolish its Committee of Correspondence failed. Instead, the committee urged adoption of a "solemn league and covenant" to refuse all British imports until the port reopened and Parliament restored chartered rights. Borrowed from Scottish Presbyterians who resisted Charles I during the crisis leading to the English Civil War, the committee's phrase seemed chosen to provoke.[25] A meeting of the colonial assembly at Salem only brought further conflict. Complaining that he could not have got a worse council or assembly, Gage described them "as little more than echoes to the contrivers of all the mischief in the town of Boston."[26]

Those contrivers quickly took over town and county governments across Massachusetts. Justices in Pittsfield and Berkshire's sheriff told Gage that they lacked the power to execute the governor's June 29 proclamation against illegal combinations. Even before seeing the proclamation, delegates had assembled to pass their own covenant. Trying to check them brought threats of tar and feathers. An armed crowd went further by seizing David Ingersoll in Great Barrington and bringing him before a committee in Connecticut that impeached him for resisting their opposition to Parliament. Weeks later they again captured him in flight and forced him to sign the Berkshire Covenant before he sought protection in Boston.[27] Gage's correspondence charts the collapse of British authority in Massachusetts during 1774. Opposition groups emerged as an alternative power structure that displaced colonial government under the Crown. By September, Gage saw no prospect of enforcing the Coercive Acts without "first making a conquest of the New England provinces."[28] British forces, however, still awaited the opening blow to avoid "some larger rebellion by giving it the name of defense."[29] Facing "not a Boston rabble but the freeholders and farmers of the country," he warned Dartmouth that "a check anywhere would be fatal and the first stroke will decide a great deal."[30] Open rebellion had begun.

The stroke Gage anticipated fell in April 1775, when fighting at Lexington and Concord threw his army on the defensive in siege lines at Boston. News reached Britain on May 28 as the government settled measures to implement the existing policy of military coercion. Well before this, though, political insiders like Charles Jenkinson and Hutchinson had observed that British opinion backed a hard line against the colonists.[31] George III privately had declared in September that "the die is now cast, the colonies must either submit or triumph." With further reports confirming the rebellion, he told North in November that "blows must decide whether they are to be subject to this country or independent; I do not wish to come to severer measures but we must not retreat."[32] He rejected as against Britain's constitution any compromise by which Americans might recognize his sovereignty with internal self-government beyond parliamentary control. America, he told Dartmouth, must be a colony of England or treated as an enemy. Placing distant possessions upon an equality with the superior state would be more ruinous than losing them. Ministers and most political figures agreed.[33] Rather than questioning parliamentary supremacy, critics in Britain focused on the way ministers exercised that power and blamed them for starting what they called a civil war. Most politicians who opposed the war that unfolded also deplored the constitutional experiment on which the Americans embarked, urging on them instead the British constitution's superiority.[34]

News of Bunker Hill made clear in London the depth of colonial resistance. A royal proclamation of August 23, modeled on the response to the Jacobite Rising of 1715, formally declared the American colonies in "open and avowed rebellion" for resisting lawful authority "and traitorously preparing, ordering, and levying war against the king." It charged not only civil and military officials but also all subjects to assist in suppressing rebellion and bringing traitors to justice.[35] "Unnatural rebellion" became a recurring phrase in parliamentary debates.[36] Telling the Commons that "no man in his senses could doubt but that America was in rebellion," Sir George Hay distinguished war against rebels from alien enemies who "owed no allegiance, no duty, no gratitude." Rebellion, by contrast, violated "every moral as well as civil tie," adding "moral guilt, and the blackest of all earthly crimes" to rapine and violence.[37] His distinction framed rebellion as an unjust assault on lawful authority. Suppressing it by force, therefore, fell within the bounds of just war. Blackstone had called the right of resistance in any but the most extreme circumstance as "a doctrine productive of anarchy, and (in consequence) equally fatal to civil liberty as tyranny itself." Society can neither be maintained nor protect civil liberty "without obedience to some sovereign power: and obedience is an empty name, if every individual has a right to decide how far he himself shall obey."[38]

Blackstone expressed what had become a normative view among British elites who rejected or sharply qualified John Locke's case for a right of resistance.[39] Locke carried more weight in America by the 1770s than in Britain, whose political culture had been shaped by Jacobite risings in 1715 and 1745. Defending the Hanoverian political order had turned British Whigs seeking a foundation for their liberties to a theory of the ancient constitution that elevated Parliament's authority in ways that made colonial arguments untenable. Locke's justification of private property and the unequal division of wealth supported the political status quo that "Court Whigs" at midcentury sought to protect, but his other arguments did not. Even those in Britain who acknowledged a theoretical right of resistance denied that conditions justifyied exercising it. Instead of seeing resistance as means of securing rights, elites and the public emphasized the danger rebellion posed by threatening to dissolve society.[40] Arguments about resistance—whether Lockean or rooted in a separate Protestant tradition—carried more weight in the American colonies, where rebellion had not posed a threat as it so recently had in Britain.[41]

Hugo Grotius, over a century before in *On the Law of War and Peace* (1625), had limited resistance to the most extreme circumstances, placing a heavy onus upon rebels to justify their actions. A promiscuous right of resistance, he warned, would bring anarchy, "a Mob where all are speakers, and no hearers." Only a king who alienated his realm, abdicated its government, designed the destruction of its people, or usurped the share of sovereignty held by a senate or people in a mixed government provided an exception. The fact that each of those cases involved rulers violating a constitution set a high barrier.[42] Emer de Vattel, writing more recently in *The Law of Nations* (1758), concurred that only a tyrant making war on the nation could be forcibly resisted in what became self-defense. He otherwise deemed violent disobedience to a sovereign—whether localized as sedition or grown to the larger scale of insurrection—a state crime, even when arising from just cause. Only the denial of justice to a people whose patience has been exhausted by intolerable evils of great and manifest injustice could excuse such defiance.[43] The jurist Sir George Hay, who defended North's measures against America in 1775, acknowledged a right to resist even lawful power exercised in arbitrary fashion against the constitution but saw no such action to excuse the colonists' armed resistance.[44] If war, as Vattel defined it, involved prosecuting right by force, then suppressing rebellion against constitutional authority as George III proclaimed was a just conflict.[45]

Besides defining the criteria that determined a just war, rules also governed the just conduct of war. The codification of practice informed by reason checked the ferocity of warfare, limited fighting to combatants, and secured protection for civilians and prisoners. Early modern jurists developed laws of war largely from custom, itself rooted in natural law and Christian teaching, but their work shaped the practices and conventions on which they drew. Within Europe at least, deliberately brutal measures against civilians, like the French devastation of the German Palatinate in 1688–89, declined.[46] Exceptions largely involved poor discipline among regular troops or actions by detachments lacking close supervision rather than directives by commanders or rulers.[47] Eighteenth-century international law, however, treated war against rebels differently from conflicts with a foreign enemy. Rebels had placed themselves outside the protection of law by their defiance of it. Any restraint or moderation in efforts to suppress them came as a concession by authorities, not by claim of right. Vattel's argument for rulers to show clemency rested on a duty to seek their subjects' good and prudential concerns about restoring peace, which differed from rights or privileges claimed by rebels. Contrasting the Duke of Alva's brutal efforts to suppress the Dutch Revolt against Philip II with Henry IV's treatment of French Huguenots underlined the emphasis.[48]

Jacobite rebellions offered a recent precedent that highlighted the contrast between war against foreign enemies and suppressing revolt. Gage and Lord Germain, who as colonial secretary directed British strategy during the American Revolution, both had fought at Culloden in 1746; Brigadier General Hugh Mercer, who served under General George Washington, had been a surgeon in the Jacobite army. Considering them an existential threat to the Hanoverian regime, the Duke of Cumberland had "denied the armed Jacobites and their supporters any consideration under the rules of war." His measures against the 1745 rising, which included ravaging the countryside and shooting prisoners, differed from George I's handling of an earlier revolt in 1715. Harshness verging on brutality sprang from Cumberland's need to end resistance so his forces could return to fight in Flanders. Concern for their own honor, however, compelled many British officers to keep promises as they would to a lawful belligerent. Their commitment to the laws of war shaded pragmatic calculations involving reprisal and prisoner exchange and served to moderate their behavior.[49] Such a utilitarian approach had been common in the 1715 rising, during which George I and his government had preferred conciliation to punishment.[50] While the laws of war allowed harsh measures in principle, pragmatism often shaped their application.

The decision to subdue the colonies involved more than a just claim to sovereignty. Even critics of the policies that had led to war by 1775 viewed the empire as vital to Britain's prosperity and great-power status; they later blamed ministers for an eclipse of national greatness as the war turned against Britain. Besides the market America provided for British goods and the export value of its produce, colonies along the Atlantic Seaboard provided food and other goods to immensely wealthy plantation colonies in the Caribbean. George III feared that American independence would force the West Indies to cast off their obedience from necessity alone, depriving Britain of funds to maintain its navy and service its public debt. Ireland would see America as an example—as indeed it did—and become the next domino to fall. The king later framed the conflict as a question of whether Britain was "to rank among the great powers of Europe, or to be reduced to one of the least considerable."[51] Those stakes justified an unprecedented projection of naval and military power across the Atlantic. George III and his ministers believed that the war for America was not only right but also necessary.

Few questioned such reasoning when the war began. Josiah Tucker, the dean of Gloucester Cathedral and noted political economist who wrote pamphlets opposing American resistance to British policy, stands out as a notable exception. While defending the justice of the Stamp Act and Parliament's right to levy taxes on and legislate for colonies, Tucker saw no way to make colonists any more obedient than they chose to be. The trouble and expense of conquering them to compel submission outweighed any benefit. Instead, Tucker urged that Britain separate unilaterally. Since America could trade with no other European state to greater advantage than Britain, independence would not change the fundamental economic relationship. Nor could rivals finance trade as readily as Britain or provide America so good a market for its own goods. Separation would give Britain the advantages of American trade without the burden of defending or governing it. Far from sympathizing with colonists, Tucker believed them feckless and self-interested. Independence, he expected, would lead them to quarrel among themselves, with some seeking renewed ties with Britain.[52] However significant in retrospect, especially for its objections to mercantilism, Tucker's case found little support. From opposing positions on America, Samuel Johnson and Burke both dismissed Tucker's proposal as wild and childish.[53]

Rather than surrender its claims, the government committed additional forces to Gage's successor, Lieutenant General Sir William Howe, for an offensive. Seizing New York would provide a more effective base for operations than Boston, from which Howe had withdrawn in March 1776. Reinforced and with further contingents arriving, Howe's army and the accompanying fleet off New York in July formed the largest expedition Britain had sent across the Atlantic. Landings on Long Island and Manhattan the next month quickly drove the colonial army back into the interior of New York and New Jersey.[54] The practical challenge had grown beyond suppressing a revolt to the more formidable problem of dismantling an enemy regime in order to end what had become a civil war. Howe thought that until they had tried their chances in battle, the Americans would not retract their demands. Defeating Washington would enable British regulars to suppress colonial militia and reestablish royal authority. Ministers and generals alike believed that without Continentals or militia to coerce them, most colonists would return to their proper allegiance. The army's task, then, was to assist the good Americans in subduing the bad.[55]

Although the term "rebels" persisted in British usage, the conflict's escalation into a civil war, which Vattel distinguished from mere rebellion, brought fighting under the laws of war.[56] Pragmatic considerations also restrained British conduct. Howe and his brother, Vice Admiral Lord Richard Howe, who commanded naval forces on the American station, held a commission to restore public tranquility. Despite the failure of their conferences with delegates sent by Congress, the brothers still aimed for reconciliation.[57] General Howe's expectation that many Americans would abandon the rebellion once defeats showed it could not succeed guided his operations. But his brother recognized that punitive naval attacks on the coast and ravaging the countryside would drive the indifferent to take up arms rather than starve. The restraint they showed, especially toward civilians, reflected their desire to end the conflict amicably as the best path to lasting peace. Successive commanders throughout the struggle rejected what Lieutenant General Sir Henry Clinton disparaged as a "war of devastation." Clinton in early 1776 had observed the need "to gain the hearts & subdue the minds of America." The Howe brothers thus combined measured force with offers of conciliation to weaken support for Congress and bring a political solution.[58]

Others within the British army in North America took a different view from their commander's preference for conciliation. Major General James Grant complained in 1775 that "leniency has had every bad effect which can be imagined" and believed it "high time to try how severity will operate." This alternative "hard school" urged a punitive approach that aimed to end hostilities sooner by making rebels appreciate the consequence of resistance. It viewed leniency as cruelty, likely to prolong a conflict that fell hardest on Loyalists. Howe's subordinate Captain Lord Rawdon urged giving soldiers liberty to ravage at will so Americans "may feel what a calamity war is." Marauding troubled many officers more for its effect on discipline than the damage to civilians. Setbacks convinced Grant by 1778 that "the torch must convince the deluded Yankees for the sword without flames will have no effect."[59] Clinton still rejected a punitive strategy despite allowing several expeditions that burned coastal towns. Tension between the conciliatory and hard schools within the army, coupled with the brutality of frontier war and the bitterness of fighting between Patriots and Loyalists, brought occasional departures from the rules of war.[60]

Concern for their own men and civilian officials of the Crown moderated the use of force, particularly once troops were captured in significant numbers. The contrast with Cumberland's response to the 1745 Jacobite rising merits attention. Rather than punishing colonists as traitors, British commanders treated them as legal belligerents to prevent reprisals. Washington had made clear to Gage that he would treat British regulars, including officers, as they treated his own men. Gage had replied that he recognized no commission not granted by the king, but he insisted that rebel prisoners, "whose lives by the law of the land are destined for the cord," were treated well. Both commanders invoked standards for the humane conduct of war, and their armies followed accepted rules of parole and prisoner exchange. Howe and later Clinton followed the same course. Washington's efforts to build the Continental Army into a professional force along European lines—and his rejection of a guerilla strategy utilizing militia—was deliberately intended to secure status as a legitimate military organization that his opponents must then recognize.[61] When compared with the savagery of the frontier war or the harsher measures often employed to crush domestic rebellion, British regulars largely fought within rules set by a developing eighteenth-century view of *jus in bello*. Unlike the pacification of the Scottish Highlands after 1745, Britain's war in America sought to restore union and harmony rather than remodel a defeated society.[62]

Victories that recovered New Jersey and much of the region around New York seemed to put British aims within reach. The Howe brothers offered pardons to Americans willing to pledge allegiance to the Crown as a step toward restoring civil government. This strategy almost succeeded; support for the American cause fell. Samuel Adams lamented in early December 1776 that perhaps a majority in the mid-Atlantic had "determined to give it up." Admitting that "our affairs are in a pretty bad way," Washington told his brother, "the game is pretty near up—owning in a great measure to the insidious arts of the enemy."[63] Crossing the Delaware to fight the British at Trenton and Princeton, however, broke the momentum the British had built along with the illusion of military invincibility. The fate of New Jersey Loyalists abandoned by the army's retreat fatally upset the Howes' policy of amnesty and reconciliation.[64] Months of skirmishing for supplies, known as the Forage War, then further undid the British victories of 1776. Howe's force stood on the defensive when the new campaign season opened. Those setbacks prompted growing dismay even before Lieutenant General John Burgoyne's surrender at Saratoga in October 1777.

British ministers and officials began reassessing their position as they found regaining control over the thirteen colonies increasingly elusive. Americans had effectively abolished the Navigation Laws by opening their ports to European commerce, which began an experiment testing the policy's value to British trade.[65] Charles Jenkinson, a commercial expert advising North, who had long taken a hard line on colonial policy, ruled out negotiating terms with America in 1777. Indeed, he proposed tightening the Navigation Laws to restrict colonial shipping to coastal trade and the direct commerce of individual colonies with Britain. Besides keeping the colonies from competing with British shipping, Jenkinson sought to limit their ability to deploy a naval force, their vessels having taken a toll on commerce since the conflict began.[66] A 1778 memorandum revisiting the case advised conquering "the Southern Provinces only" and setting a boundary along the Hudson River; New England cost more than it contributed. Recently increased exports to Canada that clearly served New England's market showed that Britain would still enjoy that region's trade outside the empire, while other mainland colonies would step in to provision the West Indies and Newfoundland. Jenkinson also believed that turning from conquest to containment would save honor while contracting the scale of operations. Regulating the internal production of colonies, he added, served no purpose if external trade was controlled and directed to British advantage.[67]

Admiral Howe's private secretary, Ambrose Serle, had reached similar conclusions in 1776 on the colonies' value, particularly the northern ones. Even with the prospect of success undimmed, he thought that, as with Spain, "our rage of colonization in countries which yield exactly the same produce with our own" had done more harm than good. Far from being useful, colonies had sapped British commerce, manufacturers, and fisheries while incurring heavy debt to secure them. After Saratoga, Serle directly invoked Tucker's plan of renouncing the colonies.[68] His response, like Jenkinson's later memorandum, showed how American events had opened space to reassess objectives. Consulted by his friend Alexander Wedderburn, solicitor general in North's administration, Adam Smith argued that losing America would not harm British security as its naval strength rested on trade with Europe. The cost of imperial defense made the American colonies a source of weakness rather than strength. Political separation would not impede commercial exchange.[69] The perceived price of losing America thus had fallen.

Evolving views of America's importance to the British imperial system guided thoughts on how far to press claims of right involving parliamentary sovereignty. The opposition member of Parliament Sir George Saville remarked in January 1777, "The cause itself wears away by degrees from a question of right and wrong between subjects, to a war between us and a foreign nation." Edward Gibbon, who supported the war, observed by August that the Americans had "almost lost the appellation of rebels." Burgoyne's surrender at Saratoga had convinced at least a portion of opinion that America had made good its claim to independence even though the war retained significant public support. The French alliance with the Americans hardened views that the colonies had become a foreign rival. Even the Massachusetts Loyalist Thomas Hutchinson began speaking of the United States rather than of merely rebellious colonies. While not accepting their independence, George III recognized the need for peace so Britain could focus on France and its threat elsewhere. Instead, he spoke of holding a position in America to keep a certain awe over the abandoned colonies.[70] Since a renewed offensive demanded more troops than Britain could send, particularly as fighting with France spread to the Caribbean, king and cabinet went on the defensive in America, using naval operations and a commercial blockade to compel terms.[71] An undercurrent that accepted separation grew as repeated setbacks made the original aim of asserting British sovereignty in North America problematic or unlikely.

North, who had hoped for a negotiated reconciliation from the start, considered peace imperative following Burgoyne's surrender and the looming prospect of French intervention. He proposed a conciliatory plan with sweeping concessions that waived Parliament's claims to tax or legislate for America; that body retained merely a power to regulate the trade of the empire. No standing army would be stationed in the colonies during peacetime nor charters modified without consent. Congress might be retained as a permanent institution so long as it did not infringe parliamentary sovereignty. A peace commission carried the terms across the Atlantic in 1778 with powers to negotiate.[72] Conceding positions that had justified war, the commission accepted American demands that British opinion had considered unthinkable just a few years before. Congress nevertheless refused to compromise on independence. General Clinton, who replaced Howe as commander in chief in North America, scoffed at the idea that Americans would accept terms as his army prepared for a retreat to

New York. Instead, the United States embraced an alliance with France that underlined the split between Britain and America while expanding the war into a global conflict. British opinion increasingly associated America with other European powers that joined the war, with Americans now a foreign enemy rather than rebellious subjects.[73] British strategy now sought victory—or at least retaining ground—in America on the cheap while securing vital Caribbean interests.

Noting vulnerabilities in the South after a detached force took Savannah, Georgia, and then held it against a Franco-American counterattack, Clinton opened a new campaign in 1780 to conquer the valuable southern colonies, where ministers thought Loyalists would provide support. Those were also the region in America, as Jenkinson had argued, most valuable to the empire. Defeat at Charleston, South Carolina, dealt a blow as disheartening to Americans as Saratoga had been for the British and seemed to shift the balance to Britain's favor. Washington's forces around New York faced increasing internal strains due to shortages of money and supplies. British officers speculated that resistance soon would collapse. The fact that the war never involved a linear series of defeats—the struggle's outcome remained uncertain as fortunes shifted on both sides—convinced the North government to persevere even as it lowered expectations. George III still resisted conceding independence to the colonies in March 1780 on the grounds that it would place Britain "into a very low class among the European states," with other powers treating it accordingly. But Cornwallis's difficulties with guerilla resistance in the Carolinas as well as his inability to destroy Continental forces under Major General Nathanael Greene at the Battle of Guilford Court House (March 1781) demonstrated the ongoing difficulties and dangers of subduing America. Although the earl's subsequent advance into Virginia created a brief panic there, Cornwallis soon found himself and his army trapped inside the Old Dominion, especially after the French naval victory off the Virginia Capes on September 5, 1781. The following month a combined Continental and French army under Washington forced Cornwallis to surrender, thus ending all hopes of British hegemony over their former colonies.[74]

As Burke had told a correspondent, "in war, *events* do everything." North received news of Cornwallis's surrender almost as a physical blow, declaring: "Oh God! It is all over." He and colleagues revised the king's speech for the opening of Parliament to acknowledge the defeat. During a House of Lords debate on the response to the address, Shelburne insisted that the struggle could not be continued. Besides the desperate state of public finances, America could not be conquered, and Britain had not an ally in Europe.[75] North, who had only remained in office under pressure from George III, realized how the political landscape had quickly changed. Despite widespread support at the start, as Gibbon observed, "the length of a fruitless contest, the loss of armies, the accumulation of debt and taxes, and the hostile confederacy of France, Spain and Holland indisposed the public to the American war, and the persons by whom it was conducted. . . . [T]he minsters who refused to bend were broken by the tempest."[76]

With majorities in the House of Commons rapidly dwindling against successive opposition motions, North resigned abruptly on March 27, 1782. George III then faced a choice between Lords Rockingham or Shelburne to form the next government, plus growing pressure to end the war on the best terms available. Realizing his own unpopularity and lack of a parliamentary following, Shelburne persuaded the king to accept Rockingham, with himself as colonial secretary and Charles James Fox as foreign secretary.[77] The new ministers, who had opposed the war, did not immediately accept a total break. Fox, who by June proclaimed unconditional independence "a wise, just, and equitable measure," had hoped the month before to retain some connection. He focused on separating America from the French and placing negotiations in his hands rather than Shelburne's. Despite his eagerness for reconciliation, Shelburne opposed granting America independence; only later did he come to accept that not even a nominal sovereignty could be retained. The good relations that would separate America from France and provide access to its markets required, in his own words, yielding to "the fatal necessity" of independence.[78]

Although the concept of just peace drew upon longstanding themes in the just war tradition, *jus post bellum* actually developed in the generations after the American Revolution. Yet early-modern discussions regarding the conclusions of military conflicts in a just fashion did stress limitations that victors were obligated to respect. Francisco Vitoria, the sixteenth-century Dominican philosopher, for instance, insisted that war should not be waged to ruin an enemy but only to obtain those just rights for which the conflict was fought. Defining peace and security, along with satisfaction for a particular injury, as the ends of war limited how a victor could impose his will upon the vanquished.[79] It also suggested principles on which to settle a compromise short of either party's clear victory.

Vattel defined peace as "that desirable state in which everyone quietly enjoyed his rights, or, if controverted, amicably discussed them by force of argument." Rather than something artificial that society imposed by force, he thought peace natural to man as the state to which both nature and human reason point. Thus, by reconciling enemies and ceasing hostilities between them, peace restored nations to their natural state.[80] Vattel spoke to the situation Britain faced when he described peace treaties as "no more than a compromise" falling short of strict justice by agreeing to equivalents that "each party shall receive in extinction of all his pretentions." Rational compromise provided an alternative to prolonging war when each party had become weary of the struggle. Vattel also described peace treaties as ending the war and abolishing the subject of it. Other quarrels might give rise to a new war, but just peace meant upholding an agreed settlement to the old dispute.[81] This understanding embedded in his reasoning joined with practical considerations to shape how Britain responded to the established fact of American independence.

When Rockingham died on July 1, 1782, George III made Shelburne prime minister in his place. The change of administration gave Shelburne the scope to pursue reconciliation through generous peace terms. He won the king's consent, if not enthusiasm, by arguing that trade could replace dominion over America. A paper in George III's own hand echoed Shelburne's view that more advantage could be reaped from trade with Americans as friends than by holding them as colonies. It significantly cited recent experience "to suppose we actually gained more by them when in actual rebellion, and the common open connection cut off, then when they were in obedience to the crown."[82] The preliminary treaty agreed to in November drew opposition for concessions to the United States, particularly on compensation for Loyalists and boundaries with Canada. Almost universal agreement to accept American independence did not mean granting it without first securing British honor and practical interests. Critics, including Jenkinson and Lord Sheffield, cast the new nation as a commercial rival to be contained and rejected Shelburne's case for the benefits of free trade. But even those asserting such a rivalry accepted that commercial advantage did not require political control. Since concluding treaties fell under royal prerogative, the opposition could not block peace with America. Shelburne had essentially won, but he was forced to resign.[83]

Negotiating with the United States as an independent rival meant abandoning Britain's central justification for fighting the war. The point already had been given up by degrees, even before Shelburne conceded independence. Silas Deane, living as an exile in London, observed how quickly the loss of America was forgotten outside party debates and pamphlets, which turned primarily on whether it was a loss at all. Ceasing to be a point for declamation, the war for America passed into history.[84] Grotius's argument for the advantage of embracing peace even at some loss to both conqueror and conquered seemed to have been proven over the next decade or two.[85] Necessity more than principle guided British acceptance of peace with its former colonies; nevertheless, the peace Shelburne concluded outlasted his career when (however begrudgingly at times) Britain acknowledged the United States as an independent country. Disputes involving trade, debts, and relations with Native Americans would bring conflicts culminating in the War of 1812, but the question of sovereignty at the heart of the American Revolution had been resolved. The United States had successfully joined the international community of independent sovereigns.

NOTES

1. Sir John Harington, *Epigrams,* bk. 4, epistle 5, in *The Letters and Epigrams of Sir John Harrington together with the Prayse of Private Life,* ed. Norman Egbert McClure (Philadelphia: University of Pennsylvania Press, 1930), 235.
2. J. C. D. Clark, *The Language of Liberty: Political Discourse in the Anglo-American World* (Cambridge: Cambridge University Press, 1994), 85–88, 107; William Blackstone, *Commentaries on the Laws of England,* 4 vols. (Oxford, 1765–69), 1:94–105, 156–57.
3. Allan Ramsay, *Thoughts on the Origin and Nature of Government. Occasioned by the Late Disturbances between Great Britain and Her American Colonies. Written in the Year 1766* (London: 1769), 20–21; Ramsay, *The Constitutional Rights of the Legislature of Great Britain, to Tax the British Colonies in America Impartially Stated* (London, 1768), 2–3. Massachusetts Loyalist Thomas Hutchinson praised the first pamphlet as "the best thing I have ever seen on the subject." Bernard Bailyn, *The Ordeal of Thomas Hutchinson* (Cambridge, Mass.: Harvard University Press, 1974), 76–78.
4. H. T. Dickinson, "The Eighteenth Century Debate on the Sovereignty of Parliament," *Transactions of the Royal Historical Society,* 5th ser., 26 (1976): 190, 201–4.
5. Richard Bourke, *Empire and Revolution: The Political Life of Edmund Burke* (Princeton, N.J.: Princeton University Press, 2015), 292–93, 302–3; Charles R. Ritcheson, *British Politics and the American Revolution* (Norman: University of Oklahoma Press, 1954), 138; William Cobbett, *The Parliamentary History of England, from the Earlier Period to 1803* 8 (Nov. 20, 1775): 997.
6. Jack P. Greene, *The Constitutional Origins of the American Revolution* (Cambridge: Cambridge University Press, 2010).
7. Eric Nelson argues that appeals to royal prerogative were more than just a rhetorical strategy and reflected concerns that factional interests might use control over Parliament to curb their liberty. See *The Royalist Revolution: Monarchy and the American Founding* (Cambridge, Mass.: Harvard University Press, 2014).
8. Benjamin Franklin to Lord Kames, Feb. 15, 1767, in *The Papers of Benjamin Franklin,* ed. Leonard W. Labaree et al., vol. 14 (New Haven, Conn.: Yale University Press, 1959–2014), 65.
9. Greene, *Constitutional Origins of the American Revolution,* 109–11.
10. E. P. Thompson, "The Moral Economy of the English Crowd in the 18th Century," *Past & Present* 50 (1970): 76–136.

11. Viscount Barrington to Sir William Draper, Sept. 1, 1768, cited in *The Persistence of Empire: British Political Culture in the Age of the American Revolution,* by Eliga H. Gould (Chapel Hill: University of North Carolina Press, 2002), 121.
12. On how policing duties affected military training and deployments, see J. A. Houlding, *Fit for Service: The Training of the British Army, 1715–1795* (Oxford: Clarendon, 1981). For operational and legal considerations, see Tony Hayter, *The Army and the Crowd in Mid-Georgian England* (London: Macmillan, 1978); and Richard Vogeler, *Reading the Riot Act: The Magistracy, the Policy and the Army in Civil Disorder* (Milton Keynes, U.K.: Open University Press, 1991).
13. David Preston, *Braddock's Defeat: The Battle of the Monongahela and the Road to Revolution* (Oxford: Oxford University Press, 2015), 75–76, 79, 85–87.
14. John Shy, *Toward Lexington: The Role of the British Army in the Coming of the American Revolution* (Princeton, N.J.: Princeton University Press, 1965), 176–81, 192.
15. Bernard to Gage, Aug. 27 1765, in *The Barrington-Bernard Correspondence and Illustrative Matter, 1760–1770,* ed. Edward Channing and Archibald Cary Coolidge (Cambridge, Mass.: Harvard University Press, 1912), 227.
16. Gage to Barrington, Mar. 10, 1768, Gage MSS, William L. Clements Library, University of Michigan, Ann Arbor.
17. Gage to Barrington, June 28, 1768, ibid.; Barrington to Gage, Aug. 1, 1768, ibid.
18. Dartmouth to the Attorney and Solicitor General, Feb. 5, 1774, in *Documents of the American Revolution, 1770–1783,* ed. K. G. Davies, vol. 8 (Shannon: Irish University Press, 1972–81) [hereafter cited as *DAR*], 37–42; Attorney and Solicitor General to Dartmouth, Feb. 11, 1774, ibid., 46–48.
19. *Parl. Hist.* 18 (Feb. 20, 1774): 321.
20. Ibid. (Feb. 2, 1774): 248; ibid. (Jan. 19, 1774): 192.
21. P. D. G. Thomas, *Tea Party to Independence: The Third Phase of the American Revolution* (Oxford: Clarendon, 1991), 62–66.
22. Dartmouth to Hutchinson, Apr. 9, 1774, in *DAR,* 90.
23. Gage to Frederick Haldimand, Apr. 4, 1774, Additional Manuscripts [hereafter cited as Add MSS] 21665, British Library, London.
24. Gage to Dartmouth, May 31, 1774, in *DAR,* 117–18.
25. For the continuity with the Wars of the Three Kingdoms as seen by both sides of the Revolution (and the reference by loyal Britons to the trouble caused by Presbyterians), see chapter 2 above.
26. Thomas, *Tea Party to Independence,* 120–22; John. R. Alden, *General Gage in America: Bring Principally a History of His Role in the American Revolution* (Baton Rouge: Louisiana State University Press, 1948), 208–9; Gage to Dartmouth, June 26, 1774, in *DAR,* 136–37.
27. Justices of Pittsfield and Sheriff of Berkshire to Gage, July 15, 1774, Gage MSS; Statement by David Ingersoll, [Aug. 1774], ibid.
28. Gage to Dartmouth, Sept. 20, 1774, in *DAR,* 197–98; Gage to Barrington, Sept. 25, 1774, Gage MSS; Gage to Dartmouth, Sept. 25, 1774, in *DAR,* 201.
29. James Robertson to Frederick Haldimand, Sept. 15, 1774, Add MSS 21665.
30. Gage to Dartmouth, Sept. 2, 1774, in *DAR,* 179–82.

31. Thomas, *Tea Party to Independence,* 229–30.
32. George III to North, Sept. 10, 1774, in *The Correspondence of George III from 1760 to December 1783,* comp. and ed. Sir John Fortescue, 6 vols. (London: Macmillan, 1927–8), 3:256; George III to North, Nov. 18, 1774, ibid., 153.
33. Thomas, *Tea Party to Independence,* 237–38.
34. P. J. Marshall, *Remaking the British Atlantic: The United States and the British Empire after American Independence* (Oxford: Oxford University Press, 2012), 63–64.
35. Ritcheson, *British Politics and the American Revolution,* 195.
36. Stephen Conway, "From Fellow-Nationals to Foreigners: British Perceptions of the Americans, circa 1739–1783," *William & Mary Quarterly,* 3rd ser., 59, no. 1 (Jan. 2000): 86.
37. *Parl. Hist.* 8 (Dec. 7, 1775): 1040.
38. Blackstone, *Commentaries,* 1:244.
39. For further discussion of Locke's argument, see chapter 2 above.
40. Clark, *Language of Liberty,* 257–58; H. T. Dickinson, *Liberty and Property: Political Ideology in Eighteenth-Century Britain* (New York: Holmes and Meyer, 1977), 123, 126, 131–32.
41. Justifications for resistance by Protestant theologians (see chapter 2 above) evoked in Britain the struggle between Charles I and Parliament in the 1640s, which ended in regicide. They failed to resonate with British sympathizers, though, while making colonial resistance all the more unjustified to its opponents, who framed the revolt as a "Presbyterian war." Clark, *Language of Liberty,* 357–58.
42. Hugo Grotius, *The Rights of War and Peace,* 3 vols., ed. with an introduction by Richard Tuck (Indianapolis: Liberty Fund, 2005), 1:338–39, 375–77.
43. Emer de Vattel, *The Law of Nations, or Principles of the Law of Nations Applied to the Conduct and Affairs of Nations and Sovereigns with Three Early Essays on the Origin and Nature of Natural Law and on Luxury,* ed. Bèla Kaposi and Richard Whitmore (Indianapolis: Liberty Fund, 2008), 104–6, 642.
44. *Parl. Hist.* 18 (Nov. 20, 1775): 995–96.
45. Vattel, *Law of Nations,* 306.
46. Wayne E. Lee, *Barbarians & Brothers: Anglo-American Warfare, 1500–1865* (Oxford: Oxford University Press, 2011), 187–89; John A. Lynn, "A Brutal Necessity? The Devastation of the Palatinate, 1688–1689," in *Civilians in the Path of War,* ed. Mark Grimsley and Clifford J. Rogers (Lincoln: University of Nebraska Press, 2002), 79–102.
47. Lee, *Barbarians & Brothers,* 193–201. The discussion of existential warfare in chapter 7 above also notes a measure of restraint exerted and influenced by formal armies and senior commanders that diminished or disappeared among nonregular forces and leaders as their distance from them grew.
48. Vattel, *Law of Nations,* 642–44.
49. Christopher Duffy, *The '45 Bonnie Prince Charlie and the Untold Story of the Jacobite Rising* (London: Cassell, 2003), 129–30, 528, 542.
50. Margaret Sankey, *Jacobite Prisoners of the 1715 Rebellion: Preventing and Punishing Insurrection in Early Hanoverian Britain* (Aldershot, U.K.: Ashgate, 2005), x, xiii.

51. Andrew Jackson O'Shaughnessy, *The Men Who Lost America: British Leadership, the American Revolution and the Fate of Empire* (New Haven, Conn.: Yale University Press, 2013), 28–29.
52. Josiah Tucker, *Four Tracts on Political and Commercial Subjects* (Gloucester, U.K.: Raikes, 1774).
53. Peter J. Stanlis, "British Views of the American Revolution: A Conflict over Rights of Sovereignty," *Early American Literature* 9 (1976): 192.
54. O'Shaughnessy, *Men Who Lost America*, 92.
55. Matthew H. Spring, *With Zeal and with Bayonets Only: The British Army on Campaign in North America, 1775–1783* (Norman: University of Oklahoma Press, 2008), 4–6, 14, 21–22.
56. Vattel, *Law of Nations*, 644–45.
57. Thomas, *Tea Party to Independence*, 317–18; Ritcheson, *British Politics and the American Revolution*, 205–8.
58. Conway, "From Fellow-Nationals to Foreigners," 90; memorandum of conversation, Feb. 7, 1776, Clinton MSS, William L Clements Library, University of Michigan, Ann Arbor; O'Shaughnessy, *Men Who Lost America*, 97–98.
59. Paul David Nelson, *General James Grant: Scottish Soldier and Royal Governor of East Florida* (Gainesville: University Press of Florida, 1993), 91–92, 131; Stephen Conway, "To Subdue America: British Army Officers and the Conduct of the Revolutionary War," *William & Mary Quarterly*, 3rd ser., 43 (1986): 394.
60. For a discussion of the brutality of frontier warfare contrasting with the approach under discussion here, see chapter 7 above.
61. George Washington to Gage, Aug. 11, 1775, Gage MSS; Gage to Washington, Aug. 13, 1775, ibid.; Conway, "From Fellow-Nationals to Foreigners," 90–92.
62. P. J. Marshall, *The Making and Unmaking of Empires: Britain, India, and America, c. 1750–1783* (Oxford: Oxford University Press, 2005), 354.
63. Samuel Adams to Elizabeth Adams, Dec. 9, 1776, in *Letters of Delegates to Congress, 1774–1789*, 29 vols., ed. Paul H. Smith (Washington, D.C.: Library of Congress, 1976–2000), 5:509–10; George Washington to Samuel Washington, Dec. 7, 1776, *The Papers of George Washington: Revolutionary War Series*, 20 vols. (to date), ed. W. W. Abbott et al. (Charlottesville: University Press of Virginia, 1985–), 7:369–71.
64. David Hackett Fischer, *Washington's Crossing* (Oxford: Oxford University Press, 2004), 344–45, 349–50.
65. Edmund George Petty Fitzmaurice, *Life of William, Lord Shelburne, afterwards First Marques of Lansdowne*, 2 vols. (London: Macmillan, 1912), 1:19.
66. Jenkinson to North, June 26, July 9, 1777, Add MSS 38306.
67. 1778 Memorandum, Add MSS 38210, ff. 187–92.
68. Ambrose Serle, *The American Journal of Ambrose Serle, Secretary to Lord Howe, 1776–1778*, ed. Edward Tatum (San Marino, Calif.: Huntington Library, 1940), 57, 66–67, 184–85.
69. Donald Winch, *Adam Smith's Politics: An Essay in Historiographic Revision* (Cambridge: Cambridge University Press, 1978), 147, 150; Adam Smith, "Thoughts on the State of the Contest with America, February 1778," in *The Correspondence of Adam*

Smith, ed. E. C. Mossner and I. S. Ross (Oxford: Oxford University Press, 1977), 377–85.

70. Conway, "From Fellow-Nationals to Foreigners," 93–94; George III to North, Mar. 26, 1778, in *Correspondence of George III,* 4:80–81.
71. Kevin J. Weddle, "'A Change of Both Men and Measures': British Reassessment of Military Strategy after Saratoga," *Journal of Military History* 77 (July 2013): 852–54.
72. Ritcheson, *British Politics and the American Revolution,* 259, 268–72.
73. Sir Henry Clinton memorandum, [May 23, 1778], Clinton MSS; Conway, "From Fellow-Nationals to Foreigners," 68.
74. O'Shaughnessy, *Men Who Lost America,* 14, 276–79; George III to North, Mar. 7, 1780, in *Correspondence of George III,* 5:30.
75. Burke to William Baker, Oct. 12, 1777, in *Correspondence of Burke,* 10 vols., ed. Thomas W. Copeland et al. (Cambridge: Cambridge University Press, 1958–78), 3:389; O'Shaughnessy, *Men Who Lost America,* 3; Fitzmaurice, *Life of William, Lord Shelburne,* 2:83.
76. Edward Gibbon, *Memoirs of the Life of Edward Gibbon, with Various Excursions and Observations by Himself,* ed. G. B. Hill (London: Methuen, 1900), 212–13.
77. John Norris, *Shelburne and Reform* (London: Macmillan, 1963), 148–53.
78. Marshall, *Remaking the British Atlantic,* 23, 40; Esmond Wright, "The British Objectives, 1780–1783: 'If Not Dominion then Trade,'" in *Peace and the Peacemakers: The Treaty of 1783,* ed. Ronald Hoffman and Peter J. Albert (Charlottesville: University Press of Virginia, 1986), 13.
79. Larry May, *After War Ends: A Philosophical Perspective* (Cambridge: Cambridge University Press, 2012), 45–46.
80. Vattel, *Law of Nations,* 651–52, 655.
81. Ibid., 662–63.
82. John L. Bullion, "George III on Empire, 1783," *William & Mary Quarterly,* 3rd ser., 51, no. 2 (Apr. 1994): 305–9.
83. Marshall, *Remaking the British Atlantic,* 50–53.
84. Ibid., 16–17.
85. Grotius, *Rights of War and Peace,* 3:1638–43.

13 NEUTRALITY, RACE, AND WARS OF EXTERMINATION

Native Americans in the Aftermath of the American Revolution

Daniel R. Brunstetter

In 1780 the Academy of Science, Letters, and Arts of Lyon sponsored an essay competition asking European intellectuals to consider the following questions: "Was the discovery of the Americas injurious or useful to the human species? If good came of it, what are the ways in which to conserve and increase them? If it produced evils, what are the ways to remedy them?"[1] While not framed in just war terms, the questions implicitly asked Enlightenment-era European intellectuals to weigh the calamities resulting from the Spanish conquest of the New World with the (perceived) benefits of the recent American Revolution. Regarding the former, the famous inquiry in the sixteenth century about just war and indigenous rights resulting from the Spanish conquest arguably revolutionized how Europeans thought about *jus ad bellum*, or when to go to war.[2] Spanish thinkers such as Francisco de Vitoria, Francisco Suárez, and Domingo de Soto lamented the massacres of indigenous populations, denied the right of Europeans to wage just war on religious grounds, and articulated the sovereign rights of "barbarians" under the law of nations. These arguments marked a significant shift in just war thinking away from the holy-war paradigm toward a more secular perspective.[3] But these concerns were of scant interest to the Enlightenment-era judges of the Academy of Lyon.

What is peculiar about this intellectual competition, sponsored by the Abbé Raynal, was that no winner was declared (for the responses were deemed too unworthy because they tended to focus too much on the calamities of the Spanish conquest). But a summary of the "right" answer was printed some years later as the *Coup d'Oeil sur les quatre concours qui ont eu lieu en l'Académie des Science Belles-Lettres et Arts de Lyon pour le prix offert par M. l'Abbé Raynal sur la découverte de l'Amérique.* In this summary, the massacre of native populations by Spanish conquistadors was duly criticized—these were not just wars against barbarians, but rather massacres committed by religious zealots and glory hunters. Yet there was something to be valorized: the American Revolution. This was presumably a just war that set the stage for the inevitable spread of democracy in the New World in the *post bellum* era:

> Those who will know how to take advantage of this great example shall never forget what they owe to America, where the standard of liberty was laid out for the entire universe; and when one asks them what the discovery of this continent produced, they will respond that it was very cruel in the beginning and that during several centuries, it compensated great evils with only weak advantages, but having softened, humanized, and enlightened the nations by happy experiences that one could not do elsewhere, [America] showed to all the true path to liberty, and that civil liberty, preferable to savage liberty, has grown deep roots in North America and has extended its branches to Europe, and will come to cover little by little all the parts of the world.[4]

But there is something troubling implied in this adulation. Speaking of the triumph of American democracy, the anonymous author writes that "with the proximate and universal regeneration for which we hope and of which we are already tasting the first fruits, one essential element is lacking: whether the Indians can participate? Will we finish by repopulating their native lands and the homeland of their ancestors only by destroying them? That is the direction towards which our clearing of the land and the progress of our colonies is pointing."[5] The answer is troubling as it highlights a future of inevitable "just" wars: "The route that all peoples should follow is too well marked for them not to see it. All those who are not enchained by the passions or besotted by vice will be civilized and free when they want to be so; *all the rest are incapable or unworthy of being so.*"[6] To the extent that this conclusion captures the Western mindset—a similar stance is seen in Thomas Jefferson's writings just before the Revolution and later in Alexis de Tocqueville's works while traveling a generation after—there is a sense that the American Revolution heralds a new era, one in which democracy and coexistence with the "savages" of the New World are incompatible.

The question of whether the Revolution was a just war or not is, of course, much debated.[7] What is interesting about the *Coup d'Oeil* is that it foretells of a postwar world in which American democracy, once established, sets a bellicose stance toward the "savages." The *jus post bellum* phase of the American Revolution came, indeed, to be defined by something of a moral imperative: the spread of democracy entails the extermination of native tribes via just war.

The *Coup d'Oeil* is not just a curious moment in intellectual history, but rather a philosophical watershed that reflects a broader trend about how the American Revolution's *jus post bellum* phase would be perceived from an Enlightenment perspective. The document's conclusions reflect a shifting understanding regarding just war against so-called barbarians implicit in one of the era's leading just war thinkers, Emer de Vattel, as well as new ideas about the link between just war, sovereignty, and the spread of democracy. Whatever agreements of neutrality or coexistence might have existed before or even during the early stages of the Revolutionary War, these became unsustainable once the Americans emerged victorious. This begs the following questions: Why did a policy of American Indian neutrality before and during the early phases of the war become impossible in the *post bellum* phase? And why did a policy of wars of extermination waged by the Americans against American Indian tribes emerge?

To answer these questions requires exploring the tensions between the principle of neutrality, the birth of democracy by "just war," and the racialization of American-"savage" relations in the *jus post bellum* phase of the Revolution. While many tribes attempted to remain neutral during the Revolutionary War, this turned out to be a doomed strategy that had dramatic effects in the postwar era. The tensions of neutrality found in Vattel's work *The Law of Nations* (1758), which was a hugely influential text on just war in the Enlightenment that held patchy influence in colonial North America (mostly among elites), combined with the perceived necessities of sovereign responsibility from the victorious American perspective and the desperate attempts by American Indians to preserve their independence in a world of democratic settler expansion, arguably influenced *post bellum* realities. This *post bellum* context tapped into troubling, underlyingly racial caveats inherent in Vattel's just war thinking that, from the American perspective, arguably could have justified wars of extermination against the Native tribes.

This conclusion raises serious concerns about the relationship between the American Revolution and the legacy of just war thinking, particularly *jus post bellum*. "Rehabilitation," among the most accepted contemporary notions of justice after war, did not apply in the eighteenth century.[8] Rather, *jus post bellum* was couched in terms of punishment and retribution (a view most contemporary just war scholars argue against), which is expressed clearly in Vattel's work. That being said, in the case of American Indians, there was an important caveat. Again, Vattel provides the theoretical insight: while a just peace could be sought with the "civilized," it might not be possible with some "savages," against whom wars of *extermination* could be waged under certain circumstances. Vattel did not mention New World peoples specifically, however; read in the context of the *post bellum* American Revolution, his ideas could have intimated something along the lines of the following: while peace was made with the British, with the cession of certain lands as part of a just retribution, wars of extermination could, under certain conditions, be justifiable against the Native tribes inhabiting these lands if they did not accept the terms of the peace. Thus did European norms of *jus post bellum* blend with racially infused ideals in the wake of the American Revolution to devastating and morally problematic effect.

Relations with American Indians before and during the American Revolution

The Treaty of Paris of 1783, negotiated between the United States and Great Britain, ended the Revolutionary War. Of significant import is that these negotiations did not include the American Indian tribes that had aligned with the British and that the British ceded territory—what is sometimes referred to as the "Old Northwest," the frontier lands that stretched from the Appalachian and Allegheny Mountains to the Mississippi River—to the fledgling United States.

From the perspective of many Native tribes, these lands were not Great Britain's to give, meaning the United States had no right to expand settlements into these territories. From the U.S. perspective, the land was obtained by right of conquest; Native tribes, because they had sided with the vanquished, were subject to the conditions of the peace treaty that ended the war. The *post bellum* era thus began with the seeds of conflict already planted. To understand how this would lead to wars of extermination requires taking a closer look at how the affected tribes came to side with the British. Doing so reveals a connection between the dilemmas of neutrality and the *post bellum* tensions poised to erupt into conflict.

The political geography of North America during the century prior to the Revolution was extremely complex. Various European imperial powers (Great Britain, France, and Spain) had laid claim to large swaths of land and had fought multiple wars. Individual Native tribes positioned themselves within these imperial disputes, playing a complicated game of diplomacy that involved neutrality and alliances, negotiations and war. They often also had their own intertribal rivalries, though there were also times of punctuated pan–American Indian alliances. Wars were fought, treaties were signed, and the game of diplomacy was renewed.

The Iroquois are a case in point. Following the peace settlement of 1701, the Iroquois began a policy of general neutrality with the French and British. This was broken on several occasions, including Queen Anne's War (1702–13), King

George's War (1744–48), and the French and Indian War (1754–63), but always resorted because they believed it was in their best interest to preserve their autonomy by not siding permanently with one colonial power over the other. This was a sage foreign policy, but it was a potentially treacherous path to follow in the context of feuding imperial rivalries. Indeed, at times, the Iroquois Confederacy, or constituent members of it, broke neutrality to align with one side or the other. But after hostilities ceased, even if the power dynamics had slightly shifted, a return to the policy of neutrality remained an option. While American Indian sovereignty was not fully conceived—the British claimed dominion over land and the peoples who lived on it by way of the Treaty of Utrecht (1713)—politically deft and militarily strong tribes such as the Iroquois were able to act like sovereign entities, making decisions and pursuing actions they perceived to be in their own interests.[9] Such political maneuvering worked insofar as the Iroquois remained a respected power that neither Britain nor France wanted to engage in full-out war, one that maintained some sense of Vatellian sovereignty (as described in chapter 3 above). To quote one French governor near the end of Queen Anne's War: "It is a matter of importance to us . . . not to be at war with that tribe if we can possibly help it, and the five Iroquois villages are more to be feared than the whole of New England."[10] According to one British official, the Iroquois believed it was prudent to "keep the balance betwixt [the English and French]. . . . [I]f the Five Nations would now observe an exact neutrality, they would be courted and feared by both sides."[11] The American Revolution, however, changed the rules of the diplomatic game. The reason is found in the dilemmas of the eighteenth-century notion of neutrality and the consequences of breaking it.

Among the most influential European texts on war and neutrality at the time was Vattel's *Law of Nations.* The book arguably influenced British and American leaders in North America, including George Washington.[12] Earlier in chapter 10, T. Cole Jones describes that while leadership on both sides accepted the restraining *jus in bello* mechanisms found in the works of Vattel (and others), the nature of warfare in colonial North America often made these difficult to implement. The same could be said of neutrality, a reality that Vattel himself was keenly aware. In Book III ("Of War") Vattel devotes an entire chapter to the "obligations and rights flowing from neutrality." He offers a clear definition: "Neutral nations are those who, in time of war, do not take any part in the contest, but remain common friends to both parties, without favouring the arms of the one to the prejudice of the other." If a nation does not show perfect impartiality, then this leads to what he calls "fraudulent neutrality," which carries with it significant consequences.[13]

Neutrality is a diplomatic strategy a nation can employ "to secure her own peace, when the flames of war are kindling in her neighborhood."[14] In colonial America the flames of war were often kindled between European powers posturing for economic or political advantages over one another with the resources of the New World pawns in a global colonial struggle. But American Indian nations were not mere pawns in a European game of diplomacy. As Colin Calloway explains, Europeans "entered a world in which various Indian groups pursued different foreign polices with regard to other Indian friends and enemies. . . . International and inter-colonial rivalries added to and complicated intertribal rivalries, turning North America into a kaleidoscope of competing, overlapping, and changing foreign policies."[15] Pursuing tribal-centric interests was, however, a tricky game when European colonial powers were at war in adjacent lands. A close reading of Vattel illuminates the tensions of neutrality that American Indian tribes would have faced from the perspective of Europeans versed in eighteenth-century laws of war.

The first challenge of neutrality involves persuading warring neighbors of one's true neutrality. Vattel concedes the right to a party at war to pursue its own self-defense by attacking any sovereign power in league with a declared enemy. He thus explains: "I should have just cause to consider that nation as leagued with my enemy; and in this case, the care of my own safety would authorize me to treat her as such."[16] The burden, it seems, is on the neutral nation to prove its *bonne foi* to remain neutral. Among the requirements for doing so is to continue trading with both powers and not refuse to one what is granted to another. "If the neutral state," writes Vattel, "grants or refuses a passage to one of the parties at war, we ought in like manner to grant or refuse it to the other, unless a change of circumstances affords her substantial reasons for acting otherwise. Without such reasons, to grant one party what she refuses to the other, would be a partial distinction, and a departure from the line of strict neutrality."[17]

This becomes complicated when put in the context of war. For example, Vattel concedes that an "innocent passage is due to all nations with whom a state is at peace, and this duty extends to troops as well as individuals."[18] But of course this is dangerous. If one foreign power demands passage of its troops for benevolent purposes, this could nevertheless be interpreted as having underlying intentions, such as attacking an enemy outpost or occupying the neutral nation's territory. Vattel was not immune to such fears:

> When the passage is not of absolute necessity, the bare danger which attends the admission of a powerful army into our territory, may authorize us to refuse them permission. We may have reason to apprehend

> that they will be tempted to take possession of the country. . . . Let it not be said with [Hugo] Grotius, that he who requires the passage is not to be deprived of his right on account of our unjust fears. A probable fear, founded on good reasons, gives us right to avoid whatever may realize it.[19]

This was a plausible scenario in the sovereign kaleidoscope of colonial North America. For example, during King George's War, the Iroquois's policy of neutrality prohibited the passage of French troops through their territory for bellicose purposes. Neutral passage was permissible "unless the French should come through our settlements to hurt our Bretheren the English, which we would not permit."[20]

Vattel was well aware of such scenarios. Thus, he contends, "if the neutral sovereign has good reasons for refusing a passage, he is not obliged to grant it." He then concludes, "The tranquility, therefore, and the common safety of nations requires that each should be mistress of her own territory, and at liberty to refuse every foreign army an entrance, when she has not departed from her natural liberties in that respect, by treaties."[21] But this is a slippery slope, for it requires judgment laced with uncertainty about the intentions of the non-neutral parties as well as observance of treaties not always signed under equal conditions. Errors of judgment or perceived breaches of treaty could be fatal, for they could signal to the refused party that the nation in question is practicing fraudulent neutrality.

The consequences of fraudulent neutrality were grave. Vattel explains that "if the refusal be evidently unjust . . . , if the passage be unquestionably innocent,—a nation may do herself justice, and take by force what is unjustly denied her." Refusing innocent passage thus would be considered a breach of neutrality, though Vattel is keenly aware of the difficulties in assessing the intentions of one's enemy: "we have already observed that it is very difficult for the passage of an army to be absolutely innocent, and the evils it may occasion, and the dangers that may attend it,—so complicated are they in their nature, and so numerous are the circumstances with which they are connected,—that to foresee and provide for every thing is next to impossible."[22] This was, in many ways, the situation that American Indian tribes faced. How should a tribe act amid feuding "brothers"? The collapse of colonial authority coupled with the emigration of land-hungry settlers that neither the British not the Americans could control threated the tribes' security and, with this, any hope of sustained neutrality.

While a few tribes sided directly with the Americans out of ideological concerns (for example, the Indians of Stockbridge and the Catawbas) and others fought settler advancements (such the Cherokees), many tribes were less committed in the beginning. Indeed, James H. O'Donnell cites the Cherokees' doomed resistance as a benchmark for other tribes to stay out of a "white man's quarrel."[23] Yet even if a tribe sought neutrality, it was required to make diplomatic decisions under conditions of uncertainty that ultimately jeopardized its impartial standing. For example, the Delawares and Shawnees pursued neutrality initially but were brutally torn asunder by American settlers; for them, the natural choice was to side with the British. The American Revolution even split the alliance that had bound the confederated tribes of the Iroquois, with some siding with the Americans and others with the British. Armstrong Starkey has described the typical stance within tribes facing evolving conditions before and during the American Revolution as one involving a generational split, with elders arguing for pacification, while younger leaders promoted armed resistance.[24]

The political solutions to the dilemmas of neutrality were not straightforward, as readers of Vattel would readily surmise. Indeed, he added caveats to his claims regarding "very uncommon cases," and the American Revolution was most certainly a case that fit this bill. One such caveat implicated American Indians' stance of neutrality. Imagine an American fighting the British and considering American Indian neutrality while reading this passage:

> But if necessity authorizes me to pass, the conditions on which the passage will be granted may be accepted or rejected, according to the manner of the people I am treating with. Suppose I am to cross the country of a barbarous, savage, perfidious nation—shall I leave myself at their discretion, by giving up my arms and causing my troops to march in divisions? No one, I presume, will condemn me to take so dangerous a step. . . . Since necessity authorizes me to pass, a kind of new necessity arises for my passing in such a posture as will secure me from any ambuscade or violence.[25]

Given the pervasive view that American Indians were "savages," then any reasonable American commander would follow Vattel's advice and invoke the policy of necessity.

Now imagine the British perspective. Vattel exhorts, "as we are not bound to grant even innocent passage except for just causes, we may refuse it to him who requires it for a war that is evidently unjust,—as, for instance, to invade a country without any reason, or even a coloured pretext."[26] From the British perspective, the American cause was unjust, meaning that American Indians ought to refuse passage of rebel troops. Placing emphasis on this interpretation would give the British reason to look unfavorably on those tribes that granted equal sovereign privileges to the Americans—that is, the equal treatment neutral nations owe to sovereign warring nations.

Finally, from the American Indian perspective, yet another reading of Vattel would send an alternative message, namely concerning the right to refuse passage to armed groups with uncertain intentions. Whether or not any Natives were versed in Vattel is beside the point; those Anglo leaders interpreting their actions would likely have been. Vattel opines that "another fear may also warrant her [a neutral] in refusing a passage, namely, that of involving her country in the disorders and calamities of war. . . . The infinite evils of such a situation are an unexceptionable reason for refusing the passage. . . . He who attempts to force a passage, does an injury to the neutral nation, and gives her most just cause to unite her arms with those of his adversary."[27] Tribes thus would be just in resisting against those Americans who tried to force their passage, though this would, of course, break their pledge of neutrality. This was, perhaps inevitably, the course of action that Native tribes concerned with protecting their own sovereign interest took during the Revolution. As Starkey observes, "Indian communities . . . were riven by questions of war or negotiation, alliance or neutrality. While they disagreed among themselves on how best to conduct their relations with their European neighbors, their goal remained the same. They were not concerned with American Independence or of the integrity of the British empire except as those issues affected their own way of life."[28]

Neutrality was, as is evident in Vattel's explications, a tension-laden foreign-policy option. In the context of the American Revolution, it proved impossible to maintain. And once neutrality is broken, then the rights of belligerents apply. This transformation has consequences, especially at a war's end. In the case of the American Revolution, those on the losing side had to abide by the terms of the treaty that concluded the conflict.

It is important to take a slight detour here to discuss eighteenth-century *jus post bellum* norms. Vattel is widely recognized for his contributions to just war thinking, with the literature focusing on how he sought to moderate *jus in bello* norms and his contribution to the secularization of just war.[29] Yet scholars tend to overlook the point that his view on *jus post bellum* also captures essential norms of the eighteenth century. When thinking about *jus post bellum* at the time of the American Revolution, it is important to recognize that much of just war thinking was framed in notions of punishment. This is especially true with Vattel. Thus, the justice after war was framed in terms of restitution or retribution—that is, making a defeated enemy pay for the damage caused. One sees this in Vattel, especially in Book IV of *Law of Nations,* which focuses on the restoration of peace. The following passage captures the essence of the prevailing view of *jus post bellum:*

> The love of peace should equally prevent us from embarking in a war without necessity, and from persevering in it after the necessity has ceased to exist. When a sovereign has been compelled to take up arms for just and important reasons, he may carry on the operations of war till he has attained its lawful end, which is, to procure justice and safety. (Book III. §28.)
>
> If the cause be dubious, the just end of war can only be to bring the enemy to an equitable compromise (Book III. §38); and consequently the war must not be continued beyond that point. The moment our enemy proposes or consents to such compromise, it is our duty to desist from hostilities.
>
> But if we have to do with a perfidious enemy, it would be imprudent to trust either his words or his oaths. In such case, justice allows and prudence requires that we should avail ourselves of a successful war, and follow up our advantages, till we have humbled a dangerous and excessive power, or compelled the enemy to give us sufficient security for the time to come.
>
> Finally, if the enemy obstinately rejects equitable conditions, he himself forces us to continue our progress till we have obtained a complete and decisive victory, by which he is absolutely reduced and subjected. (Book III. Chap. VIII. IX. XIII)[30]

Note that Book III, section 28 refers to where Vattel lays out the *jus ad bellum* criteria, thus drawing a link between *jus ad bellum* and *jus post bellum* based in justice and security. Justice, from Vattel's point of view, is viewed through the lens of retribution. Thus, Book III, chapters VIII, IX, and XIII discuss what things a victor can take from the enemy during the war as part of compensation for the damages done and to ensure future security. This all adds up to a retribution-based view of *jus post bellum* that runs contrary to twenty-first-century formulations, though insofar as Vattel is representative of the times, this helped inform the way the postwar period was imagined.

What does all this mean for the aftermath of the American Revolution? At least from an American perspective, this meant that American Indians were required to respect the stipulation that their lands had been ceded by way of treaty as compensation for the damages done during the war. That the tribes were not privy to the negotiations was apparently of no concern—their land was forfeit by right of conquest. To quote Vattel: "Immovable possessions, lands, towns, [and] provinces . . . become the property of the enemy who makes himself master of them: but it is only by the treaty of peace, or the entire submission and extinction of the state to which those towns and provinces belonged, that the acquisition is completed."[31]

The gamble—or perhaps the inevitable necessity—of making choices in times of upheaval carries a price, according to the *jus post bellum* standards of the day. In the preceding chapter, William Anthony Hay describes how Great Britain used the peace process to consolidate its remaining imperial power vis-à-vis other European powers. For American Indian tribes that sided with the British, there was indignation at being, for all intents and purposes, abandoned.

With the American star on the rise, the rules of diplomacy that had governed colonial North America began to change. Despite being militarily and financially fragile, the newly founded United States began to dictate the terms of diplomatic negotiations. Prior to the Revolution, American Indian tribes played off European powers against each other, using alliances to further their own interests, often at the expense of other Native rivals. Europeans played the game of diplomacy in a way that respected traditional indigenous customs. But the founding of the United States changed the power balance. As Calloway concludes: "The 'middle ground' arrangements that first the French and then the British had maintained with American Indian tribes dissolved as American invaders discarded old ways of conducting Indian diplomacy and attempted to dictate from a position of strength. The new nation was interested less in having Indian allies and more in having Indian land."[32] Assuming the territory was theirs by right of conquest, the Americans were indeed able to dictate the terms, and in a *post bellum* era, just war norms were such that this could be done harshly with recalcitrant foes who refused to accept the dictates of peace.

The Laws of War, Race, and Perpetual Enmity in the Wake of the Revolution

Inherent in eighteenth-century just war thinking was the perception that the rules of war applied to conflicts between civilized nations, not in those with so-called barbarians. At the dawn of international law in the sixteenth century, when the Spanish scholastics argued that even barbarians had sovereign rights, Vitoria intimated that the rules could be different when fighting "true barbarians."[33] Vestiges of this hierarchy persisted into eighteenth-century just war thinking.

Theodore Christov argues in chapter 3 that the Americans sought to exercise the right of Vattelian sovereignty to earn a place on the international stage as an equal among nations. This concept of sovereignty had a humanizing aspect that Vattel imagined would lead to the observance of justice among nations. And if war broke out, then its horrors would be limited to the extent possible by the *jus in bello* rules of war. That being said, Vattel's *Law of Nations* offers caveats to both ideals.

"If there were a people," writes Vattel, "who made open profession of trampling justice under foot,—who despised and violated the rights of others whenever they found an opportunity,—the interest of human society would authorize all the other nations to form a confederacy in order to humble and chastise the delinquents. . . . [T]he safety of the human race requires that she should be repressed."[34] Vattel's comments do not single out specific peoples, nor do they, on the surface, entail racial proclamations. But they do tap into a deeply inegalitarian element of just war thinking by suggesting that the civilized could unite against those who despised (European conceptions of) justice. When put into the context of the American Revolution, those perceived to despise justice were the "savages."

Despite periods of cultural coexistence, one area in which American Indians and Europeans were clearly distinguishable was the manner in which they *imagined* the ideals of warfare. While several previous chapters establish the ideals of European warfare, and deviations from them, in the context of the American Revolution, what is important here are two observations: first, the ideals of *jus in bello* rules, such as sparing civilians and taking care of prisoners, were aspired to by Europeans and (some) Americans in the context of inter-European conflicts (of course, these notions were far from being universally respected); and second, the perception that American Indians did not abide by the (European) rules of war but rather waged merciless warfare that ignored all civilized restraints.[35] Stories of Native savagery, especially on the frontiers, fueled this perception. Despite different cultures of warfare, the belief that European standards ought to be the universal norm placed the tribes, in the mindset of many Americans, in the category of "savages." And within the norms of European warfare, different standards of treatment were justified when dealing with such peoples.

Pondering the duties of restraint when confronting "savages," Vattel writes:

> If the people do not voluntarily submit, the state of war still persists. A conqueror who has taken up arms . . . whose intention it was to subdue a fierce and savage people, and once [and] for all to reduce an obstinate enemy,—such a conqueror may with justice lay burthens on the conquered nation, both as a compensation for the expenses of the war, and as punishment. He may, according to the degree of indocility apparent

> in their disposition, govern them with a tighter reign, so as to curb and subdue their impetuous spirit: he may even, if necessary, keep them for some time in a kind of slavery.[36]

Again, Vattel does not single out specific peoples; he only consents to such a state of affairs when more moderate ways have failed, and then only until the conquered can become citizens under a just and inclusive regime. Yet in the context of the aftermath of the American Revolution, these moderating hopes came face to face with the harsh realities of a racially divided new world order.

From the American perspective, the refusal of American Indian tribes to abide by the Treaty of Paris and vacate the ceded lands meant that the United States was justified in continuing the conflict against them. The on-the-ground reality was quite complex. Some tribes sought peaceful coexistence with the new nation but, harassed by advancing settlers who operated according to often-independent agendas, also defended themselves with force when necessary. This then led to accusations that they were not abiding by the treaty, which when coupled with accounts of brutal killings of settlers, fueled the stereotype of American Indians as "merciless savages." Other tribes refused to accept the conditions of the treaty, to which they did not consent, from the start and chose to fight (sometimes as part of a loose confederacy). There is not space here to delve into the details of this multifaceted struggle, so the focus instead will be on the ultimate consequences of this toxic situation—namely, that it rendered impossible the moderate hopes of Vattel's philosophy of war, leaving North America stagnated in the racially tinged caveats of his thought.

Thinking back to the philosophical musing at the beginning of this chapter, one can understand how the stage was set for wars of extermination. In the *Coup d'Oeil,* Enlightenment optimism sided with the ideals of the revolutionaries, who had rediscovered man's original liberty in the forests of North America and grafted it onto a newly founded democracy. To resist the spread of democracy, which Americans (and some Europeans) perceived the Natives as doing, was a sign of racial inferiority. It signaled that the two cultures could not coexist, that one would eventually come to perish by the fires of war.

After the Revolution, North America was characterized by multiple visions of sovereignty. On the one hand there was the view that American Indians were sovereign peoples, with a right to territories in which to live and with whom the fledgling United States could make treaties. This was the vestige of the colonial era, the dying embers of the "middle ground."[37] And indeed, the United States made countless treaties with numerous tribes.[38] But the value of these agreements was undermined by an alternative understanding of sovereignty gaining traction, which denied American Indians the right to occupy ancestral lands *as American Indians.* This was the view that ultimately came to dominate, and its acceptance contributed to the contextual brew feeding the wars of extermination.

Echoing ideas found in the treatises of John Locke, some Americans argued that North America was inhabited by "savages" who were, for all intents and purposes, stateless beings.[39] Locke's ideas, which parallel the viewpoint embraced by the *Coup d'Oeil,* highlight the contours of a framework that was beginning to gain a strong foothold in the philosophical imagination of Enlightenment-era thinkers and statesmen. The focus in the *Coup d'Oeil* is not on the treatment of the American Indians by settlers, which was not always magnanimous, but on how the settlers embraced a liberty possible only in North America in order to shed the yolk of European despotism: "Ever since diverse groups of Europeans, chased out of their homeland by the persecution from which they suffered, brought to America their industry, their talents, their religion, manufacturing, sciences, arts and especially their mores, America is no longer condemned to being a vast desert or savage region. When all these means, which are the true forces of humanity, are allowed to be deployed under a free sky . . . they are sure to triumph."[40]

The forests of North America provided territory, vast tracts of unused (in the Lockean sense) land on which to live and refound a society based on liberty. As Carole Pateman documents, the American colonists' arguments tapped into a philosophical tradition in which uncultivated land, or *terra nullius,* was open to appropriation.[41] She goes on to explain that American Indians "are not part of the settler contract—but they are henceforth subject to it, and their lives, lands, and nations re-ordered by it."[42] The influence of these arguments was evident on the eve of the Revolution and would grow in power and scope following the American victory. "The settler political theory that developed in the interstices of the British empire," explains Craig Yirush, "was intimately connected to the dispossession of the indigenous peoples of North America. Indeed, it was the settlers [American colonials] rather than the Crown who argued that the American Indians were, in effect, stateless, and therefore could be pushed aside in the scramble for land following the defeat of the French in 1763 and the British in 1783."[43]

The interlude between these imperial defeats offers a philosophical snapshot of American diplomatic relations with American Indians, laced with racial and bellicose overtones. In 1774, on the eve of the First Continental Congress, Thomas Jefferson penned *A Summary View of the Rights of British America* in which he argues that land ownership—what he calls "possessions" in colonial

America—is "undoubtedly of the allodial nature. . . . [E]ach individual of the society may appropriate to himself such lands as he finds vacant, and occupancy will give him title."[44] This argument made several assumptions, among them that settler rights to the land were more valid that tribal rights and that the way American Indians used the land was inferior to European uses. This view of sovereignty fueled the settler mentality, namely that lands used by American Indians were there for the taking. Moreover, it was buttressed by increasingly racialized relations in North America.

The American view of Natives was different than that of the British. While stories of indigenous brutality were common, this did not undermine, in the eyes of the British, tribal rights to sovereignty. But the settler mentality painted a different picture as savagery translated into racial inferiority. Unlike the coexistence of the "middle ground," there was a growing perception among Americans that they were living between the tyrants of the Old World and the "merciless savages" of the New World. The Declaration of Independence (1776) gives us a picture of what settlers exercising their "right" to possess vacant lands had to face on the frontier: "He [King George III] has excited domestic insurrections amongst us, and has endeavored to bring on the inhabitants of our frontiers, the merciless Indian savages, whose known rule of warfare, is undistinguished destruction of all ages, sexes and conditions."[45] What is clear here from the American perspective is that the "Indian savages" were in no manner neutral but rather bedfellows with the British. The term "merciless" is significant as is the belief that indigenous rules of war were the opposite of the "civilized" laws of European warfare. The implication seems to be that cohabitation was impossible, meaning that either the Americans had to forfeit their "right" to expand, American Indian tribes had to move, or a war in which only one would survive would ensue. But because American rights were deemed superior to those of the "savages," in their minds it fell upon the American Indians to acquiesce; if they did not, then Americans were justified in fighting for their rights to the territory. The racial implications are clear: white American settlers were superior to American Indians, who did not abide by the laws of civilization. American politics, indeed its underlying settler mentality, did not recognize nonwhite personhood as legitimate.[46] Of course, atrocities were committed by all parties involved, but the Americans believed they had civilization "on their side," which meant that their atrocities increasingly came to be seen as necessary to exterminate a barbaric foe and guarantee the protection and spread of democracy.[47]

An example is George Washington's campaign against the Iroquois during the Revolutionary War. In 1779 Washington ordered Brigadier General John

Sullivan to "lay waste all the settlements around, with instructions to do it in the most effectual manner, that the country may not merely be overrun, but destroyed."[48] This would, of course, be a violation of the European rules of war. Despite Washington's lofty belief in these civilized ideals, he recognized that the rules were difficult to enforce and surmised that, in a war against "savages," the rules did not necessarily apply. To return to Vattel: "Those who seem to delight in the ravages of war, who spread it on all sides, without reasons or pretexts, and even without any other motive than their own ferocity, are monsters unworthy [of] the name of men. They should be considered as enemies to the human race. . . . [A]ll nations have a right to join in a confederacy for the purpose of punishing and even *exterminating* those savage nations."[49] Wars of extermination run very much counter to the moderating *jus in bello* rules outlined by Vattel in *Law of Nations*, showing the dark underbelly of the racially infused European attitudes toward non-Europeans.[50] Indeed, Washington's campaign against the Iroquois is just one among many examples of the wars of extermination that would ensue.

Even though there was order in and reason to American Indian warfare (albeit different from European ways), the perception that it was pure brutality fueled the American campaigns against indigenous foes.[51] And if we accept Vattel as a source of authority, then the Americans would have seen themselves as being justified in acting as such. In just war parlance, the dictates of Vattelian humanity, designed to restrain the destructiveness of war, gave way to the necessities of a just war against a pitiless enemy. But if one takes the perspective of American Indian tribes, then the racial underpinnings of Vattel's view of just war become apparent. Despite their universalist appeal, there is a clear hierarchy that denies the identity of those placed in the category of "savages," leaving them to bear the brunt of European judgments. What is more, the rights of war also impinged on their very right to existence, for Vattel imbues the civilized with the right to exterminate the barbarians. Vattel does not specifically single out North American peoples (his examples are the clash between the Germanic tribes and Rome as well as the Turks and Tartars—all of which were groups who threatened European civilization), but when read in the context of the *post bellum* American Revolution, this viewpoint fit into a racialized world order in which whites dominated over "savages."

Following the war, the Northwest Ordinance of July 1787 sought to reestablish the borders between the United States and the Native tribes. Article III makes the following claim that, upon closer inspection, is the spark that ignited the flames of ensuing wars of extermination: "The utmost good faith shall always be observed towards the Indians; their lands and property shall never be taken from them without their consent; and, in their property, rights, and liberty, they shall never be invaded or disturbed, unless in just and lawful wars authorized by Congress."[52] On the one hand, respect was paid to American Indian sovereignty. Yet this was a notion that had been eclipsed and was receding in the wake of American expansion. On the other hand, this respect was all but doomed to be undermined by the settler mentality and subsequent claims to land that became engrained in the American mindset as well as the racialization of attitudes toward Native tribes. Americans claimed the right to wage just wars against the Natives, but this right was all but denied to the tribes, who struggled with what to do—continue to concede their land to appease the United States, try to adapt to white ways (and give up their own lifestyles), or fight back. While most tribes generally recognized that they were fighting for their survival, Americans were unable to accept or unwilling to take this perspective.[53] And one does not have to go any further than Vattel to find justification for war against resisting tribes: "The right of employing force, or making war, belongs to nations no farther than is necessary for their own defense and for the maintenance of their rights."[54] Defense of its population, settlers included, and the right to settle vacant lands within the territories it claimed by treaty as part of the *jus post bellum* settlement ending the Revolutionary War clearly fell under this heading.

As long as the American Indian tribes sought to control their own destiny and live according to traditional ways, Vattel's worldview was a blueprint for legitimized (from the American perspective) wars of extermination. The events that transpired in the Northwest Territory are a case in point. As then-governor of the Northwest Territory, Major General Arthur St. Clair, tried to negotiate with a loose confederacy of tribes led by Joseph Brant to purchase lands that had been ceded in previous treaties, settlers continued to flood the region. The talks eventually splintered after some tribes did not recognize the American right to settlement in the region and prepared to fight for their own existence.[55] In such a context of mutual mistrust, neutrality was no longer a viable option as it once had been. Lost too was the idea that should disagreements come to war, a return to neutrality afterward was a legitimate diplomatic option. Setters and Native tribes exchanged acts of brutality; the new national government under Washington then felt justified in authorizing the first major Indian war of the postrevolutionary period.[56] After initial setbacks (for example, the defeat of Brigadier General Joseph Harmar's ill-fated expedition in 1790 and St Clair's defeat in 1791), the tide of the campaign turned. Despite attempts to make peace, the war continued with Major General Anthony Wayne's offensive in 1794, which culminated in the American victory at Fallen Timbers. The Treaty of Greenville (1795) reconfigured the frontier borders as Native tribes ceded more land and moved ever westward. But the agreement proved to be hollow in the face of increased settler expansion into the Ohio River valley as white populations increased from 5,000 in 1796 to more than 230,000 by 1810.[57] Tensions mounted, and despite more periods of Native resistance—under Tecumseh for example—the pattern repeated itself until the various tribes were either driven out or destroyed.[58] The pattern predicted by the *Coup d'Oeil* thus came to its merciless fruition.

Conclusion

The *post bellum* era of the American Revolution in a sense resolved the tensions of neutrality seen in Vattel by making neutrality an impossible diplomatic course of action for American Indian tribes. It did so at the expense of the egalitarian core of the fledgling American democracy by solidifying a latent racial hierarchy in North America by which white settlers seized the right to dominate (or exterminate) Native populations. This racial framework may have existed at the margins of Vattel's just war thinking as he generally sought to provide a moral framework for the honorable adjudications of political disputes among nations and to limit the horrors of war. Yet in a changing world in which the humanity of Vattelian sovereignty was replaced by a racialized view that denied rights to American Indians, war—terrible and total wars of extermination—was the inevitable outcome so long as Natives resisted the expanding, land-greedy United States.

Tocqueville's fatalistic lament is a fitting summary of the *post bellum* context American Indian tribes faced: "Today, it is true, the American government does not take their lands away from them, but it allows them to be invaded. In a few years, doubtless, the same white population that now presses on them will be on their heels in the solitudes of Arkansas . . . and as sooner or later they will run out of land, they will have to resign themselves to dying."[59] Regardless of whether the American Revolution was just, the *post bellum* phase broke with the diplomatic patterns that had governed colonial North American for more than a century, ringing in a new era of "just"—ultimately racialized—warfare. But it did so in a way that was ironically consistent with the moral contours of *jus post bellum* of the time, what Vattel described as paying retribution for injuries caused. From the American perspective, wars of extermination against Native tribes were a just means to obtain their rights to land acquired by conquest, ceded by treaty, but populated by recalcitrant "savages" who did not respect the terms of the proper peace between Great Britain and the United States.

For American Indians, who were ignored in the *just post bellum* settlement, the possibilities were bleak.[60] Tocqueville's lament echoes the viewpoint expressed by American Indian representatives from the Wynadots, Seven Nations of Canada, Delawares, Shawnees, Miamis, Ottowas, Chippewas, Senecas, Potowatomis, Conoys, Munsees, Nanticokes, Mahicans, Mississaguas, Creeks and Cherokees speaking to American commissioners in 1793. Their poignant words sum up the injustice of the *post bellum* situation, capturing the moment when the notion of sovereignty characterizing the diplomacy of the "middle ground" was eclipsed by a different view of sovereignty motivated by the inexorable spread of the racially infused American democracy:

> Brothers, you have talked to us about concessions. It appears strange that you should expect any from us, who have only been defending our just Rights against your invasion; We want Peace; Restore us to our Country and we shall be Enemies no longer. . . . Look back and view the lands from whence we have been driven to this spot, we can retreat no further, because the country behind hardly affords food for its present inhabitants. And we have therefore resolved, to leave our bones in the small space, to which we are now confined.[61]

NOTES

1. *Coup d'Oeil sur les quatre concours qui ont eu lieu en l'Académie des Science Belles-Lettres et Arts de Lyon pour le prix offert par M. l'Abbé Raynal sur la découverte de l'Amérique,* in *Avantages et désavantages de la découverte de l'Amérique,* ed. Hans Jürgen Lüsebrink and Alexandre Mussard (Saint Etienne, France: Publications de l'Université de Saint Etienne, 1994), 129. All translations of the *Coup d'Oeil* are my own.
2. Anthony Pagden, *The Fall of Natural Man: The American Indian and the Origins of Comparative Ethnology* (Cambridge: Cambridge University Press, 1986); Anthony Pagden, "Dispossessing the Barbarians: The Language of Spanish Thomism and the Debate over Property Rights of the American Indians," in *The Languages of Political Theory in Early Modern Europe,* ed. Anthony Pagden (Cambridge: Cambridge University Press, 1987), 79–98.
3. James Turner Johnson, *Just War Tradition and the Restraint of War: A Moral and Historical Inquiry* (Princeton, N.J.: Princeton University Press, 1981). On the ways in which European norms and ideas about the ethics of war have been transmitted over time, see the contributions in Daniel Brunstetter and Cian O'Driscoll, eds., *Just War Thinkers: From Cicero to the 21st Century* (New York: Routledge, 2017).

4. *Coup d'Oeil,* 142.
5. Ibid., 144.
6. Ibid., 145 (my italics).
7. For example, see chapters 6 and 11 above. Compare also two differing views: Eric Patterson and Nathan Gill, "The Declaration of the United Colonies: America's First Just War Statement," *Journal of Military Ethics* 14, no. 1 (2015): 7–34; and Gregg Frazer, "The American Revolution: Not a Just War," *Journal of Military Ethics* 14, no. 1 (2015): 35–56.
8. Brian Orend, *The Morality of War,* 2nd ed. (Petersborough, Ont.: Broadview, 2013), esp. chap. 6. For alternative conceptions, see Alex J. Bellamy, "The Responsibilities of Victory: *Jus Post Bellum* and the Just War," *Review of International Studies* 34 (2008): 601–25.
9. Dale Miquelon, "Ambiguous Concession: What Diplomatic Archives Reveal about Article 15 of the Treaty of Utrecht and France's North American Policy," *William and Mary Quarterly,* 3rd ser., 67, no. 3 (2010): 459–86.
10. Quoted from Wayne Aquila, *The Iroquois Restoration: Iroquois Diplomacy on the Colonial Frontier, 1701–1754* (Detroit: Wayne State University Press, 1983), 91.
11. Quoted from ibid., 124.
12. Eliga H. Gould, "Zones of Law, Zones of Violence: The Legal Geography of the British Atlantic, circa 1772," *William and Mary Quarterly,* 3rd ser., 60, no. 3 (2003): 471–510.
13. Emer de Vattel, *The Law of Nations* (Indianapolis: Liberty Fund, 2008), 523. On neutrality more broadly speaking, see Stephen C. Neff, *The Rights and Duties of Neutrals: A General History* (Manchester, U.K.: Manchester University Press, 2000).
14. Ibid., 526.
15. Colin G. Calloway, *New Worlds for All: Indians, Europeans, and the Remaking of Early America* (Baltimore: The John's Hopkins University Press, 1997), 117.
16. Vattel, *Law of Nations,* 527.
17. Ibid., 537.
18. Ibid., 534.
19. Ibid., 536.
20. Quoted from Aquila, *Iroquois Restoration,* 94. For Aquila's general discussion to ascertain the complexities of such a stance, see ibid., 93–100.
21. Vattel, *Law of Nations,* 535.
22. Ibid.
23. James H. O'Donnell, *Southern Indians in the American Revolution* (Knoxville: University of Tennessee Press, 1973), 34–53.
24. Ibid., 116–18.
25. Vattel, *Law of Nations,* 537.
26. Ibid., 541.
27. Ibid., 538–39.
28. Armstrong Starkey, *European and Native American Warfare, 1675–1815* (Norman: University of Oklahoma Press, 1998), 113. See also Colin G. Calloway, *The American Revolution in Indian Country* (Cambridge: Cambridge University Press, 1995).

29. For a general study, see Theodore Christov, "Vattel," in Brunstetter and O'Driscoll, *Just War Thinkers,* 156-67. On just war and sovereignty in Vattel, see James Turner Johnson, *Sovereignty: Moral and Historical Perspective* (Washington, D.C.: Georgetown University Press, 2014), 97.
30. Vattel, *Law of Nations,* 654–55.
31. Ibid., 596.
32. Calloway, *New Worlds for All,* 133.
33. Daniel Brunstetter, *Tensions of Modernity: Las Casas and His Legacy in the French Enlightenment* (New York: Routledge, 2012), 43–45.
34. Vattel, *Law of Nations,* 297–98.
35. For a view that offers insight into how some Native tribes understood war and security, see Neta C. Crawford, "A Security Regime among Democracies: Cooperation among Iroquois Nations," *International Organization,* 48, no. 3 (Summer 1994): 345–85.
36. Vattel, *Law of Nations,* 599.
37. Richard White, *The Middle Ground: Indians, Empires, and Republics in the Great Lakes Region, 1600–1815* (Cambridge: Cambridge University Press, 1991).
38. Robert A. Williams Jr., *The American Indians in Western Legal Thought: The Discourses of Conquest* (Oxford: Oxford University Press, 1990).
39. For a discussion, see ibid., 249–51.
40. *Coup d'Oeil,* 143.
41. Ibid., 36–37.
42. Carole Pateman, "The Settler Contract," in *The Contract and Domination,* ed. Carole Pateman and Charles Mills (Cambridge: Polity, 2007), 56.
43. Craig Yirush, *Settlers, Liberty, and Empire: The Roots of Early American Political Theory* (Cambridge: Cambridge University Press, 2011), 270.
44. Thomas Jefferson, *A Summary of the Rights of British America. Set Forth in Some Resolutions Intended for the Inspection of the Present Delegates of the People of Virginia* (Williamsburg, 1774), 21.
45. Quoted from Cynthia A. Kierner, ed., *Revolutionary America: Sources and Interpretation* (Upper Saddle River, N.J.: Prentice Hall, 2003), 137–39.
46. Charles Mills, *The Racial Contract* (Ithaca, N.Y.: Cornell University Press, 1997), 19–30.
47. On this subject, see Wayne E. Lee, *Barbarians and Brothers: Anglo-American Warfare, 1500*–1865 (Oxford: Oxford University Press, 2011), 171–231.
48. Quoted from Barbara Alice Mann, *George Washington's War on Native America* (Westport, Conn.: Praeger, 2005), 56.
49. Vattel, *Law of Nations,* 487 (my italics). See also the racialized exception to the *jus in bello* rule of sparing the life of an enemy who surrenders: "When we are at war with a savage nation, who observe no rules, and never give quarter, we may punish them in the persons of any of their people whom we take . . . and endeavor . . . to force them to respect the laws of humanity." Ibid., 544.
50. On Vattel's view of *jus in bello,* see Christov, "Vattel," 163–65.

51. For a discussion of war norms in colonial North American, see John Grenier, *The First Way of War: American War Making on the Frontier, 1607–1814* (Cambridge: Cambridge University Press, 2005).
52. Northwest Ordinance, July 13, 1787, *The Avalon Project,* Lillian Goldman Law Library, Yale School of Law, http://avalon.law.yale.edu/18th_century/nworder.asp, accessed Mar. 1, 2016.
53. Colin G. Calloway, *Crown and Calumet* (Norman: University of Oklahoma Press, 1987), 198–99.
54. Vattell, *Law of Nations,* 483.
55. For a discussion, see Wiley Sword, *President George Washington's Indian War: The Struggle for the Old Northwest, 1790–95* (Norman: University of Oklahoma Press, 1985), 59–78.
56. Reginald Horsman, *Expansion and American Indian Policy, 1783–1812* (Lansing: Michigan State University Press, 1967), 84–85.
57. Colin G. Calloway, *The Shawnees and the War for America* (London: Viking Penguin, 2007), 109.
58. Ethan Schmidt's account of the postrevolutionary plight of the Cherokees, Creeks, Chickasaws, Choctaws, Catawbas, Abenakes, Stockbridges, and Iroquois makes for somber reading. See *Native Americans in the American Revolution: How the War Divided, Devastated, and Transformed the Early American Indian World* (Santa Barbara, Calif.: Praeger, 2014), 157–72. See also Sword, *President George Washington's Indian War,* 299–313; and Calloway, *Crown and Calumet,* 240–57.
59. Alexis de Tocqueville, *Democracy in America,* trans. Harvey Mansfield and Delba Winhtrop (Chicago: University of Chicago Press, 2002), 322–23.
60. Calloway, *American Revolution in Indian Country,* 292–301.
61. Colin G. Calloway, ed., *The World Turned Upside Down: Indian Voices from Early America* (Boston: Bedford Books, 1994), 183.

CONTRIBUTORS

ANDREAS HARALD AURE is associate professor at Trondheim School of Law, Trondheim, Norway. He is the author of *The Right to Wage War: The Reception of Grotius 50 Years after "De Jure Belli ac Pacis"* (Berliner Wissenschaftsverlag, 2015); and "Hugo Grotius: Individual Rights as the Core of Natural Law," in *Philosophy of Justice,* edited by Guttom Fløistad, vol. 12 of Contemporary Philosophy: A New Survey (Springer Verlag, 2015); and journal articles in Norwegian and German. Dr. Aure has also edited works (in Norwegian) by Hugo Grotius, Ludvig Holberg, and Wilhelm von Humbolt.

DANIEL R. BRUNSTETTER is associate professor of political science at the University of California, Irvine. He is the author of *Tension of Modernity: Las Casas and His Legacy in the French Enlightenment* (Routledge, 2012) as well as coeditor (with Jean-Vincent Holeindre) of *The Ethics of War and Peace Revisited: Moral Challenges in an Era of Contested and Fragmented Sovereignty* (Georgetown University Press, 2017) and (with Cian O'Driscoll) *Just War Thinkers: From Cicero to the 21st Century* (Routledge, 2017). Brunstetter has also published numerous journal articles and book chapters, including most recently "The Decision to Use Military Force in Recent Moral Argument," in *The Ashgate Research Companion to Military Ethics,* edited by James Turner Johnson and Eric D. Patterson (Ashgate, 2015).

BENJAMIN L. CARP holds the Daniel M. Lyons Chair of American History as associate professor of early American history at Brooklyn College of the City University of New York. He is the author of *Defiance of the Patriots: The Boston Tea Party and the Making of America* (Yale University Press, 2010), which won the Society of the Cincinnati Cox Book Prize in 2013; and *Rebels Rising: Cities and the American Revolution* (Oxford University Press, 2007); and coeditor (with Richard D. Brown) of *Major Problems in the Era of the American Revolution, 1760–1791: Documents and Essays,* 3rd edition (Wadsworth, Cengage Learning, 2014). He has written articles for *Early American Studies, Civil War History,* and the *William and Mary Quarterly.* He has previously taught at Tufts University and the University of Edinburgh.

THEODORE CHRISTOV is associate professor of honors, history, and international affairs at George Washington University in Washington, D.C. His book *Before Anarchy: Hobbes and His Critics in Modern International Thought* (Cambridge University Press, 2015) examines the debates over international relations in the works of Thomas Hobbes, Samuel Pufendorf, and Emer de Vattel. Christov has also published articles in various academic journals and edited collections.

JONATHAN DEN HARTOG is associate professor of history at the University of Northwestern–Saint Paul, Minnesota. He is author of *"Patriotism and Piety": Federalist Politics and Religious Struggle in the New American Nation* (University of Virginia Press, 2015). He has also published articles in *Early American Studies,* the *Journal of Church and State,* and the *Faulkner Law Review* as well as several essays in edited volumes.

JACK P. GREENE is John Carter Brown Library Researcher-in-Residence at Brown University and the Andrew W. Mellon Professor Emeritus in the Humanities at Johns Hopkins University. Author of more than a dozen books on early America and the Atlantic world, his works include *Peripheries and Center: Constitutional Development in the Extended Polities of the British Empire and the United States, 1607–1789* (University of Georgia Press, 1986) and *The Constitutional Origins of the American Revolution* (Cambridge University Press, 2010). Greene's most recent works are *Evaluating Empire and Confronting Colonialism in Eighteenth-Century Britain* (Cambridge University Press, 2013) and *Settler Jamaica in the 1750s: A Social Portrait* (University of Virginia Press, 2015).

PHILLIP HAMILTON is professor of history at Christopher Newport University in Virginia. He is author of *The Making and Unmaking of a Revolutionary Family: The Tuckers of Virginia, 1752–1830* (University of Virginia Press, 2003), *Serving the Old Dominion: A History of Christopher Newport University* (Mercer University Press, 2011), and *The Revolutionary War Lives and Letters of Lucy and Henry Knox* (Johns Hopkins University Press, 2017). In addition, Hamilton has published articles in the *William and Mary Quarterly* and the *Virginia Magazine of History and Biography.* He is currently writing a biography of the Revolutionary War general Henry Knox.

WILLIAM ANTHONY HAY is associate professor of history at Mississippi State University and a fellow of the Royal Historical Society. He is the author of *The Whig Revival, 1808–1830* (Palgrave 2005) and editor of *Is There Sill a West? The Future of the Atlantic Alliance* (University of Missouri Press, 2007). Hay also recently completed a biography of Robert Banks Jenkinson, 2nd Earl of Liverpool, Britain's prime minister from 1812 to 1827, and is currently writing a book on British strategy and policy during the American Revolution.

T. COLE JONES is an assistant professor of early American history at Purdue University. He is the author of *Captives of Liberty: Enemy Prisoners of the American Revolution* (University of Pennsylvania Press, forthcoming), which explores how Americans dealt with political and military prisoners during the Revolutionary War. Jones has also published articles in the *New England Quarterly,* the *Journal of the Early Republic,* the *Journal of Military History,* and *Common-Place.*

MARK EDWARD LENDER is professor emeritus at Kean University. He is author or coauthor of ten books in American military, social, and institutional history, including (with James Kirby Martin) *A Respectable Army: The Military Origins of the Republic, 1763–1789* (3rd ed., Wiley, 2015), *The War for American Independence: A Reference Guide* (ABC-CLIO, 2016), and (with Garry Wheeler Stone) *Fatal Sunday: George Washington, the Monmouth Campaign, and the Politics of Battle* (University of Oklahoma Press, 2016), winner of the Society for Military History's 2017 Distinguished Book Award and a finalist for the George Washington Prize.

JAMES KIRBY MARTIN is the Hugh Roy and Lillie Cranz Cullen University Professor of History at the University of Houston. He is the author, coauthor, or editor of twelve books, among them *Benedict Arnold, Revolutionary Hero: An American Warrior Reconsidered* (New York University Press, 1997), (with Mark Edward Lender) *A Respectable Army: The Military Origins of the Republic, 1763–1789* (Harlan Davidson, 1982, 2nd. ed., 1986), (with Joseph T. Glatthaar) *Forgotten Allies: The Oneida Indians and the American Revolution* (Hill and Wang, 2006); and most recently (coedited with David L. Preston) *Theaters of the American Revolution: Northern, Middle, Southern, Western, Naval* (Westholme, 2017) He is currently completing two books, *The Remarkable American Revolution: A Narrative History* (with Sheila Skemp), and *The Temptation of George Washington: The Newburgh Conspiracy and Revolutionary Leadership.* Among his other professional activities, Martin serves as a historian adviser to the Oneida Indian Nation of New York.

GLENN A. MOOTS is professor of political science and philosophy at Northwood University in Midland, Michigan, and served as William E. Simon Visiting Fellow in the James Madison Program at Princeton University in 2013–14. He is author of *Politics Reformed: The Anglo-American Legacy of Covenant Theology* (University of Missouri Press, 2010); essays in *American Political Thought, Locke Studies, Perspectives on Political Science,* and *Hebraic Political Studies;* as well as chapters in edited collections on colonial American religion. Moots served as guest editor for a special 2015 issue of the *Journal of Military Ethics* on the American Revolution.

VALERIE ONA MORKEVIČIUS is an associate professor of political science at Colgate University. She is the author of *Realist Ethics: Just War Traditions as Power Politics* (Cambridge University Press, forthcoming). Her earlier work on the ethics of rebellion has appeared in *Ethics and International Affairs* (2013) as well as in several edited volumes. Morkevičius was a 2010–11 resident fellow at the Stockdale Center for Ethical Leadership at the U.S. Naval Academy.

JOHN D. ROCHE is an assistant professor of history at the U.S. Air Force Academy. He is currently revising his dissertation, "'[America] may be conquered with more Ease than governed': The Evolution of British Occupation Policy during the American Revolution," for publication. Roche's research interests include Atlantic, military, and colonial American history.

WILLIAM P. TATUM III has served as the official government historian of Dutchess County, New York, since 2012. His scholarly work explores British state formation in the eighteenth century, with special emphasis on the role of the military justice system and the army in this process. Tatum has taught at Brown and served as the Sol Feinstone Scholar at the David Library of the American Revolution.

INDEX